CONTENTS

PART ONE
BLOOD MOON
Its Origins and Its Oeuvre in 62 photo-accessorized pages

page 1

PART TWO
DARWIN PORTER
Recording the Scene from the Peripheries of Show Biz

In the Beginning
    Lash La Rue, Sophie Tucker, Movies as therapy during World War II, Senator George Smathers and JFK. Lucille Ball and Eleanor Roosevelt at the U. of Miami, *The Miami Herald*, and hard-drinking, pre-gentrifiation days with Harry Truman and the Pink Triangle in Key West   page 63

Arts Industry Socialite Stanley Mills Haggart and his links to Hedda Hopper   page 73

Madison Avenue's Zeal for Celebrity Endorsements:
    Pumping up Sales with William Holden, Debbie Reynolds, and Joan Fontaine   page 75

The Frommer Guides as a Celebrity Confessional   page 76

In Praise of Older Women: Their Beauty, their Savvy, and their Resources. The Confessions of
    Burt Reynolds. **Plus** Hedy Lamarr, Anne Baxter; and Ruth Warrick   page 77

Lessons from Darwin Porter on the Fine Art of "Walking" (i.e., Escorting) Celebrity *"Grandes Dames"*
    to Parties and Social Events   page 78

The Magnolia-Scented Saga of Greta Keller, Pola Negri, and Jolie Gabor   page 79

Introducing the Queen of Off-Broadway: Lucille Lortel, matriarch and goddess of Christopher Street   page 80

Hustling a Bodybuilder: The Sword & Sandals saga of Stanley Cranston and Steve Reeves   page 81

Mae Murray: The Self-Enchanted Dancer With the Bee-Stung Lips   page 81

The Most Famous Actress of 1941: Junior Miss (aka Patricia Peardon):
    Her widely heralded appearance on the cover of LIFE coincided with the Japanese
    Bombardment of Pearl Harbor.   page 82

How Darwin's business partner and mentor (an insider from the glory days of silent films)
    introduced him to Arthur Miller, the world famous playwright, then the husband of Marilyn
    Monroe, and how it led to a thwarted involvement (and inside view) of Milton Green's
    Marilyn Monroe Productions.   page 83

MONARCHS IN HIDING: **Visit Portugal.** How Darwin, then an emissary of The Frommer Guides,
    researched the Royal Hideaways of the Portuguese Riviera. Piercing the entourages of
    the Pretenders to the Thrones of France, Italy, and Spain, A-List Celebrities
    who romanced the bisexual (deposed) King of Italy; his long-suffering wife, Giovanna
    de Savoia; Magda Lupescu (the despised everyday citizen who married the deposed
    King of Romania); and Amalia Rodriguez, the nightclub entertainer who became
    the Queen of Fado.   page 85

Poor Little Rich Girl: The embarrassing tale of Woolworth Heiress BARBARA HUTTON & her MATADOR, 24-year-old ANGEL TERUEL .... page 91

Marlene Dietrich's most implacable rival, GRETA KELLER: Her years-long status as Darwin's housemate, how she handled the scariest overlords of the Third Reich, how she had to escape from Nazi Germany on 30 minutes' notice; her lavender marriage to the bisexual actor who was blackmailing Howard Hughes; and how she introduced Darwin to the filmmaker cited as "the most brilliant producer of propaganda films in the history of moviemaking, Leni Riefenstahl. .... page 92

Howard Hughes' scandalous titty film: *The Outlaw*, and the sad and sorry "blackmailers tend to get killed" saga of David Bacon. .... page 94

WHEN DIVAS CLASH: The fight over ROBERT TAYLOR when TAMARA GEVA (*the Great Russian Ballerina and ex-wife of George Balanchine*) is assaulted in a theater lobby by BARBARA STANWYCK. .... page 99

TELL IT TO TALLULAH: The story behind the story of Bankhead's failed marriage to John Emery, and how Tamara Geva ferociously struggled to keep him. .... page 101

ROBERT TAYLOR: Greta Garbo described him as "So beautiful, So dumb." .... page 103

OLD WOUNDS (in this case, because of Robert Taylor) NEVER HEAL: More about TAMARA GEVA vs. "BLOODY BABS" STANWYCK .... page 104

HEDY (in *Ecstasy*) LAMARR: The Bizarre Story of the International Intrigue and Censorship Problems Whirling Around the Most Beautiful Woman in the World .... page 104

JACK DEMPSEY, The World's Heavyweight Boxing Champion, and his Widely Publicized Dalliance with MAE WEST .... page 108

More about Darwin's friendship with JACK DEMPSEY .... page 109

MAE WEST: Size Mattered. Race and Notoriety Didn't. Her links to Mickey Hargitay, Steve Cochran, Bugsy Siegel, Cary Grant ("I knew he was homosexual before he did!"), Harry Houdini, and Duke Ellington .... page 111

HOW HENRY WILLSON, Hollywood's Gay Svengali, Created the Beefcake Craze of the 1950s. He Renames the Men he "discovers" and morphs them into Heartthrobs. He also discovers LANA TURNER .... page 112

BEEFCAKE BLUES: Darwin reviews "guys gone wrong in the fleshpots of show-biz," and the occasional career he helped to steer right: Guy Madison, John Derek, Craig Stevens, Ty Hardin, Kerwin Matthews, Yale Summers, Clint Walker, Dack Rambo, Doug McClure, Chad Everett, Mike Connors (think "*Mannix*"), Rory Calhoun, and the age of Sputnik's ultimate heartthrob, Tab Hunter .... page 113

TROY DONAHUE, the Self-Destructive Pin-up Boy of Pop Culture .... page 125

Star-Crossed Lovers: ROBERT WAGNER & NATALIE WOOD. During their heyday, the only couple more famous was "Jack and Jackie" .... page 128

NATALIE WOOD & JAMES DEAN: Rebels With a Curse: Live Fast, Die Young and Violently. Nick Adams, Sal Mineo, & Natalie Wood: "Who's Sleeping with Jimmy Tonight?" .... page 133

SEARCHING for the female lead (Judy) of *Rebel Without a Cause*: How the outcome was affected by Nicholas Ray's Casting Couch. How Jayne Mansfield and Unsinkable Tammy (Debbie Reynolds) lost the coveted role. .... page 136

Let the (Gay) Games Begin: James Dean and His Rise to Fame.

BLOOD MOON PRODUCTIONS
ITS ORIGINS, ITS *OEUVRE*, ITS SOURCES, & ITS LEGACY

This 250-page 'wild card,' combines aspects of a catalogue with a memoir, an autobiography, and a manual for Media Studies. It was inspired by new (and in many cases, horrifying) realities in North America's book distribution patterns. It's also a late-in-life effort to document our company's research methods. How did two (eccentric but agile) writers manage to accumulate so many gossipy, historically compelling *exposés*?

This is it...our best shot at compiling, for estate purposes and as an effort to revise our distribution networks, a CATALOGUE of our *oeuvre*.

How things got DOWN and LOW at Blood Moon will never happen again. Our story is unique. Here's our spin on the quirky small press that brazenly recorded tell-all tales that many other venues would have refused to publish.

We present it as a bookseller's catalogue on steroids. We've added narratives that illustrate our investigative techniques...and insights into the high-flying *milieux* in which—for a few decades, at least—we thrived.

Perhaps it's also a mournful testimonial to the value of old-fashioned "up-close-and-personal," (i.e. "non Internet") conversations. In our case, many them were with living witnesses to dramas-within-dramas that were crucial to that all-American phenomenon known as SHOW BIZ.

Many thanks for your interest. May your lives be happy, and may all your hopes and dreams come true.

—Danforth Prince
President and Founder
BloodMoonProductions.com

"Packed with enough gossip to fuel a carload of *Kaffeeklatsches* on both sides of the Atlantic, this book is accessorized with grasping, arts-industry tales of 'who did what to whom,' during the Golden Age of Show Biz."
—Darwin Porter

BLOOD MOON PRODUCTIONS

Its Origins, Its Oeuvre, Its Sources, Its Legacy

Darwin Porter and Danforth Prince

ISBN 978-1-936003-94-5
Unless otherwise stated, all texts are
© 2025 Blood Moon Productions, Ltd.

Book covers, designs, and layouts by Danforth Prince

THIS BOOK IS DEDICATED TO VERNON HENRY (1960-2025)

and to anyone who ever embarassed themselves in public
during their pursuit of a career in publishing, show biz, the music industry, politics,
or the creative arts. Its galleys were composed and laid out on Quark Express.
It was manufactured in the USA, and it's distributed worldwide through Ingram, Amazon.com,
Barnes & Noble.com, and through internet vendors everywhere.

Jack Simmons "The Hawk" Glides Into Jimmy's Life. TV Star Vampira and her televised calls from the grave.	page 139
Role-playing and Method Acting during an audition: Sal Mineo Makes Pornographic Love to Jimmy Dean in full view of Nick Ray as a demonstration of their onscreen chemistry.	page 140
CASTING ISSUES during the pre-production of James Dean's classic: The search for a Henpecked Husband, a Tarantula Mother, a 1950's Sitcom Mom, & an Incestuous Father. The 1950s weren't as dull as you might have thought.	page 141
More than a Bromance: DENNIS HOPPER	page 143
"Me Tarzan, You Jimmy" — Johnny Weissmuller to James Dean	page 144
METHOD MANIA: Jimmy Rages Through Some of the Most Iconic Film Sequences In the History of Cinema. *Walpurgisnacht* on the set of *Rebel without a Cause*	page 146
James Dean's long-term effect on Elvis Presley	page 156
The Murky, Suspicious, & Unexplained Death of Sex Kitten/Screen Goddess NATALIE WOOD Death in a Dinghy WHO DID IT?	page 159
ROCK HUDSON: EROTIC FIRE A Truck Driver and Master Seducer Morphs Into a PHALLIC SYMBOL and OBJECT OF LUST for Love-Starved Teenage Girls and Gay Men	page 166
Tony Randall: The Most Unfunny Man in Show-Biz	page 171
GAY EXTORTION: How Rock Hudson coped with blackmail from the unscrupulous lesbian he married	page 173

PART THREE
ANITA FINLEY

Portrait of a Lady: She made Baby Boomers (their care, maintenance, and marketing) the focus of her career

page 177

PART FOUR
DANFORTH PRINCE

Behind the Scenes of a Celebrity Exposé Publisher

page 183

Hookers, Road Kill, & Panning for Gold in the Klondike: The Early Days of the Trump Dynasty	page 184
Puritanical America the Way It Used to Be *(i.e., the Genealogical Origins of a Publishing Maverick)*	page 184
The Complicated Celluloid Saga of BUTTERFLIES IN HEAT	page 185
Chasing Butterflies (Celebrity Endorsements)	page 186
Literary License: The Sordid Story of Jay Garon	page 186
Casting Wars: Wannabes for the film adaptation of Darwin Porter's hustler, Numie Chase: Perry King, Jan Michael Vincent, Christopher Jones, Matt Collins	page 187
Casting Wars: Round Two: Gloria Swanson: Egomaniacal, Temperamental, and Very Very Grand	page 188
Rita Hayworth: The Decline and Fall of the Love Goddess	page 188

AND THE WINNER IS: Barbara Baxley	page 189
Joan Blondell vs. Pat Carroll	page 189
Gay? Gay-for-Pay?	
The Commodore vs. Orson Welles	page 190
Eartha Kitt as a Black Trans-sexual	page 190
Rainy Nights in Georgia with THE GEORGIA LITERARY ASSOCIATION	page 191
Razzle Dazzle: A Libertine Romp as a Sequel to *Butterflies in Heat*	page 192
SILENT DEBAUCHERY: Soundless Films "on the Down Low"	page 192
Homosexuals with Southern Twangs: *Rhinestone Country*: A Novel about Closeted Lives South of the Mason-Dixon Line	page 193
BLOOD MOON: A Novel about What Happens When the Moon Turns to Blood	page 193
Blood Moon "Discovers" the Fine Art of Biography with A Double Dose of Humphrey Bogart	page 193
BLOODY WONDERFUL	
KATHARINE THE GREAT: The Secret Life of Katharine Hepburn	page 194
Bad Boy, Megastar, Sexual Outlaw: UNZIPPING MARLON BRANDO	page 195
HOWARD HUGHES is What Happens When a Demented Billionaire Pulls Strings in Hollywood	page 195
JACKO	page 196
Heeeere's Merv!	page 197
Heathcliff & Scarlett (*aka* Larry and Viv)	page 197
The Kennedys: The Gift that Keeps on Giving. All The Gossip Unfit to Print	page 197
Fabulous Frank, *the Boudoir Singer*	page 198
J. Edgar Hoover & Clyde Tolson: High Jinx and Gay Trysts at the FBI	page 198
"La Liz," SuperDiva: Elizabeth Taylor, *There Is Nothing Like a Dame*	page 199
Pornographic America: *Inside Linda Lovelace's Deep Throat*	page 199
Eva, Magda, and Zsa Zsa: THE GABORS, Bombshells from Budapest, Great Courtesans of the 20th Century	page 200
UNHOLY TRIO: Pink Triangle, The Feuds and Private Lives of Tennessee Williams, Gore Vidal, & Truman Capote.	page 201
Blood Moon's Presidents Club (This Time, It's THE REAGANS)	page 201
MORE from Blood Moon's Presidents Club: THE CLINTONS (*So This Is That Thing Called Love*) Get a Celebrity *Exposé* of Their Own	page 202
Peter O'Toole: Hellraiser, Sexual Outlaw, Irish Rebel	page 202
Jimmy, Lad, We Hardly Knew 'Ye: The Public vs. The Private James Dean	page 203
Presidents Club Bad Boy, THE DONALD, The Man Who Would Be King	page 203
LUSCIOUS LANA: Hearts and Diamonds Take All	page 204
Getting a Piece of the Rock: EROTIC FIRE	page 204
Playboy's HUGH HEFNER: Empire of Skin. All Those Bunnies	page 205
Princess Leia and Unsinkable Debbie Reynolds in Hell	page 205
Kirk Douglas: The Life & Death of a Hollywood Horndog	page 205
The Highest-Grossing MegaStar of the '80s: BURT REYNOLDS	page 206
GOING GLOBAL (Selling Celebrity to the Chinese)	page 206
When the World Was Young: GLOBETROTTING	page 207
MEGASTARS UNCENSORED AND UNVARNISHED: Lana and Rock	page 208
Blood Moon's Invasion of Babylon and its Detour to Gomorrah	page 209
CELEBRITY and the IRONIES OF FAME: **Blood Moon's Magnolia House Series**	page 212
WHO MURDERED SHOW BIZ'S MOST FAMOUS BLONDE?: An excerpt, with names and mug shots, lifted directly from the pages of one of our best-sellers	page 215
The Seductive Sapphic Exploits of Hollywood's Greatest Lover: **MERCEDES DE ACOSTA.** Everything you ever wanted to know about *Über*-glam and Lesbians in the Golden Age of Show-Biz.	page 221
TOO MANY DAMN RAINBOWS: Judy Garland & Liza Minnelli	page 222

LUCY & DESI vs. The Ricardos: Everyone Had Something to Say about Them   page 223

FONDA *(Père)* and His Counter-culture, Movie Star Children: TRIPLE EXPOSURE   page 227

HOLLYWOOD REMEMBERED: What it is, why we wrote it, and why it's Gone With the Wind   page 227

PART FIVE
COMING ATTRACTIONS
What's New and What's Next from Blood Moon Productions

The King of Hollywood (CLARK GABLE in Three Volumes)   page 233
    Volume One: CLARK GABLE, King of Hollywood (1901-1938)
    Volume Two: GONE WITH THE WIND (1938-1939). *Frankly, My Dear, He DID Give a Damn*
    Volume Three: CLARK GABLE: Where Love Has Gone *(1940-1961)*

A Double-Barreled Overview of the Sexiest, Most Fantasy-Adaptable Actor in Golden Age Hollywood   page 235
    Volume One (1901-1939): GARY COOPER, The Montana Mule
    Volume Two (1940-1961): GARY COOPER, High Noon in Hell

MEDIA BUZZ Media is Buzzing for What's Next at Blood Moon. (HINT: It's gonna vaguely resemble what we did with Blood Moon's BABYLON series)   page 236

Blood Moon's STARDUST Series: A Startling Two-Volume Overview of Why NYC was, during the 60s, and 70s, Truly Great

    Volume One: **STARDUST. From Off-Off Broadway to Hollywoo**d: *Lucille Lortel, Joseph Papp, and the Explosive Birth of the Modern Theatre*   page 237

    Volume Two : ***X-Rated Manhattan in the Jaded 1970s***. *Sybaritic Denizens of the Night Thrive in an Emporium of Exotica & Erotica*   page 240

Blood Moon's INSIDE BROADWAY, a publishing triptych with MORE about THE AMERICAN THEATER
    Anticipating Publication, beginning in 2028   page 242

    Volume One: ***Broadway Actors, Directors, & Playwrights Who Lit Up the Great White Way***
    Volume Two: ***Broadway Damsels, Dames, & Divas: They Gave Us So Many Enchanted Evenings***
    Volume Three: ***Babes (Male and Female) on Broadway.*** *Mystique, Ego, Triumph, and Tragedy*

GOMORRAH: IT'S BACK.   page 244

    Volume One was published in 2024. Two additional installments are almost ready for their closeup:
    Volume Two of Three: *SLIMELIGHT—Nobody's Perfect. Hidden Tales from Celebrity Boudoirs*
    Volume Three of Three: *ONLY ANGELS HAVE WINGS: More Hidden Tales from Celebrity Boudoirs*

And after that, after all the others on this page have been processed, we'll churn out Blood Moon's finale:

ERROL FLYNN, THE TASMANIAN DEVIL Golden Age Hollywood's Phallic Symbol   page 245

BLOOD MOON PRODUCTIONS

AND THE CELEBRITY ASSOCIATIONS THAT MADE ITS PUBLICATIONS POSSIBLE

www.BloodMoonProductions.com

Entertainment about Fame and How America Interprets its Celebrities

"We present this as an exhilarating but mournful overview of an age when gossip got registered (and amplified) in confrontational, face-to-face (non-Internet) ways."

—Danforth Prince

PART ONE

Blood Moon: Its Origins & Its *Oeuvre*

Blood Moon Productions originated in 1997 as The Georgia Literary Association, a vehicle for the promotion of obscure writers from America's Deep South. Today, Blood Moon is based in New York City, and staffed with writers who previously devoted their energies to THE FROMMER GUIDES, a trusted name in travel publishing.

Blood Moon has demonstrated a remarkable knack for publicity. Its titles have been widely reviewed by the U.S. and U.K's broadsheet newspapers and/or tabloids, and four of its biographies were extensively serialized by the largest-readership publications of the U.K., *The Mail on Sunday* and *The Sunday Times*. Other serializations of Blood Moon's titles have appeared in Australia's *Women's Weekly* and *The Australian*.

Our corporate mission involves researching and salvaging the oral histories of America's entertainment industry--those "off the record" events which at the time might have been defined as either indecent or libelous, but which are now pertinent to America's understanding of its origins and cultural roots.

For more about us, click on *www.BloodMoonProductions.com*, or refer to the pages which immediately follow.

Thanks for your interest, and happy reading.

BEFORE THE MEMORIES FADE

How decades as the most visible and prolific writers at *The Frommer Guides* turned Darwin Porter and Danforth Prince into celebrity-chasing adventurers on location in Europe, California, The Caribbean, and the World at Large

The point we want to make in this introduction is that before Blood Moon Productions ever existed, its writers devoted themselves to the research ond production of many titles within the world-renowned **FROMMER TRAVEL GUIDES.**

The venue was unique. As their designated representatives to most of Europe, the Caribbean, and large swaths of the USA, we saw the world, experienced its cultural and aesthetic wonders, worked hard, and had a fabulous time.

But in 2013, the party ended. After a recession and radical changes in how Americans opted to educate itself about their travel tastes and options, the Frommer guides were curtailed, sold and re-sold (multiple times) and endured radical reductions of their budgets and titles. **A way of life had ended. Inevitably, we had already seen the beginning of the end. (Who could have possibly missed it?) As such, we had already begun the (painful) process of "re-formatting' our research headquarters (historic Magnolia House in Staten Island) and morphing it into the headquarters of a bold new publishing venue with a unique, "celebrity-centric" mission statement....i.e., Blood Moon Productions.**

Our Ongoing Obsession with the American Concept of Celebrity and Fame

Even during the heyday of the postwar travel industry, we'd been consistently fascinated by the concept of celebrity and fame in America. And *(full disclosure)*, we had occasionally used our niche at Frommer as a vehicle (or disguise) for the meeting and greeting of celebrities. Tourist authorities in Sweden, Italy, and/or France cooperated with requests we made for introductions to, for example, **Ingrid Bergman, Gina Lollabrigida, and Brigitte Bardot** (among many others) each of whom were willing to be identified with "the best and brightest" of their respective cultural scenes.

So when the Frommer guides as we had known them collapsed, we "fell" into a celebrity-indulgent cocoon whose foundations had already been more or less defined and established.

Here, then, as laid out within the pages of this book, is the story of what happened AFTER the travel party ended, AFTER the Frommer Guides imploded, and when we, as the "keeper of the secrets" and writers of most of the Frommer series were forced to pursue other venues.

As such, we present, through this book, a History (or Biography) of the publishing venture we built, sweated, and labored over AFTER THE BEGINNING OF OUR END at the Frommer Guides, during the tumultuous final years of "The American Century."

It's been a helluva story. Throughout our administration of Blood Moon's experimental saga, we've showcased an alternative (counterculture) spin on the Entertainment industry that would never have been endorsed by Hollywood overseers of previous decades. Here lies the heart—and it's been a helluva ride.

Now, while we still remember and **LEST WE FORGET,** here it is—a detailed historical record of the complicated independing publishing venue we conceptualized and built.

We give you, in the pages that follow, our story. Best wishes to all of you, with thanks for your interest.

Darwin Porter

Danforth Prince

IN THE BEGINNING

Blood Moon originated in Georgia as a testimonial to the illustrious literary traditions of the gothic Deep South

The Georgia Literary Association

Cinematic, Radically Experimental "Pop Publishing"

—the kind you wouldn't necessarily expect from the Deep South

---

Blood Moon originated from the distribution-related needs of two writers (Darwin Porter and Danforth Prince) whose priorities had, until then, been dominated by their writing obligations at the Frommer Guides.

By the mid-1990s, travel journalism (as the world had known it) had changed forever by the rise of the internet and changing consumer demographics. Reacting, swiftly but not without some twinges of terror, we shifted our productive focus toward pop fiction—much of it set in the Deep, gothic South—and celebrity biographies.

To make this work, we needed a new corporate structure and a distribution network. The business entity that evolved was named after the State of Georgia, the authors' residence at the time, We envisioned the GLA as a vehicle for the renaissance of the gothic ironies that Flannery O'Connor (who will forever be linked to Savannah) had indelibly associated with the Deep South.

Thus originated the Georgia Literary Association. Danforth Prince designated himself as its president /publisher and launched some experimental, "pop culture entertainments" set in, among others, Savannah, Key West, the hollers of country-music Nashville, and other mostly Southern locales of romantic (and perhaps mystical) appeal.

Some of our efforts were condemned and vilified. Others were frenziedly promoted by the counterculture press, both in Georgia and nationwide. And a few sold way beyond expectations, eventually evolving, thanks in part to increased international recognition and a growing fan base, into cult classics.

Each of those early, quasi-experimental "pop publishing" titles is now proudly included in the backlist of Blood Moon Productions, Ltd. The half-dozen pages that immediately follow are devoted to descriptions of those early, sometimes very successful, experimental titles.

Distribution during these early years was fulfilled by Bookazine in the US, and Turnaround in the UK and Europe

From the Georgia Literary Association, in cooperation with Manor Books, the Florida Literary Association and Blood Moon Productions

THE RENAISSANCE OF A CULT CLASSIC

BUTTERFLIES IN HEAT

Darwin Porter

You first heard about it in the 70s, when it was the most notorious and gossipped-about book in Key West. Now it's back.

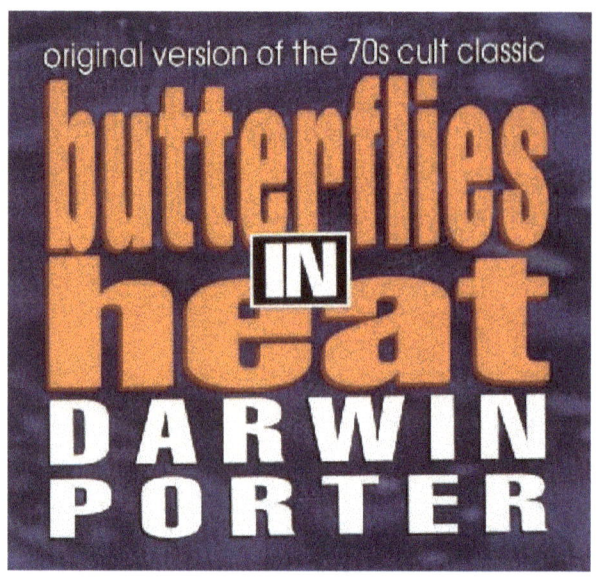

"Darwin Porter writes with an incredible understanding of the milieu-- hot enough to singe the wings off any butterfly"
—**James Kirkwood**, co-author, **A Chorus Line**

"How does Darwin Porter's garden grow? Only in the moonlight, and only at midnight, when man-eating vegetation in any color but green bursts forth to devour the latest offerings"
—**James Leo Herlihy**, author of **Midnight Cowboy**

"I'd walk the waterfront for Numie (the hustler protagonist of Butterflies in Heat) any day."
—**Tennessee Williams**

> "We know from the beginning that we're getting into a hotbed that has morbid fascination for potential readers. The novel evolves, in fact, into one massive melée of malevolence, vendetta, and e-v-i-l, stunningly absorbing alone for its sheer and unrelenting exploration of the lower depths."
> **BESTSELLERS**

"The most SCORCHING novel of the BIZZARE, the FLAMBOYANT, the CORRUPT since Midnight Cowboy. The strikingly beautiful blond hustler, Numie, has come to the end of the line. Here, in the SEARING HEAT of a tropical cay, he arouses PASSIONS that explode under the BLOOD-RED SUN."

Manor Reviews

This title, a cult classic now in its **16th printing**, has sold steadily to a coterie of Darwin Porter fans since its inauguration in 1976, when it was the thing EVERYBODY in Key West was talking about, and the inspiration for the movie (**The Last Resort, aka Tropic of Desire**) that EVERYBODY wanted to be in—including Eartha Kitt and "The Marlboro Man," Matt Collins.

Butterflies in Heat, by Darwin Porter. A novel about malevolence, vendetta, morbid fascination, and redemption.
ISBN 1-877978-95-7.

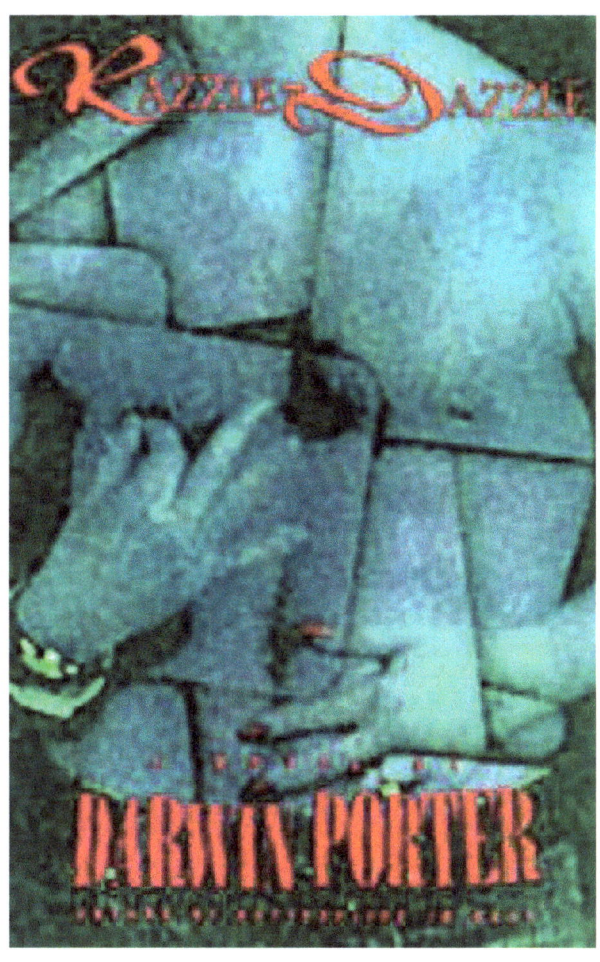

And Then there was *Butterflies in Heat*'s Sequel,

Darwin Porter's

Razzle-Dazzle

SUPER-RICH SHERRY AND HER BOYS SET OUT ON A GAY ROMP TO FILM *BUTTERFLIES IN HEAT* IN KEY WEST— BUT AN ILL WIND WAS BLOWING NORTH FROM THE CARIBBEAN

Why can't we have our own Danielle Steele, Jackie Collins, and John Grisham—all rolled into one sexy, delectable read? Gay lit has emerged from the closet! Darwin Porter welcomes us to the millennium. We've arrived!
—George S. Mills

Bizarre and Brilliant! Savage and Brutal! Money and Power, Violence & Sex! Wickedly Funny! An Explosive, Intriguing, and DAZZLING Novel!

"This novel reads like a whirlwind. One has so much fun with this mean-and-lean page-turner that one at first overlooks what a gripping, compelling suspense thriller it is—on multiple levels."
—*Books Today,* Atlanta

"Savvy, crisp portraits of characters on the make in the fleshpots of "The Last Resort" of Key West. It ensnares the reader."
—*Advance Reviews*, New York

"Darwin Porter makes Truman Capote look like a Disney-boycotting redneck at a Southern Baptist Convention."
—*Time Out*, London

Jesse Helms must not read this novel. He'll denounce it from the Senate floor as a threat to Western civilization. And Bill Clinton will probably sue for sexual harrassment."
—*Fab Magazine*, Toronto

"Darwin Porter is the Tennessee Williams of today—that is, if "Tom" were born in 1972."
—*Nat og Dag*, Copenhagen

"There's something here for everyone here...Sadists, size queens, romance readers, thrill seekers, Bi's, gossip-mongers, defenders of the *paparazzi,* and bedmates of Cuban men."
—*Siegessaule*, Berlin

"If Dino and his father, Rafael, are typical of Cuban manhood, book me on the next flight to Havana."
—*La Noche,* Barcelona

Original ISBN 1-877978-96-5, Revised ISBN 9-781877-978968

Wild, orgiastic nights in pre-code Hollywood

Hollywood's Silent Closet

Darwin Porter

The first book of its kind, it's the most intimate and most realistic novel about sex, murder, blackmail, and degradation in early Hollywood ever written.

"The Little Tramp" **Charlie Chaplin** (right) was one of the most recklessly debauched players in Hollywood. Read all about it, here.

Disillusioned In her later years, "America's Sweetheart" **Mary Pickford** (left) declared herself a recluse and virtually never left her bedroom.

An anthology of star-studded scandal from Tinseltown's very gay and very lavender past, it focuses on Hollywood's secrets from the 1920s, including the controversial backgrounds of the great lovers of the Silent Screen.

Valentino, Ramon Novarro, Charlie Chaplin, Fatty Arbuckle, Pola Negri, Mary Pickford, and many others figure into eyewitness accounts of the debauched excesses that went on behind closed doors. It also documents the often tragic endings of America's first screen idols, some of whom admitted to being more famous than the monarchs of England and Jesus Christ combined.

"The *Myra Breckinridge* of the Silent-Screen era. Lush, luscious, and langorously decadent. A brilliant primer of *Who Was Who* in early Hollywood."

Gay Times, London

Millions of fans lusted after **Gary Cooper** (left) and **Rudolph Valentino** (right) but until the release of this book, **The Public Never Knew.**

A compelling, door stopping paperback, 7" x 10" with 746 pages and 60 vintage photos
ISBN 978-0-9668030-2-0

A banquet of information about the pansexual intrigues of Hollywood between 1919 and 1926 compiled from eyewitness interviews with men and women, all of them insiders, who flourished in its midst. Not for the timid, it names names and doesn't spare the guilty. If you believe, like Truman Capote, that the literary treatment of gossip will become the literature of the 21st century, then you will love **Hollywood's Silent Closet.**

BLOOD MOON

An Artfully Brutal Tale of Psychosis, Sexual Obsession, Money, Power, Religion, and Love.
Darwin Porter

In 2008, this title was designated as one of the ten best horror novels ever published
in a survey conducted by the British literary club ***Boiz Who Read***

*"**Blood Moon** reads like Dynasty on steroids. A compelling psycho-sexual adventure of three beautiful men
meeting on the fast road to hell."* —Buddy Hamilton

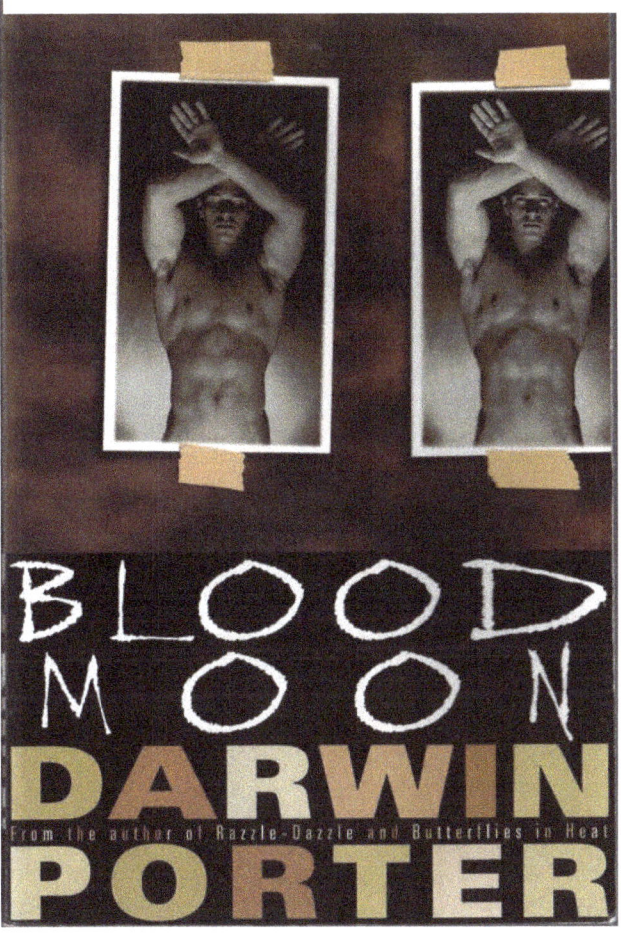

GEORGIA LITERARY ASSOCIATION

"In the gay genre, Blood Moon does for the novel what Danielle Steele and John Grisham have been publishing in the straight world for years."

—Frank Fenton

Rose Phillips, Blood Moon's charismatic and deviant evangelist, and her shocking but beautiful gay son, Shelley, were surely written in hell. Together, they're a brilliant—and jarring—depiction of a fiercely aggressive Oedipal couple competing for the same male prizes.

Blood Moon exposes the murky labyrinths of fanatical Christianity in America today, all within a spunky context of male eroticism. If you never thought that sex, psychosis, right-wing religion, and violence aren't linked, think again.

"**Blood Moon** reads like an IMAX spectacle about the power of male beauty, with red-hot icons, a breathless climax, and erotica that's akin to Anaïs Nin on Viagra with a bump of meth."

—Eugene Raymond

**A controversial, compelling, and artfully potboiling paperback that describes
what really happens when the Moon Turns to Blood.**
ISBN 978-0-9668030-4-4

Rhinestone Country

An Erotic Thriller about Love and the Music Industry   Darwin Porter

All that glitter, all that publicity, all that applause, all that pain...

The *True Grit* of show-biz novels, *Rhinestone Country* is a provocative, realistic, and tender portrayal of the Country-Western music industry, closeted lives south of the Mason-Dixon line, and three of the singers who clawed their way to stardom.

"Beautifully crafted, Rhinestone Country sweeps with power and tenderness across the racial, social, and sexual landscapes of the Deep South. This is a daring and dazzling work about trauma, deception, and pain, all of it with a Southern accent."
                                                                        —**Bookazine**

"Let's play the guessing game. Which legend in country music was the inspiration for the character of Pete Riddle? A mouthwatering speculation."
                                                                        —**Island News**

"From the Georgia Literary Association, a gay and erotic treatment of the Country-Western music industry. Nashville has come out of the closet at last!"	Rhinestone Country reads like a scalding gulp of rotgut whiskey on a snowy night in a bowjacks honky-tonk. --**Mississippi Pearl**

Softcover, with a Southern accent, some memorable men and down-home women, and a whole lot of pathos

569 pages   ISBN 978-0-9668030-3-7

Midnight in Savannah

A Horrifying, Bittersweet Novel about Sexual Eccentricities in the Deep South

Darwin Porter

The author, Darwin Porter, a native of North Carolina and Florida, is co-author of *The Frommer Guides* to the City of Savannah and the State of Georgia. During his research there for those guidebooks, he formed some startling conclusions about The Deep South, Savannah, and that city's most famous murder.

This is the more explicit, and more entertaining, alternative to John Behrendt's Savannah-based *Midnight in the Garden of Good and Evil*. Decadent but bemused, it's a saga of corruption, greed, sexual tension, and murder that gets down and dirty in the Deep Old South.

If you've ever felt either traumatized or eroticized south of the Mason-Dixon Line, you should probably read this book.

For more than a year after its publication in 2000, it was one of the best-selling counterculture novels in Georgia and the Carolinas. Newspapers throughout the South, both gay and straight, editorialized on this, the book that satirized THE BOOK that changed the face of tourism in Savannah for all time.

Eugene Raymond, a filmmaker in Nashville, writes, "Porter disturbs by showing the world as a *film noir* cul-de-sac. Corruption has no respect for gender or much of anything else."

"In MIDNIGHT, both Lavender Morgan (at 72, the world's oldest courtesan) and Tipper Zelda (an obese, fading *chanteuse* taunted as 'the black widow') purchase lust from sexually conflicted young men with drop-dead faces, chiseled bodies, and genetically gifted crotches. These women once relied on their physicality to steal the hearts and fortunes of the world's richest and most powerful men. Now, as they slide closer every day to joining the corpses of their former husbands, these once-beautiful women must depend, in a perverse twist of fate, on sexual outlaws for *le petit mort*. And to survive, the hustlers must idle their personal dreams while struggling to cajole what they need from a sexual liaison they detest. Mendacity reigns. Physical beauty as living hell. CAT ON A HOT TIN ROOF's Big Daddy must be spinning in his grave right now."
—**Eugene Raymond**

"If you're not already a Darwin Porter fan, this novel will make you one! We've come a long way, baby, since Gore Vidal's The City and the Pillar." —**Time Out for Books**

"An artfully brutal saga of corruption, greed, sexual tension, and murder, highlighted by the eccentricities of the Deep South. Compulsive Reading." —**The Georgia Literary Assn.**

"I've just booked the next flight to Savannah! Nothing like a good Georgia boy on a chilly night in Dixie!" —**Out!**

A supremely entertaining paperback that will haunt you long after your return from Georgia. 498 pages

ISBN 978-0-9668030-1-3

THE SECRET LIFE OF
HUMPHREY BOGART

THE EARLY YEARS (1899-1931)

DARWIN PORTER

Darwin Porter's myth-shattering biography (the first of a two-part set) gives a controversial CLOSEUP of a young, hot, and humpy Bogart, pre-Casablanca, pre-Bacall, pre-*African Queen*, revealing for the first time what was under the trenchcoat of history's most famous movie star.

This is the most revealing book ever written about the undercover lives of movie stars during the 1930s. Learn what America's most visible male star was doing during his mysterious early years on Broadway and in Hollywood at the dawn of the Talkies--details that Bogie worked hard to suppress during his later years with Bacall.

The subject of more than 80 radio interviews by its author, and widely covered by both the tabloids and the mainstream press, it's based on never-before-published memoirs, letters, diaries, and interviews from men and women who either loved Bogie or who wanted him to burn in hell. No wonder Bogie, in later life, usually avoided talking about his early years.

Serialized in three parts by Britain's *Mail on Sunday*, it demonstrates that Hollywood's Golden Age stars were human, highly sexed, and at least when they were with other Hollywood insiders, remarkably indiscreet.

"This biography has had us pondering as to how to handle its revelations within a town so protective of its own...This biography of Bogart's early years is exceptionally well written."
—JOHN AUSTIN, *HOLLYWOOD INSIDE*

"In this new biography, we learn about how Bogart struggled for stardom in the anything goes era of the Roaring 20s.
—*THE GLOBE*

"Porter's book uncovers scandals within the entertainment industry of the 1920s and 1930s, when publicists from the movie studios deliberately twisted and suppressed inconvenient details about the lives of their emerging stars."
—*TURNER CLASSIC MOVIE NEWS*

"Laced with facts and based on solid, credible research, this is a historically important text that will eventually evolve into required reading for anyone interested in Hollywood's Golden Age. The book is beautifully written."
—LAURENCE HAZELL, PhD. University of Durham (UK)

"We can only hope that Darwin Porter doesn't run into Lauren Bacall in a dark alley!"
—SALON.COM

The Secret Life of Humphrey Bogart, The Early Years (1899-1931)
Softcover. 527 pages, with photos. ISBN 0-9668030-5-1

THEN WE WENT BIGTIME

In 2010, Darwin Porter and Danforth Prince
—disliking the regional connotations of The George Literary Associatiion—
formally restructured their publishing platform as

BLOOD MOON PRODUCTIONS, Ltd.

The new entity's distribution was assigned to the National Book Network.
The titles consigned to their care are described on the pages that immediately follow.

DARWIN PORTER

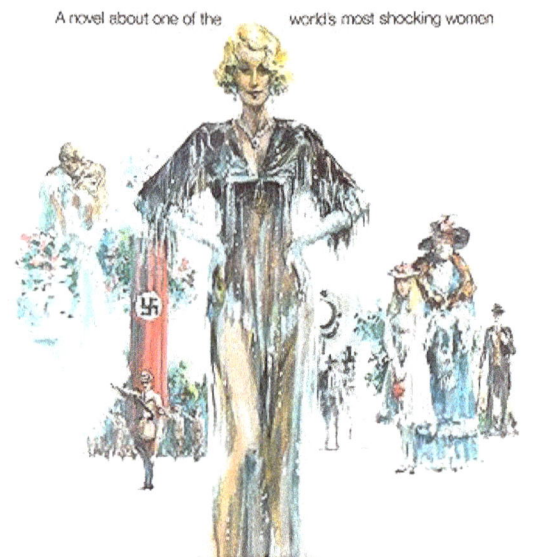

A novel about one of the world's most shocking women

Marlene Dietirch

Darwin Porter's
MARIKA

A bestselling novel about one of the world's most spectacular (and talked-about) women

"The wrenching opening chapter of Marika is one of the most personally resonant reading experiences of my life."

—**Tamara Geva**, Soviet and later American actress, ballet dancer, choreographer, and ex-wife of dancer-choreographer George Balanchine.

Inspired by the lives of three of the 20th Century's most fascinating women—**Marlene Dietrich, Greta Garbo**, and **Hedy Lamarr**—this is the story of "Marika Kreisler," a smart, dark-souled and "seismically seductive" enchantress.

Set against the backgrounds of Berlin, Vienna, London, New York, and Hollywood, Marika is the unvarnished story of one of the world's extraordinary women. At thirteen, she was sold off to an ancient Polish count. Based on an incredible capacity to survive, she endured Nazi Germany (including Hitler's and Goebbel's seductive attentions) in time to morph into one of the world's greatest movie stars.

Who is Marika Kreisler? She's the real woman behind the legends of Dietrich and Garbo, an actress-chanteuse whose life spans seven decades of tragedy and triumph, from her childhood thralldom to a lecherous husband five times her age, to the nightmare of a World War I Berlin prison, to her nude debut in a film made by her grandmother's gigolo lover, to the glamour and infamy of her experiences in show-biz, and at the front, during World War II.

Marika—an innocent, a temptress, a legend. There never has been, there never will be, another like her.

"A wonderful, big, passionate novel about an extraordinary woman who at times eerily reminds one of Marlene Dietrich—Marika is a remarkable characer, and Marika is a stunner of a book!"

—**Burt Hirschfeld**, author of Fire Island and Aspen

ISBN 0-87795-175-6

Originally published by Arbor House, this book's copyright is now administered by Blood Moon Productions. Shortly after its publication, its Dutch translation **(Der Weg Naar de Top)** was designated as BOOK OF THE MONTH in The Netherlands.

Darwin Porter's

VENUS

A novel inspired by the life of Anaïs Nin

Orinally published by Arbor House, its copyright is now controlled by Blood Moon Productions

Anaïs Nin captured significant insights into the psychology of the female personality. As a *roman à clef*, *Venus* defines her dilemmas, her ambitions, her motivations, and her notoriety.

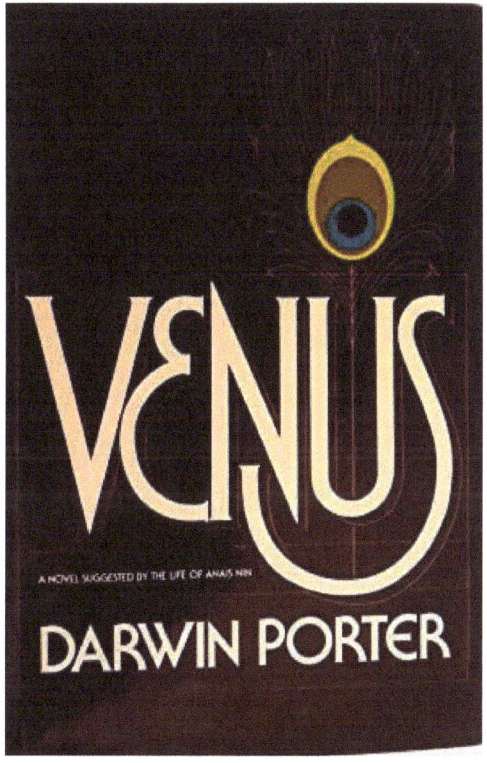

Here is a superb novel about eros and art, and the subculture that basked in both, suggested by the life of the brilliant (and notorious) feminist revolutionary, Anaïs Nin.

In a search for artistic fulfillment that takes her from the poverty of a Brooklyn tenement to the elegant literary salons of Paris, Espérance de Acosta, labeled as a pornographer and banned by censors, constructs a dazzling life in the face of every conceivable hardship and obstacle. In a world dominated by men, she struggles to discover her own sexuality, her artistic soul—and, above all, herself as an independent spirit.

Set against the backdrops of Paris' Latin Quarter and the avant-garde circles of New York, *Venus* captures all the sensuality, passion, and hedonism of the soul-searching lost generation.

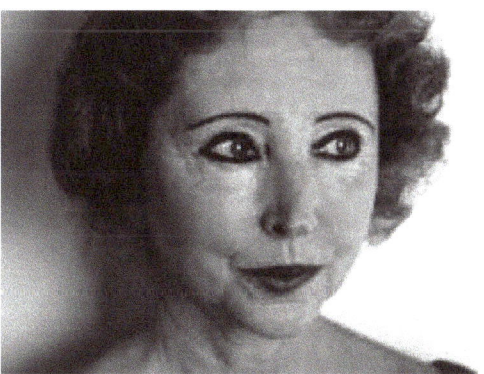

Pornographer, diarist, literary lion, bigamist, and intimate friend of Darwin Porter: **Anaïs Nin**
ISBN 0-87795-366-X
Originally published by Arbor House, this book's copyright is now administered by Blood Moon Productions

Anaïs Nin
(1903-1977)
Renowned writer Anaïs Nin operated her printing press here in the 1940s, where she personally helped produce some of her earliest publications, including their artwork and typeface, regarding these as an extension of her creative process. Her work here helped connect her to a larger publisher and wider audience, eventually inspiring generations of writers and thinkers.

PLACED BY VILLAGE PRESERVATION

The commemorative plaque affixed to 17 East 13th Street, NYC

DID YOU KNOW? That Blood Moon's **Darwin Porter** "rolled around in the hay" with the legacy of Humphrey Bogart not once, but TWICE.

Both of the **"BOGART BIOPSIES'** he produced generated massive tabloid publicity, in part because their revelations at the time were NEW, SCANDAL-SOAKED, and directly culled from the HOLLYWOOD UNDERGROUND.

Left photo:
**Humphrey Bogart,
The Early Years (1899-1931),**
back when his films were Pre-Code and *risqué*
ISBN 0-9668030-5-1

Right photo:
**Humphrey Bogart,
the Making of a Legend.**

What was the secret of his spectacular popularity? and what REALLY lay beneath his trenchcoat?
ALL of that's here, as aggressively promoted the week of its publication by some of the biggest newspapers and tabloids in the world.
ISBN 978-1-936003-14-3

HOW THE TABLOIDS HUMPED FOR BLOOD MOON'S PAIRED OVERVIEWS OF BOGIE

In the early stages of its publishing life, Blood Moon's frenemies sometimes rebuked it for "Courting and Romancing" the Tabloids. But our humping paid off. The Daily Mail and its weekend counterpart, The Mail on Sunday, along with the National Enquirer, The Globe, The Examiner, The New York Daily News, and publications across Europe all delivered SCADS of early publicity. We've replicated some of the coverage that the press lavished on our double-volumed release of revelations about "Hunky Humpy" Bogart.

HERE'S THE SECOND OF DARWIN PORTER'S
TWO-VOLUME SET OF BOOKS ABOUT BOGIE

HUMPHREY BOGART
THE MAKING OF A LEGEND
BY DARWIN PORTER

Startling New Information about Golden Age Hollywood that Readers Had Never Seen Before

Whereas Humphrey Bogart is always at the top of any list of the Entertainment Industry's most famous actors, very little is known about how he clawed his way to stardom from Broadway to Hollywood during Prohibition and the Jazz Age.

This radical expansion of one of Darwin Porter's pioneering biographies begins with Bogart's origins as the child of wealthy (morphine-addicted) parents in New York City, then examines the scandals, love affairs, breakthrough successes, and failures that launched Bogart on the road to becoming an American icon. Drawn from original interviews with friends and foes who knew a lot about what lay beneath his trenchcoat, this exposé covers Bogart's life from his birth in 1899 till his marriage to Lauren Bacall in 1945. It includes details about behind-the-scenes dramas associated with three mysterious marriages, and films such as *The Petrified Forest, The Maltese Falcon, High Sierra,* and *Casablanca.* Read all about the debut and formative years of the actor who influenced many generations of filmgoers, laying Bogie's life bare in a style you've come to expect from Darwin Porter. Exposed with all their juicy details is what Bogie never told his fourth wife, Lauren Bacall, herself a screen legend.

Bogart with **Ingrid Bergman** in *Casablanca* (1942), the film that made each of them a legend.

This revelatory book is based on dusty unpublished memoirs, letters, diaries, and often personal interviews from the women—and the men—who adored him. There are also shocking allegations from colleagues, former friends, and jilted lovers who wanted the screen icon to burn in hell. All this and more, much more, in Darwin Porter's exposé of Bogie's startling secret life.

Bogie (left photo) with three relatively unknown wives, *left to right*, **Helen Mencken, Mary Philips,** and **Mayo Methot.**

Humphrey Bogart, The Making of a Legend
Darwin Porter
A "cradle-to-grave" hardcover, 542 pages, with hundreds of photos
ISBN 978-1-936003-14-3. $27.95

You already know about what *Kate Remembered*, because there are a LOT of "deferential and obsequious whitewashes" already in print.

BUT HERE AT LAST IS AN UNVARNISHED ACCOUNT OF WHAT KATHARINE HEPBURN DESPERATELY WANTED TO FORGET

KATHARINE THE GREAT
A LIFETIME OF SECRETS REVEALED

DARWIN PORTER

Katharine Hepburn was the most obsessively secretive actress in Hollywood.

Her androgynous, pan-sexual appeal usually went over big with movie audiences-- until those disastrous flops when it didn't. This book tells the how and why of Kate Hepburn's most closely guarded secrets.

There's a carload of other biographies about Hepburn that eiher got the facts wrong or whitewashed them to the point where there's almost been a consistent act of academic sabotage.

But here at last is a biography that isn't afraid to wrestle with the outrageous ego and ferociously guarded privacy of Hollywood's most mysterious *Über-diva*:

Katharine Hepburn.

Katharine Hepburn was Hollywood's most successful, most eccentric, and most phobically secretive actress.

Here's the OTHER side of her life, exposed at last.

A gossippy tell-all that fans of Old Hollywood find fascinating.
558 pages, with photos
ISBN 0-9748118-0-7

Last year, Darwin Porter dumped The Secret Life of Humphrey Bogart on us, and we lapped up every sentence of it, despite some doubt about its veracity…His avowed sources were there, reliable and substantiated, amassed over several years and guarded until such time that the subjects had shed these mortal coils. Now, once again, the author draws upon his vast storehouse of notes and quotes regarding the movie stars of an earlier period—notes and quotes that could never be published in the time of the good old, bad old days of studio fiefdom, when damage contral was the name of the game.
This time out, Katharine Hepburn is the subject, …and the inner workings of a studio (RKO in the early 30s) in that period are relished."

--Conrad J. Doerr in Palm Springs' BOTTOM LINE

*D*arwin Porter's biography of Katharine Hepburn cannot be lightly dismissed or ignored. Connoisseurs of her life would do well to seek it out as a forbidden supplement" — The Sunday Times (London)

"Behind the scenes of her movies, Katharine Hepburn played the temptress to as many women as she did men, ranted and raved with her co-stars and directors, and broke into her neighbors' homes for fun. And somehow, she managed to keep all of it out of the press. As they say, *Katharine the Great* is hard to put down."
—The Dallas Voice

"The door to Hepburn's closet has finally been opened. This is the most honest and least apologetic biography of Hollywood's most ferociously private actress ever written."
—Boomer Times /Senior Life

BRANDO UNZIPPED

Darwin Porter

This "entertainingly outrageous" (FRONTIERS MAGAZINE) biography provides a definitive, blow-by-blow description of the "hot, provocative, and barely under control drama" that was the life of America's most famous Postwar actor.

"Lurid, raunchy, perceptive, and certainly worth reading...One of the ten best show-biz biographies of 2006."
—*The Sunday Times (London)*

"<u>Yummy</u>. An irresistably flamboyant romp of a read."
—*Books to Watch Out For*

"Astonishing. An extraordinarily detailed portrait of Brando that's as blunt, uncompromising, and X-rated as the man himself."
—*Women's Weekly*

"This shocking new book is sparking a major reassessment of Brando's legacy as one of Hollywood's most macho lotharios."
—*Daily Express (London)*

"As author Darwin Porter finds, it wasn't just the acting world Marlon Brando conquered. It was the actors, too."
—*Gay Times (London)*

"*Brando Unzipped* is the definitive gossip guide to the late, great actor's life."
—*The New York Daily News*

Marlon's Men
as reviewed by London's *Gay Times*

"He was considered one of the most dynamic and imposing actors of his generation, but as author Darwin Porter finds, it wasn't just the acting world that Marlon Brando conquered...It was the actors, too."

As serialized in the UK by THE SUNDAY TIMES and in Australia by *Women's Weekly* and *The Australian* Translations now available in French, Dutch, and Portuguese

FOREWORD MAGAZINE'S Book of the Year AWARD FINALIST

A definitive and artfully lurid hardcover with 625 indexed pages and hundreds of photos   ISBN 978-0-9748118-2-6.

FRANK SINATRA
THE BOUDOIR SINGER
All the Gossip Unfit to Print from the Glory Days of Ol' Blue Eyes

"When Sinatra dies, they'll donate his zipper to the Smithsonian." —Dean Martin

"F-R-A-N-K-I-E-E-E-E! Take my virginity!," screamed a bobby-soxer in midtown Manhattan in 1943

"Every time I sing a song, I'm actually making love on stage. Call me 'The Boudoir Singer.'" —Frank Sinatra

"He was no Joe DiMaggio in bed" said Marilyn Monroe.

"Mais oui! The Mercedes-Benz of men!" said Marlene Dietrich.

"A complete shit!" claimed Lauren Bacall when he dumped her at the aisle.

"Our problems were never in bed," said Ava Gardner, his greatest love. *"We were always great in bed: 10 pounds of Frank, 110 pounds of cock."*

"He's the most fascinating man in the world. Don't stick your hand in his cage." —Tommy Dorsey

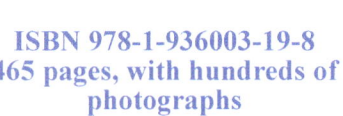

Who, exactly, was this mercurial, enigmatic man? For this compendium of show-biz scandal, Darwin Porter, former bureau chief and entertainment columnist for *The Miami Herald*, drew upon a tresure trove of celebrity contacts he accumlated over the years. This award-winning tell-all has everything you ever wanted to know about Sinatra—and more.

ISBN 978-1-936003-19-8
465 pages, with hundreds of photographs

DAMN YOU, SCARLETT O'HARA
The Private Lifes of Laurence Olivier and Vivien Leigh

Darwin Porter and Roy Moseley

This book tears away the velvet curtain previously draped over the reputations of this famous team, exposing with searing insights the depths of their sexual excess and interpersonal anguish. Some of the most iconic figures of the 20th century move through chapters that highlight a revelation on every page.

Hot, Shocking, Meticulously Researched, and Winner of FOUR Distinguished Literary awards since its controversial release in February of 2011.

Here, for the first time, is a biography that raises the curtain on the secret lives of (Lord) **Laurence Olivier**, known for his interpretation of the brooding and tormented Heathcliff of Emily Brontë's *Wuthering Heights*, and **Vivien Leigh,** who immortalized herself with her Oscar-winning portrayals of Scarlett O'Hara in Margaret Mitchell's *Gone With the Wind*, and as Blanche DuBois in Tennessee Williams' *A Streetcar Named Desire*.

Even though the spotlight shone on this famous pair throughout most of their tabloid-fueled careers, much of what went on behind the velvet curtain remained hidden from view until the publication of this ground-breaking biography. The PRIVATE LIVES (to borrow a phrase from their gossipy contemporary, Noël Coward) of this famous couple are exposed with searing insights into their sexual excess and personal anguish.

Dashing and "impossibly handsome," Laurence Olivier was pursued by some of the most dazzling luminaries, male and female, of the movie and theater worlds. The influential theatrical producer David Lewis asserted, "He would have slept with anyone." That included Richard Burton, who fell madly in love with him, as did Noël Coward. Lord Olivier's promiscuous, emotionally disturbed wife (Viv to her lovers) led a tumultuous off-the-record life whose paramours ranged from the A-list to men she picked up off the street. None of the brilliant roles depicted by Lord and Lady Olivier, on stage or on screen, ever matched the power and drama of personal dramas which wavered between Wagnerian opera and Greek tragedy. *Damn You, Scarlett O'Hara* is the definitive and most revelatory portrait ever published of the most talented and tormented actor and actress of the 20th century.

Darwin Porter is the co-author of this seminal work. Winner of numerous awards for his headline-generating biographies, he has shed new light on Marlon Brando, Steve McQueen, Paul Newman, Katharine Hepburn, Humphrey Bogart, Merv Griffin, Michael Jackson, and Howard Hughes.

Roy Moseley, this book's other co-author, maintained a decades-long association with the famous couple, nurturing them through their tumultuous triumphs, emotional breakdowns, and streams of suppressed scandal.

This award-winning book has received accolades from the following:
San Francisco Book Festival 2011, Honorable Mention for Biography
Paris Book Festival 2011, Winner, BEST BIOGRAPHY
New York Book Festival 2011, Honorable Mention for Biography
Beach Book Festival 2011, Grand Prize Winner for BEST SUMMER READING of 2011

ISBN 978-1-936003-15-0   Hardcover, 708 pages, with photos

THERE IS NOTHING LIKE A DAME

"BRUNETTES ARE BETTER, AND BRUNETTES HAVE MORE FUN,"

says Danforth Prince, President of Blood Moon Productions, about the release, this week, of his company's hot new biography of Hollywood's ultimate brunette, Elizabeth Taylor.

It's the publishing industry's most comprehensve overview of scandals associated with the world's most famous (brunette) movie star. ELIZABETH TAYLOR, with detailed descriptions of incidents that the Über-Goddess would NEVER have tolerated during her lifetime

WHAT A DAME!

Her enemies described her as the Serpent of the Nile.   WE think, however, that she was an *Uber*-Diva and Mega-Celebrity who redefined hedonism and pop culture in America.

IT'S ALL HERE

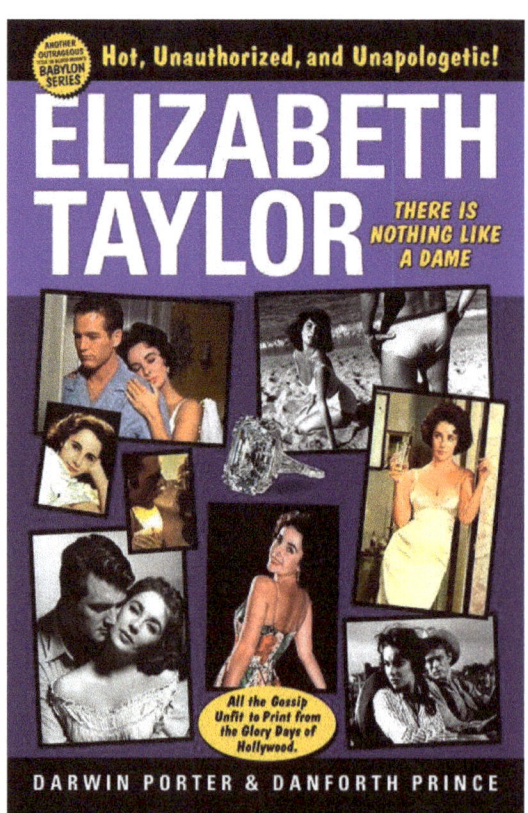

Sympathetic but shocking—a richly detailed roster of revelations and insights into LA LIZ and her ongoing role within America's Entertainment Industry during the peak of its muscle and power.

Her scandals—and a lot more—are exposed in a saga that's both sympathetic and shocking. This book contains enough irony, drama, and detail to fascinate anyone who's ever been intrigued with the lore and legend of the 20th Century's most notorious *femme fatale.* **All of them are included within this ode to a great Dame and a fabulous movie star.**

"I'm called a scarlet woman. That's wrong. I'm positively purple."
—Elizabeth Taylor

"Before they wither, Elizabeth Taylor's breasts will topple empires."
—Richard Burton

"I can't write an honest version of my own memoirs, because if I did, too many people would sue me."
—Elizabeth Taylor

TAYLOR: HOT, UNAUTHORIZED, UNAPOLOGETIC

ISBN 978-1-936003-31-0
600 pages, with photos

What did STEVE McQUEEN really have to do to make it in Show Biz? Finally—A COOL Biography that was too HOT to be published during the lifetime of its subject.

KING of COOL —TALES OF A LURID LIFE

"This book is potentially dangerous for middle-aged men."
—*The Sunday Times* (London)

The drama of Steve McQueen's personal life far exceeded any role he ever played on screen. Born to a prostitute, he was brutally molested by some of his mother's "johns," and endured gang rape in reform school. His drift into prostitution began when he was hired as a towel boy in the most notorious bordello in the Dominican Republic, where he starred in a string of cheap porno films. Returning to New York before migrating to Hollywood, he hustled men on Times Square and, as a "gentleman escort" in a borrowed tux, rich older women.

And then, sudden stardom as he became the world's top box office attraction. The abused became the abuser. "I live for myself, and I answer to nobody," he proclaimed. "The last thing I want to do is fall in love with a broad."

Thus began a string of seductions that included hundreds of overnight pickups--both male and female. Topping his A-list conquests were James Dean, Paul Newman, Marilyn Monroe, and Barbra Streisand. Finally, this pioneering biography explores the mysterious death of Steve McQueen. Were those salacious rumors really true?

    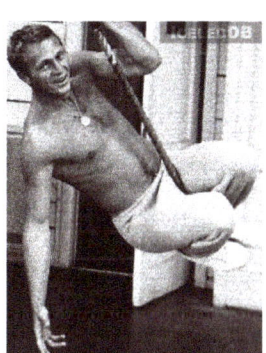

STEVE MCQUEEN
King of Cool, Tales of a Lurid Life
Darwin Porter
ISBN 978-1-936003-05-1   A carefully researched, 466-page hardcover with dozens of photos

MERV GRIFFIN, A LIFE IN THE CLOSET

Darwin Porter

This is the first unauthorized biography of Merv Griffin, a failed Big Band singer and unsuccessful actor who unexpectedly rewrote the rules of America's broadcasting industry.

Along the way, he met and befriended virtually everyone who mattered, made billions operating casinos and developing jingles, contests, and word games, and became the richest man on TV. All of this while maintaining a male harem and a secret life as America's most famously closeted homosexual.

This startling insight into the ways and means of the broadcasting industry is from a controversial writer whose previous work virtually re-defined the art of the celebrity biography,

In this comprehensive biography--the first published since Merv's death in 2007--celebrity biographer Darwin Porter reveals the amazing details behind the richest and most successful talk show host in the history of America's entertainment industry.

"Darwin Porter told me why he tore the door off Merv's closet.......*Heeeere's Merv!* is 560 pages, 100 photos, a truckload of gossip, and a bedful of unauthorized dish."

Cindy Adams, The NY Post

"Darwin Porter tears the door off Merv Griffin's closet with gusto in this sizzling, superlatively researched biography...It brims with insider gossip that's about Hollywood legends, writ large, smart, and with great style."

Richard LaBonté, BOOKMARKS

Most of his viewers (they numbered 20 million per day) thought that **Merv Griffin**'s life was an ongoing series of chatty segués--amiable, seamless, uncontroversial.
But things were far more complicated than viewers at the time ever thought. Here, from the writer who unzipped **Marlon Brando**, is the first post-mortem, unauthorized overview of the mysterious life of **the richest and most notorious man in television**

HOT, CONTROVERSIAL, & RIGOROUSLY RESEARCHED
HERE'S MERV!

Darwin Porter, Hardcover, with photos
ISBN 978-0-9786465-0-9

It's Blood Moon's *Babylon Series*

Outrageous overviews of exhibitionism, sexuality, and sin as filtered through 85 years of Hollywood indiscretion.

Three of them are already in print. Others are on the way.

HERE'S VOLUME ONE OF THREE
Hollywood Babylon It's Back!

"From the Golden Age of beautiful bombshells and handsome hunks to today's sleaziest, most corrupt, and most deliciously indecorous hotties, this is the hottest compilation of inter-generational scandal in the history of Hollywood.

As they were unfolding, these stories were known only within Hollywood's most decadent cliques. But all of that changed with the release of this series.

Dishing with abandon, the authors spare no one—especially not the dead. Marilyn Monroe had an affair with Ronald Reagan. Marilyn also had a tryst with Joan Crawford but refused to make it an ongoing affair. James Dean showed a disconcerting interest in a 12-year-old boy in the early 1950s. Lucille Ball launched herself into show business as a hooker, and her husband Desi Arnaz had a fling with Cesar Romero. Cary Grant had an incestuous relationship with his stepson, Lance Reventlow. And this, by the way, is only the tip of the iceberg."

—**Rush & Molloy, The NY Daily News**

"The American movie industry is always eager for the spotlight if the close-up is flattering and good for business. But Hollywood may get more than it bargained for with **Hollywood Babylon's** compendium of stories, rumors, and myths. Virtually every page features one kind of train wreck or another, usually accompanied by spectacularly lurid photographs. Darwin Porter and Danforth Prince provide a hair-raising list of compromises and strategically granted sexual favors as proof that some stars will do anything for a part. Try as you might, you won't be able to stop turning the pages. In revealing so many facts previously under wraps, this book, in fact, raises the question of how much more remains hidden."

—**Shelf Awareness/ Bookselling News**

"These books will set the graves of Hollywood's cemeteries spinning" Daily Express

Hollywood Babylon-It's Back!
Darwin Porter and Danforth Prince
Hardcover, 408 outrageous pages, with hundreds of photos

ISBN 978-0-9748118-8-8

HERE'S VOLUME TWO OF THREE-PART SERIES
HOLLYWOOD BABYLON STRIKES AGAIN!
THE PROFOUNDLY OUTRAGEOUS VOLUME TWO OF BLOOD MOON'S BABYLON SERIES

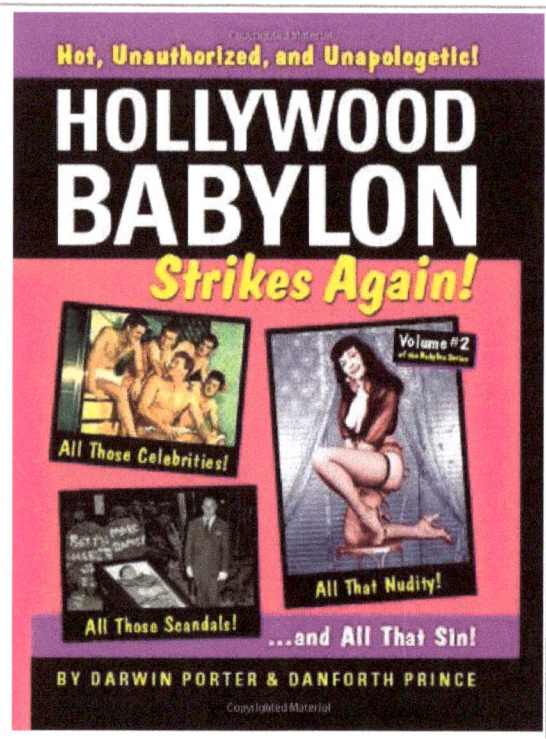

"You know, everyone thinks Hollywood is a cesspool of epic proportions today, but please! It's always been that way. And if you love smutty celebrity dirt as much as I do (and if you don't, what's wrong with you? Ya got morals or something?), then have I got a book for you!"
—**The Hollywood Offender**

"Despite Babylon's many explicit photos, the real meat (haha, you see what I did there?) of the book is the stories of old Hollywood that further prove that the whole place needs to be wiped out by an act of God. How crazy and depraved was Hollywood back then? Hold onto your f****** hat."
—**from blogsite I Don't Like You in that Way (HOLLYWOOD IS INSANE)**

"This is the best classic scandal bible on Hollywood ever published. And believe me, I;'ve read hundreds...It's a must for anyone who's ever been to the movies or watched TV."
—**David Hartnell**

"The reader is truly spoiled for choice when selecting the high (or low) points in HBIB, but the standout chapters involve Lucille Ball (who was apparently aptly named in her pre-Desi days), Bette Davis (who may very well have caused the delayed death of her second husband by clobbering him with a lamp), Ava Gardner (who enjoyed hanging out with hookers—just to talk. Really), Cary Grant and heiress Barbara Hutton (and Barbara's son Lance and Cary...), and Nick Adams ('60s TV star whose suicide might have been arranged by the Memphis Mafia. I'm already contemplating what Porter and Prince could have planned for future volumes."
—**The Pride Edition of Seattle Gay News, June 20, 2008**

"It's the more outragious accusations from this book that linger in the mind: That James Dean was having it off with a 12-year-old boy, Cary Grant was f****** his stepson. Nick Adams was murdered because he was writing a tell-all autobiography, Errol Flynn raped his son Sean, Marcello Mastroianni was regularly blown by Pope Paul VI. Lucille Ball was a hooker, and (sadly) Tony Randall was a self-loathing 'faggot.' This is one hell of a gossip bible."
—**Barry Lowe in SX News** (Australia)

Winner of the Los Angeles Book Festival's Best Nonfiction Title of 2010, and the New England Book Festival's Best Anthology for 2010.

"These books will set the graves of Hollywood's cemeteries spinning"   Daily Express

Hollywood Babylon Strikes Again!
Darwin Porter and Danforth Prince
Hardcover, 380 outrageous pages, with hundreds of photos

ISBN 978-1-936003-12-9

HERE'S VOLUME THREE OF AN AWARD-WINNING THREE-PART SERIES

HOLLYWOOD BABYLON WITH DETOURS TO GOMORRAH

THE PROFOUNDLY OUTRAGEOUS THIRD VOLUME OF BLOOD MOON'S BABYLON SERIES

OUT OF THE CELLULOID CLOSET—HOMOSEXUALITY IN THE MOVIES

Hip, Funny, & Informative.
The most comprehensive anthology of GLBTQ film descriptions and reviews ever published.

DID YOU KNOW? That before the worldwide breakout of Covid, Blood Moon launched what was envisioned as an ongoing series of guidebooks to gay & lesbian film, replete with special features, gossip about "When Divas Clash," insights into intra-industry *brouhahas*, AND the Blood Moon Awards.

Winner of the New England Book Festival's Best GLBT Title of 2010, and winner of coveted nominations from Foreword Magazine for its Book of the Year (Performing Arts), from the Benjamin Franklin Awards for "Best GLBT nonfiction title." It also won an Honorable Mention from the Hollywood Book Festival.

Volume One (published 2006)
ISBN 978-0-9748118-4-0

Volume Two (published 2007)
ISBN 978-0-9748118-7-1

The Collector's Edition
An indispensible sourcebook.
ISBN 978-0-9748118-9-5

WHAT THE CRITICS SAID

"Authoritative, exhaustive, and essential, it's the queer girl's and queer boy's one-stop resource for what to add to their feature-film queues. The film synopses and the snippets of critic's reviews are reason enough to keep this annual compendium of cinematic information close to the DVD player. But the extras--including the special features and the Blood Moon Awards--are butter on the popcorn."
—*Richard LaBonte, Books to Watch Out For*

"Blood Moon's Guide to Gay and Lesbian Film is like having access to a feverishly compiled queer film fan's private scrapbook. Each edition is a snapshot of where we are in Hollywood now. It's also a lot of fun..."
— *Gay Times (London)*

"Startling. It documents everything from the mainstream to the obscure, detailing dozens of queer films from the last few years."
—*HX (New York)*

"Includes everything fabu in the previous years' movies. An essential guide for both the casual viewer and the hard-core movie watching homo."
—*Bay Windows (Boston)*

"From feisty Blood Moon Productions, this big, lively guidebook of (mostly) recent gay and gayish films is not meant to be a dust-collecting reference book covering the history of GLBT films. Instead, it's an annual running commentary on what's new and what's going on in gay filmmaking."
—*Mandate*

MORE ABOUT
50 Years of Queer Cinema
500 of the Best GLBTQ Films Ever Made
(See Previous Page)

It's a comprehensive paperback designed as a reference source for private homes & libraries. 534 pages, with film reviews, gossip, special features, insider dish, and hundreds of photos. **ISBN 978-0-9748118-9-5**

AN INDISPENSIBLE REFERENCE SOURCE FOR FILMS ABOUT

The Love that Dare Not Speak Its Name

As late as 1958, homosexuality couldn't even be mentioned in a movie, as proven by the elaborate lengths the producers of Tennessee Williams' swampy Cat on a Hot Tin Roof took to evade the obvious fact that its hero, Paul Newman, was playing it gay. And in spite of the elaborate lengths its producers took to camouflage its lavender aspects, in-the-know viewers during the late 50s realized all along that Joe E. Brown was fully aware that Jack Lemmon wasn't a biological female ("nobody's perfect!") in Some Like it Hot (1959).

That kind of baroque subterfuge ended abruptly in 1960, when cinema emerged from its celluloid closet. With the release of Boys in the Band in 1970, gay cinema had come of age. It was queer and here to stay. Decades later came Brokeback Mountain, Transamerica, and Milk.

This comprehensive anthology documents it all, bringing into focus a sweeping rundown of cinema's most intriguing Gay, Lesbian, Bisexual, Transgendered, and "Queer Questioning" films that deserves a home next to the DVD player as well as on the reference shelves of public libraries. Crucial to the viability of this book is the fact that new DVD releases have made these films available to new generations of viewers for the first time since their original release.

More than just a dusty library reference, this book shamelessly spills 50 quasi-closeted years of Hollywood secrets—all of them in glorious technicolor.

"In the Internet age, where every movie, queer or otherwise, is blogged about somewhere, a hefty print compendium of film facts and pointed opinion might seem anachronistic. But flipping through well-reasoned pages of commentary is so satisfying. Add to that physical thrill the charm of analysis that is sometimes sassy and always smart, and this filtered survey of short reviews is a must for queer-film fans.

"In part one, Porter and Prince provide a succinct "A to Z romp" through 500 films, with quick plot summaries and on-point critical assessments, each film summed up with a pithy headline: *Yossi & Jagger* is "Macho Israeli Soldiers Make Love, Not War."

"The films surveyed in part two are quirkier fare, 160 "less publicized" effort , including—no lie—*Karl Rove, I Love You*, in which gay actor Dan Butler falls for 'George W. Bush's Turd Blossom.'

"Essays on **Derek Jarman, Tennessee Williams, Andy Warhol, Jack Wrangler, Joe Gage** and others—and on how *The Front Runner* never got made—round out this indispensable survey of gay-interest cinema."

—RICHARD LABONTE, BOOK MARKS/QSYNDICATE

CORRUPTION, MENDACITY, & PUNITIVE HANKY PANKY FROM WITHIN THE FBI

J. EDGAR HOOVER & CLYDE TOLSON

INVESTIGATING THE SEXUAL SECRETS OF AMERICA'S MOST FAMOUS MEN AND WOMEN

Darwin Porter

CRIMINAL ACTIVITIES AND VOYEURISTIC MANIA FROM AMERICA'S CHIEF LAW-ENFORCEMENT OFFICER

It was 1928. Into FBI Director **J. Edgar Hoover**'s Office walked a job applicant. *Clyde Tolson*, fresh from America's Corn Belt. He was handsome, macho, well-built, and soft-spoken. Later, he'd be called "the Gary Cooper of the FBI."

Hoover sat up and took immediate notice of Tolson's commanding presence, especially his piercing black eyes. After an hour of chatting with Tolson, Hoover proclaimed, "Our bureau needs more men like you."

When Hoover invited Tolson to his home for dinner that night, the meal would mark the beginning of thousands served over the next forty years. Before the rooster crowed, Hoover had been nicknamed "Speed," and Tolson was called "Junior." In public, of course, Tolson referred to Hoover as "The Boss."

But as Tolson, one drunken night, told their "fag hag," **Ethel Merman:** "When we go home and shut the door, I'm the boss."

For their sexual amusement, but often for blackmail purposes, Junior and Speed became intimately familiar with the obscene files of the FBI. Illegal wiretaps and hidden microphones were used to destroy their enemies.

"Hoover ruled as the head of America's Gestapo," claimed an angry **Harry S Truman**. Through nine different presidents, Hoover kept his job, even blackmailing **Dwight D. Eisenhower**.

The files he accumulated on "my worst enemy," **Eleanor Roosevelt**, silenced her opposition to him. As time went by, Hoover and Tolson opened a celebrity version of Pandora's box, learning the darkest secrets of **Errol Flynn** (was he a Nazi?), **Marilyn Monroe, Elvis Presley, the Kennedys, Marlon Brando, Rock Hudson**, and especially **Martin Luther King, Jr.**, among countless others.

"For decades, America has been in the grip of two homosexual lovers," **Lyndon B. Johnson** told his pal, **Florida Senator George Smathers**. "And there's not a God damn thing I can do about it. He's got us by the *cojones*, and he'll never let go."

For nearly half a century, this peculiarly private man, who carefully guarded his own dark secrets, held virtually unchecked public power. He manipulated every president from **FDR** (*"Sometime, J. Edgar, we'll catch you with your pants down"*) to **Richard Nixon**. He used illegal wiretaps and hidden microphones to destroy anyone who opposed him. And just for fun, he and bedmate Clyde Tolson investigated America's greatest entertainers, including **Marilyn Monroe** and **Elvis Presley**; its greatest scientists (including **Albert Einstein**), and its greated civil rights leaders.

Darwin Porter's saga of power and corruption has a revelation on every page—cross dressing, gay parties, sexual indiscretions, hustlers for sale, alliances with the Mafia, and criminal activity by the nation's chief law enforcer.

It's all here, with chilling details about the abuse of power on the dark side of the American saga.
But mostly it's the decades-long love story of America's two most powerful men who could tell presidents "how to skip rope." (Hoover's words.)

*Darwin Porter has been fascinated by J. Edgar Hoover, the Justice Department, and the American concept of fame since he worked as an entertainment columnist for **The Miami Herald**. Since then, he's evolved into one of the most acclaimed celebrity biographers in the world.*

ANOTHER HELLUVA GOOD READ FROM DARWIN PORTER   ISBN 978-1-936003-25-9

LANA TURNER

The Sweater Girl, Celluloid Venus, Sex Nymph to the G.I.s who won World War II, and Hollywood's OTHER Most Notorious Blonde

Beautiful and Bad,
Her Full Story Has Never Been Told. UNTIL NOW!

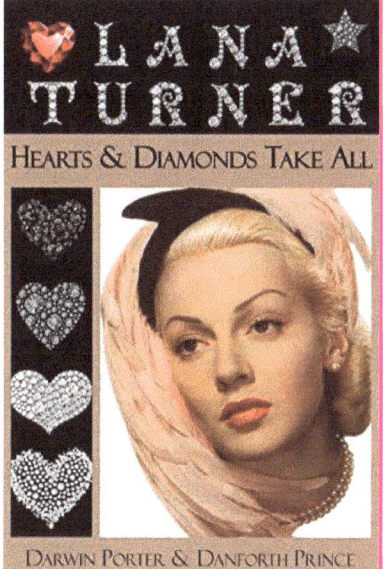

Lana Turner was the most scandalous, most copied, and most gossiped-about actress in Hollywood. When her abusive Mafia lover was murdered in her house, every newspaper in the Free World described the murky dramas with something approaching hysteria.

Blood Moon's salacious but empathetic new biography exposes the public and private dramas of the girl who changed the American definition of what it REALLY means to be a blonde.

Here's how CALIFORNIA BOOKWATCH and THE MIDWEST BOOK REVIEW described the mega-celebrity as revealed in this book:

"Lana Turner: Hearts and Diamonds Take All belongs on the shelves of any collection strong in movie star biographies in general and Hollywood evolution in particular, and represents no lightweight production, appearing on the 20th anniversary of Lana Turner's death to provide a weighty survey packed with new information about her life.

"One would think that just about everything to be known about The Sweater Girl would have already appeared in print, but it should be noted that Lana Turner: Hearts and Diamonds Take All offers many new revelations not just about Turner, but about the movie industry in the aftermath of World War II.

"From Lana's introduction of a new brand of covert sexuality in women's movies to her scandalous romances among the stars, her extreme promiscuity, her search for love, and her notorious flings - even her involvement in murder - are all probed in a revealing account of glamour and movie industry relationships that bring Turner and her times to life.

"Some of the greatest scandals in Hollywood history are intricately detailed on these pages, making this much more than another survey of her life and times, and a 'must have' pick for any collection strong in Hollywood history in general, gossip and scandals and the real stories behind them, and Lana Turner's tumultuous career, in particular."

Lana Turner, Hearts & Diamonds Take All
Winner of the coveted "Best Biography" Award from the San Francisco Book Festival

Darwin Porter and Danforth Prince
Softcover, 622 pages, with photos. ISBN 978-1-936003-53-2

Carrie Fisher & Debbie Reynolds
Princess Leia & Unsinkable Tammy in Hell

It's history's first comprehensive, unauthorized overview of one of the greatest mother-daughter acts in showbiz history, Debbie Reynolds ("hard as nails and with more balls than any five guys I've ever known") and her talented, often traumatized daughter, Carrie Fisher ("one of the smartest, hippest chicks in Hollywood"). Evolving for decades under the unrelenting glare of public scrutiny, each became a world-class symbol of the social and cinematic tastes that prevailed during their heydays as celebrity icons in Hollywood.

It's a scandalous saga of the ferociously loyal relationship of the "boop-boop-a-doop" girl with her intergalactic STAR WARS daughter, and their iron-willed, "true grit" battles to out-race changing tastes in Hollywood.

Loaded with revelations about "who was doing what to whom" during the final gasps of Golden Age Hollywood, it's an All-American story about the price of glamour, career-related pain, family anguish, romantic betrayals, lingering guilt, and the volcanic shifts that affected a scrappy, mother-daughter team—and everyone else who ever loved the movies.

"Feeling misunderstood by the younger (female) members of your gene pool? This is the Hollywood exposé every grandmother should give to her granddaughter, a roadmap like Debbie Reynolds might have offered to Billie Lourd."

—Marnie O'Toole

"Hold onto your hats, the "bad boys" of Blood Moon Productions are back. This time, they have an exhaustively researched and highly readable account of the greatest mother-daughter act in the history of show business: Debbie Reynolds and Carrie (Princess Leia) Fisher. If celebrity gossip and inside dirt is your secret desire, check it out. This is a fabulous book that we heartily recommend. It will not disappoint. We rate it worthy of four stars."
—MAJ Glenn MacDonald, U.S. Army Reserve (Retired), © MilitaryCorruption.com

"How is a 1950s-era movie star, (TAMMY) supposed to cope with her postmodern, substance-abusing daughter (PRINCESS LEIA), the rebellious, high-octane byproduct of Rock 'n Roll, Free Love, and postwar Hollywood's most scandal-soaked marriage? Read about it here, in Blood Moon's unauthorized double exposé about how Hollywood's toughest (and savviest) mother-daughter team maneuvered their way through shifting definitions of fame, reconciliation, and fortune."

—Donna McSorley

Winner of the coveted "Best Biography" Award from the 2018
New York Book Festival

Carrie Fisher & Debbie Reynolds,
Unsinkable Tammy & Princess Leia in Hell
Darwin Porter & Danforth Prince

630 pages Softcover with photos. ISBN 978-1-936003-57-0

THIS IS WHAT HAPPENS WHEN A DEMENTED BILLIONAIRE LANDS IN HOLLYWOOD

From his reckless pursuit of love as a rich teenager to his final days as a demented fossil, Howard Hughes tasted the best and worst of the century he occupied. Along the way, he changed the worlds of aviation and entertainment forever. This biography reveals inside details about his destructive and usually scandalous associations with other Hollywood players.

HOWARD HUGHES, HELL'S ANGEL

Darwin Porter

Set amid descriptions of the unimaginable changes that affected America between Hughes's birth in 1905 and his death in 1976, this book gives an insider's perspective about what money can buy--and what it can't.

"The Aviator flew both ways. Porter's biography presents new allegations about Hughes' shady dealings with some of the biggest names of the 20th century"
—*New York Daily News*

"Darwin Porter's access to film industry insiders and other Hughes confidants supplied him with the resources he needed to create a portrait of Hughes that both corroborates what other Hughes biographies have divulged, and go them one better."
—*Foreword Magazine*

"Thanks to this bio of Howard Hughes, we'll never be able to look at the old pinups in quite the same way again."
—*The Times* (London)

Contrary to popular Hollywood legend, producer Howard Hughes did not seduce **Jane Russell** during the making of the controversial *The Outlaw*. Instead, he ordered **Jack Beutel**, cast as Billy the Kid, to join him in bed.

Howard Hughes lavished gifts and introduced a **young Robert Taylor**, *depicted above*, to a life of flying high in airplanes, sailing yachts, and "being devoured" in bed.

Billie Dove *(photo, left)* the grandest silent screen diva of her era, became his lover...until she gave him syphilis

Winner of a respected literary award from the Los Angeles Book Festival, this is an astonishing tale of outrageous fortune, unbouonded ambition, and tragic greed.
814 pages, with photos **ISBN 978-1-936003-13-6**

ANNOUNCING BLOOD MOON'S PRESIDENTIAL SERIES

DID YOU KNOW? That books about Presidential (or pre-Presidential) scandals are as much a part of Blood Moon's repertoire as the ones we've associated with movie stars?

If you're in the mood for salacious (and underpublicized) overviews of what really went on in POTUS rumpus rooms, or if you're interested in embarassments that show Presidents (or pre-Presidents, before they were elected) and their Ladies as less than saintly, check out Blood Moon's quintet of Presidential *exposés* within the pages of this catalogue.

THE KENNEDYS

ALL THE GOSSIP UNFIT TO PRINT

A Staggering Compendium of Indiscretions Associated With Seven Key Players in the Kennedy Clan; A Cornucopia of Relatively Unknown but Carefully Documented Scandals from the Golden Age of Camelot. Jaw-dropping, a myth-shattering overview of a family consumed by its own passions.

Darwin Porter & Danforth Prince

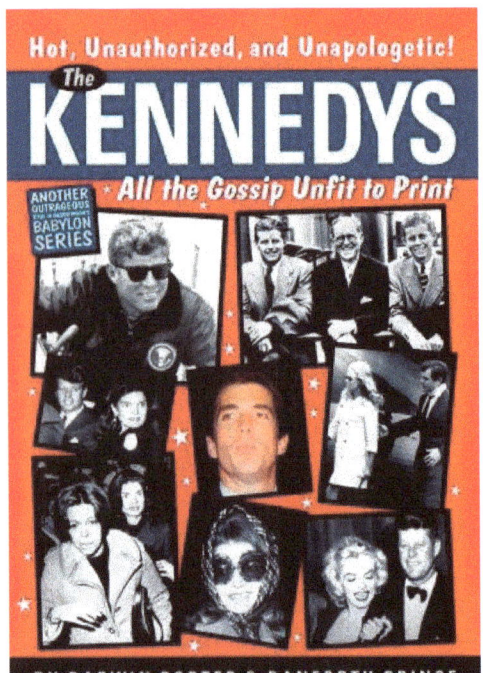

The great enemy of truth is very often not the lie—deliberate, contrived, and dishonest, but the myth—persistent, persuasive, and unrealistic."
—John F. Kennedy

"God, I hate Camelot. I've begged Jackie to tell them to play something else, but it's like talking to a goddamn brick wall."
—JFK, on the Marine String Orchestra playing at the White House.

"A vulgar slut, a publicity seeker, an egomaniac, a self-promoter, a vicious bitch, an unbalanced drug addict, an alcoholic whore, a dime-a-dance floosie"
—Jacqueline Kennedy on Marilyn Monroe

"Listen, honey, if it wasn't for me, your boyfriend wouldn't even be in the White House."
—Sam Giancana to Judith Campbell Exner

"The greatest twenty seconds of my life."
—Angie Dickenson, describing JFK

"JFK was a man thoroughly out of control, thoroughly out of his depth, and maybe thoroughly out of his mind.. He was just a hoodlum Prince of Camelot. He was the incarnation of Sodom and Gomorrah."
—Seymour Hirsch, *The Dark Side of Camelot*

The Kennedys were the first true movie stars to occupy the White House. They were also Washington's horniest political tribe, and although America loved their humor, their style, and their panache, we took delight in this tabloid-style documentation of their hundreds of staggering indiscretions.

Keepers of the dying embers of Camelot won't like it, but Kennedy historians and aficionados will interpret it as required reading.

Hardcover, with hundreds of photos and 450 meticulously researched, highly detailed, and very gossipy pages with more outrageous scandal than 90% of American voters during the heyday of Camelot could possibly have imagined.

ISBN 978-1-936003-17-4.

LOVE TRIANGLE
Ronald Reagan, Jane Wyman, & Nancy Davis

HOW MUCH DO YOU REALLY KNOW ABOUT THE REAGANS?

THIS BOOK TELLS EVERYTHING ABOUT THE SHOW-BIZ SCANDALS THEY DESPERATELY WANTED TO FORGET.

Unique in the history of publishing, this scandalous TRIPLE BIOGRAPHY focuses on the Hollywood indiscretions of former U.S. president Ronald Reagan and his two wives. A proud and Presidential addition to Blood Moon's Babylon series, it digs deep into what these three young and attractive movie stars were doing decades before two of them took over the Free World.

As reviewed by Diane Donovan, Senior Reviewer at the California Bookwatch section of the Midwest Book Review: "Love Triangle: Ronald Reagan, Jane Wyman & Nancy Davis may find its way onto many a Republican Reagan fan's reading shelf; but those who expect another Reagan celebration will be surprised: this is lurid Hollywood exposé writing at its best, and outlines the truths surrounding one of the most provocative industry scandals in the world.

"There are already so many biographies of the Reagans on the market that one might expect similar mile-markers from this: be prepared for shock and awe; because Love Triangle doesn't take your ordinary approach to biography and describes a love triangle that eventually bumped a major Hollywood movie star from the possibility of being First Lady and replaced her with a lesser-known Grade B actress (Nancy Davis).

"From politics and betrayal to romance, infidelity, and sordid affairs, Love Triangle is a steamy, eye-opening story that blows the lid off of the Reagan illusion to raise eyebrows on both sides of the big screen.

"Black and white photos liberally pepper an account of the careers of all three and the lasting shock of their stormy relationships in a delightful pursuit especially recommended for any who relish Hollywood gossip."

In 2015, LOVE TRIANGLE, Blood Moon Productions' overview of the early dramas associated with Ronald Reagan's scandal-soaked career in Hollywood, was designated by the Awards Committee of the HOLLYWOOD BOOK FESTIVAL as Runner-Up to Best Biography of the Year.

LOVE TRIANGLE:
Ronald Reagan, Jane Wyman, & Nancy Davis
Darwin Porter & Danforth Prince
Softcover, 6" x 9", with hundreds of photos. ISBN 978-1-936003-41-9

BILL & HILLARY
So This Is That Thing Called Love

Confused about how to interpret their raucous pasts?
This uncensored tale about a love affair that changed the course of politics and the planet is of compelling interest to anyone involved in the slugfests and incendiary wars of THE CLINTONS.

This is both a biographical coverage of the Clintons and a political *exposé*; a detailed, weighty exploration that traces the couple's social and political evolution, from how each entered the political arena to their White House years under Bill Clinton's presidency.

"Containing gossip, scandal, and biographical sketches, it delves deeply into the news and politics of its times, presenting enough historical background to fully explore the underlying controversies affecting the Clinton family and their choices.

"Sidebars of information and black and white photos liberally peppered throughout the account offer visual reinforcement to the exploration, lending it the feel and tone of both a gossip column and political piece—something that probes not just Clinton interactions but the D.C. political milieu as a whole.

"The result may appear weighty, sporting over five hundred pages, but is an absorbing, top recommendation for readers of both biographical and political pieces who will thoroughly enjoy this spirited, lively, and thought-provoking analysis."
— THE MIDWEST BOOK REVIEW

***

Shortly after its release in December of 2015, this book received a literary award *(Runner-up to Best Biography of the Year)* from **the New England Book Festival.** As stated by a spokesperson for the Awards, "The New England Book Festival is an annual competition honoring excellence in books, with particular focus on projects that deserve closer attention from the academic community. Congratulations to Blood Moon and its authors, especially Darwin Porter, for his highly entertaining analysis of Clinton's double-barreled presidential regime, and the sometimes hysterical over-reaction of their enemies."

BILL & HILLARY
So This Is That Thing Called Love
Darwin Porter & Danforth Prince
Softcover, with photos.   ISBN 978-1-936003-47-1

PLAYBOY'S HUGH HEFNER
EMPIRE OF SKIN

THE COMPREHENSIVE, UNAUTHORIZED *EXPOSÉ* THAT EVERY SURVIVOR OF THE SEXUAL REVOLUTION WILL WANT TO READ
DARWIN PORTER & DANFORTH PRINCE

Hugh Hefner, the most iconic Playboy in human history, was a visionary, an empire-builder, and a pajama-clad pipe-smoker with a pre-coital grin.

In 1953, he published his first edition of *Playboy* with money borrowed from his puritanical, Nebraska-born mother. Marilyn Monroe appeared on the cover, with her nude calendar inside.

Rebelling against his strict upbringing, he lost his virginity at the age of 22.

His magazine, punctuated with nudes and studded with articles by major literary figures, reached its zenith at eight million readers. As a "tasteful pornographer," Hef became a cultural warrior, fighting government censorship all the way to the U.S. Supreme Court. As the years and his notoriety progressed, he became an advocate of abortion, LGBT equality, and the legalization of marijuana. Eventually, he engaged in "pubic wars" with Bob Guccione, the flamboyant founder of *Penthouse,* which cut into Hef's sales.

Lauded by millions of avid readers, he was denounced as "the father of sex addiction," "a huckster," "a lecherous low-brow feeder of our vices," "a misogynist," and, near the end of his life, "a symbol of priapic senility."

During his heyday, some of the biggest male stars in Hollywood, including Warren Beatty, Sammy Davis, Jr., Mick Jagger, and Jack Nicholson, came to frolic behind Hef's guarded walls, stripping nude in the hot tub grotto before sampling the rotating beds upstairs. Even a future U.S. president came to call. "Donald Trump had an appreciation of Bunny tail," Hef said.

Hefner's last Viagra-fueled marriage was to a beautiful blonde, Crystal Harris, 60 years his junior. "There's nothing wrong in a man marrying a girl who could be his great-granddaughter," he was famously quoted as saying.

This ground-breaking biography, the latest in Blood Moon's string of outrageously unvarnished myth-busters, was the first published since Hefner's death at the age of 91 in 2017. It's a provocative saga, rich in tantalizing, often shocking detail. Not recommended for the sanctimonious or the faint of heart, and loaded with ironic, little-known details about the trendsetter's epic challenges and the solutions he devised.

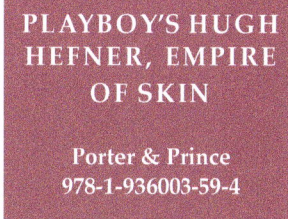

PLAYBOY'S HUGH HEFNER, EMPIRE OF SKIN

Porter & Prince
978-1-936003-59-4

PINK TRIANGLE

THE FEUDS AND PRIVATE LIVES OF
TENNESSEE WILLIAMS, GORE VIDAL, TRUMAN CAPOTE,
& FAMOUS MEMBERS OF THEIR ENTOURAGES

This book, the only one of its kind, reveals the backlot intrigues associated with the literary and script-writing enfants terribles of America's entertainment community during the mid-20th century.

It exposes their bitchfests, their slugfests, and their relationships with the glitterati—Marilyn Monroe, Brando, the Oliviers, the Paleys, U.S. Presidents, a gaggle of other movie stars, millionaires, and international *débauchés*.

This is for anyone who's interested in the formerly concealed scandals of Hollywood and Broadway, and the values and pretentions of both the literary community and the entertainment industry.

"A banquet... If PINK TRIANGLE had not been written for us, we would have had to research and type it all up for ourselves...Pink Triangle is nearly seven hundred pages of the most entertaining histrionics ever sliced, spiced, heated, and serviced up to the reading public. Everything that Blood Moon has done before pales in comparison. Given the fact that the subjects of the book themselves were nearly delusional on the subject of themselves (to say nothing of each other) it is hard to find fault. Add to this the intertwined jungle that was the relationship among Williams, Capote, and Vidal, of the times they vied for things they loved most—especially attention—and the times they enthralled each other and the world, [Pink Triangle is] the perfect antidote to the Polar Vortex."
—**Vinton McCabe** in the *NY JOURNAL OF BOOKS*

"Full disclosure: I have been a friend and follower of Blood Moon Productions' tomes for years, and always marveled at the amount of information in their books—it's staggering. The index alone to Pink Triangle runs to 21 pages—and the scale of names in it runs like a Who's Who of American social, cultural and political life through much of the 20th century."
—**Perry Brass** in *The Huffington Post*

"We Brits are not spared the Porter/Prince silken lash either. PINK TRIANGLE's research is, quite frankly, breathtaking. PINK TRIANGLE will fascinate you for many weeks to come. Once you have made the initial titillating dip, the day will seem dull without it."
—**Jeffery Tayor** in *The Sunday Express (UK)*

PINK TRIANGLE—THE FEUDS AND PRIVATE LIVES OF
TENNESSEE WILLIAMS, GORE VIDAL, TRUMAN CAPOTE,
AND FAMOUS MEMBERS OF THEIR ENTOURAGES

DARWIN PORTER & DANFORTH PRINCE

SOFTCOVER, 700 PAGES, WITH PHOTOS   ISBN 978-1-936003-37-2

THEY CALLED HIM "THE ROCK."

ROCK HUDSON

IN THE DYING DAYS OF HOLLYWOOD'S GOLDEN AGE, ROCK HUDSON WAS THE MOST CELEBRATED PHALLIC SYMBOL AND LUST OBJECT IN AMERICA. THIS BOOK DESCRIBES HIS RISE, FALL, AND THE INDUSTRY THAT CREATED HIM.

Rock Hudson charmed every casting director in Hollywood (and movie-goers throughout America) as the mega-star they most wanted to share PILLOW TALK with. This book describes his rise and fall, and how he handled himself as a closeted but promiscuous bisexual during an age when EVERYBODY tried to throw him onto a casting couch.

Based on dozens of face-to-face interviews with the actor's friends, co-conspirators, and enemies, and researched over a period of a half century, this biography reveals the shame, agonies, and irony of Rock Hudson's complete, never-before-told story.

In 2017, the year of its release, it was designated as winner ("BEST BIOGRAPHY") at two of the Golden State's most prestigious literary competitions, the Northern California and the Southern California Book Festivals.

It was also favorably reviewed by the *Midwestern Book Review, California Book Watch, KNEWS RADIO, the New York Journal of Books*, and the editors at the most popular Seniors' magazine in Florida, *BOOMER TIMES*.

 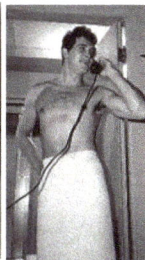 

Pansexual and promiscuous, Rock Hudson managed to perform, again and again and again, both onscreen and in private. Read all about his rise and fall, and the industry in which, for a while at least, he thrived.

ROCK HUDSON EROTIC FIRE

Darwin Porter & Danforth Prince
Softcover, 624 pages, with dozens of photos, 6" x 9" ISBN 978-1-936003-55-6

BURT REYNOLDS
PUT THE PEDAL TO THE METAL

How a Nude Centerfold Sex Symbol Seduced Hollywood

In the 1970s and '80s, Georgia-born Burt Reynolds —the highest-grossing movie star of his era— represented a new breed of movie star.

Charming and relentlessly macho, he was a good old Southern boy who made hearts throb and audiences laugh. He was Burt Reynolds, a football hero and a guy you might have shared some jokes with in a redneck bar. After an impressive but tormented career, rivers of negative publicity, a self-admitted history of bad choices, and a spectacular fall from Hollywood grace, he died in Jupiter, Florida, at the age of 82 in September of 2018.

For five years, both in terms of earnings and popularity, he was the number one box office star in the world. *Smokey and the Bandit* (1977) became the biggest-grossing car-chase film of all time. As he put it, perhaps as a means of bolstering his image, "I like nothing better than making love to some of the most beautiful women in the world." Perhaps he was referring to his romantic and sexual involvements with dozens of celebrities from New Hollywood. More unusual dalliances occurred with Marilyn Monroe, whom he once picked up on his way to the Actors Studio in New York City. Love with another VIP came in the form of that "Sweetheart of the G.I.s," Dinah Shore, sparking chatter. "I appreciate older women," he once said in a moment of self-revelation. According to Sally Field, "Burt still lives in my heart." But then she expressed relief that, because of his recent death, he never read what she'd said about him in her memoir.

Men liked him too: He played poker with Frank Sinatra; shared boozy nights with John Wayne; intercepted a "pass" from closeted Spencer Tracy; talked "penis size" with Mark Wahlberg; went "wench-hunting" with Johnny Carson; and threatened to kill Marlon Brando, to whom his appearance was often compared. He also hung out with Bette Davis. ("I always had a thing for her.")

His least happy (some said "most poisonous") marriage—to Loni Anderson—was rife with dramas played out more in the tabloids than in the boudoir. According to Reynolds, "She's vain, she's a rotten mother, she sleeps around, and she spent all my money."

This biography—the first comprehensive overview of the "redneck icon" ever published—reveals the joys and sorrows of a movie star who thrived in, but who was then almost buried by the pressures and insecurities of the New Hollywood. A tribute to "truck stop" America, it's about the accelerated life of a courageous spirit who "Put His Pedal to the Metal" with humor, high jinx, and pizzazz. He predicted his own death: "Soon, I'll be racing a hotrod in Valhalla in my cowboy hat and a pair of aviators." On his tombstone, he wanted it writ: "He was not the best actor in the world, but he was the best Burt Reynolds in the world."

BURT REYNOLDS
PUT THE PEDAL TO THE METAL

Darwin Porter & Danforth Prince; ISBN 978-1-936003-63-1;   450 pages with photos

LINDA LOVELACE
INSIDE LINDA LOVELACE'S DEEP THROAT
Degradation, Porno Chic, and the Rise of Feminism

Darwin Porter

The most comprehensive biography ever written of an adult entertainment star, her tormented relationship with Hollywood's underbelly, and how she changed forever the world's perceptions about censorship, sexual behavior patterns, and pornography.

Darwin Porter, author of more than thirty critically acclaimed celebrity exposés of behind-the-scenes intrigue in the entertainment industry, was deeply involved in the Linda Lovelace saga as it unfolded in the 70s, interviewing many of the players, and raising money for the legal defense of the film's co-star, Harry Reems.

In this book, emphasizing her role as an unlikely celebrity interacting with other celebrities, he brings inside information and a never-before-published revelation to almost every page.

"This book drew me in..How could it not?" Coco Papy, Bookslut.

The Beach Book Festival's Grand Prize Winner for Best Summer Reading of 2013"

Runner-Up to "Best Biography of 2013"
—The Los Angeles Book Festival

Another hot and insightful commentary about major and sometimes violently controversial conflicts of the American Century,
from Blood Moon Productions.

Inside Linda Lovelace's Deep Throat

Darwin Porter

Softcover, 640 pages, 6"x9" with photos. ISBN 978-1-936003-33-4

PAUL NEWMAN

The Man Behind the Baby Blues
His Secret Life Exposed

Drawn from firsthand interviews with insiders who knew Paul Newman intimately, and compiled over a period of nearly a half-century, this is the world's most honest and most revelatory biography about Hollywood's pre-eminent male sex symbol.

This is a respectful but candid cornucopia of once-concealed information about the sexual and emotional adventures of an affable, impossibly good-looking workaday actor, a former sailor from Shaker Heights, Ohio, who parlayed his ambisexual charm and extraordinary good looks into one of the most successful careers in Hollywood.

Whereas the situations it exposes were widely known within Hollywood's inner circles, they've never before been revealed to the general public.

But now, the full story has been published—the giddy heights and agonizing crashes of a great American star, with revelations and insights never before published in any other biography.

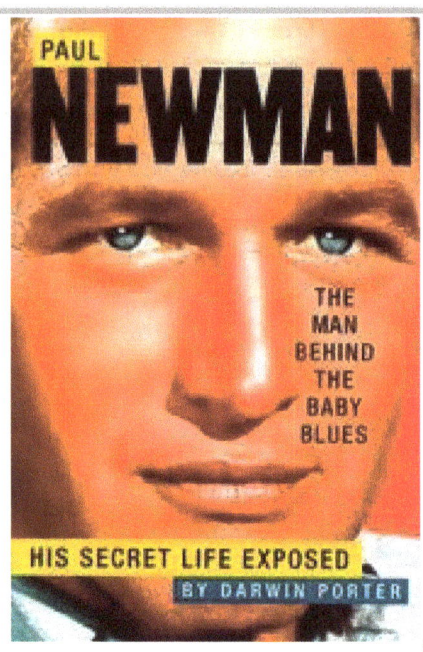

***

"Paul Newman had just as many on-location affairs as the rest of us, and he was just as bisexual as I was. But whereas I was always getting caught with my pants down, he managed to do it in the dark with not a paparazzo in sight. He might have bedded Marilyn Monroe or Elizabeth Taylor the night before, but he always managed to show up for breakfast with Joanne Woodward, with those baby blues, looking as innocent as a Botticelli angel. He never fooled me. It takes an alleycat to know another one. Did I ever tell you what really happened between Newman and me? If that doesn't grab you, what about what went on between James Dean and Newman? Let me tell you about this co-called model husband if you want to look behind those famous peepers."

—Marlon Brando

PAUL NEWMAN
The Man Behind the Baby Blues,
His Secret Life Exposed, by Darwin Porter
Recipient of an Honorable Mention from the
New England Book Festival
Hardcover, 520 pages, with dozens of photos.
ISBN 978-0-9786465-1-6

BLOOD MOON'S RESPECTFUL FAREWELL TO A GREAT AMERICAN MOVIE STAR

KIRK DOUGLAS
MORE IS NEVER ENOUGH
Darwin Porter & Danforth Prince

Dripping with Testosterone, a Young Horndog Sets Out to Conquer Hollywood

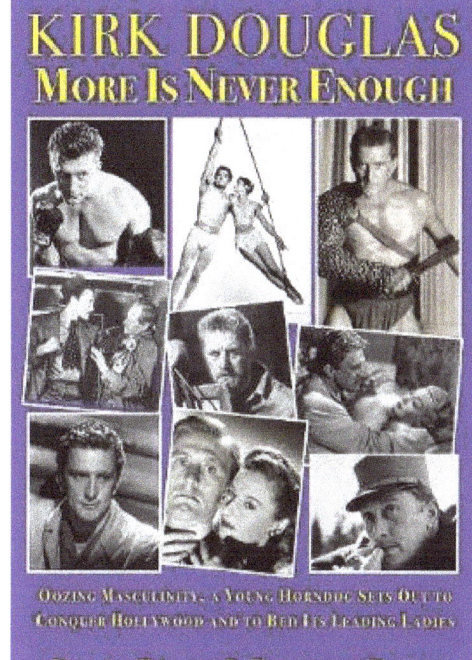

Of the many male stars of Golden Age Hollywood, Kirk Douglas became the final survivor, the last icon of a fabled, optimistic era that the world will never see again. When he celebrated his birthday in 2016, a headline read: LEGENDARY HOLLYWOOD HORNDOG TURNS 100.

He was both a charismatic actor and a man of uncommon force and vigor. His restless and volcanic spirit is reflected both in his films and through his many sexual conquests.

Douglas was the son of Russian-Jewish immigrants, his father a collector and seller of rags. After service in the Navy during World War II, he hit Hollywood, oozing masculinity and charm. Conquering Tinseltown and bedding its leading ladies, he became the personification of the American dream, moving from obscurity and (literally) rags to riches and major-league fame.

The *Who's Who* cast of characters roaring through his life included not only a daunting list of Hollywood goddesses, but the town's most colossal male talents and egos, too. They included his kindred hellraiser and best buddy Burt Lancaster, John Wayne, Henry Fonda, Billy Wilder, Laurence Olivier, Rock Hudson, and a future U.S. President, Ronald Reagan, when winning the highest office in the land was virtually unthinkable.

Over the decades, he immortalized himself in film after film, delivering, like a Trojan, one memorable performance after another. He was at home in *film noir*, as a western gunslinger, as an adventurer (in both ancient and modern sagas), as a juggler, as Tennessee Williams' "gentleman caller," as a Greek super-hero from Homer's *Odyssey*, and as roguish sailor in the Jules Verne yarn, exploring the mysteries of the ocean's depths.

En route to his status as a myth and legend, his performances reflected both his personal pain and the brutalization of the characters he played, too. In *Champion* (1949), he was beaten to a fatal bloody pulp. As the sleazy, heartless reporter in *Ace in the Hole* (1951), he was stabbed with a knife in his gut. As Van Gogh in *Lust for Life* (1956), he writhed in emotional agony and unrequited love before slicing off his ear with a razor. His World War I movie, *Paths of Glory* (1957) grows more profound over the years. He lost an eye in *The Vikings* (1958), and, as the Thracian slave leading a revolt against Roman legions in *Spartacus* (1960), he was crucified.

All of this is brought out, with photos, in this remarkable testimonial to the last hero of Hollywood's cinematic and swashbuckling Golden Age, an inspiring testimonial to the values and core beliefs of an America that's Gone With the Wind, yet lovingly remembered as a time when it, in many ways, was truly great.

KIRK DOUGLAS: MORE IS NEVER ENOUGH
Darwin Porter & Danforth Prince;   ISBN 978-1-936003-61-7;   550 pages with photos.

Honoring the 60th Anniversary of his Violent and Early Death

JAMES DEAN: TOMORROW NEVER COMES

Darwin Porter & Danforth Prince

America's most enduring and legendary symbol of young, enraged rebellion, James Dean continues into the 21st Century to capture the imagination of the world.

After one of his many flirtations with Death, which caught up with him when he was a celebrity-soaked 24-year-old, he said, "If a man can live after he dies, then maybe he's a great man." Today, bars from Nigeria to Patagonia are named in honor of this international, spectacularly self-destructive movie star icon.

Migrating from the dusty backroads of Indiana to center stage in the most formidable boudoirs of Hollywood, his saga is electrifying.

A strikingly handsome heart-throb, Dean is a study in contrasts: Tough but tender, brutal but remarkably sensitive; he was a reckless hellraiser badass who could revert to a little boy in bed.

A rampant bisexual, he claimed that he didn't want to go through life "with one hand tied behind my back." He demonstrated that during bedroom trysts with Marilyn Monroe, Rock Hudson, Elizabeth Taylor, Paul Newman, Natalie Wood, Shelley Winters, Marlon Brando, Steve McQueen, Ursula Andress, Montgomery Clift, Pier Angeli, Tennessee Williams, Susan Strasberg, Tallulah Bankhead, and FBI director J. Edgar Hoover.

Woolworth heiress Barbara Hutton, one of the richest and most dissipated women of her era, wanted to make him her toy boy.

Tomorrow Never Comes is the most penetrating look at James Dean to have emerged from the wreckage of his Porsche Spyder in 1955.

Before setting out on his last ride, he said, "I feel life too intensely to bear living it." *Tomorrow Never Comes* presents a damaged but beautiful soul.

JAMES DEAN
Tomorrow Never Comes
Darwin Porter & Danforth Prince
Softcover, with photos. ISBN 978-1-936003-49-5

PETER O'TOOLE

Hellraiser, Sexual Outlaw, Irish Rebel
Darwin Porter & Danforth Prince

When it was published, early in 2015, this book was widely publicized in the *Daily Mail*, the *New York Daily News*, the *New York Post*, the *Midwest Book Review, The Express (London), The Globe*, the *National Enquirer*, and in equivalent publications worldwide

One of the world's most admired (and brilliant) actors, Peter O'Toole wined and wenched his way through a labyrinth of sexual and interpersonal betrayals, sometimes with disastrous results. Away from the stage and screen, where such films as *Becket* and *Lawrence of Arabia*, made film history, his life was filled with drunken, debauched nights and edgy sexual experimentations, most of which were never openly examined in the press. A hellraiser, he shared wild times with his "best blokes" Richard Burton and Richard Harris. Peter Finch, also his close friend, once invited him to join him in sharing the pleasures of his mistress, Vivien Leigh.

"My father, a bookie, moved us to the Mick community of Leeds," O'Toole once told a reporter. "We were very poor, but I was born an Irishman, which accounts for my gift of gab, my unruly behavior, my passionate devotion to women and the bottle, and my loathing of any authority figure."

Author Robert Sellers described O'Toole's boyhood neighborhood. "Three of his playmates went on to be hanged for murder; one strangled a girl in a lovers' quarrel; one killed a man during a robbery; another cut up a warden in South Africa with a pair of shears. It was a heavy bunch."

Peter O'Toole's hell-raising life story has never been told, until now. Hot and uncensored, from a writing team which, even prior to O'Toole's death in 2013, had been collecting under-the-radar info about him for years, this book has everything you ever wanted to know about how THE LION navigated his way through the boudoirs of the Entertainment Industry IN WINTER, Spring, Summer, and a dissipated Autumn as well.

Blood Moon has ripped away the imperial robe, scepter, and crown usually associated with this quixotic problem child of the British Midlands. Provocatively uncensored, this illusion-shattering overview of Peter O'Toole's hellraising (or at least very naughty) and demented life is unique in the history of publishing.

PETER O'TOOLE
Hellraiser, Sexual Outlaw, Irish Rebel

Darwin Porter & Danforth Prince
Softcover, with photos. ISBN 978-1-936003-45-7

THOSE GLAMOROUS GABORS

BOMBSHELLS FROM BUDAPEST, GREAT COURTESANS OF THE 20TH CENTURY

DARWIN PORTER & DANFORTH PRINCE

Zsa Zsa, Eva, and Magda Gabor transferred their glittery dreams and gold-digging ambitions from the twilight of the Austro-Hungarian Empire to Hollywood. There, more effectively than any army, these Bombshells from Budapest broke hearts, amassed fortunes, lovers, and A-list husbands, and amused millions of voyeurs through the medium of television, movies, and the social registers. In this astonishing "triple-play" biography, designated "Best Biography of the Year" by the Hollywood Book Festival, Blood Moon lifts the "mink-and-diamond" curtain on this amazing trio of blood-related sisters, whose complicated intrigues have never been fully explored before.

***

"You will never be Ga-bored…this book gives new meaning to the term compelling. Be warned, Those Glamorous Gabors is both an epic and a pip. Not since Gone With the Wind have so many characters on the printed page been forced to run for their lives for one reason or another. And Scarlett making a dress out of the curtains is nothing compared to what a Gabor will do when she needs to scrap together an outfit for a movie premiere or late-night outing.

"For those not up to speed, Jolie Tilleman came from a family of jewelers and therefore came by her love for the shiny stones honestly, perhaps genetically. She married Vilmos Gabor somewhere around World War 1 (exact dates, especially birth dates, are always somewhat vague in order to establish plausible deniability later on) and they were soon blessed with three daughters: Magda, the oldest, whose hair, sadly, was naturally brown, although it would turn quite red in America; Zsa Zsa (born 'Sari') a natural blond who at a very young age exhibited the desire for fame with none of the talents usually associated with achievement, excepting beauty and a natural wit; and Eva, the youngest and blondest of the girls, who after seeing Grace Moore perform at the National Theater, decided that she wanted to be an actress and that she would one day move to Hollywood to become a star.

"Given that the Gabor family at that time lived in Budapest, Hungary, at the period of time between the World Wars, that Hollywood dream seemed a distant one indeed. The story—the riches to rags to riches to rags to riches again myth of survival against all odds as the four women, because of their Jewish heritage, flee Europe with only the minks on their backs and what jewels they could smuggle along with them in their decolletage, only to have to battle afresh for their places in the vicious Hollywood pecking order—gives new meaning to the term 'compelling.' The reader, as if he were witnessing a particularly gore-drenched traffic accident, is incapable of looking away."

—*New York Review of Books*

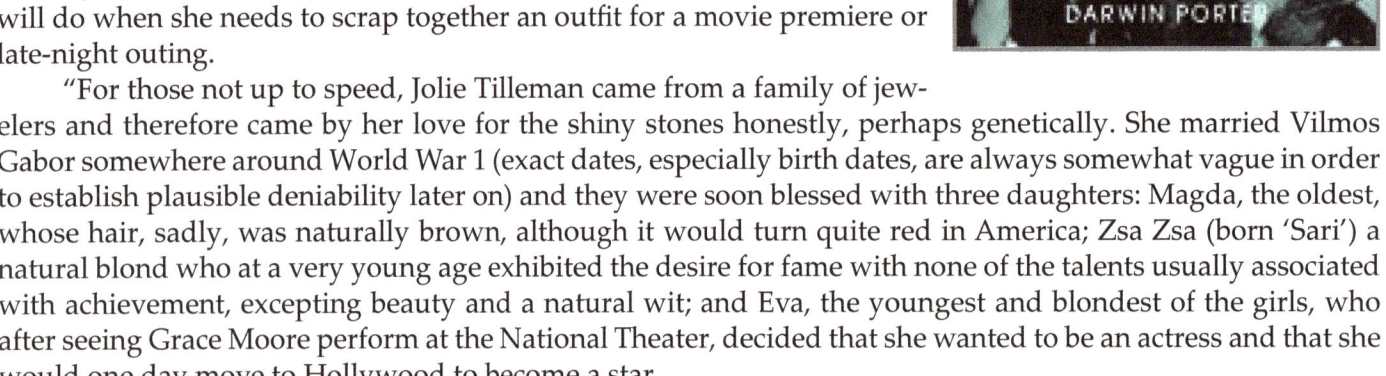

THOSE GLAMOROUS GABORS
BOMBSHELLS FROM BUDAPEST, GREAT COURTESANS OF THE 20TH CENTURY
Darwin Porter & Danforth Prince
Softcover, 730 pages, with hundreds of photos   ISBN 978-1-936003-35-8

A COMPREHENSIVE BIOGRAPHY OF THE ONCE-MOST-FAMOUS ENTERTAINER IN THE WORLD

JACKO

The Social and Sexual History of Michael Jackson

This is the world's most unbiased report on the trials and tribulations of a performer whose fame surpassed, in some places, that of either the U.S. President or Jesus Christ. From investigative reporter Darwin Porter—the biographer who Unzipped Marlon Brando and brought Babylon back to Hollywood.

It illuminates the life of The Gloved One from cradle to grave, including his meteoric rise to fame, insights into his fall from grace, and the desperate but ongoing attempts to revive his career. Published post-mortem to MJ's tragic death in June of 2009, it provides shocking insights into his triumphs and disasters, and an estate that will be disputed for decades.

An award-winning finalist in Foreword Magazine's BOOK OF THE YEAR contest, this is unlike any other biography of the superstar ever written.

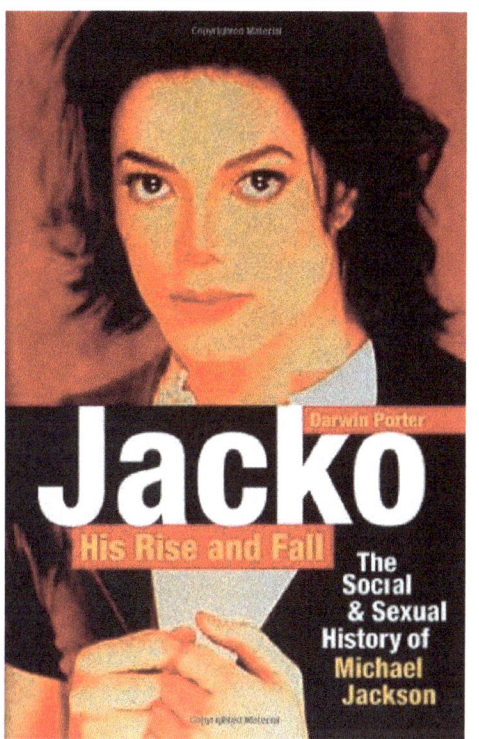

"I'd have thought that there wasn't one single gossippy rock yet to be overturned in the microscopically scrutinized life of Michael Jackson, but Darwin Porter has proven me wrong. Definitely a page-turner. But don't turn the pages too quickly. Almost every one holds a fascinating revelation."
—**Richard LaBonte.** *Books to Watch Out For*

"Don't stop till you get enough. Darwin Porter's biography of Michael Jackson is dangerously addictive."
—*The London Observer*

This biography was authored by Darwin Porter and originally released in 2007, during the lifetime of MJ, who presumably was aware of its existence and opted to allow its sale and distribution to proceed without any legal protests or publicly expressed objections.

At the time of its release, it was the only significant biography of Michael Jackson published during the previous fifteen years, a remarkable circumstance, considering the superstar's widespread fame and controversies.

Post-millennium, Michael became an object of ridicule and scorn, hounded by the press and bleeding from a river of lawsuits. This book examines the mechanics of his decline, as it describes an American icon who wandered into a treacherous Garden of Eden and tasted its forbidden fruit.

In this book, Michael interacts with an all-star cast whose members included Elizabeth Taylor, Katharine Hepburn, Jane Fonda, Madonna, Princess Di, Mick Jagger, Paul McCartney, Diana Ross, Brooke Shields, Sammy Davis Jr., Johnnie Cochran, Sophia Loren, Frank Sinatra, Fred Astaire, Cary Grant,. Mae West, Liberace, Lisa Marie Presley, and that dad of hers.

"I've become the victim of my own fame," Michael lamented to these friends while reminding them, when he was still alive, of the words he wanted engraved on his tombstone: **DON'T JUDGE ME.**

JACKO, His Rise and Fall
The Social and Sexual History of Michael Jackson

Darwin Porter
ISBN 978-0-9748118-5-7   Hardcover   542 pages, with photos.

Getting to Know Blood Moon's
MAGNOLIA HOUSE SERIES

DID YOU KNOW?

THAT THE ORIGINS OF OUR MAGNOLIA HOUSE SERIES WERE INSPIRED BY DONALD TRUMP?

We spent the early months of 2016 laboring over a guidebook to the Fame and Fury of Donald Trump. We envisioned it as a "compendium of cringe." Source material derived from recaps of TV news and from reporting by *The New York Times, The NY Daily News,* and the *New York Post,* but with the "seasonings" for which Blood Moon is famous.

NBN's "rank and file" was prepped and primed, optimistic about high-volume sales, and flush with impressive advance orders. **WHAT COULD POSSIBLY HAVE GONE WRONG?**

Without warning, days before its widely publicized release, the NBN flipped, refusing to get involved. Their awkwardly orchestrated betrayal sabotaged months of advance planning.

We regrouped. Ours was not the first ambitious publishing vision sabotaged by issues and players associated with THE DONALD. In the days that followed, we arranged for alternative distribution of the title.

Interestingly, **The Man Who Would Be King** went on to win multiple literary awards and many stunning reviews. Seven years later, we repackaged and re-released it on the 4th of July, 2024, in advance of Trump's "comeback" second term.

We present this as an explanation of the real-life trauma associated with the creation of Blood Moon's Magnolia House Series. With the understanding that none of the books within that series has ever been associated with the NBN, they incorporate many of our best, most seasoned, and most mature titles. Most have been extensively reviewed, and some have won impressive literary awards. It is with that understanding that we present, on the pages that immediately follow, descriptions of each of the titles within the series.

What Is Magnolia House?

Built in stages between 1830 and 1866, and closely associated with the ambitions and traumas of the Civil War, it's our resident headquarters, a landmarked "*grande dame*"with memories to sustain and stories to tell.

In the months that followed, we crafted and produced a double-volumed overview of the building's history. They relay its celebrity associations from before our tenure there, and also during the decades we occupied the premises.

Introducing Blood Moon's
MAGNOLIA HOUSE
and the Series that Bears its Name

Two turn-of-the 20th-century views of Staten Island's Historic Magnolia House

HOW DO YOU DESCRIBE A BOOKISH, MAGNOLIA-SCENTED LANDMARK?

As depicted below, **Volumes One and Two** of Blood Moon's **Magnolia House Series** were conceived as affectionate testimonials to a great American monument, **MAGNOLIA HOUSE**, our company's nurturing and very tolerant historic home in Staten Island (NYC) It has a raft of stories to tell—some of them about how it adapted to the publishing industry's radically changing tastes, times, circumstances, and values.

VOLUME ONE (ISBN 978-1-936003-65-5) focuses on its construction by a prominent lawyer during the booming (Northern) economy before the Civil War; its Gilded-Age purchase by the widow of the Surgeon General of the Confederate States of America; and later, its role as a branch office of THE FROMMER GUIDES during the heyday of the American travel industry. It was an era rich with insights into the celebrity secrets their reporters on the job in "London, Paris, and "Hollywood on the Tiber" (privately, until now) unveiled, years later, through Blood Moon Productions.

VOLUME TWO (ISBN 978-1-936003-73-0) is an *haute* celebrity romp through the half-century of Broadway, Hollywood, and publishing scandals swirling around Magnolia House's visitors and their frenemies…a "Reporters' Notebook" with everything that arts industry publicists didn't want fans and critics to know about at the time.

**Each of these books is a celebration of the fast-disappearing
PRE-COVID AMERICAN CENTURY,**
And both are available now through internet purveyors worldwide.

from BLOOD MOON PRODUCTIONS at MAGNOLIA HOUSE
Award-Winning Entertainment about
America's Legends, Icons, & Celebrities

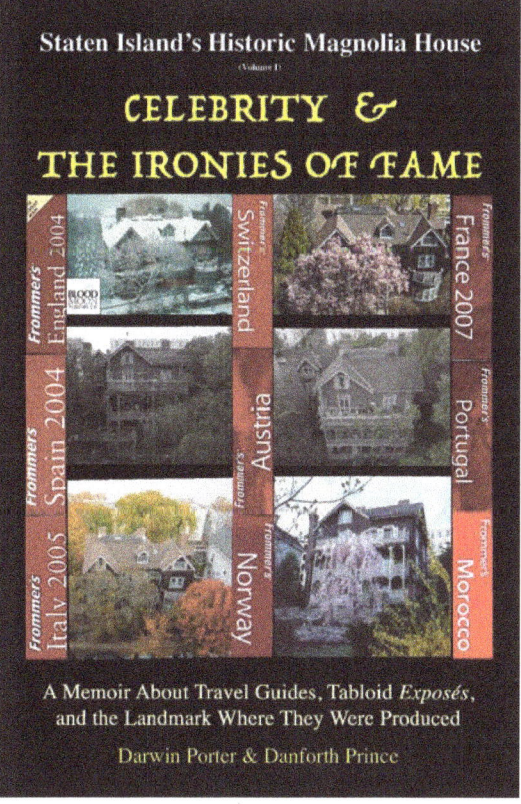

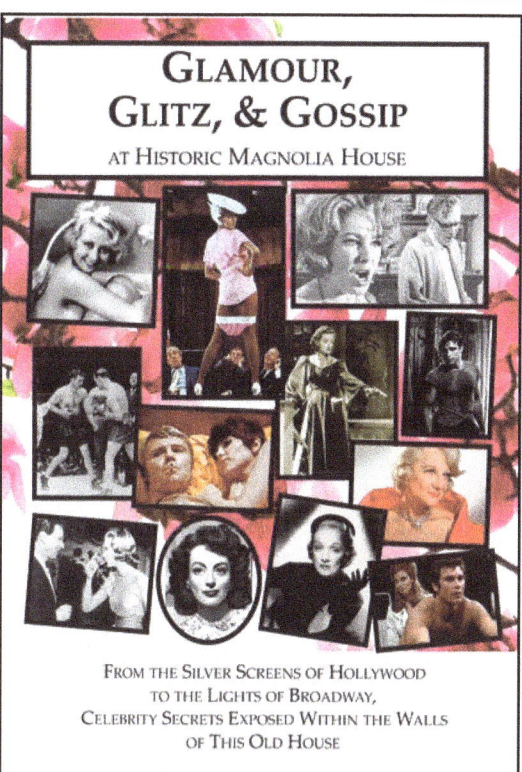

DONALD TRUMP
IS THE MAN WHO WOULD BE KING

This is the most famous book about our incendiary President you've probably never heard of.

Winner of three respected literary awards, and released three months before the Presidential elections of 2016, it's an entertainingly packaged, artfully salacious bombshell, a scathingly historic overview of America during its 2016 election cycle, a portrait unlike anything ever published on CANDIDATE DONALD and the climate in which he thrived and massacred his political rivals.

Its volcanic, much-suppressed release during the heat and venom of the 2016 Presidential campaign has already been heralded by the Midwestern Book Review, California Book Watch, the Seattle Gay News, the staunchly right-wing WILS-AM radio, and also by the editors at the most popular Seniors' magazine in Florida, BOOMER TIMES, which designated it as one of their BOOKS OF THE MONTH.

TRUMPOCALYPSE: *"Donald Trump: The Man Who Would Be King* is recommended reading for all sides, no matter what political stance is being adopted: Republican, Democrat, or other.

"One of its driving forces is its ability to synthesize an unbelievable amount of information into a format and presentation which blends lively irony with outrageous observations, entertaining even as it presents eye-opening information in a format accessible to all.

"Politics dovetail with American obsessions and fascinations with trends, figureheads, drama, and sizzling news stories, but blend well with the observations of sociologists, psychologists, politicians, and others in a wide range of fields who lend their expertise and insights to create a much broader review of the Trump phenomena than a more casual book could provide.

"The result is a 'must read' for any American interested in issues of race, freedom, equality, and justice—and for any non-American who wonders just what is going on behind the scenes in this country's latest election debacle."

Diane Donovan, Senior Editor, California Bookwatch

DONALD TRUMP, THE MAN WHO WOULD BE KING

WINNER OF "BEST BIOGRAPHY" AWARDS FROM BOOK FESTIVALS IN NEW YORK, CALIFORNIA, AND FLORIDA
Darwin Porter and Danforth Prince

Softcover, with 822 pages and hundreds of photos. ISBN 978-1-936003-51-8.
DARWIN PORTER & DANFORTH PRINCE

 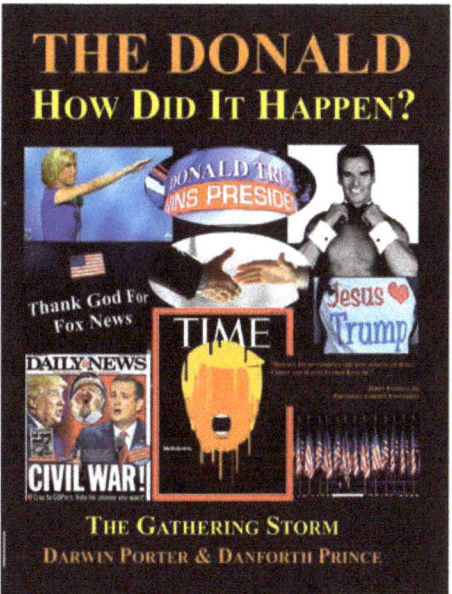 

BLOOD MOON ANNOUNCES THE RELEASE OF THE SECOND EDITION OF ITS 2016 OVERVIEW OF DONALD TRUMP'S FIRST BID FOR THE WHITE HOUSE

THE DONALD: HOW DID IT HAPPEN?

AVAILABLE EVERYWHERE, IN TIME FOR NEW INDICTMENTS FROM FEDERAL AND STATE PROSECUTORS

Blood Moon proudly announces the release, on August 4, 2023, of a revised new edition of its award-winning celebrity overview of how THE DONALD—a loudmouthed, pussy-grabbing TV star, casino kingpin, and real estate mogul—became President of the United States. ISBN 978-1-936003-90-7. A BIG paperback with a BIG (8.5" x 11") footprint. Available after August 4th through Amazon.com and at internet booksellers everywhere.

BLOOD, SWEAT, TEARS, & THE DONALD: HOW WE DID IT
Danforth Prince, President, Blood Moon Productions

This is a revised edition of a book which we hastily issued, with the (thwarted) expectation of elevated sales, seven years ago, just two "high stress, high-anxiety" months before Donald Trump won the Presidential election of 2016.

What could possibly have gone wrong? Moments before its anticipated release, perhaps with political motivations of its own, our then-distributor, the National Book Network, abruptly switched strategies and refused to sell it, throwing into last-minute chaos our carefully orchestrated hopes and dreams.

Hurriedly, we gathered our marbles and released it instead through alternative (but less extensive) distribution channels.

Within a few months, it garnered impressive reviews, a handful of prestigious literary awards, and cautious applause from both sides of the political divide.

Now, on the eve of Donald Trump's bid for a second Presidential term, we believe that some of the mysteries associated with SECOND TERM ("Comeback") DONALD lie in early clues he dropped, many of which we recorded in this book.

We present it to readers as a Rosetta Stone, an insight into VINTAGE TRUMP and THE WAY WE WERE at the time of thiw book's first introduction to the reading public, way back in 2016.

This is a historic overview of THE DONALD and HOW HE DID IT, a horrified but compelling memoir for future generations.

God Bless Us All, and God Bless America. We salute, with reverence, the American concepts of Democracy, Free Speech, Prosperity, and Justice for All.

THE DONALD

HOW DID IT HAPPEN?
The Gathering Storm
Porter & Prince

Blood Moon Proudly Defines this as #9 in its Magnolia House Series

This book is dedicated to the unsung heroes of the American Century, the hardworking men and women, some of them pawns of fate, who collectively succeeded at making America great.

DANCING FOOLS

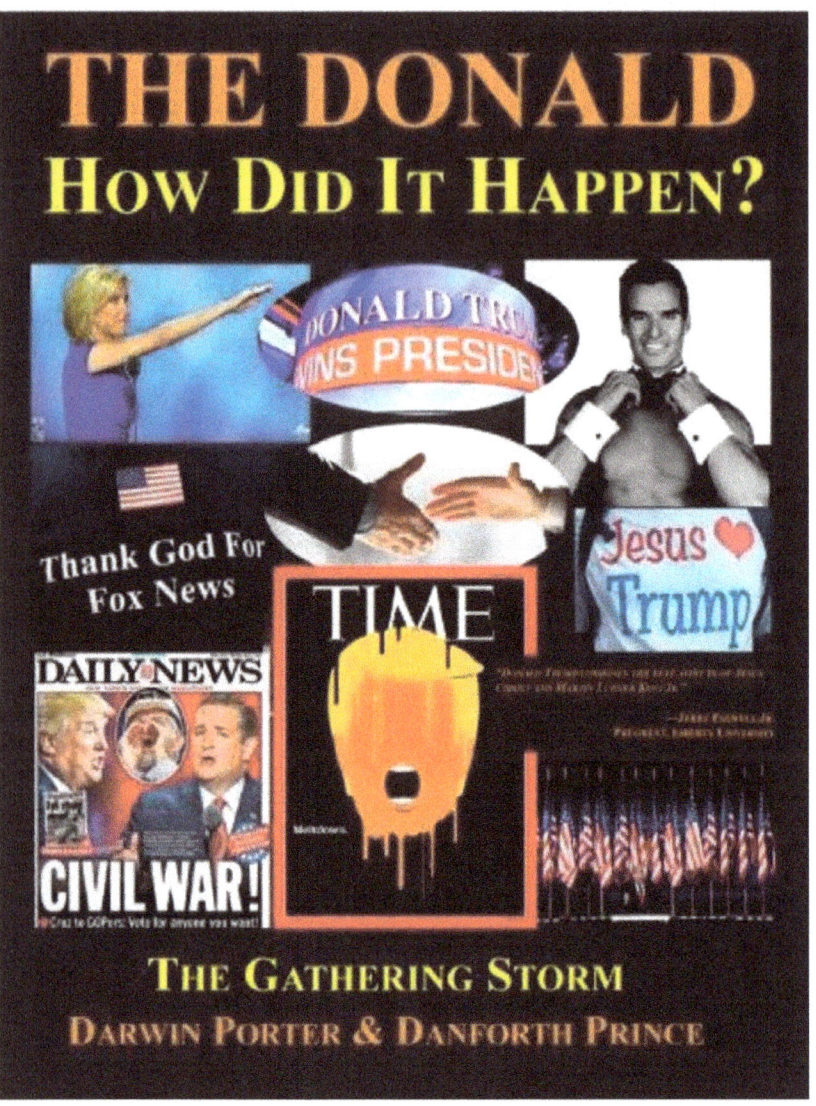

In 2023, six years after its original publication in September of 2016, and as he was plotting his second Presidential term, we reformatted *THE MAN WHO WOULD BE KING* to reflect circumstances associated with Trump's repetitive cycle of "dumpster fires." Then we renamed it:

THE DONALD: HOW DID IT HAPPEN?
The Gathering Storm

(ISBN 978-1-936003-90-7)

THE DONALD: HOW DID IT HAPPEN?
The Gathering Storm

Softcover, with 280 "oversized (8 1/2" x 11") pages and hundreds of photos. ISBN 978-1-936003-90-7. Available now from Ingram, Amazon.com and other purveyors, worldwide.

AS THEY RELATE TO OUR PRESENT AND FUTURE PUBLISHING AGENDAS

Let's talk about **Twosomes, Twins, "Paired Sets," "Double-Bright Moons," Triplets, and (GASP) Quintets.**

Blood Moon has been cited as "dauntingly prolific," with a knack for multiple children. Here are some of our "matched sets," most of them already published, but others of which are clearly marked for release in the medium-term future. We're mentioning this as it relates to the players described on the following page. **THE FONDAS**: **Father** (Henry), **Daughter** (Jane), and **Bad Boy** (Peter) For more on them, the family that brought inter-generational conflicts, Hollywood style, to center stage throughout the rebellious 60s and the sexual 70s, please turn the page.

LUCY X2
(I.E., THE RICARDOS, INCLUDING DESI)

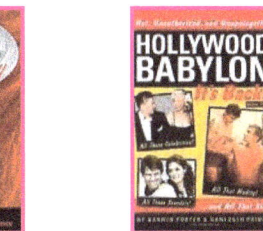

A JUICY TRIPTYCH OF BABYLONS

TRIPLE-PLAY GUIDES TO GLBTQ FILMS

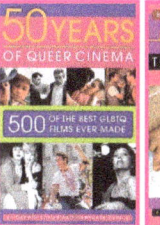  

OUR DOUBLE DOSE OF DONALD MEANS DOUBLE THE FUN!

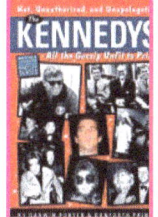    

GOMORRAH ON THE POTOMAC
(A ROLLICKING PRESIDENTIAL QUINTET)

THE FONDAS:
TRIPLE EXPOSURE IN TWO VOLUMES

THE FACE OF BLOODY AND BEAUTIFUL THINGS TO COME ALREADY WRITTEN, WITH EDITORIAL COMPLETION BEGINNING IN SIX MONTHS AND EXTENDING OVER INTO A PERIOD OF TWO YEARS,

 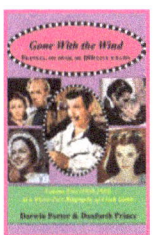 

A THREE-VOLUME CELEBRATION OF CLARK GABLE

A DOUBLE-WHAMMIED EDITORIAL ROLL IN THE HAY WITH "HIGH NOON IN HELL" GARY COOPER

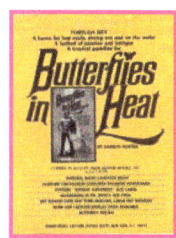 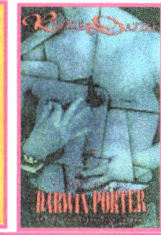

AND LEST WE FORGET, FROM LONG AGO AND FAR AWAY:
BUTTERFLIES IN HEAT, A CULT CLASSIC, WITH ITS SOUTH FLORIDA SEQUEL, RAZZLE-DAZZLE.

WHAT DOES NEW YORK CITY SHARE IN COMMON WITH L.A. AND SAN FRANCISCO?
THEIR RESPECTIVE BOOK AWARD FESTIVALS EACH APPLAUDED
HOW BLOOD MOON DEFINED THE FONDAS: HENRY, JANE, AND PETER

BOOK AWARD NEWS:

THE FONDAS: TRIPLE EXPOSURE
A ROLLICKING, DOUBLE-BARRELLED OVERVIEW OF A VERY FAMOUS AMERICAN FAMILY

On July 25, 2023, the Awards Committee at the prestigious **NEW YORK BOOK FESTIVAL** defined Darwin Porter and Danforth Prince's double-volume overview of **THE FONDAS** as **WINNER of their BEST BIOGRAPHY OF THE YEAR** Award.

Their decision arrived in the immediate aftermath of the hotly contested **San Francisco Book Festival**, where the same double-volumed set was defined as RUNNER UP to Best Biography of the year, too.

The most comprehensive (and to some, shocking) overview of their lives ever published—it brings new life and an upgraded cultural importance to this talented and influential trio of biologically related stars.

WHO WERE THE FONDAS?: During the climactic peak of Classic Hollywood, **Henry Fonda** was the reassuring archetype of the American male—at least on film. In private, he married five times (two of his wives committed suicide), soldiered on through active military service in the Pacific during World War II, and seduced legendary ladies (*or dragons, depending on your point of view*) who included Bette Davis, Jean Harlow, Greta Garbo, Joan Crawford, Lucille Ball, and Marlene Dietrich.

His very outspoken daughter, Jane, led a tumultuous, scandal-soaked life of her own, one indelibly linked to the "New Wave" and "New Hollywood" of the 60s, 70s, and 80s. Spectacularly famous in Europe and the U.S., she morphed from a bilingual onscreen sex kitten into the notorious "Hanoi Jane," later making a film comeback as an Oscar winner. Her love affairs embraced everyone from Warren Beatty to the Black Panthers.

The least-known, perhaps least "likable" member of this tumultuous trio, **Peter Fonda** led a privileged life laced with drugs, high adventure, and seductions—a thrill-seeking "Easy Rider" racing across the landscapes of the 1960s, 70s, and 80s as the "Bad Boy Gone Wild"—often bringing with it a "wafty and pointless psychedelia."

THE FONDAS—It's all here in two delicious volumes. If you want to know what went on in Hollywood after the klieg lights went off, consider reading them. The private "ecstatic and agonized" lives of a celebrity-soaked entertainment industry pro, his daughter, and his son are documented as never before, lives set on fire by triumph, tragedy, passion, heartbreak, wide acclaim, scalding denunciations, and suicides.

IN 2022, IN HONOR OF THE 40TH ANNIVERSARY OF HENRY FONDA'S DEATH, BLOOD MOON PRODUCTIONS RELEASED VOLUME ONE OF A TWO-PART BIOGRAPHY CELEBRATING THE LIFE AND CAREER OF ONE OF THE AMERICAN CENTURY'S MOST CELEBRATED ACTORS

HENRY FONDA

DARWIN PORTER AND DANFORTH PRINCE

TWO MONTHS LATER, IT WON THE COVETED
BEST BIOGRAPHY AWARD FROM THE HOLLYWOOD BOOK FESTIVAL

Throughout his forty-five year career, **Henry Fonda**—a stable, reassuring archetype of the American male—never gave a bad performance. immortalizing himself in such films as *Young Mr. Lincoln, The Grapes of Wrath,* and *Mister Roberts*. The torments of his introverted private life vied with his on-screen dilemmas. Personal dramas included five wives (two of whom committed suicide) and involvements in many of the seminal events (including active service in the Navy during World War II) of the 20th Century. His affairs starred such megadivas as Lucille Ball, Joan Crawford, and Bette Davis, and with his second wife, Frances Seymour, he founded a Hollywood dynasty with movie star children, Jane and Peter.

This, **Volume One (1905-1960)** covers Henry's origins in Depression-era Nebraska, his rise to fame, his complicated dynamics with other celebrities, and his middle-aged years navigating his passion for acting with the business realities of Hollywood.

Volume Two (1961-1982), also available now, covers his complicated relationships with his famous and newsworthy daughter, Jane, and his (deceased) son, Peter.

Together, these books give the clearest, most detailed overview of this great American actor ever published.

All this and more from Blood Moon Productions, an award-winning publishing enterprise that specializes in exposing long-suppressed secrets hidden during Hollywood's Golden Age.

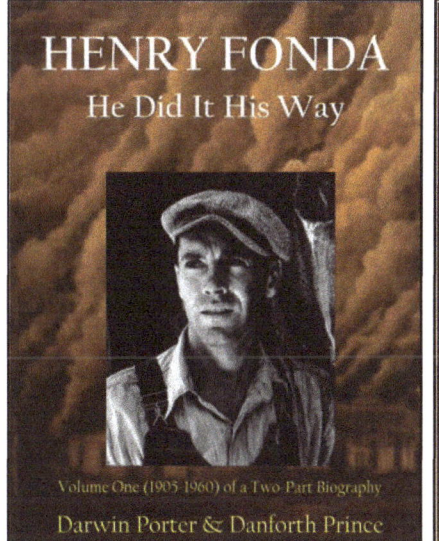 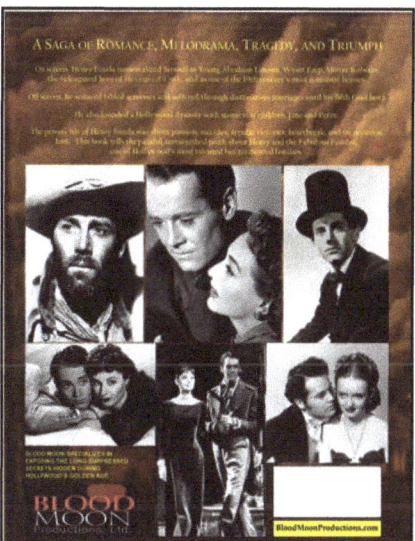

HENRY FONDA: HE DID IT HIS WAY
Volume One (1905-1960) of a Two-Part Biography

Darwin Porter & Danforth Prince   345 pages, with hundreds of photos
ISBN 978-1-936003-84-6

A YEAR LATER, ON FLAG DAY, 2023, IN TIME FOR A GREAT AMERICAN HOLIDAY, BLOOD MOON RELEASED VOLUME TWO OF ITS TWO-PART BIOGRAPHY OF THE AMERICAN CENTURY'S MOST CELEBRATED CINEMATIC DYNASTIES

THE FONDAS—HENRY, JANE, & PETER

TRIPLE EXPOSURE   INTERTWINED SAGAS OF DYSFUNCTION, TRAGEDY, AND TRIUMPH

Throughout his forty-five year career, Henry Fonda,—a stable, reasuring archetype of the American male—never gave a bad performance. Personal tragedies included five wives (two of whom committed suicide) and affairs which starred such mega-divas as Lucille Ball, Joan Crawford, and Bette Davis.

This, **Volume Two (1961-1982)**, of Blood Moon's FONDA project, turns klieg lights on three emotionally intertwined mega-celebrities, two of them Oscar winners: The lanky and boyish American hero, **Henry**; his beautiful daughter, "the eternal rebel," **Jane**; and his son, **Peter,** a preppy-looking thrill-seeker indelibly linked to the "bad boy on a bike" narratives of the 60s.

It's the second, and final, installment of Blood Moon's coverage of the FABULOUS FONDAS, one of Hollywood's most talented but tormented families. It reflects the private agonies of a father, daughter, and son engulfed by the divisions of their respective generations and the ironies of the American Experience.

**THE FONDAS: HENRY, JANE, & PETER
TRIPLE EXPOSURE**
Volume Two (1961-1982) of a Two-Part Biography
360 pages, with hundreds of photos
Available everywhere on June 14, 2023 through Ingram, Amazon, Barnes & Noble, and online booksellers everywhere   ISBN 978-1-936003-86-0

It joins Volume One, HENRY FONDA: HE DID IT HIS WAY (1905-1960). the already-available winner of a Best Biography of the Year award from the Hollywood Book Festival. Together, as a pair, this two-volume set gives the clearest, most detailed, and clearly unvarnished overview of the Fondas ever published.

Established in 2004 by writers formerly associated with THE FROMMER GUIDES, **Blood Moon Productions** is an independent publishing enterprise dedicated to researching, salvaging, and preserving the oral histories of "The American Century."

As described by **The Huffington Post,** "Blood Moon, in case you don't know, is a small publishing house on Staten Island that cranks out Hollywood gossip books, about two or three a year, usually of five, six-, or 700-page length, chocked with stories and pictures about people who used to consume the imaginations of the American public, back when we actually had a public imagination. That is, when people were really interested in each other, rather than in Apple 'devices.' In other words, back when we had vices, not devices."

Blood Moon is one of the most prolific show-biz presses in the world, with a backlist of almost 50 titles, each an overview of seminal characters who affected the course of human history.   For more information about its exciting line of award-winning celebrity biographies and film guides, click on

www.BloodMoonProductions.com

Judy Garland & Liza Minnelli
Too Many Damn Rainbows

Judy and Liza were the greatest, most colorful, and most tragic mother-daughter saga in show biz history. They live, laugh, and weep again in the tear-soaked pages of this remarkable biography. Darwin Porter and Danforth Prince have compiled a compelling "post-modern" spin.

According to Liza, "My mother—hailed as the world's greatest entertainer—lived eighty lives during her short time with us."

Their memorable stories unfold through eyewitness accounts of the typhoons that engulfed them. They swing across glittery landscapes of euphoria and glory, detailing the betrayals and treachery which the duo encountered almost daily. There were depressions "as deep as the Mariana Trench," suicide attempts, and obsessive identifications on deep psychological levels with roles that include Judy's Vicky Lester in *A Star is Born* (1954) and Liza's Sally Bowles in *Cabaret* (1972).

Lesser known are the jealous actress-to-actress rivalries. Fueled by klieg lights and rivers of negative publicity, they sprouted like malevolent mushrooms on steroids.

As Judy faded into the 1960s, Liza roaringly emerged as a star in her own right. "I did it my way," Liza said. She survived the whirlwinds of her mother's drug addiction with a yen for choosing all the wrong men in patterns that weirdly evoked those of Judy herself.

For millions of fans, Judy will forever remain the cheerful adolescent (Dorothy) skipping along a yellow brick road toward the other side of the rainbow. Liza followed her down that hallucinogenic path, searching for the childhood, the security, and the love that eluded her.

Judy Garland, an icon whose memory is permanently etched into the American psyche, continues to thrive as a cult goddess. Revered by thousands of die-hard fans, she's the most poignant example of both the manic and depressive (some say "schizophrenic") sides of the Hollywood myth.

Deep in her 70s, Liza is still with us, too, nursing memories of her former acclaim and her first visit as a little girl to her parents at MGM, the "Dream Factory," during the Golden Age of Hollywood.

Judy Garland & Liza Minnelli: Too Many Damn Rainbows
Darwin Porter & Danforth Prince
Softcover, 6" x 9", with hundreds of photos.   ISBN 9781936003693

THE SEDUCTIVE SAPPHIC EXPLOITS OF
MERCEDES DE ACOSTA
HOLLYWOOD'S GREATEST LOVER

IF YOU ASSUMED THAT THE GREATEST LOVERS ARE MEN, some of the most famous "cult goddesses" of the early- and mid-20th-Century might emphatically disagree.

At Magnolia House, in the final years of her life, the celebrated, notorious, and once-fabled Spanish beauty, **MERCEDES DE ACOSTA** (1892-1968) was a frequent visitor. To Darwin Porter, she confessed and recited fabulously indiscreet stories about her romantic same-sex exploits among the theatrical and cinematic elite of New York, London, Paris, and Hollywood.

It reveals "Sapphic Standards" from the heyday of Silent Film and the early Talkies that no other book—even her own (Here Lies the Heart, *published in 1960)— ever dared to make public.*

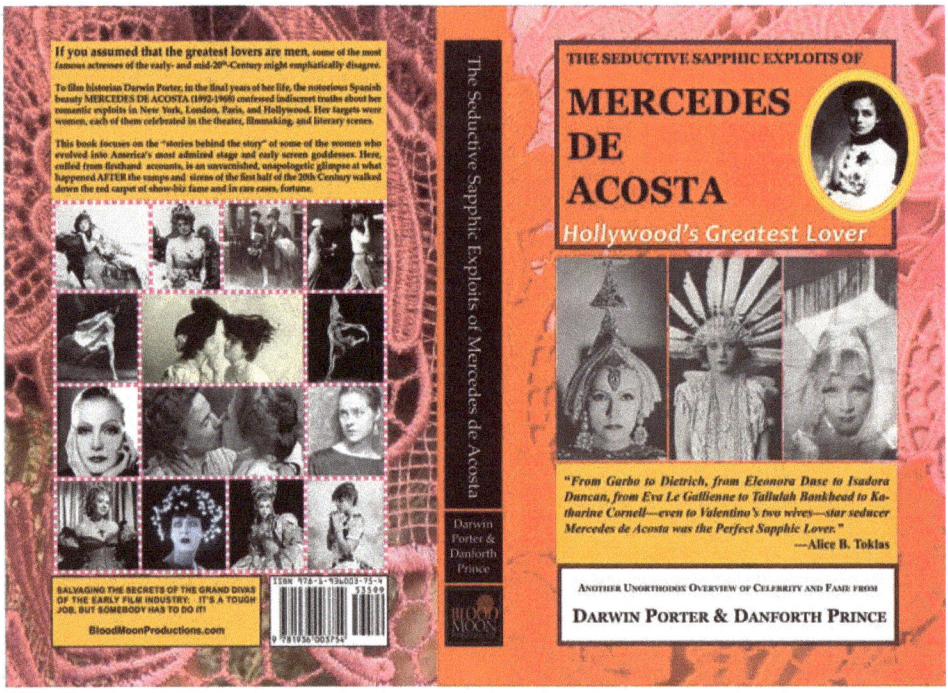

Mercedes de Acosta's love affairs were with women, each a figurehead in art, the theater, and the filmmaking and literary scenes. They included Greta Garbo, Marlene Dietrich, Nazimova, Gertrude Stein, Alice B. Toklas, Eva Le Gallienne, Tallulah Bankhead, Jeanne Eagels, Katharine Cornell, Eleanora Duse, Isadora Duncan, and both of Valentino's wives. This is probably the best portrait of *avant-garde* Broadway and early 20th-century filmmaking ever published. Read all about it in the most recent installment of Blood Moon's MAGNOLIA HOUSE SERIES

THE SEDUCTIVE SAPPHIC EXPLOITS OF
MERCEDES DE ACOSTA
HOLLYWOOD'S GREATEST LOVER

Darwin Porter and Danforth Prince   ISBN 978-1-936003-75-4.
A pithy, photo-packed softcover with 474 pages and many dozens of photos

Blood Moon Productions proudly announces A NEW EDITION of its 2014 compilation of lurid, vintage scandals from the Golden Age of Camelot. It focusses on the most watched, most enigmatic, and most controversial woman of the 20th Century, and it's called

JACQUELINE KENNEDY ONASSIS
Her Tumultous Life & Her Love Affairs

Porter & Prince

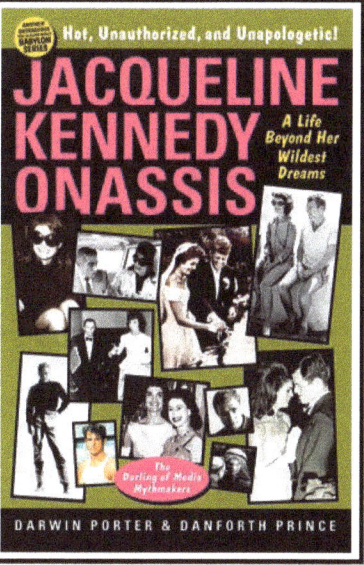

JACKIE INVADES "WASHINGTON BABYLON," EUROPE, & BEYOND

This is a new edition of the most compelling compilation of cash-soaked ambition, sexual indiscretion, and social embarrassment about a former first lady ever published,

Available now from **Ingram** and from **Amazon.com** worldwide, in honor of one of America's favorite Valentines.

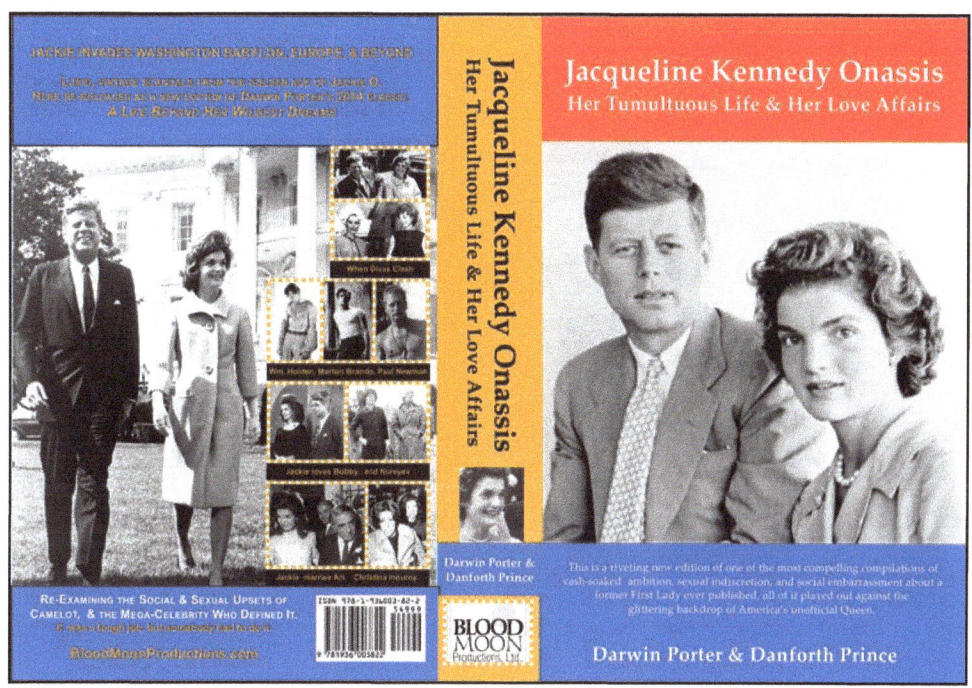

JAQUELINE KENNEDY ONASSIS
Her Tumultuous Life & Her Love Affairs

Conceived in direct and sometimes defiant contrast to the avalanche of more breathlessly respectful testimonials to the life and legacy of "America's Queen," this book is the latest installment in Blood Moon's endlessly irreverent MAGNOLIA HOUSE series.

RE-EXAMINING THE SOCIAL AND SEXUAL UPSETS OF CAMELOT AND THE MEGA-CELEBRITY WHO DEFINED IT.

It was a tough job, but somebody had to do it.

LUCILLE BALL & DESI ARNAZ

BECAME THE MOST CELEBRATED DUO IN THE HISTORY OF TELEVISION
IN TWO VOLUMES, BLOOD MOON HAS RELEASED THE MOST STARTLING, CANDID, AND UNVARNISHED OVERVIEW OF THEIR LIVES EVER PUBLISHED.

Half of America gathered every Monday night around the little black box in their living rooms to watch the antics of Lucy and Ricky Ricardo, a Cuban bandleader with his wacky, high-spirited wife.

The early struggles of Lucy and Desi were epic. As a girl, she at times was literally chained in her backyard in Jamestown, New York. As a teenager, she broke away and earned a reputation as "The Jamestown hussy," riding around with Johnny DeVita, a local hoodlum.

Born to wealth and privilege in Cuba, Desi, at the age of twelve, was escorted to the local bordello by his father to lose his virginity.

His family lost everything in the Cuban Revolution and fled to America. In Miami, Desi got a job cleaning out canary cages. He was eventually hired by bandleader Xavier Cugat because, "I beat hell out of those Afro-Cuban drums."

Meanwhile, in Manhattan, Lucy was struggling to break into show business, hustling "sugar daddies" and stage-door Johnnies who gave her money and gifts. Once, when desperate, she became a nude model. "A gal's gotta eat."

In the 1930s, she made it to Hollywood and worked making films for RKO. The executives used her as a gussied-up hooker to "entertain" out-of-town film exhibitors.

[Ultimately, she got her revenge. In one of the most ironic "fiscal revolutions" in show-biz history, she bought the studio.]

Drifting to Hollywood, Desi spotted Lucy on a sound stage "dressed like a two-dollar whore who had been badly beaten by her pimp." Their tempestuous marriage, characterized by long separations, staggered along for two decades.

By the early 1950s, the careers of both Desi and Lucy had headed south. There was a lot of resistance among TV executives who objected to his Cuban accent. But *I Love Lucy* was launched nevertheless and shot up in the ratings like a rocket, morphing into the most successful sitcom in TV history.

"With gold arriving in wheelbarrows" (Desi's words), they bought the four-block RKO Studios. Desilu Productions was launched, becoming the largest motion picture and television studio in the world.

In 1960, after their divorce, Lucy appraised her husband: "He is a Jekyll and Hyde type. He drinks, gambles, and chases the broads from thirteen to thirty, even Carrie Fisher. He's awash in broads, lots of booze, and that gay actor, Cesar Romero, is his devoted slave. Desi is destructive, but always building something. If it's big, he has to break it down."

"Love?" she asked. "I was always falling in love with the wrong man. Even Desi."

Desi, too, summed up his many years of marriage: "We were anything but Lucy and Ricky Ricardo on the tube. Those guys had nothing to do with us. Lucy and I dreamed of success, fame, and fortune. Guess what? **It all led to hell."**

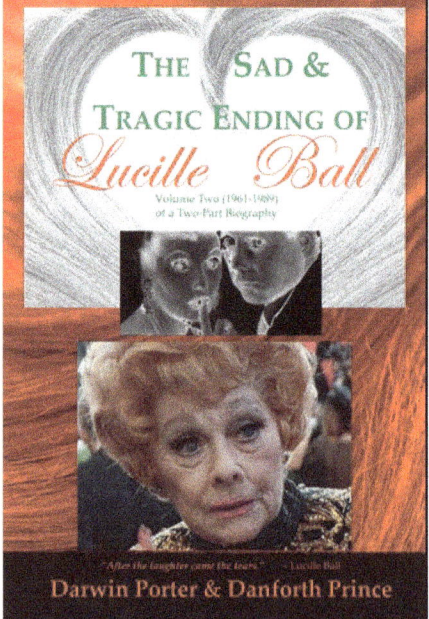

LUCILLE BALL & DESI ARNAZ

THEY WEREN'T
LUCY AND RICKY RICARDO
VOLUME ONE (1911-1960)
OF A TWO-PART BIOGRAPHY

Darwin Porter and Danforth Prince
ISBN 978-1-936003-71-6
Softcover, 530 pages, with photos,
available everywhere now

THE SAD &
TRAGIC ENDING OF

LUCILLE BALL

VOLUME TWO (1961-1989)
OF A TWO-PART BIOGRAPHY

Darwin Porter and Danforth Prince
ISBN 978-1-936003-80-8
Softcover, 550 pages, with photos, available
everywhere now

THIS BOOK ILLUSTRATES WHY GENTLEMEN PREFER BLONDES, AND WHY MARILYN MONROE WAS TOO DANGEROUS TO BE ALLOWED TO GO ON LIVING.

Less than an hour after the discovery of Marilyn Monroe's corpse in Brentwood, a flood of theories, tainted evidence, and conflicting testimonies began pouring out into the public landscape.

Filled with rage, hysteria, and depression, "and fed up with Jack's lies, Bobby's lies," Marilyn sought revenge and mass vindication. Her revelations at an imminent press conference could have toppled political dynasties and destroyed criminal empires. Marilyn had to be stopped…

Into this steamy cauldron of deceit, Marilyn herself emerges as a most unreliable witness during the weeks leading up to her murder. Her own deceptions, vanities, and self-delusion poured toxic accelerants on an already raging fire.

"This is the best book about Marilyn Monroe ever published."

—**David Hartnell,** Recipient, in 2011, of New Zealand's Order of Merit (MNZM) for services to the entertainment industry, as defined by Her Majesty, Queen Elizabeth II.

Winner of literary awards from the New York, Hollywood, and San Francisco Book Festivals

"Darwin Porter is fearless, honest and a great read. He minces no words. If the truth makes you wince and honesty offends your sensibility, stay away. It's been said that he deals in muck because he can't libel the dead. Well, it's about time someone started telling the truth about the dead and being honest about just what happened to get us in the mess in which we're in. If libel is lying, then Porter is so completely innocent as to deserve an award. In all of his works he speaks only to the truth, and although he is a hard teacher and task master, he's one we ignore at our peril. To quote Gore Vidal, power is not a toy we give to someone for being good. If we all don't begin to investigate where power and money really are in the here and now, we deserve what we get. Yes, Porter names names. The reader will come away from the book knowing just who killed Monroe. Porter rather brilliantly points to a number of motives, but leaves it to the reader to surmise exactly what happened at the rainbow's end, just why Marilyn was killed. And, of course, why we should be careful of getting exactly what we want. It's a very long tumble from the top."

—ALAN PETRUCELLI, Examiner.com, May 13, 2012

Marilyn: Don't Even Dream About Tomorrow
Sex, Lies, Murder, and the Great Cover-up, by Darwin Porter
ISBN 978-1-936003-79-2   A Revised Edition of Darwin Porter's Investigative Classic from 2012
Marilyn at Rainbow's End

BOOK RELEASE NEWS

Blood Moon's
Hollywood Remembered
Glitz, Glamour, Triumph, & Tragedy

*How Blood Moon Productions captured the attention of
The American Tabloids during the decline of
The Entertainment Industry's Golden Age*

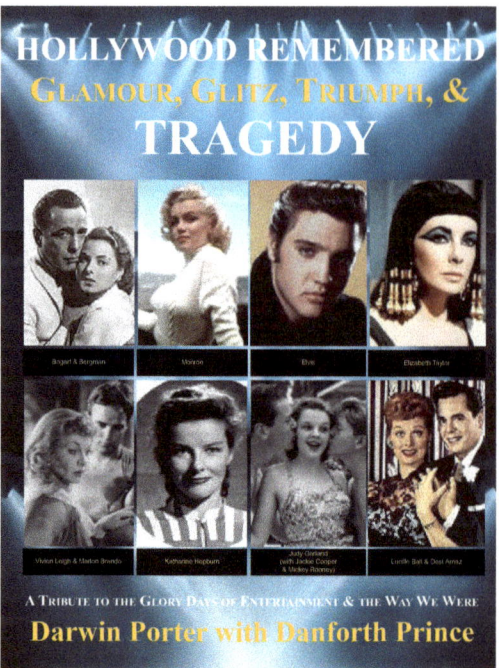

Blood Moon Productions (www.BloodMoonProductions.com) proudly announces the release of *Hollywood Remembered*, a 500-page compendium of "short stories" inspired by **Darwin Porter's** long exposure to the backlot intrigues of the entertainment industry's "Hollywood Heyday."

It's envisioned as an oversized coffee table book of enduring interest to anyone who ever loved classic films and the scandalous intrigues associated with its players. It's not for the timid. Pages are splashed with incisive commentary and photographs of a fabulous era swept away by changing times.

Its inspiration derived from twenty years of Darwin Porter's monthly contributions to *Boomer Times*, a glossy magazine and "Sunday supplement" of *The Miami Herald's* subscribers in Dade and Broward Counties, Florida. It was spearheaded by **Anita Finley**, a South Florida gerontologist who doubled as a spokesperson for her state's "politically connected' population of Baby Boomers.

According to Blood Moon's president, Danforth Prince, "The core values of **Anita Finley** and **Darwin Porter**—who define Baby Boomers as "Old-Time Hollywood's Greatest Fans"—always dovetailed neatly. This book is envisioned as a joint celebration of the staggering literary output of both *Boomer Times* and **Blood Moon Productions**. As such, we've dedicated it to **Ms. Finley**. The *Grande Dame* of Florida's Boomers.

"We also envision this as an **autobiography of Blood Moon Productions** and an end-of-life tribute to its creative director, **Darwin Porter**. If not for his archival skills, many once-underground truths about The American Century would have died with their last first-hand witnesses. But thanks in part to Porter's staggering descriptive output, thousands of once-repressed facts have been recorded and digitalized for future historians and fans. In fact, for the Library Trades, we've categorized this one-of-a-kind new book as a resource for MEDIA STUDIES.

"With a release expected on that Greatest of American Holidays, The 4th of July, Blood Moon's *HOLLYWOOD REMEMBERED* will challenge traditional beliefs about celebrities and the sociologies that nurtured them. "

With a special tribute to the celebrities whose luminous images still enthrall us on movie screens today, thanks for taking a look at this portrait of the ferociously unfettered "indie" that briefly reigned as a magnet for tabloid publicists, and as one of the hottest independent publishing ventures in the world.

**Blood Moon's HOLLYWOOD REMEMBERED:
Glitz, Glamour, Triumph, & Tragedy**

By Darwin Porter with Danforth Prince
ISBN 978-1-936003-92-1

In bookstores everywhere and online, worldwide, on the 4th of July 2024

This is the story behind the story of the small, scrappy independent press,
Blood Moon Productions,
whose celebrity *exposés* (more than 50 of them) generated *tsunamis* of tabloid flash during the decline of the entertainment industry's golden age.

It's a story about Media, the Hollywood Dream Factory, and the clumsy, treacherous juggernaut known as FAME. It's about the fantasies that the entertainment industry crafted, and the secrets it conspired to conceal.

It offers an "on the down low" view of entertainers who delighted us, who captured our imaginations, and who paid heavy prices for the pedestals on which we placed them.

It's also a memorial to belief systems and values that in many cases have
Gone With the Wind.

From "Deep in December" of our lives *(or, if we're lucky, from Deep in September)*,
we offer it as a tribute to the way we were.

Here it is…*Hollywood Remembered*…an idiosyncratic, scrappy anthology
like nothing that's ever been seen before. It says a lot about the American version
of Fame and/or Infamy that you might not have expected.

Happy reading…and may your memories burn bright.

www.BloodMoonProductions.com

**CHALLENGING THE STATUS QUO'S
BELIEFS ABOUT CELEBRITY
AND THE IRONIES OF FAME**

**IT'S A TOUGH JOB,
BUT SOMEBODY'S GOT TO DO IT.**

As described in Blood Moon's Biography of MARILYN MONROE

MARILYN VS. THE KENNEDYS

Some Like It Hot

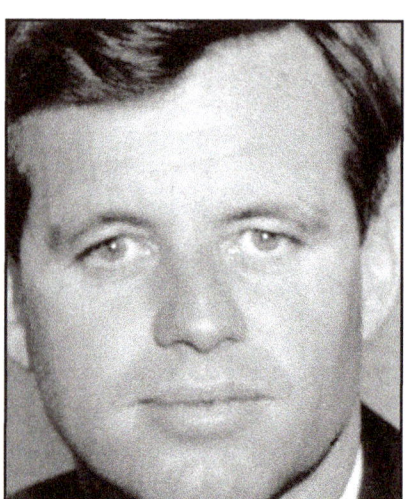

Marilyn Monroe made the rounds, going through all the Kennedy men, beginning with **Jack Kennedy** *(upper left)* in 1946. When she met Senator Kennedy years later at a Hollywood party, he didn't remember deflowering **Norma Jean Baker.** But, in fairness to the senator, in 1946 she didn't look like the woman who had turned herself into Marilyn Monroe. She was also accompanied by her husband, Joe DiMaggio. "Joe and Jack were like roosters when they came together," Marilyn later recalled.

Sometimes Sammy Davis Jr. served as "the black beard," escorting Marilyn to a party at the home of Peter Lawford, though she later disappeared with Jack. When **Joe Kennedy** *(lower left photo)* first seduced Marilyn, she was so little known she was referred to as "a minor starlet." When his son was running for president, Marilyn told Joe, "It would be nice to have a president who looks so young and good looking."

John Miner, an associate clinical professor at the University of Southern California Medical School, heard the tapes recorded for Marilyn's psychiatrist, Dr. Ralph Greenson. Miner later claimed, "Marilyn was very explicit about the sexual relationship she had with both **Jack and Robert**." It wasn't until 2010 that her relationship with **Teddy Kennedy** *(lower right)* was revealed in F.B.I. reports.

PART TWO

DARWIN PORTER

"Recording the Scene"
from the Peripheries of Showbiz

The most famous person you've never heard of, He's what would have happened if Walter Winchell had fathered a child with Hedda Hopper.

As Analyzed by Danforth Prince

"At many of the parties I attended, I was the only one there who wasn't famous."

—Darwin Porter

Darwin Porter has published more books than any other writer in America.

Although he's best-known these days for his celebrity biographies, for more than a half-century (from 1960 to 2013), he was the world's leading travel writer, working steadily, under contract, for at least five of the biggest publishing magnates in the world: Simon & Schuster, Macmillan, Inc., Prentice Hall, IDG, and some of their short-lived spin-offs, including Hungry Minds. For several years, he was employed by John Wiley & Sons after Simon & Schuster (founded in 1807) sold the Frommer travel guides to them.

HOW DID IT BEGIN?

In the late 1950s, as Europe continued boot-strapping itself from the rubble and ashes of World War II, the late Arthur Frommer wrote and self-published an edgy, experimental travel guide (*Europe on $5 a Day*) that launched an industry. It sold 330,000 copies of its inaugural edition and morphed into a key informational resource during the postwar travel boom.

Young, plucky Darwin, then in his early twenties, fresh from a gig as a Bureau Chief (in Key West) for *The Miami Herald,* happened—through connections and some lucky timing—to arrive early on the scene.

The glass ceiling shattered. Hysterically preoccupied with other business ventures, Frommer hired him to research and write the first guidebook that included his name as a formal part of the title. The resulting budget guide to England (*Frommer's England on $5 and $10 a Day*, which Darwin co-authored with the peripheral, somewhat non-involved Stanley Haggart) was such a success that its founding premise

> *"There are guilty pleasures. Then there is the master of guilty pleasures, **Darwin Porter**. There is nothing like reading him for passing the hours. He is the Nietzsche of Naughtiness, the Goethe of Gossip, the Proust of Pop Culture. Darwin knows all the nasty buzz anyone has ever heard whispered in dark bars, dim alleys, and confessional booths. And lovingly, precisely, and in as straightforward a manner as an oncoming train, his prose whacks you between the eyes with the greatest gossip since Kenneth Anger. Some would say better than Anger."*
>
> **Alan Petrucelli**
> *The Entertainment Report,*
> *Stage and Screen Examiner,*
> *Examiner.com*

Whereas **Arthur Frommer** established the Frommer trademark and authored the first in its series, the shoe-leather and on-site gruntwork for many of the titles that followed were soonafter assigned to **Darwin.** In 2007, fourteen years before Frommer's death, the "on $5-a-day' price promise" had morphed into "from $85 a-day," and Darwin was still listed as one of its authors. That was in part because many of the texts he'd composed through the course of 40 years were recycled.

soldiered on. As the decades passed, it survived 53 annual revisions. That was followed with a popular budget guide to London, followed by a blizzard of other guidebooks covering various regions within the U.K.

Dozens upon dozens of other travel guides to the individual countries of Europe followed, all of them authored by Darwin. Among the most popular were *Frommer's France* and *Frommer's Italy.*

In 1982, the publisher hired me, Danforth Prince, as co-author with Darwin. Together, in the decades that followed, we created an avalanche of best-selling travel guides.

Ironically, although Arthur Frommer, the series' namesake, was no longer either the publisher or author of any of them, some of the photos in his 2024 obituaries depict him alongside show-stopping copies of those titles.

Meanwhile Frommer, who was by then NOT involved in their redactions or research, used the fame derived from his early budget guide to Europe to launch other travel-related businesses: They included package deals, brick-and-mortar hotels in Amsterdam, Copenhagen, Curaçao, and Aruba, and a travel agency. He pumped sales at each of them through frequent appearances on TV and radio.

Impossibly over-scheduled, since he was too busy running enterprises in New York, he hired Darwin—inexorably, title by title—to update the capitals of Europe he had featured in early editions of his guidebook,

Darwin's involvement continued for decades to come, thriving long after Frommer sold his series, in 1977, to Simon & Schuster for a reported $4 million dollars.

Simon & Schuster sustained a one-hour meeting with Arthur Frommer, during which he was fired. Future editorial updates were assigned to eight other writers. Simon & Schuster sold the Frommer guides to IDG Books in 1999, who sold it to John Wiley & Sons Publishing in 2001, who sold it to Google in 2012.

In the beginning, Simon & Schuster also "cleaned house," firing many other editors and writers. Only Darwin remained from the original staff. To Darwin, at that point, was assigned the authorship of a broad spectrum of Frommer guides to the major destinations of the world. These guides became famous throughout America and Europe, some readers referring to them as "The Bibles of Travel."

He was given the daunting task of researching and writing guidebooks to the countries (and city guides to the major urban centers) of Europe, including London, Paris, Rome, Venice, and Florence.

As a guidebook writer, Darwin covered country after country, developing a guidebook to Germany with separate spinoff guides to Berlin and Munich. His authorship of a guide to Switzerland and Liechtenstein morphed into a separate guidebook to Zurich. His authorship of a guide to Spain expanded into separate guidebooks to Madrid, Barcelona, and Andalucia.

Darwin "re-united" the Austro-Hungarian Empire after the appearance of his guidebook to *Frommer's Austria & Hungary*. From that emerged an eventual spinoff of a separate guide to Vienna.

At one point Darwin was hired to craft a guidebook for the then-booming "touristic invasion" of Scandinavia. It emerged in the form of an "all-in-one" combined guide to the far north of Europe, incorporating the touristic allure of Denmark, Sweden, Norway, Finland, Iceland, and Greenland. That colossal, "doorstopping" compilation was eventually subdivided even further. Denmark, Sweden, and Norway were split off into separate guidebooks

CELEBRITY AND THE IRONIES OF FAME

Stanley Mills Haggart, a socialite and art director who had met everyone in Hollywood when it was still a small town, was instrumental in introducing young Darwin to worlds he'd never seen before, One of those worlds involved "brokering" Darwin's introduction to **Arthur Frommer.**

For the remaining 25 years, until his death in 1980, Stanley's name was cited, alongside Darwin's, as a co-author of many guidebooks within the fast-expanding family of Frommer guides, even though Darwin—trained in the pressure-cookers of *the Miami Herald*—did 90% of the labor and spilled 100% of the blood, sweat, and tears.

Ironically, whereas Arthur Frommer remained a visible presence after writing his "famous first' and a handful of others, he was fired by **Simon & Schuster** a few weeks after they acquired his name and imprint.

For the next 40 years, Darwin labored to produce, on time, on budget, and on demand, a raft of guidebooks that bore the Frommer name.

Stanley Haggart (photo, left) became legendary for his easy access to movie stars from the silent era. Part of that derived from his gregarious, socially adept mother, **Maria Jane Haggart** (photo above).

Feeling stifled after she became widowed, she migrated from Lawrence, Kansas with her teenaged son, Stanley, in tow, to experiment with life far from the strictures she had known.

Hollywood was her final destination. There, she bought a house in Laurel Canyon, close to the movie colony where everyone, back then, knew everyone.

As it happened, columnist **Adela Rogers St. Johns** was her confidant and next-door neighbor, and her circle of friends was wide.

Before the end of her life, she rented that house to a parade of actors, four of whom were noteworthy as having co-starred with **Greta Garbo** in four of her seminal films. (They included **Antonio Moreno, Lars Hansen, Lewis Stone,** and **Conrad Nagel**)

Later, she helped usher her *avant-garde* and bohemian son, Stanley, into employment as on on-site researcher for the legendary gossip columnist, **Hedda Hopper**. Stanley later transmitted his files and research notes to Darwin, who used them as source material within some of his biographies.

of their own, and separate city guides were compiled, by us, to Copenhagen and Stockholm.

In the spirit of the then-booming travel market, a pioneering, "experimental" Frommer Guide was eventually published on the then-Soviet Bloc nations of Czechoslovakia, Bulgaria, Poland, Ukraine, and Romania.

By the 1980s, tourism was exploding to the islands of the West Indies. Darwin stepped into the breach, spending many months researching Bermuda, The Bahamas, and the islands of the Caribbean from Puerto Rico to Trinidad. These warm-weather destinations were so popular that Darwin was eventually contracted to produce separate overviews—trademarked and distributed as Frommer guides—to Puerto Rico, Jamaica, Barbados, the Dominican Republic, the Cayman Islands, and even the (then fast-emerging) Turks & Caicos.

FROM WHAT AND FROM WHERE DID DARWIN ORIGINATE?

Darwin, at 20, the youngest bureau chief in the history of *The Miami Herald*.

Darwin Porter came into the world in the Blue Ridge Mountains of North Carolina, the son of Numie Porter, who had recently married Darwin's mother, the then-20-year-old Hazel Phillips. Tall, rugged, and handsome, Numie led people to believe that he was in his 20s. Two months after their wedding, Hazel discovered that he was only 17.

Before America entered World War II, Numie found work at the U.S. Department of Commerce in Wilmington, N.C. In 1942, after America declared war on Japan and Germany, he was murdered.

[Along with two other employees of the same agency, he was kidnapped, tied to a tree, doused with gasoline, and ignited. Neither the murderers nor their motives were ever uncovered, but it was speculated that the victims had uncovered a nest of Nazi spies entrusted with the sabotage of vital East Coast ports. A tragedy that horrific left wounds.]

From there, with the dual intention of surviving and of supporting the war effort, Hazel migrated to manufacturing jobs in Richmond and Norfolk. Her contemporaries later evaluated her looks as something akin to a brunette version of Jayne Mansfield. Once, when she and "baby Darwin" were waiting for a train at the railway station in Richmond, a sailor approached her and said, as part of a seductive pickup, "**Lady, you could stop an eight-day clock.**" It was a line that Darwin committed to memory for life.

The train's departure had been delayed for a late-arriving V.I.P. As young Darwin and Hazel watched, then-President Franklin D. Roosevelt emerged from the back seat of a limousine. Staff members lifted him from the car into a wheelchair before wheeling him into a secure area of the about-to-depart train. As Hazel and Darwin found spots in one of the second-class cars, Darwin called out to him, "You've been holding up the train!"

Cheerfully, FDR waved at the kid, saying, "Sorry, young fellow. I've got a war to win!"

LEST WE FORGET Here's then-president **Franklin Delano Roosevelt,** looking as he did from around the time **6-year-old Darwin** *(inset photo)* admonished him for delaying the departure of his train.

***

Before the end of World War II, Hazel would marry again, twice, two more marriages that each ended tragically. The last word she ever received from her second husband, Clarence Huskins, came from the muddy bat-

As an wartime adolescent trying to figure out the strange but approving whistles that servicemen frequently aimed at his mother, **young Darwin** paid attention to PINUPS, and followed (as in **Betty Grable**) the personal histories of the girls who got whistled at—especially if they later evolved into movie stars.

Here's a midwar view of a mechanic painting, as a morale-builder, and in designs tacitly approved by the Pentagon, a pinup ("Little Gem") onto the nose of a fighter plane.

tlefields of Belgium. He was about to have both of his legs amputated. She never heard from him again. He may have died in an air raid.

Her third husband, a Navy man named Steve Rogers, was a sailor aboard a vessel that suffered a direct hit from a Japanese torpedo. He disappeared forever into the waters of the Pacific.

After the war, Hazel, by then working bussing tables in the breakfast room of a hotel in Washington, D.C., had a reunion with her childhood sweetheart, Harold Triplett, and soonafter married him. It was her fourth marriage.

He left her after eight months, migrating to Hollywood with a male photographer. Later in life, Hazel and "Tripp" reconnected, and ended their lives together in Florida.

Darwin's first-ever up-close-and-personal with a movie star. It happened at the Liberty Theater in North Wilkesboro, NC. Darwin was a loosely supervised seven-year-old. The star of that weekend's matinee was **Lash LaRue**. Years later, when he fell on bad days, Darwin came to his rescue.

***

At an early age, Darwin developed a passion for movie stars, no doubt inherited from his mother, and no doubt encouraged by their role as highly visible morale-builders during World War II. Both of them were film addicts, seeing (sometimes side-by-side) almost every major movie released during the years immediately after World War II.

Their favorites were Bette Davis, Joan Crawford, Gary Cooper, and Clark Gable. They were also devoted to Barbara Stanwyck, Claudette Colbert, and Marlene Dietrich. They also saw every film featuring Rita Hayworth, Judy Garland, and a young Elizabeth Taylor. In the years to come, Darwin would write tell-all biographies of some of these stars, and make it a focused point to "hang out" with screen legends.

The first movie star he met was at a theater in his native North Wilkesboro, North Carolina. He was whip-tossing Lash LaRue making personal appearance tours in small-town movie theaters throughout America.

The owner of the Liberty Theatre, a friend of Hazel, arranged a date with her and this somewhat sinister-looking cowboy hero. He always dressed in black, wearing a rakishly tilted Stetson and with a whip strapped to his hip.

About a decade later, in 1961, Darwin came to the rescue of his screen hero when LaRue was arrested by Miami police on charges of vagrancy, public drunkenness, and possession of illegal drugs. "For old times' sake," Darwin bailed him out of jail and moved him into a small apartment building he owned at the time. Before the end of his life, LaRue's failed marriages reached a grand total of ten.

LaRue was merely the first movie star Hazel and Darwin knew. Soon, a cavalcade of stars would pass through their lives. They had relocated to Miami Beach, where Hazel had found work as a "Girl Friday" to Miss Sophie Tucker, hailed as "The Last of the Red Hot Mamas."

Nearly every celebrity who visited Miami Beach called on "Miss Sophie."

Many male stars were attracted to the buxom and affable Hazel, none more notable that Frank Sinatra. He gave "Baby Darwin" a ten-dollar bill and told him to "get lost." Decades later, Darwin would write a biography of Sinatra, entitling it "The Boudoir Singer."

For some reason, Miss Tucker was the favorite singer of then-actor Ronald Reagan. *[You might have thought it would be Doris Day, whom he was dating at the time. He had recently filmed* Storm Warning *(1951) with Day and Ginger Rogers. It premiered in Miami. With hopes of marrying her, he was smitten with Day at the time. Confusingly, he was also dating MGM starlet Nancy Davis, who, as has been revealed in many sources, was secretly known as "The Fellatio Queen of Hollywood." Author Kitty Kelley wrote the first major-league exposé of Davis.*

Although Reagan had originally wanted to marry Day, Nancy informed him that she was pregnant. Ever the gentleman, he wed her instead.

During the final months of the Reagan presidency, with his cognitive powers receding, Nancy, for a few months at least, became the most powerful woman on the planet.]

Since Day wasn't available because of a picture commitment, horndog Reagan invited an emerging starlet (Marilyn Monroe) to accompany him to Miami Beach, where he would call on Miss Tucker.

Divorced from Jane Wyman at the time, Reagan at first had fallen in love with actress Adele Jurgens, who

Who Was Sophie Tucker?

1. **The Last of the Red Hot Mammas** and a noted entertainer in the 1940s in the fast-emerging postwar boomtown of Miami Beach
2. The employer of Darwin's mother, Hazel, who was her personal assistant and "Girl Friday"
3. The show-bizzy *duenna* of Miami Beach who regularly received social calls from ardent fans who included **Ronald Reagan, Frank Sinatra,** and virtually every other entertainer visiting for either work or for play, and
4. Something of an "unofficial godmother" to the star-struck frighteninlgly precocious: adolescent then known as Freddie Porter.

was making a movie, *Ladies of the Chorus.* He had given her a diamond engagement ring.

In the movie, Marilyn Monroe played the beautiful and cooperative daughter of Jurgens, who portrayed a burlesque queen. When Reagan arrived on the set, Jurgens was completing a scene. While he was waiting for her to wrap up the scene, the future U.S. President met Marilyn. It was "Hello, Marilyn, Goodbye Adele."

Hazel and Darwin met both Reagan and his date (Marilyn). Little did Darwin know at the time that he would one day write a popular *exposé* of Marilyn, revealing new details about her untimely death. He would also write *Love Triangle,* the cynical show-biz and political saga of Reagan and his two wives, Jane Wyman and Nancy Davis.

Hazel also sustained an affair with Victor Mature that began after he made a personal appearance at the Olympic Theatre on Flagler Street in Miami. Onscreen, he was known for his muscular frame, toothy smile, slick waving hair, and macho allure.

Victor Mature in 1942, around the time he was dating Darwin's mother. He appears here, all smiles, with **Rita Hayworth.**

Mature's involvement with Hazel was brief. Late one night, Rita Hayworth slipped into town to begin an affair with him, adding him to a list of conquests that would include Robert Mitchum, Tyrone Power, James Stewart, and aviator Howard Hughes. Hayward would later marry famously eccentric husbands who included Orson Welles and Prince Aly Khan.

Darwin also met actor Wendell Corey after Hazel became involved with him romantically and sexually. An almost forgotten man today, in his heyday, he was the leading man to such stars as Joan Crawford and Barbara Stanwyck.

Darwin's first visit to a movie set occurred in South Florida when *Slattery's Hurricane* (1949) was being filmed with Richard Widmark, Linda Darnell, and Veronica Lake. Hazel was hired as an aide to Darnell, who was drinking heavily and not remembering her lines.

Wendell Corey, another of Hazel Triplett's dates, appears on the right restraining **Barbara Stanwyck** and on the left romancing **Joan Crawford.**

On the set of that film, Hazel began secretly dating Widmark within a hideaway suite at the Helen Mar Hotel. He was on the dawn of a legendary career. She had first thrilled to him when he made the *film noir, Kiss of Death* (1947) in which he was cast as the cackling villain, Tommy Udo, who pushes Mildred Dunnock, in her wheelchair, down a long, steep, flight of stairs.

"Richard wasn't at all like that screen persona," Hazel said. "A real gentleman, loving and considerate."

She would connect with him again on very intimate terms when he made *Don't Bother to Knock* with Marilyn Monroe in 1951. "I was so delighted that he preferred me to Marilyn."

It was on the set of *Slattery's Hurricane* that young Darwin became enraptured with Veronica Lake and her peek-a-boo hair style. "We slipped away whenever she was free and went to this little stand where we devoured the best hamburgers in the State of Florida."

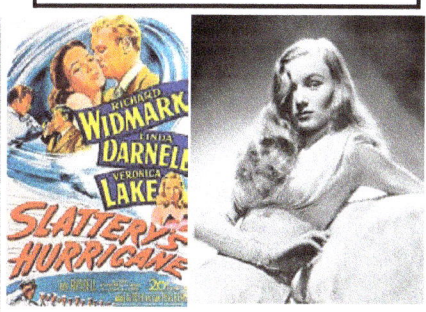

Left photo: **Richard Widmark** with **Linda Darnell** in *Slattery's Hurricane* (1949). Far right photo: **Veronica Lake.** Darwin helped her with her memoirs, years after they met, thanks to his mother, when he was in college.

Later, he would work on her memoirs when her star light went out in Hollywood and she ended up as a bartender.

Hazel eventually fell in love with the handsome, dashing, and very rich Harry Hunt, who was six years younger than she was. As their affair intensified, he invited her to come and live with him in West Virginia.

Entrenched in his new and exciting life in Miami, Darwin did not want to go. Hazel, therefore, agreed to leave her 13-year-old son behind in Miami after Harry paid his rent for the coming year and provided him with adequate spending money.

Darwin attended Miami High School, where he became the editor of the school newspaper and also the editor of its literary magazine, *Silhouette.*

While still in high school, one of Darwin's best friends was Robert Graham, the president of the student body. In later life, Graham became the Governor (and later Senator) from Florida.

When Bill Clinton was running for president, Graham told Darwin that the following morning, he was going to be named as his vice-presidential running mate. Darwin remained glued to the TV news when word came that Clin-

Darwin's friend, confidant, and classmate at Miami High: **Bob Graham,** Governor (and later, Senator) from Florida

ton had named Al Gore instead as his running mate.

During his senior year at Miami High, Darwin won a four-year journalism scholarship to the University of Miami. Before the end of his sophomore year, he had taken over the editorial direction of the university's award-winning newspaper, *The Miami Hurricane.* He also became president of several clubs.

Darwin inaugurated a policy of inviting famous people, visiting Miami or Miami Beach at the time, to be fêted at the University.

His biggest conquest involved persuading Eleanor Roosevelt to visit the campus. She was staying at the Fontainebleu Hotel on Miami Beach. She was viewed as a living legend and treated accordingly. Darwin later wrote a profile of her entitling it "Portrait of a Great Lady." She later wrote him a note of thanks.

The former first Lady did not disappear from Darwin's life. He renewed his acquaintance with her in Manhattan during a visit to his newly coined friend, Tallulah Bankhead.

Miss Bankhead, a few days later, arranged for Darwin to escort Mrs. Roosevelt to a political rally at Sheridan Square in Greenwich Village. He also attended three other events with her, one of which featured George Jessel as master of ceremonies. Jessel introduced Mrs. Roosevelt "as the greatest lady of the 20th Century."

Like many Hollywood actors, First Lady **Eleanor Roosevelt** got deeply involved in supporting the war effort too. Here, about a decade before she got to know Darwin, she holds a bouquet of roses as she stands with **Sabu**, the India-born star of the 1937 British adventure film, *The Elephant Boy.* At this point in his life, he was a soldier attached to Fort Meade, MD.. The venue was FDR's birthday celebration at a USO post Washington, D.C. in January of 1944

As editor of the university newspaper, Darwin continued to invite visiting celebrities as guest lecturers. Except for Elvis Presley, most of them accepted. His manager, Col Tom Parker, turned down the invitation.

Other visitors, including Adlai Stevenson and Nat King Cole, accepted.

Other than Mrs. Roosevelt, Darwin's biggest triumph involved persuading Lucille Ball and Desi Arnaz to attend. Because of their hit TV show, *I Love Lucy*, they were the most popular stars in America at that time.

Darwin later said, "I soon learned they were nothing like the Ricardos they played on television." In time, he would write a two-volume biography about their agonizing, sometimes triumphant lives.

A significant moment in Darwin's college-aged life came when he was put in charge of "Youth for Smathers" throughout the state of Florida. The reference involved Senator George Smathers (*aka "Gorgeous George"*), a notoriously promiscuous "babe magnet."

Smathers' closest friend was then-Senator from Massachusetts, John F. Kennedy. One afternoon, Smathers invited Darwin to accompany him to Palm Beach, where they would meet and talk to John Kennedy and his wife, the lovely Jacqueline.

The afternoon went beautifully and became one of Darwin's greatest memories. As time went by, he would one day write separate thick (and scandal-soaked) biographies of each of these magnetic personalities.

Darwin was "enrolled" as **Lucille Ball** and **Desi Arnaz's** "handler" and tour guide during their studio-sanctioned visit to the University of Miami. In real life, they weren't ANYTHING like the Ricardos. Years later, he wrote about it.

During that encounter in Palm Beach, Darwin had been stunned to see both of them attired in pink pants. Since then, pink pants have become relatively widespread on golf courses, etc. But back then, if a boy walked down the street wearing a pair, an unruly group of males was likely to surround him, call him a faggot, and possibly beat him up.

En route back to Miami, the Senator asked Darwin what he thought of JFK as a possible Democratic nominee for the presidency.

"I thought both JFK and Jacqueline were gracious, even charismatic. But he is far too sophisticated to be elected president," he said.

Years later, at a party at the home of Tennessee Williams in Key West, Darwin relayed the story of his meeting with "Jack and Jacqueline." At the party were such guests as Stanley Mills Haggart, Gore Vidal, novelist James Leo Herlihy, producer Walter Starcke, and businessman Bill Johnson.

"I've got a better story than that," Tennessee quipped. "When Gore here took me to meet Kennedy in Palm Beach, when we were alone beside the pool, I fellated him

In Palm Beach, when "Gorgeous George" Smathers, then Senator from Florida, introduced Darwin, as president of "Youth for Smathers" to a young and vibrant **JFK and his bride, Jacqueline.** Darwin thought they were too hip and sophisticated to ever get elected. Here, they appear in 1953.

in the dressing room."

"I know that," Gore said. "In fact, I told Jack that you found his ass attractive. When I passed on that remark to the *complimentee*, Jack replied, 'How exciting!'"

At the university, through one of his visiting professors (Wilson Hicks, the retired Executive Editor of *Time-Life, Inc.*) Darwin attracted the attention of the managing editor of *The Miami Herald.* He immediately hired Darwin as a staff writer, assigning him to Palm Beach. Darwin later described it as "the most exciting venue of my life."

In his capacity as a feature and news writer, he attended star-studded parties, later saying, "At many of them, I was the only person there who was not rich and famous."

Thanks to his status with *The Miami Herald,* Darwin appeared on the guest list of parties thrown by Frances Langford, a singer and actress who was popular during the golden age of radio. During World War II, she became known as the "G.I. Nightingale," an armed forces sweetheart who entertained troops touring with Bob Hope.

She had divorced her first husband, matinee idol Jon Hall.

From 1955 to 1986, she was wed to Ralph Evinrude, President of Outboard Marine Corporation. The couple lived on their estate in Jensen Beach and built a Polynesian-style restaurant and marina on Indian River.

"She threw the best parties in Florida," Darwin said. "At some of them, Langford performed."

She was responsible for introducing Darwin to Gertrude Macy, the Broadway producer. When Macy met him, she was on the verge of migrating for a six-month gig in Manhattan and was in search of a house-sitter during her absence.

Darwin gladly accepted the invitation. To his surprise, he found that her sumptuous bed was suspended by gold-plated chains from the ceiling. One could ease out of it and plunge directly into a "canal" that funneled into an (outdoor) swimming pool.

Macy became known for her contributions to the American theater. A ferocious feminist vaguely associated with the department store empire that bears her family's name, she morphed herself into the producer of shows which included Betty Hutton, Gene Kelly, Alfred Drake, Ray Bolger, Arthur Godfrey, and Gordon MacRae. She also co-produced *I Am a Camera* with Julie Harris, which was later adapted into the movie musical *Cabaret* with Liza Minnelli. Macy also managed the career of the great Katharine Cornell, who vied for the title of "Queen of Broadway."

At a party in Palm Beach, Darwin was introduced to the Duke and Duchess of Windsor, one of the most infamously stylish couples in the world. The Duke (*aka the former King of England, Edward VIII*) had abdicated his throne "to marry the woman I love."

They weren't anything like what Darwin had imagined. In his words, "They were the dullest couple you ever wanted to meet. Dull, Dull. Dull."

Decades later, Darwin learned more about what was really going on behind the scenes with the Duke and his American-born Duchess. "I was offered, for publication (for a genuinely daunting pricetag) the startling memoirs of Hollywood's most popular pimp, Scotty Bowers, who had written a tell-all that contained stunning, first-hand revelations. A deal with me was never concluded. Instead, Grove Press dared to issue the book in 2012."

One of its major *exposés* centered on Scotty as the supplier of high-testosterone young men to service the sexual needs of the Duke; and of lithe and beautiful young women to the Duchess.

Over the course of many years, Scotty also supplied males (including himself) for the sexual pleasure of Spencer Tracy; and a bevy of some 150 ladies to the boudoir of Katharine Hepburn. Scotty himself seduced everyone from Vivien Leigh to Edith Piaf and sustained a *ménage à trois* with then-roommates Cary Grant and Randolph Scott. From Cole Porter to Vincent Price, Scotty's list of conquests-for-pay goes on and on, embracing Montgomery Clift, Rock Hudson, and Errol Flynn.

Scotty "tricked" with Noël Coward when he visited Hollywood from London, and supplied "young gals" to Desi Arnaz. On three occasions, he sent bodybuilder Steve Reeves to the bed of George Cukor. The parade also embraced Ramon Novarro, Tyrone Power, and Charles Laughton. Scotty also "supplied" actor Cornel Wilde to J. Edgar Hoover, long-term director of the F.B.I. Hoover had met the studly actor during a visit he made to the set of *The Greatest Show on Earth* (1952), an extravaganza that also starred Betty Hutton.

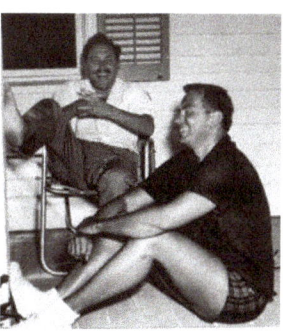

FRENEMIES WHO GOSSIP

Gore Vidal *(foreground)* with **Tennessee Williams** in Key West, during Darwin's tenure there as bureau chief of *The Miami Herald*.

How and Why was Darwin hired as a Bureau Chief at the tender age of 20?

Because after his retirement, **Wilson Hicks**, the "Father of Modern Phot-Journalism:" and former Executive Editor of Time-Life, had joined the faculty of the University of Miami and recommended him to the Editor-in-Chief of *The Miami Herald*.

NOTORIOUS

The Duke of Windsor and His Duchess in 1940

Darwin later wrote an *exposé* biography of the FBI director, the most extensive ever published on his notorious and gay private life.

Darwin hated giving up the rich social life of Palm Beach when he was named as the *Miami Herald's* bureau chief in Key West, covering the Florida Keys from Key Largo (the setting for the Humphrey Bogart/Lauren Bacall movie) to Marathon. He was the youngest bureau chief in the newspaper's history.

Key West wasn't the remote outpost he thought it to be. *Avant-garde* and arts-soaked, it would forever change his life. Ernest Hemingway had felt at home here until he was lured to nearby Cuba. Darwin later became a best friend of the author's son, the deeply troubled Gregory Hemingway, who wished that he had been born female.

Scotty Bowers, Hollywood hustler, pimp, and "procuror to the stars," poses in the 1950s with models & starlets **Valerie Vernon** (left) and **Constance Dowling**.

Right from the beginning, Darwin got to visit the set where *Operation Petticoat* (1959) was being filmed. It starred Cary Grant and Tony Curtis. The female lead was played by heiress Dina Merrill, the daughter of the multi-millionaire E.F. Hutton and the multi-millionaire socialite Marjorie Merriweather Post.

Dina grew up at Mar-a-Lago, which she would later sell to the television actor Donald Trump for $7 million. Donald Jr. today claims it's worth one billion.

Darwin and Dina developed a friendship that lasted for years, although they would go for months without seeing each other. However, in 1981, he showed up to see her perform as a stage actress in Tennessee Williams' *Suddenly, Last Summer.* Later, he invited her to Sardi's for a late-night supper. That was the last time he ever saw her.

Soon after his arrival in Key West, Darwin was granted "the greatest interview of my life from the man who for a time was the most powerful person who had ever lived." His name was Harry S Truman.

The ex-president arrived in Key West for his farewell visit. The port had been his vacation retreat during his presidency.

He was the guest of the sheriff, John Spottswood. He arranged for Darwin to go on morning walks with the former president, with the Secret Service hovering nearby, beginning at 6AM.

On one of these mornings, young Darwin interviewed Truman about his decision to order "Little Boy" aboard the *Enola Gay* and flown to the skies above Japan. The bombing of Hiroshima marked the beginning of the Atomic Age.

Ernest ("Papa") Hemingway with his transsexual youngest son-turned-daughter, then known as **Gregory,** in Cuba in the 1950s.

In 1960, Darwin shared a hotel room with him as Hurricane Donna almost wiped Key West off the map.

Truman said, "My military chiefs told me that America would lose half a million men in a land invasion of Japan. Apparently, they were going to fight to the death. I made the decision and went to bed without losing any sleep. I knew I had made the best decision for the American people"

Thus, because he was only 21 at the time, Darwin, as of this writing, remains the only reporter still alive who got to talk to Truman about Hiroshima.

The morning after his article was published in *The Miami Herald*, Truman, during his morning walk, told Darwin, "You misspelled my name. You put a period after the S in Harry S Truman. My family could not agree on a middle name—Shipped or Solomon—so an S without a period was used instead."

***

In Key West, Darwin would soon form friendships with that town's writers, actors, and artists—some of them famous throughout America. Many of them would open new worlds for him.

He was startled to learn that he was living next door to Tennessee Williams, then at the peak of his fame and the best-known playwright in America. They formed a bond that would survive until the playwright's death in 1983.

At the time, many stars were flying into Key West with hopes of persuading him to cast them in one of his dramas. Tennessee would always maintain he had to work until two every afternoon, and Darwin would entertain his guests, perhaps persuading them to agree to a

During his presidency, **Harry S Truman**, pictured whith his dour wife, **Bess**, used Key West as a vacation retreat. Months before his death, he decided to pay a farewell visit.

He was an early morning riser, up at 6am. Based, it was said, on the advice of his physician, he started his mornings with a shot of bourbon and a large glass of orange juice. Then he'd take a brisk walk, usually with the Secret Service, members of his staff, and from time to time, a member of the press. One of them was young **Darwin Porter**, Key West bureau chief of *The Miami Herald.*

formal interview for publication in *The Miami Herald.*

One of the visitors to Key West was Marlon Brando, who had practically immortalized himself in the Broadway play and in its later Hollywood adaptation, *A Streetcar Named Desire.* The actor wanted to learn about any plays that Tennessee might have in development, possibly thinking he might be ideal to star as another character as strong as Stanley Kowalski.

Assigned to entertain Brando, Darwin asked his friend Bill Johnson and his lover, Johnny Frels to sail with Brando and himself to a deserted island off the coast of Key West.

En route, they stopped and boarded the wreckage of a naval ship that had sunk during World War II. A large part of its hull remained above water.

On the otherwise uninhabited island, Brando removed all his clothes and started running along the beach. "If only I had brought my camera," Darwin lamented. In years to come, one of Darwin's all-time best-sellers was his *exposé* of the actor's life, *Brando Unzipped.*

Frank Merlo *(left)* with **Tennessee Williams** at their home in Key West. They usually included Darwin in their parties and intrigues.

Darwin's parade of stars and authors continued. Even Gloria Swanson arrived in town with the expressed intention of starring in *Sweet Bird of Youth.* Paul Newman showed up, as did Geraldine Page and Rip Torn. Authors who visited Tennessee included Gore Vidal, Carson McCullers, William Inge, and Truman Capote, more outrageous than he'd ever been before.

In New York, where Tennessee and his long-time companion, Frankie Merlo, had an apartment, the list of guests who attended their parties was impressive. Frankie saw that Darwin got invited. There, he met Katharine Hepburn, who would become the subject of one of Darwin's future biographies.

A galaxy of world-class stars and directors paraded in and out of Tennessee's apartment: Elia Kazan, Anne Jackson, Eli Wallach, Robert Redford, Natalie Wood, Jane Fonda, Anna Magnani, Burt Lancaster, Shelley Winters, Margaret Leighton, Hermione Baddeley, Josh Logan, and literary agent Audrey Wood.

Marlon Brando getting ready to rape Blanche du Bois.

Darwin got to meet his favorite actress, Bette Davis, who had signed to appear as the lead in Tennessee's latest play, *The Night of the Iguana.*

His greatest adventure with Tennessee was yet to come, when they drove to Mexico to visit the set of the film adaptation of his play, *The Night of the Iguana,* starring Ava Gardner, Richard Burton, Sue Lyon, and Margaret Leighton. Elizabeth Taylor was also on location, perhaps protecting her husband from a bevy of females. Many evenings were spent with director John Huston.

Darwin bonded with Ava, a fellow "Tarheel" from North Carolina. He also got to know Elizabeth Taylor, who would be the subject of one of his future biographies.

It was while on location that cast and crew heard the news: President John F. Kennedy had been assassinated in Dallas.

In time, Darwin would write *Pink Triangle,* in which he traced the odyssey of not only Tennessee but of Gore Vidal and Truman Capote, exploring their intrigues, feuds, and romantic competition.

Indomitable, Strident, and Macho **Katharine Heburn**

Darwin also went with Tennessee to a suburb of London to visit the set of the movie, *Suddenly, Last Summer,* starring Elizabeth Taylor, Katharine Hepburn, and Montgomery Clift. It explored a world of what the press called "degenerates obsessed with rape, homosexuality, and cannibalism."

The playwright admitted that he thought Taylor was miscast. In contrast, he had nothing but praise for Hepburn as Violet Venable.

Darwin's experience watching the filming of *Suddenly, Last Summer* would later appear in his separate biographies of both Hepburn and Taylor.

Whenever he could, during his on-site research for the Frommer Guides, Darwin would visit the sets of movies being filmed in Europe. During his research of *Frommer's Rome,* he visited the sound stage where Twentieth Century Fox was filming the 1963 version of *Cleopatra,* an elaborate confection where Elizabeth Taylor admitted she fell in love with Richard Burton.

On location in Spain and Morocco for the Frommer Guides, Darwin also followed Peter O'Toole during the filming of *Lawrence of Arabia* (1962). Excerpts from those experiences—and from many others—were later recorded in his biography

Richard Burton with **Ava Gardner** in *The Night of the Iguana*

of O'Toole.

***

If the managing editor of *The Miami Herald* had known in advance that Key West would soon become a major news beat, he might have assigned a reporter with more experience. Fidel Castro was launching the Cuban Revolution, a guerilla war against the forces of then-president Fulgencio Batista.

By 1959, Batista loyalists were fleeing the country. Many of them were flooding into the nearby port of Key West.

As Darwin greeted the refugees for story material, he recalled that the first arrivals had been "imported" aboard yachts, sometimes wearing mink coats and diamonds. As the weeks went by, refugees seemed increasingly destitute, and to an increasing degree, from the middle and lower classes.

The United States tried assassination and an economic embargo, leading to the ill-fated Bay of Pigs Invasion in 1961. During that "on-the-brink-of-a-World-War," Castro aligned with the Soviet Union and allowed (some say "encouraged") the Soviets to import nuclear weapons into Cuba.

Having relocated by then from Florida to New York, Darwin still occasionally visited his home on William Street in Key West's Old Town. "Locals feared they were going to have an atomic bomb dropped directly on their town."

***

It was in Key West that Darwin interviewed a rising young novelist and playwright, James Leo Herlihy. He had just finished touring the country with his latest play, *Crazy October*, starring Tallulah Bankhead, Joan Blondell, and Estelle Winwood. Although it never made it to Broadway, it played to packed houses during its nationwide tour.

That interview marked the beginning of Darwin's life-long friendship with Herlihy. As an added surprise, Darwin learned that Herlihy had arranged for Tallulah to be housed for an extended vacation within the home of his socialite friend, Virginia Peirce. That night, Tallulah and Darwin dined together, marking the debut of Darwin's long relationship with that flamboyantly outspoken (and famously debauched) eccentric. Their friendship lasted until her death in 1968.

"This belle from Alabama has to be the most fascinating woman I've ever met," Darwin said. "After her return to Manhattan, I put her to bed many a drunken night, and sometimes counseled her telephonically during some of her hours-long drugged and drunken reveries. I've been around stars all my life, but none, before or since, were like Tallulah."

Darwin was especially intrigued when Tallulah discussed her former conquests. They ranged from Sir Winston Churchill to Johnny (*Tarzan*) Weissmuller, from Gary Cooper to John Barrymore—quite a roster of roosters. She was also bisexual, seducing Marlene Dietrich, Katharine Cornell, Billie Holliday, and Hattie McDaniel, who won an Oscar for her portrayal of Mammy in *Gone With the Wind* (1939).

"Tallulah was the most terrifying actress I ever befriended, but also the most fascinating," Darwin claimed. "I spent many a night with her and her coterie of friends and acquaintances. She had dedicated her performance in the play, *Midgie Purvis,* to Stanley Mills Haggart, my mentor. After the show, she invited us to her townhouse in midtown Manhattan, where she entertained Paulette Goddard and the novelist, Erich Maria Remarque. You don't forget an evening like that!"

Later, in Hollywood, Darwin met and befriended Tallulah's co-star in *Crazy October*, Joan Blondell. Blondell and Darwin became close friends, with Blondell later staying in Darwin's Magnolia House on Staten Island during her visits to New York City.

The daughter of vaudevillians, she personified show business in all those films where she ws sassy and wisecracking. Blondell sustained two famous marriages, one to actor-director Dick Powell until June Allyson stole him away. She later wed producer Mike Todd, who later became the third Mr. Elizabeth Taylor. She once told Darwin, "Bing Crosby promised to marry me but never did."

324 William Street, Darwin's former home in Key West, a few blocks from where Tennessee Williams lived with Frank Merlo.

He bought it for $8,000 in the early 60s. Sixty years later, its asking price was $3.2 million. When he bought it, a local contractor told him, "All this place needs is a match," supposedly a reference to burning the derelict down, for insurance purposes.

Tallulah Bankhead *(right)* eliciting a bawdy laugh from **Hedda Hopper.**

According to Darwin, "Tallu had the worst case of 'potty mouth' of anyone I knew."

"I suppose you could say that Tallulah is a tramp in the most elegant sense," claimed Tennessee Williams.

A wonderful, wisecracking blonde, **Joan Blondell**

In addition to *Crazy October,* Herlihy had written a novel, *All Fall Down,* whose adaptation into a film incorporated scenes shot in Key West. The movie starred Warren Beatty, Angela Lansbury, Eva Marie Saint, Karl Malden, and Brandon De Wilde. Its screenplay was by William Inge, who, Darwin learned, had fallen madly in love with Beatty, a then-on-the-rise neophyte. "It didn't do him much good. Beatty would, in time, seduce half the women in Hollywood. To name-drop a few: Elizabeth Taylor, Madonna, Joan Collins, Cher, Jane Fonda, Barbra Streisand, and both Jacqueline Kennedy and her sister, Lee Radziwill."

Inge, who later became a friend of Darwin's, also wrote another script for Beatty called *Splendour in the Grass,* co-starring Natalie Wood. Beatty had an affair with her.

Darwin also visited the set where Tennessee Williams' *The Roman Spring of Mrs. Stone* was being filmed. Beatty tackled the role of a Roman gigolo involved with an older, affluent widow, Mrs. Stone, as portrayed by Vivien Leigh.

Three homosexual playwrights—James Leo Herlihy, William Inge, and Tennessee Williams, launched the film career of Warren Beatty, who became known as Hollywood's Casanova. Over the years, Darwin planned to write a dual bio of the brother and sister acting team of Beatty and his sister, Shirley MacLaine, but too many other contracts popped up.

As a novelist, Herlihy became best known for his provocative novel, *Midnight Cowboy.* Its initial sale as a novel flopped, earning him only $20,000 in royalties.

However, the break of his life occurred when director John Schlesinger picked up a paperback version of *Midnight Cowboy* and read it aboard one of his flights to London.

When he returned to Hollywood, he hired Waldo Salt to write the screenplay. It went before cameras with Jon Voight playing the hustler, Joe Buck. His co-star, portraying Ratso Rizzo, was Dustin Hoffman.

Sylvia Miles, one of Darwin's best friends, was cast as a hooker who turns the tables on the gullible Buck.

Midnight Cowboy became the first X-rated film to win an Oscar for Best Picture of the year. Both Voight and Hoffman were nominated for the Best Actor Academy Award, losing it to John Wayne for *True Grit.* Miles was nominated for Best Supporting Actress, losing to Goldie Hawn for *Cactus Flower.*

Herlihy earned $800,000 for the film rights. Regrettably, his attorney invested the money in a fraudulent real estate deal in Florida, with the promise that it would avoid income tax. The money was lost. Herlihy later committed suicide.

***

Stanley Mills Haggart was the set designer who had worked on the aesthetics of *Crazy October's* national road show. Born in 1910 in Kansas, he had moved to Hollywood around 1915 after the death of his father. His gregarious, socially adept mother, Maria Jane Haggart, got a job working in the costume department of MGM. Haggart and his mother lived in Benedict Canyon (Los Angeles), immediately next door to the widely syndicated entertainment columnist, Adela Rogers St. Johns.

During the peak years of Golden Age Hollywood, Haggart became closely associated with the arts colonies of both Los Angeles and Manhattan. In the mid-1960s, he acquired a house in the Old Town of Key West, Florida. He had it restored. It had once belonged to his friend, Gloria Swanson, an "army brat" during the era when her father was in the military and stationed in Key West.

Later, Darwin acquired that same property from Haggart.

At the time he met Darwin, Haggart had divorced the English socialite, Phyllis Krystal and was dating the rising young actress, Anne Bancroft. Bancroft would later break off their engagement and marry Mel Brooks. She and Haggart, even after her marriage to Brooks, maintained their friendship.

Haggart later said, "I arrived in Hollywood when it was just a small town. Everybody knew everybody else. I even got to meet Mary Pickford and Charles Chaplin."

Although there was a difference in their ages, he became the best friend of child actor Philippe de Lacy.

Haggart visited the set of *Love,* the 1927 silent film based on Leo Tolstoy's novel, *Anna Karenina.* In it, De Lacy played the son of Greta Garbo. Between takes, Garbo, Haggart, and De Lacy played games together.

[In 1961, in Manhattan, Darwin and Haggart co-hosted a dinner for Garbo in which she was reunited with a now-fully-

Upper photo: **Warren Beatty** with **Eva Marie Saint** in *All Fall Down* (1962), and

Lower photo: with **Vivien Leigh** in *The Roman Spring of Mrs. Stone* (1961)

Jon Voight with **Sylvia Miles**, each cast as streetwalkers, each simulating foreplay, in ***Midnight Cowboy*** (1969)

Anne Bancroft, as Mrs. Robinson, with **Dustin Hoffman** in *The Graduate* (1967)

grown-up De Lacy. By then, he had morphed into an account executive for the advertising agency, J. Walter Thompson.

Darwin recalled the night as "that enchanted evening." In time, he became a "Garbo addict," viewing all of her films, silents and talkies alike, in some cases two or three times.

Years later, Darwin would accompany Tennessee Williams to Greta Garbo's elegant but subdued apartment in Manhattan.

The playwright had written a film scenario for a new drama which he thought might persuade Garbo to return to the screen, which she had abandoned after the commercial failure of Two-Faced Woman *(1941).*

Listening intently while drinking straight vodka, Garbo, at the end of the reading, imperiously rose to her feet: "Gentlemen," she said. "It is time for you to go. As for the script, give it to Joan Crawford."

En route back to Tennessee's apartment, he told Darwin, "Garbo has the cold quality of an icy mermaid…or something."

Greta Garbo with **Philippe de Lacy** in *Love* (1927), a film adaptation of Tolstoy's *Anna Karenina*.

As a late teenager, Haggart became an extra in silent movies, earning from $5 to $10 a day. He got to meet some of the major stars of the silent screen, luminaries such as Norma Talmadge, Colleen Moore, John Gilbert, Gloria Swanson, Rod La Rocque, Vilma Banky, Constance Bennett, and Ramon Novarro.

His last role as an extra involved dancing around Fred Astaire and Ginger Rogers with a swarm of other (formally dressed) dancers in *Top Hat* (1935).

In the 1930s, he met Randolph Scott, who got him work as an extra in films and later hired him as the manager and manservant of the home he shared with Cary Grant.

Haggart later became "the Leg Man" for columnist Hedda Hopper, the journalistic rival of Louella Parsons. Haggart and her son, William Hopper, would pound the night beat from club to club, seeking scandal for Hopper's upcoming syndicated columns. *(Hopper herself famously retired every night at ten.)* Much of the more shocking data they gathered could not be printed in Hedda's column.

Fred Astaire in **Top Hat (1935). Stanley Haggart,** Darwin's mentor who later passed on many of the stories was a member of the chorus.

Haggart, however, saved all his revelations, which were later inherited by Darwin, who put them to use in the composition of the biographies he produced during the 21st Century.

After time as a radio announcer in Trinidad during World War II, Haggart migrated back to Manhattan, where for two years he worked as a male model, posing for magazine layouts.

There, he befriended another young model, Betty Bacall, learning that she was having an affair with a young and unknown wannabe actor, Kirk Douglas.

Of course, she later became Lauren Bacall, married to Humphrey Bogart—who was later the subject of one of Darwin's best-selling biographies.

After World War II, Haggart ventured into publishing, working as an art director at *Family Circle*. In 1946, with his assistant, Louise Sloane, he was assigned to write and illustrate, with photos, a feature article about a young couple's upcoming June wedding. The assignment involved radically re-decorating the home of the bride's parents for her upcoming nuptials. The magazine editors' meddling was so disruptive that the newlyweds-to-be almost called off their engagement.

The adventures of Haggart and Sloane were later adapted into a play by magazine editors Eileen Tighe and Graeme Lorimer called *Feature for June*. Paramount acquired the rights in June of 1945 for $50,000. However, by July of 1947, the rights were sold to Warners for a comedy called *June Bride* starring Bette Davis. After Fred Astaire and Cary Grant each rejected the role, the male lead went to Robert Montgomery.

Later in his life, especially during the course of his mentorship of Darwin, Haggart sometimes hosted rather lavish parties. To them, he invited some of the stars of Golden Age Hollywood, the ones he'd met during his early days in the film colony and during his time he worked for Hedda Hopper.

Through Stanley's introductions, Darwin recalled conversations with Mary Astor, Loretta Young, Irene Dunne, Lillian Gish, Linda Darnell, William Haines, Louise Brooks, Luise Rainer, Ginger Rogers, Fay Wray, and Hedy Lamarr. *[Ironically, for years, Lamarr and Darwin shared the services of the same literary agent, and ran into one another at the parties he hosted, too.]*

CELEBRITY ENDORSEMENTS
How Darwin's Gig with an Advertising Agency led to Encounters with Movie Stars, and how

WILLIAM HOLDEN
Admitted He'd Been a Male Whore,

Why DEBBIE REYNOLDS,
Broke and Destitute, Had to Live in Her Car, and how

JOAN FONTAINE & DARWIN PORTER
learned that they had something in Common:
A Shared Dislike of Her Sister, Olivia de Havilland

CELEBRITY ENDORSEMENTS FROM MADISON AVENUE

Joan Fontaine

For a few years during the early days of television, Darwin worked in the frenzied trenches of New York's Madison Avenue, then the marketing and advertising capital of the world. His writing and editorial talents were subcontracted by a television production company known as TV Graphics whose clients, among many others, include Grey Advertising and Pepsi-Cola. Its manager, Sydney Greenhaus, quickly recognized young Darwin's talent for fulfilling the whims of movie stars.

TV Graphics specialized in celebrity endorsements, and as such, hired many film and TV personalities to hype consumer products. Darwin's job included arranging diversions and recreation for them. That included favored seats at restaurants and Broadway openings, invitations to parties, and helping them—when it was called for—to light up the town.

One of these assignments involved working with Joan Fontaine. They shared something in common: Their mutual dislike of her actress sister, Olivia de Havilland.

Fontaine later became an avid reader of Darwin's celebrity biographies, especially what he'd written about her in his biography of the billionaire film mogul and aviator, Howard Hughes.

Another memorable experience involved work as an arranger for William Holden who, even then, had a teeny weeny problem with alcohol. One drunken night he told Darwin, "When I was a young actor, just starting out in Hollywood, I dated and serviced older actresses. Back then, you might have called me a male whore."

[After Holden's status as a major movie star became more secure, the "glam quotient" of his seductions got classier and more upscale. Intimacies ensued with Grace Kelly, Susan Hayward, Rita Hayworth, Shelley Winters, Lucille Ball, Dorothy Lamour, Barbara Stanwyck...even Jacqueline Kennedy.

[Notice of coverage to come: Darwin, based on some of those conversations, will preview details of Holden's abundant and complicated love life in an upcoming release within his Gomorrah series.]

William Holden

Because of other priorities [especially the deluge of contracts being offered by The Frommer Guides], Darwin's involvement in TV advertising ended in the late 1960s. But before it did, his last assignment involved the orchestration of a TV commercial that cast Debbie Reynolds as a spokesperson for Singer Sewing Machines. The supposition involved her as the last of a long line of matriarchs who had dressed their children with garments they'd whipped together with a Singer.

She was an unexpected casting decision, but she threw herself into the campaign, delivering her lines and the message with style. She needed the money, confessing that she was broke, and that her many (very complicated) business interests had flopped, all of them more or less at the same time. For a while, she was sleeping overnights in her car.

Darwin would later write a combined mother/daughter biography of Debbie and her daughter, Carrie Fisher, entitling it *Unsinkable Tammy and Princess Leia in Hell*.

Gene Kelly with Debbie Reynolds

DARWIN PORTER WRITES THE FIRST FROMMER GUIDE

No introduction Haggart ever made to Darwin had the impact of his presentation to Arthur Frommer, who had suddenly become famous as the author of *Europe on $5 a Day*.

Preoccupied with other business interests, Frommer hired Stanley Haggart and Darwin to write $-a-Day guides to major countries of Europe. Haggart was not a writer, but a good researcher. As Frommer's name became better known, Darwin was hired to write the first Frommer guide that bore the Frommer name, *Frommer's Guide to England*, thereby launching the world's most popular guidebook series.

In a summary, published years later, *The Wall Street Journal* unequivocally stated that the Frommer Guidebooks, during the course of their publishing history, had sold 75 million books.

Ironically, Darwin's gig with the Frommer Guides endured, at high speeds, for 53 years. Sometimes to his regret, he had to postpone his passion for the research and composition of biographies of movie stars who had starred in the films he had devoured as an adolescent.

As late as 2006, Darwin and his co-author (me, Danforth Prince) were listed among the authors of *Frommer's Europe* on $85 a Day.

It launched an empire

SHOULD THE DYNASTIC ORIGINS OF
THE DONALD
(AND HIS CHILDREN) GET SCRIPTED AND FILMED IN HOLLYWOOD?

How the Inherited Fortune of Donald Trump Was Accumulated during the Alaska Gold Rush, When His Grandfather Sold Liquor, Decaying Meat from the Carcasses of Frozen Horses and Mules, and Over-the-Hill Whores to Miners.

In September of 2016, Blood Moon published the first edition of *Donald Trump, The Man Who Would Be King*. At the time, Trump was running for President of the United States against Hillary Clinton. He told friends, "I don't expect to win. I'm doing it for the publicity."

Our book opened with the founding, in southwest Germany's Rhineland, of a dynasty whose name varied but included Drumb, Tromb, Trum, Trumpff, Drumpf, Dromb, and finally, Trump.

It began with Friedrich Trump, grandfather of The Donald, who was a player in the Klondike and Alaska Gold Rush. He never planned to (personally and physically) prospect for gold. Instead, his fortune derived from selling goods and services

Prostitutes migrating to the gold fields of Alaska and the Yukon during its gold rush. Many were imported by Friedrich Trump, grandfather of the current U.S. President.

Friedrich Trump's **Arctic Hotel,** with an attached restaurant and brothel, circa 1897. It became known for its fleas; "road kill" masquerading as sirloin; overpriced whores; and massive profits as a lynchpin of the Trump family dynasty.

Navigating the frozen waters of Alaska and the Yukon during its gold rush, and outfitting the ill-equipped men who did it.

Who knew, at the time, what all those profits would catalyze?

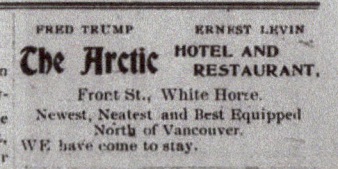

Grandparents of the Dynasty that conquered the world. **Friedrich Trump,** paternal grandfather of The Donald, and **Elisabeth Christ,** the girl he returned to Germany to marry in 1902.

that just-arrived prospectors would (desperately and immediately) need in the frozen north. That included lodgings in barely heated flophouse hotels, scammy restaurants, excavating tools, liquor, and the services of over-the-hill prostitutes imported from Seattle. Ingredients for the steaks and meats he served derived from the carcasses of overburdened horses and mules which had been worked to death along the trails and mountain passes of the frozen north.

The Donald's grandfather eventually returned to New York City with $400,000, a vast amount of money at the turn of the 20th Century. There, he shifted his focus to real estate in an era when the population of the Outer Boroughs was exploding with new arrivals from other parts of the world.

DYNASTIC DONALD

Hailed as "America's Savior" and condemned as "The Anti-Christ," The Donald will remain fixated in the nation's collective consciousness as "The Master of Schmaltz." Of merit within history's appraisal will be an overview of how the family's fortune got started.

The Trump Dynasty's Origins During Alaska's Gold Rush

A movie about Trump's grandfather, Friedrich, might become wildly successful. He thrived in the Frozen North by supplying equipment, liquor, and aging but still hot *tamales* to desperate and drunken miners flush with gold dust and nuggets. Johnny Depp was suggested as the star who could convincingly portray the notorious price gouger, pimp and whoremonger.

Aging but still-seductive actresses who come to mind as an 1890s version of Belle Watling (the whorehouse madam in Clark Gable's *Gone With the Wind*) is long indeed. **Sharon Stone? Julianne Moore? Salma Hayek? Penelope Cruz?**

IN PRAISE OF OLDER, STILL-SEDUCTIVE WOMEN
Burt Reynolds, Hedy Lamarr, and Anne Baxter

Burt Reynolds, known for his abiltiy to self-satirize and for a sexual style many described as "charming," in a promotion for *Gator* (1976)

Darwin once drove from Fort Lauderdale to Jupiter, Florida, to interview Burt Reynolds, the top box office star of the tumultuous 1970s. He would later write the most revealing and comprehensive biography of the actor ever written: ***Burt Reynolds: Put the Pedal to the Metal.*** Although they had little in common, they got along beautifully.

Reynolds was frank about the women who had passed through his life. "To put it in vulgar terms," he said, "you might say that they've come and gone. Although I've been labeled as one, I was not a super stud."

Nonetheless, Reynolds' record of seductions seems to deny that. After all, he seduced everyone from Marilyn Monroe to Elizabeth Taylor. The list is long: Lucie Arnaz, Kim Basinger, Candice Bergen, Jill Clayburgh, Catherine Deneuve, Sally Field, Lorna Luft, Sarah Miles, Mamie Van Doren, Tammy Wynette.

Dolly Parton denied having an affair with him during the making of *The Best Little Whorehouse in Texas* (1982): "We were too much alike. We both wear wigs and high heels, and we both have a roll around the middle."

Reynolds made a surprise revelation. He was not the first man invited by *Cosmopolitan* to pose as a nude centerfold. Steve McQueen, Clint Eastwood, and Joe Namath rejected the offer. "Actually, I regret that I posed for that damn centerfold."

Darwin and Reynolds, though compatible, and friendly during

Hedy Lamarr as the centerpiece of a group of admiring U.S. Servicemen at a fundraiser at the Hollywood Canteen during World War II.

The ironies of her situation as an early porn star and later, the wife of an Austrian munitions supplier to the Nazis are shocking, indeed. Hollywood transformed her. Only in America, kids…only in America.

the afternoon they spent together, had little in common—except for one thing. Each of them appreciated the charms of older women. They agreed that because a woman is over 50, that doesn't mean she has lost her sexual allure and seductive harm.

During the course of their conversation, Reynolds admitted, "I have, for example, always had the hots for Bette Davis."

Of course, the world at large learned of Reynold's attraction to older women during his long-enduring affair with the singer Dinah Shore. "If anyone ranks as the love of his life, it would be that vivacious singer," Darwin said.

Dinah Shore

Comedienne **Judy Carne**, the "Sock-it-to-me Girl"

From 1943 to 1962, Shore was married to actor George Montgomery, whom she "rescued" from the boudoir of Hedy Lamarr. After her divorce, she began a long affair with Frank Sinatra. He frequently went for weeks without seeing her, and then unexpectedly show up at her doorstep. She later married tennis pro Maurice F. Smith. Almost from the beginning, that marriage was unsuccessful.

She never married again, but had a series of affairs with, among others, Eddie Fisher, Bing Crosby, and Rod Taylor.

Beginning in 1971, she launched an affair with Burt Reynolds, who was twenty years her junior. Lasting six years, she cited it later as her greatest love affair.

Reynolds married twice, first to the English *comedienne,* Judy Carne, who claimed, "He had a divine little ass," and later, an ill-fated (and very expensive) union with Loni Anderson. He also became famously linked to Sally Field, his costar in *Smokey and the Bandit* (1977).

Here is a preview of some of the movie stars of yesterday that Darwin knew, conversed with and/or interviewed, and loudly reassured that they still maintained their allure even after producers and directors stopped calling.

***

Lessons from Darwin Porter on the Fine Art of "Walking"
(i.e., Escorting)
Celebrity *"Grandes Dames"* to Parties and Social Events

For years and years, Darwin was seen in New York, Hollywood, and London escorting older actresses to parties, premieres, and major event. Pre-requisites for the job, it was widely understood, involved some cardinal rules and some unforgivable no-no's.

Here are Darwin Porter's rules on **HOW TO BE A WALKER:**

1)   Dress and act appropriately *(no flip-flops, no T-shirts, no recreational drugs, unless they ask for them specifically). Be educated enough to become a discreet foil and conversationalist for the older diva. Even if she's irreverent and foul-mouthed, treat her like the* **grande dame** *she's become (or yearns to be). Know in advance that she's likely to be dolled up in the finery of her peak years. Always be ready for (her) photo-ops. Never leave your "date" alone at table, in the event that a* **paparazzi** *might rush and and snap her picture as an unaccompanied loner. Laugh, be clever but not too clever, and be available.*

2)   *Be rich enough to pay for, in an unostentatious way, most transportation, restaurant bills, and theater tickets, and be secure enough to handle their manias, emotional demands and sometimes oversized egos*

3)   *Never break a date with a glamour gal of yesteryear—especially if you're breaking a date less upscale or intriguing than the one you really wanted. Memories are long, and trivializations—real or imagined—are rarely forgiven.*

4)   *Read up on the glamour gal's filmography and theatrical repertoire, and know enough about Golden Age Hollywood to be supportive during their remembered rages. Discretion and loyalty matter.*

5) When in doubt, talk about your escort's high glam triumphs. Never belittle.

***

Anne Baxter, the granddaughter of Frank Lloyd Wright, was at the top of Darwin's list of interesting celebrities to escort. Darwin had been captivated by her ever since her performance as Eve Harrington in *All About Eve* (1950) opposite **Bette Davis** as the egomaniacal stage diva, Margo Channing.

He first met Baxter when the fabled Russian ballerina, **Tamara Geva**, visited her, bringing Darwin with her, for a weekend at her home in Connecticut.

That marked the beginning of many weekend visits Darwin made to her home. Together, they watched her TV appearance, co-starring with Tyrone Power, in *The Razor's Edge* (1945).

Anne Baxter *(right)* as Eve with **Bette Davis** and **Gary Merrill** in *All About Eve* (1950),

Over the years, Baxter worked with stars or directors who included Wallace Beery, Orson Welles, Billy Wilder, John Hodiak (her future husband), Tallulah Bankhead, Paul Muni, Fred MacMurray, Claude Rains, Clark Gable, Gregory Peck, and Montgomery Clift.

Darwin was with Baxter in 1971 during the opening night of her replacement of Lauren Bacall in *Applause,* the musical stage adaptation of *All About Eve.*

***

Greta Keller, the most celebrated *chanteuse* of Europe in the 1930s, was a close friend and housemate (at Darwin's Magnolia House, on Staten Island) of Darwin.

One summer, before she left Staten Island to spend the summer in her native Vienna, she asked Darwin to "look after" **Pola Negri**," the fabled, high-drama diva of the Silent Screen. Negri had rented Greta's penthouse apartment in Manhattan. It shared an outdoor terrace with another close friend of Darwin's, actor **Van Johnson.**

Translated from the German, the title of this CD is *"GRETA KELLER AND HER SONGS."*

A Poland-born actress of the stage and silent screen, Negri became famous worldwide for her work in Silent pictures, where she challenged Gloria Swanson as the reigning vamp of Hollywood. Often cast as an overwrought *femme fatale,* she became one of the leading female sex symbols of her era.

After he met her, Darwin was captivated. He escorted her wherever she wanted to go: Sardis, the 21 Club, and the final swan songs of The Stork Club.

As a former vaudevillian, Negri was fascinated by Broadway plays. Sometimes, she was recognized by aging movie fans, who remembered her heyday in the 1920s. She was always willing to sign autographs.

Darwin was intrigued to hear her talk about the glamour of her previous life, especially in Hollywood of the Silent era. For a time, as one of the richest actresses in the film industry, she lived in a mansion modeled after the White House.

Three Silent-Era views of the self-enchanted film star **Pola Negri.** *Left photo,* as the female lead in *Mania, The Story of a Cigarette Girl (*1918), revered today as a significant film within Germany's early repertoire of silent films. *Center photo* as "the ultimate vamp;" and *right photo* as a Spanish dancer interacting with her then-*fiancé* **Rudolph Valentino** shortly before his death in 1926.

She once claimed, "I introduced painted toenails to America. At first, some women thought my toes were bleeding."

Her second husband had been Prince Serge Mdivani, one of the famous "marrying Mdivani brothers" from the Soviet nation of Georgia. Seemingly without scruples, they became notorious for wedding famous heiresses and bleeding them of their money.

In her heyday, Negri was known for numerous affairs, including with Charlie Chaplin, singer-actor Russ Colombo (until he left her for Carole Lombard), Rod La Rocque (when he wasn't seducing a man), and directors

Raoul Walsh and Ernst Lubitsch.

Her most notorious affair was with Rudolph Valentino, *aka* "The Sheik." She caused a media sensation in Manhattan at his funeral, strategically fainting near his coffin, facing the cameras, and morphing his death rites into a publicity event for herself. She also ordered a mammoth floral arrangement whose blossoms spelled out her name (**P-O-L-A**) and which was prominently displayed on top of his coffin.

After silents morphed into talkies, she never regained the fame she'd enjoyed in silent films. Eventually, she returned to Germany to make pictures for UFA. There, she developed a reputation as Adolf Hitler's favorite actress.

When the French magazine, *Pour Vous,* asserted that she was the mistress of the *Führer,* she sued them—and won—for libel.

In 1949, Billy Wilder offered her the role of Norma Desmond in *Sunset Blvd.*, which would be released the following year. She rejected the role, later learning that it had also been offered to Greta Garbo, Mary Pickford, Norma Shearer, and Mae West. The role went, of course, to Gloria Swanson, who lost the Oscar that year to Judy Holliday for *Born Yesterday.*

Throughout the course of her career, Negri drew mixed reviews as an actress, the harshest condemnation coming from Tallulah Bankhead. "Negri is a lying lesbo! A Polish publicity hound She has a mustache and can't act herself out of a paper bag."

Rumored as bisexual, Negri eventually retired to San Antonio, Texas, where she lived her final years with Margaret Webster, the oil heiress and former radio star.

Negri died there in 1987 at the age of 90.

Among her final comments was "The old Hollywood I knew was the stuff of dreams. It has long since vanished."

***

One night, **Lucille Lortel**, the Queen of Off Broadway, asked Darwin if he would escort actress Ruth Warrick to a dinner party she was hosting at Sardi's in Manhattan's theater district. To Darwin, she represented a 1940s movie star who had morphed herself into a daytime TV star.

After that introduction, Darwin became Warrick's frequent escort. She had risen to prominence when cast as Emily Norton Kane, the embittered wife of the character played by Orson Welles in *Citizen Kane* (1941). It was obvious to everyone who saw it that the film was a thinly veiled overview of America's then-richest press baron, William Randolph Hearst.

Over the years, Darwin had admired Warrick's performance in such films as *Daisy Kenyon* (1947) starring Joan Crawford and Henry Fonda.

Warrick had sustained unsuccessful marriages to five different men, but one night admitted to Darwin that her favorite lovers had been Douglas Fairbanks Jr., Anthony Quinn, and Dana Andrews.

Darwin did not watch daytime TV soap operas, and he didn't realize at first how much star power Warrick had. Then he invited her to the premiere of a Broadway play devoted to the French singer, Edith Piaf. They reached their seats just as the curtain was about to rise. She looked stunning in a white gown and diamonds. There arose a palpable buzz from the audience. It seemed that everybody was whispering "There's Phoebe Tyler."

Suddenly, Darwin realized that Warrick's character of Phoebe Tyler Wallingford, the "symbolic foundation" of the hit ABC-TV daytime series, *All My Children,* had made her a household name. She played the character regularly from 1970 until her death in 2005. The role made her so famous that she entitled her autobiography, published in 1980, *The Confessions of Phoebe Tyler.*

Warrick was a strong supporter of Democratic presidents who included Lyndon B. Johnson and Jimmy Carter. In 1980, after Carter was defeated by Ronald Reagan, she wrote the ex-president a letter that thanked him for his efforts.

She showed his response to Darwin: Carter told her that "If he had hired her as his speechwriter, it would have sent Ronald

Philanthropist, show-biz socialite, Broadway producer and "Queen of Off-Broadway" **Lucille Lortel,** owner of Greenwich Village's ***Theatre de Lys*** (aka, ***"The Lucille Lortel"***), during the peak years of her friendship with Darwin Porter.

Two views of **Ruth Warrick**, *left* as the repressed and eresentful wife of the billionaire played by **Orson Welles** in *Citizen Kane* (1941) and *right* as **Phoebe Tyler,** presiding matriarch of the daytime soap, ***All My Children***, in which she starred from 1970 until her death in 2005.

Reagan back to Hollywood to make more bad movies."

***

Darwin had been introduced to **Stanley Cranston**, an insurance appraiser for art and antiques, during one of his visits to Hollywood. Years later, in New York, Darwin hired him for some estate-related issues of his own.

"Cranston was a flamboyantly gay cross between Everett Edgar Horton and Franklin Pangborn. He seemingly knew everybody, specializing in legends."

Darwin learned later that his sexual specialty involved hiring musclemen for their sexual services, paying them "top dollar" in a ferociously competitive market. Cranston preferred contestants from the Mr. America and the Mr. Universe contests. As he confided to Darwin, his alltime greatest "conquest" was the night he "rented" **Steve Reeves**.

A professional actor and bodybuilder, Reeves became celebrated in the mid-1950s as the focal point of Italian-made "sword-and-sandal" films, in which he portrayed Hercules, Goliath, and Sandokan. At the peak of his career, he was the highest-paid actor in Europe. By 1960, he ranked, for a while at least, as the Number One box office attraction in America.

Reeves went on to become Mr. America in 1947, Mr. World in 1948, and Mr. Universe in 1950.

As revealed in several widely distributed media outlets, Reeves struggled financially before money started flooding into his bank accounts. As a young (heterosexual) bodybuilder, he became a "gay for pay" client of wealthy men, although (by his account) he found the work distasteful.

During his early career as an antiques appraiser "with connections" in Manhattan, Cranston once flew Reeves from L.A. to New York for sexual liaisons he'd arranged between Reeves and some of his rich clients in the art and antiques trade. When the extended bacchanales were over, Reeves flew back to Los Angeles with $100,000 in his pocket. Adjusted for inflation, that would be a tidy sum in today's currency.

According to Darwin, "I never knew who I might encounter when I had business with Cranston in Manhattan. He seemed to have a gift for instant familiarity with celebrities. It might be an over-the-hill star of the silent screen or one the world's former top-notch boxing champions."

Late one afternoon, at cocktail hour, Darwin arrived in Cranston's apartment and found him deep in dialogue with the once very famous silent film diva, **Mae Murray**. In the 1920s, she'd been hailed as "The Girl with the Bee-Stung Lips" and "The Blonde Goddess of the Silver Screen." A New Yorker, Murray started out in the chorus line of the Ziegfeld Follies. She later became a performer in clubs in both America and Europe. One of her early dance partners was Rudolph Valentino.

Darwin later became intrigued by her and took her out on several occasions. She talked about (and was concerned about) only herself, her life, and her career. Had Darwin ever composed a biography of her life and achievements, he might have subtitled it *The Self-Enchanted*.

"Mae was the motivation that led me to write *Hollywood's Silent Closet*, an overview of the backlot intrigues of Silent-era Hollywood," Darwin said.

From 1918 to 1925, she was married to producer

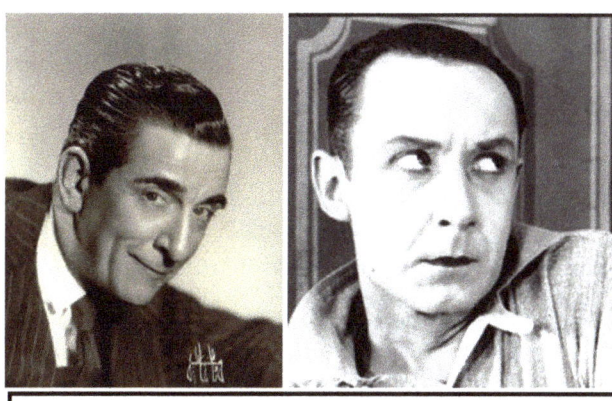

Although there was no photograph of him available, the antiques appraiser, **Stanley Cranston** evoked a mixture of two Hollywood's character actors **Edward Everett Horton** (left photo) and **Franklin Pangborn** (right photo)

A PHYSICAL LEGEND

Steve Reeves (*aka* Hollywood's "sword-and-sandal" fill-in for Hercules, Sandokan, and Goliath)

Mae Murray. *photo left* in **1915**, the coquettish focal point of an ad campaign for *Florenz Ziegfeld's Follies. Photo right:* An exaggerated tango with **John Gilbert** *in The Merry Widow* (1925)

Robert Z. Leonard. It took a long time, but she finally got her wish and overcame her husband's original objections and cast Valentino, in 1919, in two of her pictures—*The Delicious Little Devil* and *Big Little Person.* Originally, and continuing for years, Leonard had referred to Valentino as "that goddamn Italian faggot gigolo."

After the day's shoot, Murray would slip away to Valentino's low-rent, cramped apartment and have sex with him. "The devil tried to charge me, of all things!" she told Darwin. "But I told him that I had earned his sexual services by getting him cast in two of my movies."

Murray's biggest hit would be *The Merry Widow* (1925), in which she danced with John Gilbert under the direction of Erich von Stroheim. [*Stanley Haggart himself, as will be later repeated, was an uncredited extra in that big-budget, high-schmaltz extravaganza.*]

"After I finished doing those movies with Rudi, he moved on, seducing Dorothy Gish and the actor, Richard Barthelmess," Murray claimed.

After Murray left New York, Darwin never saw her again.

In 1964, he read in the newspaper that she had gotten off a Greyhound bus in St. Louis. Disoriented, she thought she'd arrived in Manhattan.

She ended up in the Motion Picture Retirement Home in Woodland Hills, California. There, she died in 1965 at the age of 79. Her glory days had ended long before that.

***

Darwin first met the actress **Patricia Peardon** at a party hosted by Tennessee Williams and his lover, Frank Merlo, at their New York apartment. She had just finished performing in that play as part of a nationwide tour of Williams' *Cat on a Hot Tin Roof.* It had been brought to the screen with Elizabeth Taylor as Maggie the Cat opposite Paul Newman.

Peardon had arrived without an escort, and Darwin volunteered to take her home. There, she invited him in for a drink and, as he remembered, "We must have talked until three o'clock in the morning." The actress and the author became instant friends.

At the time, he knew little about her career, because she was a sculptor when he met her. As the weeks went by, he learned more and more about her.

Born in Paterson, New Jersey, the daughter of a U.S. Naval Commander, Peardon had become an actress at the age of eight, appearing on radio as Snow White. At the age of 12, she toured with Katharine Hepburn in

Based on her portrayal of a perky teenager in *Junior Miss*, Broadway star **Patricia Peardon** was thrilled with the news that the editors at *Life* had opted to feature her on the cover of their edition of December 15, 1941.

Ironically, that edition also contained breaking news from the Japanese bombing of **Pearl Harbor,** a war-mongering crisis that had occurred on December 7, only a week before.

Perhaps the editors realized that their edition was too far into production to swap out the cover.

Jane Eyre, a stage production of the Theatre Guild. The older actress and the aspirant juvenile became lifelong friends. "Kate was the major inspiration for my becoming an actress," Peardon said.

Her breakthrough role came when she was 17 and appeared on Broadway as Judy Graves in *Junior Miss* (1941). *Time* magazine wrote that she "tears into the role of Judy with engaging gusto." Theater critic Richard Watts described Peardon as "Part gawky enough, just blooming enough, and just pretty enough for the part."

She was featured on the cover of *Life* magazine on December 15, 1941, just days after the Japanese attacked Pearl Harbor. She later toured with *Junior Miss* as the first USO-sponsored play to tour Europe.

Over the years, she frequently appeared in classics, many by Shakespeare, including *King Lear* and *Twelfth Night*. In regional theater, she performed in such plays as *Uncle Vanya* and *The Seven-Year Itch*.

In 1968, the Library of Congress commissioned Peardon to star in a 100th anniversary commemoration of *Little Women*. A one-woman show, it celebrated the life and times of author Louisa May Alcott.

Darwin often went for vacations at her cottage on Martha's Vineyard, and she sometimes was his guest at his winter home in Key West.

One of his most memorable afternoons with Peardon was when he went with her to call on Katharine Hepburn. It was the first of several encounters that Darwin had with Hepburn over the course of many years. Even as a boy, he had been fascinated by her, and he began collecting data on her career and private life and career that led to the groundbreaking bio that he entitled *Katharine the Great*. When it was published in 2004, it created a media blitz.

Marilyn Monroe Wants
"A Hell of a Lot More Dough"

Darwin's mentor, Stanley Mills Haggart, had formed a friendship with **Arthur Miller** that dated back to the late 1930s. The men would see each other on and off for decades to come. Darwin was present at their final meeting when they encountered each other at the *première* of *After the Fall* on January 23, 1964 at the ANTA Theatre on Washington Square in Manhattan's Greenwich Village.

The play was a deeply personal view of Miller's marriage to Marilyn Monroe. The name he assigned the character she inspired was "Maggie."

In some quarters, the play was met with outrage for his "betrayal" of Marilyn through unflattering insights gleaned during the intimacies of their marriage.

Writing in the *New Republic*, Robert Brustein wrote: "*After the Fall is a 3½ hour breach of taste, a confessional autobiography of embarrassing explicitness. There is a misogynistic strain in the play which the author does not seem to recognize. He has created a shameless piece of tabloid gossip, and act of exhibitionism which makes us all voyeurs, a wretched piece of dramatic writing.*"

Arthur Miller was born in 1915 into a Polish-Jewish family in Manhattan's Harlem. He grew up to become one of the the greatest dramatists of the 20th Century.

Haggart always made it a point to show up at the *premières* of Miller's latest play, often with a fading movie star on his arm. Some of his most memorable theatrical moments involved the *premières* of *All My Sons* (1947); *The Crucible* (1953); and *A View from the Bridge* (1955). Miller's tragedy, *Death of a Salesman* (1949), is interpreted as one of the best plays of the 20th Century.

As a loyal friend, Haggart stood by Miller through his triumphs, embarrassments, and tragedies, including when he was blacklisted throughout the movie colony for alleged communist empathies and affiliations.

Haggart was more than a bit surprised when Miller announced that he was going to marry Marilyn Monroe. Whereas Haggart had met Monroe in the late 1940s. Miller met her through Elia Kazan during the filming of *As Young as You Feel* (1951). In it, she had a small part as the "other woman" to the husband of the character played by Constance Bennett.

At the time, Miller was married to Mary Slattery, whom he divorced in 1956 so that he could marry Marilyn. Thirty-five years old, he was a decade older than his new wife.

In another surprise more, Marilyn converted to Judaism as a demonstration of loyalty to her new husband. She later confided to her close friend, actress Susan Strasberg, "I identify with Jews. Everyone's always out to get them, no matter what they do...like me."

Darwin Porter's mentor, **Stanley Mills Haggart,** had been a close friend and encourager of the famous playwright, **Arthur Miller** for decades. Part of that friendship derived from Haggart's short-lived partnership with **Milton Greene**, Marilyn's most intuitive and perceptive photographer.

When Miller married **Marilyn Monroe**, Darwin—also a huge fan of Miller's Broadway sucesses—got pulled into the vortex...in part because of legal entanglements (and an eventual lawsuit) between Haggart and Greene.

In the late 1940s, Haggart had configured himself as a business partner of **Milton H. Greene** (1922-1985). In their joint venture, they worked together on the writing, setups, filming, and production of television commercials.

Haggart learned that his new partner, Greene, had been pulled into the science and art of photography since the age of 14. Gradually, Greene worked his way up the ladders of the advertising industry until, at the age of 23, he was known as "The *Wunderkind* of Color Photography," with a knack for making established celebrities look expressive and fabulous on film. His subjects included Elizabeth Taylor, Frank Sinatra, Grace Kelly, Audrey Hepburn, Ava Gardner, Catherine Deneuve, Sammy Davis Jr., Judy Garland, and Marlene Dietrich. Throughout the 1950s, his work appeared in fashion layouts in both *Harper's Bazaar* and *Vogue*.

Greene's most famous link to a star began in 1953 when Marilyn Monroe posed for him for a layout in *Look* magazine. They struck up a friendship that led to some business ventures. Haggart, soon to be a part of some of those ventures, joined the two of them for dinner one night at *The 21 Club* in Manhattan.

MARILYN MONROE PRODUCTIONS

As it was being organized and defined, Haggart was eager to join, as a partner with Greene, the entity known as Marilyn Monroe Productions. And for a while at least, he did.

That entity was formed, by Greene, as a response to Marilyn's loudly articulated resentment that she was making only $1,800 a week while Fox was raking in millions. She was eager to complete the obligations of her contract with Fox, and then to launch out on more lucrative terms as a principal within the new organization that bore her name. Haggart noted that she was bored with the "dumb blonde" roles she'd been regularly assigned by Fox. Instead, she desperately wanted to be co-starred with first-class dramatic actors like Richard Burton and Marlon Brando, preferably in highbrow theatrical classics, including some by classic Russian and British masters.

Eventually, by the time Marilyn was shooting *The Seven Year Itch* (1955) in New York City, she was living with Greene and his wife, Amy, a former fashion model, at their home in Connecticut.

When she wasn't working, Marilyn spent time reading *The Brothers Karamazov* by Dostoyevski. In frantic pursuit of her showbiz dreams, she uncovered *haute* roles that she felt would be ideal if supplied with suitable co-stars and teachers. With the understanding that her bank accounts were almost empty but that she was probably the most valuable show-biz talent of her era, Greene agreed to pay all her expenses. Together, they formed Marilyn Monroe Productions, inviting Haggart to join as one of the shareholders and directors. .

Inevitably, Greene and Haggart sank into an quarrel over expenses, and they broke off their partnership Darwin later referred to the collapse of their partnership as one of the biggest fiscal mistakes of Haggart's life.

Greene, through Marilyn Monroe Productions, would go on to produce *Bus Stop* (1956), co-starring Marilyn with Don Murray. *[Originally, Elvis Presley wanted to play the horny cowboy opposite Marilyn, but Col. Tom Parker nixed the idea.]*

Greene would go on to produce *The Prince and the Showgirl* (1957), which (disastrously) teamed her onscreen with Laurence Olivier.

Greene and Marilyn also collaborated during about 55 photo sessions. One of them featured her wearing a ballet *tutu*. It was designated by *Time-Life* as one of the three "most popular and most seen" images of the 20th Century.

In the weeks that flanked the *première* of *The Prince and the Showgirl*, Marilyn and Greene decided to end their partnership.

Whereas Marilyn died under mysterious circumstances in August of 1962, Greene lived until the age of 63, dying of lymphoma in August of 1985.

Meanwhile, Haggart's friendship with Arthur Miller (and his frustrated and unhappy wife, Marilyn) continued. Haggart visited him on the set of Marilyn's final picture, *The Misfits* (1960). It would also go down in history books as the final film of her childhood idol, Clark Gable, who would die shortly after the completion of its film-

Displayed above is a check drawn on **Marilyn Monroe Productions,** payable to Marilyn (for $404.30) and signed by **Milton Greene**, Marilyn's favorite photographer and one of the investors in MM Productions.

Darwin Porter's business partner and mentor, **Stanley Haggart,** was also a partner and investor in that legal entity. Darwin, as it happened, was also the heir to Haggart's estate.

For decades after Haggart and Greene, with acrimony, parted ways, Darwin regretted that he didn't (or couldn't) get more intimately involved. "If I had, I might have been able to save Marilyn and owned a part of the rock, too. Yet Stanley's proximity to Marilyn gleaned MANY insights into the emotional *tsunamis* roaring around Marilyn during that co-dependent period of her career. And the anecdotes Stanley told about Arthur Miller's composition of, among others, *Death of a Salesman* and the inevitable collapse of their marriage during her filming of **The Misfits** will remain tatooed on my brain forever."

In going it alone, **Marilyn** was single-handedly taking on the all-powerful studio system. The immediate reaction at Twentieth Century-Fox was outrage. She appears here with **Milton Greene**.

Greene morphed into the producer of *The Prince and the Showgirl*, a fiscal and critical disaster released in 1957.

It retains the dubious honor as having the most emotionally fraught sound stage of any movie in Marilyn's repertoire. It also became the business venture that drove her British co-star, Laurence Olivier, the most celebrated Shakespearean actor in the U.K., into dark depressions and uncontrollable rages.

ing.

From Las Vegas, Darwin drove Haggart to the film's otherwise deserted location. There, Darwin had several memorable conversations with Gable, subject of his future three-volume biography.

Right from the beginning of filming, it became clear that Marilyn's marriage to Miller was crumbling.

Darwin would later write *Marilyn: Sex, Lies Her Murder, & the Great Cover-Up.* In it, he detailed the results of a 20-year investigation of her death by Milo Speriglio, hailed as "The King of Hollywood Detectives."

MISFITS: Marilyn with **Clark Gable.** He died shortly after the completion of that film

visit Portugal

WHERE KINGS SOUGHT REFUGE AFTER THEY'D LOST THEIR THRONES

HOW DARWIN RESEARCHED THE ROYAL HIDEAWAYS OF
THE PORTUGUESE RIVIERA

Maria Pia of Savoy with her husband, **King Luis I of Portugal,** at a masquerade party, perhaps at Estoril, in 1865.

The Portuguese Riviera, west of Lisbon, is known locally as the Costa do Sol. Its main resort is Estoril, the glamorous but subdued home of some of the wealthiest people in Europe. As a resort, it has been frequented by international celebrities and movie stars of stage and screen.

Edward VIII came here with his new bride, the Duchess of Windsor, after he'd abandoned his throne for "the woman I love."

During World War II, in which Portugal remained neutral, ex-kings fled here after Nazi troops stormed and took over their kingdoms. Estoril became a retreat of European aristocracy: "a flock" of dukes, princes, counts, barons, and their titled ladies.

Bordering Estoril, Cascais was put on the map in the 1870s by King Luis I of Portugal. He established a summer residence for his family here, opening onto the sea. Portuguese aristocrats followed, and the resort blossomed.

World War II was an epic event, but particularly ironic in Estoril. Nazi officers drank in the same bars as Allied soldiers from England and America.

In 1941, the author, Ian Fleming, arrived, and found it a teeming center of espionage. "Everybody was spying on everybody else," he said. "An idea came to me one night. Thus, my James Bond 007 master spy was born."

Ian Fleming, creator of JAMES BOND, gleaned his inspiration from time, during the war, in the espionage hotbeds of Lisbon, Estoril, and Cascais

"I didn't order dry martinis anywhere except in Estoril," he said. "Usually, I like my gin wet. But sitting in a low antique chair at the wood-paneled Spy's Bar at the Hotel Palacio, nothing but a dry gin martini will do."

[*Spy's Bar is still here today, offering a menu of 23 gins, not just Gordon's.*]

A supremely comfortable watering hole of postwar royal intrigue, **The Hotel Palacio** in Estorial

In Estoril, the Palacio became the retreat of exiled royalty fleeing lost kingdoms as German tanks rolled through their capitals, confiscating power. Sometimes, they escaped with just the clothes on their backs…and their jewelry. Lacking local currency, they often paid their hotel bills in gold, rubies, and diamonds.

The Count of Paris, "pretender" to the throne of France, held what was arguably the most prestigious title. Had he still ruled, he'd have been identified as Henri VI. He was recognized in royal circles as the descendant in the male line of France's "Citizen King," Louis Philippe d'Orléans, who ruled until 1848. French Royalists also regarded the Count of Paris as the rightful heir to Henri de Bourbon, the last descendant of King Louis XV.

The now deceased Count of Paris was born in 1908 in France, but grew up in Morocco on his family's plantation, raising livestock and crops.

The French government would not permit his family to live in France, so their European homestead became an estate near Brussels.

In 1926, the Count became the Dauphin of France in *prétence* when his father was designated as the Orléanist claimant to the throne.

By 1939, with the outbreak of World War II in Europe, the Count joined the French Foreign Legion fighting in North Africa.

In the winter of 1942, French Royalists clustered around the Count, planning a future coup, hoping to overthrow any government Charles de Gaulle might form after the Allies defeated the Nazis.

They wanted to restore a king to rule over France, and the Count, as the pretender to the throne, heartily endorsed their plan. However, **General Dwight Eisenhower**, the Allied commander, nixed the idea, asserting "those days of Louis XIV, the Sun King, or Marie Antoinette, his wife, are gone forever—and will not return."

In 1950, the travel ban against the Count of Paris was rescinded, and he returned to France from exile, purchasing a château in Amboise in the Loire Valley.

Father & Son Pretenders to the throne of France:

Left: **Prince Henri d'Orléans (1908-1999),** The Count of Paris, and Duke of France, was the Orléanist pretender to the defunct French throne as **King Henri VI of France.** French historians interpret him as the legitimate heir of Prince Henri de Bourbon, Count of Chambord (1820-83), the last patrilineal descendant of Louis XV.

Right is his son, also **Prince Henri d'Orleans (1933-2019)**, with basically the same titles and the same claims, to the monarchy of France. His moniker, had he lived and if politics in the French Republic had radically changed, would have been **Henri VII.**

He became a spendthrift, supporting residences in Morocco, Brazil, and Estoril. Faced with mounting bills, he had to spend a lot of his family's wealth, including jewelry, paintings by Old Masters, and centuries-old antiques, some of which had been rescued from Versailles.

Over dinner at the Estoril Palacio, the Count of Paris was rather blunt in assessing his current position in life: "I was a lowly farm boy growing up in Morocco. Now I preside in name only over a once great kingdom. My ancestors once owned a huge hunk of the United States. They should never have sold it."

At the end of the dinner, he rose to his feet, an act that was immediately replicated by everyone else at the dinner party, including Darwin Porter. First-timers at such an event had been carefully instructed in royal protocol.

"I have to get up at four in the morning to milk my cows," the pretender to the throne of France said, before leaving.

In 1984, the Count officially declared that his son, Henri VII, had forfeited his right to inherit his title because he had divorced his first wife and married a second one outside the Catholic Church. But two years later, he rescinded his mandate.

The Count of Paris died of prostate cancer at the age of 90 in Dreux, France. His son became the pretender to the Throne of France. This heir apparent, Prince Jean, Duc de Vendôme, was born in 1933.

He also assumed the title Duc de France, which was in use one thousand years ago.

Darwin was once asked by his editor at Simon & Schuster to write a book about the ex-royals in exile, including the Count of Paris. He always used the Palacio as his headquarters. Danforth Prince followed suit when assigned to write travel guides to Lisbon and also for the country of Portugal.

Darwin's friend was **Raymond Raybon** the American-born press and public relations director of the Palacio, and he made certain that Darwin was included in any reception or dinner party orchestrated for a former king.

At one dinner event, Darwin bowed low when he was introduced to the **Count of Barcelona**. Born in June of 1913 at the Royal Palace of La Granja, he was the third son and designated heir of **King Alfonso XIII of Spain** and **Victoria Eugenie of Battenberg**.

The Count's father was forced into exile when the Second Spanish Republic was proclaimed in 1931. His brothers renounced the throne, making Don Carlos next in line to the defunct royal seat. He bore the title of Prince of Asturias.

He served in the British Navy in 1935, stationed in Bombay. With the coming of the Spanish Civil War, Don

Carlos remained in exile, and the Fascist dictator, Francisco Franco, became the ruler of Spain.

In 1935, through the efforts of Victor Emmanuel of Italy, Juan Carlos met his future wife, Doña Maria de las Mercedes de Borbón Dos-Sicilias y Orléans.

Franco declared Spain a monarchy in 1947, although he would remain as dictator until his death. But he passed over the ascension to the throne of Don Carlos and named his son, Juan Carlos, as the future king. After Franco's death, he became king. Perhaps as a consolation prize, Juan Carlos designated his father as Count of Barcelona. Born in 1938, Juan Carlos had married Princess Sophia of Greece and Denmark in 1962.

At the previously mentioned dinner party in Estoril, the Count of Barcelona did not conceal his loathing of Franco. "My son will rule instead of me," he said.

"There was a sadness in his voice," Darwin recalled. "I think he loved his son but resented him at the same time. He seemed to think his son, through no fault of his own, had taken from him his right to rule over a country he still loved,."

The Count of Barcelona died in April 1993. Given a state funeral, he was buried with honors in the Royal Crypt at the Monastery of San Lorenzo del Escorial, near Madrid. His wife survived him by seven years.

Don Juan (1913-1993) Prince of Asturias, Count of Barcelona, and pretender to the throne of Spain

***

The deposed king that Darwin most wanted to meet was **Umberto II, the exiled King of Italy**, the last monarch to ever sit on that throne. He had been Italy's ruler for only 34 days, from May 9 to June 12 of 1946.

For years, Darwin had heard scandalous stories spread about him, and felt he'd make an intriguing chapter in his book on the ex-monarchs.

Umberto was the only son of five children of King Victor Emmanuel III and Queen Elena. But trouble lay ahead during Umberto's brief reign. A successful referendum voted to abolish the monarch, and Italy was declared a Republic. Umberto fled to Cascais in Portugal, never to set foot in Italy ever again.

Umberto had been born in the Castle of Racconigi in Racconigi, Italy (in the Piedmont, near Turin) in 1904. By 1930, he had married Princess Marie José of Belgium, but it was what was called a "lavender marriage." It was a continuation of many unsuccessful attempts to conceal his homosexuality. The attempt failed.

Two views of Umberto II (aka "The May King") the exiled King of Italy, *left photo*, with Princess Maria Jose of Belgium in 1930, and *right photo*, as he appeared in 1944 After their (forced) abdication from the throne of Italy, they separated, with Umberto remaining in Portugal, and with Maria-José moving to Switzerland with their four children.

In exile, the king and his former queen separated, although they sometimes met for special occasions.

Mussolini had once had detectives file a dossier on Umberto's homosexual affairs, most often with soldiers in the Italian Army. Perhaps he planned to use it for blackmail. During the war, many Italian newspapers had run exposés of their king's homosexuality. His sexual preference had become an issue during the post war referendum to decide if Italy wanted to abolish the monarchy.

The PR director at the Palacio had arranged a 10AM meeting for Darwin with the former king within his residence in Cascais.

"It was more like a villa than a palace, and a handsome young man, rumored to be the king's lover, showed us into the living room," Darwin said. "Apparently, Umberto had forgotten about the appointment and emerged sleepily from his bedroom in his jockey shorts, not even bothering to put on his silk robe, which the young man soon brought to him. Coffee was served."

During the hours Darwin spent there, Umberto surprised him with details of his private life. "Why not?" he said. "It's hardly a secret. A ton of newsprint has made that clear to the world."

But before that, he spoke of Hitler, of Mussolini, of Eisenhower, of his parents, and his life in exile. He said that a former lieutenant in the Portuguese army kept him supplied with a series of young soldiers. "He knows my type and is never

Benito Mussolini Fascist dictator of Italy, claimed, "There are still some imbeciles and criminals who think Germany will be defeated. I tell you this: Hitler will triumph. If Italy runs short of money, sell our masterpieces of art. I've always detested that period in history when these so-called great works of art were created by a series of perverts."

wrong in the choices he picks for me. Each soldier leaves with a hundred-dollar bill, which is good for men used to living on a soldier's pay."

He surprised both Darwin and PR director by telling them he had had some notable high-profile affairs with both Luchino Visconti and Jean Marais.

"Sometimes, celebrities seek me out just for the distinction of saying they have gone to bed with the former King of Italy." He cited Porfirio Rubirosa as his favorite "conquest."

He also claimed affairs with three male Italian movie stars, but "discretion prevents me from naming them."

He also cited as his "most exciting week ever spent with celebrities" was when Freddy McEvoy and his best friend, Errol Flynn, showed up on his doorstep. "Pure, unadulterated debauchery."

In that day, the celebrities' names were widely known. But for those born to an earlier generation, a quick thumbnail sketch might be in order.

[Most of the world knew (or once knew) who Errol Flynn was, the great lover and swashbuckler of such hits as Captain Blood, The Adventures of Robin Hood, and Don Juan.]

A-List Mega-Celebrities who Romanced a Bisexual King

Left photo Italian film director **Luchino Visconti,** hailed as "the father of cinematic neorealism;" and right photo: **Jean Marais**, a household name in France and winner of the French Legion of Honor for his contribution to French cinema.

The other men on Umberto's list of lovers are lesser-known today. **Luchino Visconti** was an Italian theater, opera, and cinema director known for such first-rate pictures as the 1960 *Rocco and His Brothers*, the 1963 *The Leopard*, and the 1971 *Death in Venice*. Although he looked like a burly, macho truck driver, he made no secret of his homosexuality. Other lovers of Visconti included director **Franco Zeffirelli** and the Austrian actor **Helmut Berger**. Visconti, who smoked 120 cigarettes a day, died in Rome of a stroke at the age of 69.

Handsome and studly **Jean Marais**, a star of more than 100 French films, was hailed in the Parisian press as "a French God, our answer to the Viking warriors." He was also a writer, director, and sculptor. The famous French writer **Jean Cocteau** discovered him in 1937, and he and Marais were lovers until the author's death in 1963.

Marais lived on until 1998, dying at the age of 84 in Cannes. Two years earlier, the government had awarded him membership in the French Legion of Honor for his enormous contribution to French cinema.

Flynn's best friend and sometimes lover was **Frederick McEvoy**, an Australia-born sportsman and socialite. When not in bed with Flynn, he married several rich heiresses. He was given the nickname "Suicide Freddy" because of his love of danger, both in sports and in life.

The spectacularly debauched swashbuckling movie hero **Errol Flynn** *(left)* poses at a society wedding with **"Suicide Freddy" McEvoy**, the Australian-born *bon vivant*, sportsman, and heiress hunter.

Both moved easily within the Portuguese orbit of Umberto II.

Along with **Porfirio Rubirosa**, McEvoy was called "The Playboy of the Western World." The two men often indulged in a contest to see which one of them had the larger penis, as each of them was celebrated for their endowments. Women who became intimate with each of them claimed that they were exactly equal in size and dimensions.

Rubirosa, born in the Dominican Republic, was called "The World's Greatest Lover," marrying two of the planet's richest women, tobacco heiress **Doris Duke** and Woolworth heiress **Barbara Hutton**.

Waiters in Paris called giant peppermills "Rubirosas." He was fond of seducing Hollywood stars, notably **Zsa Zsa Gabor, Ava Gardner, Susan Hayward, Eartha Kitt, Joan Crawford, Jayne Mansfield, Marilyn Monroe**, and **Kim Novak**, as well as the Argentine dictator, **Evita Perón.**

He told Umberto, "I consider a day in which I make love only once a wasted day. If a woman is not available, although they usually are, I will grab some young man and send him to heaven…or else to the hospital."

***

No royal he ever met captured the imagination of Darwin as effectively as did **Magda Lupescu, aka, Princess Elena of Romania**. Darwin first met her at the Palacio Estoril and continued to see her as summers went by. "Her Highness walked exactly like Mae West did in those sexually suggestive movies of the 1930s. Her skin was milky white, exactly the color of the gowns she always wore. She had a sharp wit and enjoyed off-color jokes. Her hair may have turned grey, but you wouldn't know it. It was the same color as the hair of Rita Hayworth in the 1940s. I don't want to call her eyes green. Chartreuse would be more apt. When she came into a room, all talk halted as eyes turned to watch her make an entrance."

Magda was forever linked to **King Carol II of Romania**. She first met him in 1923 when he was a Crown Prince. Their notorious (and long-enduring) affair began two years later. He was already married, and so, since they had little concern in concealing it, their adulterous affair became tabloid fodder.

Under intense pressure, Carol II renounced his rights to the throne and abdicated in 1926. He was forced into exile, but after a coup, he returned in 1930 when he was "restored" as king.

He soon sent for Magda, who resumed her status as his mistress. As such, she was known as the power behind the throne. His reign was marred by one scandal after another.

Once again, in 1940, he was forced to flee from Romania when it entered World War II on Hitler's side. By then exiled, the deposed king finally took Magda as his wife. It was his third marriage and her second.

Together, they lived in Estoril until his death in 1953. She never remarried, but for the next 24 years, she remained a glittering component of many exclusive dinner parties and galas along the Portuguese Riviera.

According to Darwin, "Instead of dominating a chapter within my book, Magda deserved a fully-fleshed-out book of her own. What a woman! What a life!"

Because of media censorship in Romania, very few people knew about involvement of **Magda Lupescu** with then **Crown Prince Karol II**. But in 1925, a photographer in Milan snapped a picture of them together and published it. Almost overnight, Lupescu became one of the most notorious women in Europe.

***

Another royal who deserved a chapter in Darwin's book was **Giovanna of Savoy**. Born in 1907, she was the daughter of King Victor Emmanuel III of Italy.

In 1930, she married **Tsar Boris III of Bulgaria** in Assisi, Italy. Their wedding was attended by **Benito Mussolini**.

Their marriage would endure until 1943 when Boris died during the traumatic depths of World War II. Bulgaria was occupied by the invading Soviets, who gave Giovanna 48 hours to either leave the country or face arrest and permanent imprisonment.

She fled, first to the Kingdom of Egypt and later, to Madrid. Eventually, she settled in Estoril. "She remained a *grande dame* to the very end," Darwin said. "Whenever she entered a room at a party at the Palacio, everyone bowed before her Highness. Sometimes she appeared with her son, Simeon II. She seemed to live in the past, as she witnessed one royal house after another fall, many because of the influence of the Soviets. She seemed perpetually lost in nostalgia, dreaming of a richer day when kings and queens ruled with elaborate protocols over eastern Europe. She remained aristocratic and elegant, holding high her rather sharp nose. It became quickly obvious that she had escaped the Soviet régime of Bulgaria with the royal jewels intact. She had the most penetrating eyes."

She remained as a social and historic "monument" in Estoril until the first weeks of the 21st Century, when she died at the age of 90. The world she had grown up in had long since Gone With the Wind.

Giovanna de Savoia at the Royal Palace in Sofia in 1939, with her husband, **Boris III of Bulgaria** (was he poisoned by Hitler?) and thier children, **Simeon** and **Marie Louise**.

***

Not all the towering figures Darwin met during his summers in Estoril were of royal blood. His mentor, Stanley Haggart, was a devotee of fado, the "national musical style" of Portugal. Darwin spent many a night enraptured by musical manifestations of "*saudade*." [*Saudade*, a sentiment claimed by the Portuguese as an emo-

Two views of **Amália Rodrigues**, Portugal's Queen of Fado

tional state that's uniquely Portuguese, is a sense of mourning for love and empires lost.]

For years, he remained a devoted fan of **Amália Rodriguez**. Born in Pena, a parish of Lisbon, in 1920, she rose within the nation's consciousness to the position of *Rainha de Fado* aka *"Queen of Fado."* Often she toured outside Portugal for performances in Spain, Mexico, and France. In 1953, she became the first major Portuguese artist to appear on American TV. A year later, she was a featured star at the Mocambo Club in Hollywood.

Outside of Portugal, the densest concentration of her fans was in France. Fans mobbed the Olympia Theater in Paris for her appearances. Charles Aznavour wrote a fado in French just for her.

Throughout her career, she also appeared in films, bringing fado to wider audiences. Darwin first saw her onscreen in the arthouse movie *The Enchanted Islands* (1964), which had been based on a short story by Herman Melville.

Grace Kelly   **Zsa Zsa Gabor**

Rodriguez later became a financial contributor to the Portuguese Communist Party. That earned her the ire of dictator Antonio Salazar. Oddly enough, he detested fado and hated Rodriguez, referring to her as "that creature."

Darwin spent many a night listening to her perform in the clubs of Lisbon, a city to which he wrote guidebooks, updated bi-annually, for many years.

In the 1970s, she gained fans in countries as diverse as Japan and Italy. She even learned to sing in Italian.

"As time passed, I noticed a change in her voice," Darwin said. "It became lower in pitch, but she sang with a new and greater intensity. My alltime favorite of her repertoires became '*Ser Quem Era*,' a song whose title translates as 'I'd Like to Be Who I Was.'"

In October of 1999, Rodriguez died at age 79 at her home in Lisbon (now a museum). The nation's Prime Minister declared three days of national mourning.

***

Darwin was in Estoril when the latest James Bond thriller, *On Her Majesty's Secret Service* (1969), was being filmed at the Palacio. This was the first James Bond movie shot without 007 himself, Sean Connery. Taking over for the Scot was a newcomer from Australia, George Lazenby. *[Originally, Sean Connery was to have reprised his now-familiar role alongside the French sex kitten, Brigitte Bardot. What a movie that would have been!]*

The Australian James Bond, 007 **George Lazenby** in *On Her Majesty's Secret Service* (1969)

On Darwin's last visit, he met and talked with some of the staff members who had been late teenaged bellhops when he'd met them. Now they were old and gray, planning their retirements.

Many memories were evoked, including the varieties of high heels that had clanked against the marble floors. **Grace Kelly, Princess of Monaco**, came to mind, and the silent screen vamp, **Gloria Swanson**, later to star in the classic *Sunset Blvd.* in 1950. Everyone on the staff remembered the arrival of **Zsa Zsa Gabor** dressed in shocking pink.

In the bar, Darwin sat in the same seat once warmed by the Count of Barcelona who had come by every afternoon for his dry martini.

But outside, the modern world had intruded. Darwin noted that Estoril's old-fashioned **Hotel Atlántico** had been torn down. During the war, it had been the favorite of Nazi officers.

In its place was a gray hulk, the Intercontinental.

That moonlit night, Darwin walked along the beach where the romantic poet, Lord Byron, had once trod.

Gloria Swanson *(right)* with "The object of her affection, **William Holden,** as they appeared in *Sunset Blvd.* (1950).

WHAT OTHER MEGA-CELEBRITY WAS A VISITOR LIKELY TO ENCOUNTER ON THE PORTUGUESE RIVIERA?

ANSWER:

BARBARA HUTTON & HER MATADOR,

24-year-old ANGEL TERUEL

The twilight of a tabloid goddess is bitterly evident in this shocking photograph of an aging "professional socialite" (**Woolworth heiress Barbara Hutton**) on her last legs.

Here she is seen in 1972 with the handsome Spanish matador, twenty-four year old **Angel Teruel.** Draped in a mink stole, Hutton was sixty years old when the photo was taken but her so-called friends cattily remarked that she looked eighty-five.

Hailed in Madrid as the greatest bullfighter since Dominguin, Teruel was known in Spain for killing bulls in the arena, and for being a bull at night with the ladies. Hutton fell for him and, although she hated the brutality of bullfighting, had a bodyguard carry her to a front row so she could watch her beloved. As she aged, she wore more and more diamonds to the *corrida*. Teruel would present her with the blood-soaked ear of the bull at the end of the fight. In return, she showered him with gifts such as a gold-and-diamond ring and a new Rolls-Royce.

Hutton was bitterly attacked in the Spanish press for "tempting our national hero of the ring by waving her ill-gotten Woolworth millions in his bedazzled eyes." She got the point and bid her lover *adios* before fleeing back to the *casbah* of Tangier. In Tangier, party guests and her own staff were systematically looting her treasures, and her bank accounts dropped precariously.

One of the world's richest women died bankrupt on May 11, 1979, at the age of sixty-six. There were only ten mourners at her funeral, which took place at the Woodlawn Memorial Cemetery in the Bronx. One obit claimed, "America's Gilded Age officially ended today with the death of its last standard-bearer, *Miss Barbara Hutton*. Peace at last for the troubled heiress."

Former Resident of MAGNOLIA HOUSE and
"Mad About the Boy,"
She was Hitler's Favorite Cabaret Singer,
And an Implacable Rival of Europe's
OTHER Lili Marleen, Marlene Dietrich

Her Name Was

GRETA KELLER

Famous for Being Famous, She was Darwin's Conduit to Other Celebrities

As a boy growing up in Miami Beach, Darwin had been captivated by the *lieder* voice of the Viennese *chanteuse*, **Greta Keller**. Her voice was said "to carry the charm of the

Parisian woman but never lost the heart of the girl from Vienna."

Her fans claimed that her voice "was in a style that evoked Marlene Dietrich."

Actually, it was the other way around. On the Viennese stage in 1929, Greta had been the star of the musical *Broadway*, with Marlene in the chorus line.

Once, at the airport in Berlin, Greta encountered Marlene carrying her records. "I'm going to sing in my next picture," Marlene said. "You don't mind if I imitate you? Surely you don't."

Darwin lived in the home of another singer, Sophie Tucker. His mother worked for her, and Sophie owned most of Greta's recordings.

In the 1970s, Darwin, by now living at Magnolia House on Staten Island, heard that Greta was starring at Town Hall in Manhattan. He rushed to buy a ticket to attend Greta's concert.

When it was over, he went backstage to meet his idol, and found her extremely ingratiating, especially when he told her he was her number one fan.

The legacy of **Greta Keller** is so deeply entwined with the arts scene of Vienna that authorities there opted to mark her former home, on the Singerstrasse, as a touristic monument with a commemorative plaque. Translated from the German, it reads: *In this house, for many years, lived GRETA KELLER (1903-1977), Songstress and Vinyl Recording Artist.*

Ironically, she was also a resident guest, for a period of at least two years, at Magnolia House, **Darwin Porter's** Victorian home on Staten Island. There, he recorded and edited her memoirs, ingested her firsthand observations about the cabaret scenes of Berlin and Vienna during the Weimar Republic; savored her introductions to historic figures who included **Leni Riefenstahl** and **Jolie Gabor,** and wrote a *roman a clef* based on elements from the lives of **Greta Keller, Marlene Dietrich,** and **Pola Negri.**

He invited her and her young male companion (from Munich) to lunch at Magnolia House the following day. He would drive into Manhattan to pick them up.

After their arrival at St. Marks Place, their friendship developed quickly. Before the end of the day, he had agreed to ghost write two books for her—one a cookbook *Food for Love*, based on her recipes from the kitchens of Old Vienna. The other would be her memoirs, with the understanding that it would be entitled Germany's Other Lili Marleen.

Within weeks, Greta came to reside at Magnolia House, and he began to interview her, recording their dialogues on tape.

Born in 1903 in Vienna, Greta became a singer and actress early in life. By the 1930s, she had evolved into one of the most visible chanteuses in Europe, centered in Berlin just as Hitler rose to power. Richard Wagner was his favorite composer, but Greta was his favorite singer.

She became a close friend of many theatrical personalities, including the German actor, Conrad Veidt, a major figure in German silent films because of his sinister, commanding, and rather floridly baroque style. She had an affair with him.

[*Veidt is remembered chiefly today for co-starring with Humphrey Bogart in Casablanca (1942). Coinciden-*

Conrad Veidt "playing against type" as a Nazi officer in the classic film, *Casablanca* (1942)

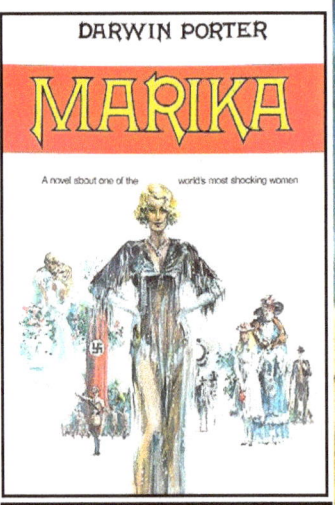

Inspired to some degree by his conversations with **Greta Keller**, *Marika*, by **Darwin Porter,** was designated as "Book of the Month" in the Netherlands.

As a bisexual, **Greta** sustained an affair with **Joan Crawford** during Joan's filming of *Reunion in France* (1942) with John Wayne.

tally, Vera Viola Maria Veidt (Conrad's daughter) would one day live with Darwin during a three-month sojourn at his home in Key West.]

A bisexual, Greta also launched an affair with the Polish actress, Pola Negri, the former vamp of the silent screen. A long-time rival of Gloria Swanson, Pola sustained affairs in Hollywood with both Valentino and Charlie Chaplin, as well as with her favorite director, Ernst Lubitsch.

After her Hollywood career faltered, Pola returned to Germany and worked for UFA, now under the direction of the Nazi propaganda minister, Josef Goebbels.

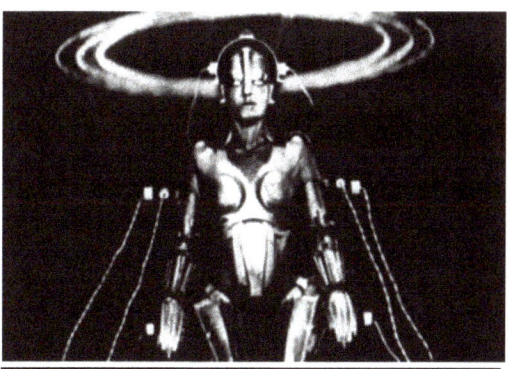

In the 1920s, **UFA** produced *avant-garde*, now classic films like **Fritz Lang's** *Metropolis*.

[UFA, the abbreviated name of Universum Film-Aktien Gesellschaft, a Berlin-based movie studio that made technically and artistically outstanding films during the silent era. UFA, for a while, at least, was among the best equipped and most modern movie production companies in the world.

On the brink of ruin in the aftermath of World War I—to some degree a result of disastrous import/export policies, it was bought in 1927 by Alfred Hugenberg, an ardent supporter of Adolf Hitler. He demanded that UFA devote itself to films that promoted German propaganda and the Nazi ideal. The Nazi-controlled German government bought UFA in 1937 and thereafter tightly controlled film content through its support of highly politicized directors who included Leni von Riefenstahl, master propaganda artist for the Third Reich. A handful of avant-garde directors were able to produce high-quality, apolitical films within this difficult milieu, but basically, UFA ceased to exist after the defeat of Germany in 1945. A new company called UFA was launched in 1956, but it eventually went bankrupt.]

One day in 1937, while dining in a neighborhood tavern in Berlin, Greta received an emergency phone call from Veidt. He warned her that Goebbels had learned that she was a Jew—something she'd never widely publicized within the anti-Semitic fervor of Germany in the late 1930s—and that she had better leave Berlin (and Germany) at once. "Take a plane anywhere it's going. The Gestapo is searching your apartment now. HURRY!"

The next plane out of Berlin was to Amsterdam, and Greta was on it. Safely outside of Germany, she booked passage aboard a ship sailing to New York.

En route, Greta had a shipboard romance with Ernest Hemingway.

After her arrival in Manhattan, she got an immediate cabaret booking at the Algonquin Hotel. Almost every night, Greta Garbo came to hear her sing, and the two (bisexual) divas had an affair.

Greta Keller had married a musician, Joe Sargent, in 1928, but when his alcoholism grew more visible, they divorced.

She would not marry again until 1942, when she wed actor David Bacon.

His murder the following year is still listed as one of the ten most mysterious murders in Hollywood history. [For details, see below.]

David Bacon (1914-1943), Greta Keller's murdered husband, in character as the serialized hero, *The Masked Marvel*, shortly before his death.

A closeted homosexual and a deeply disillusioned protégé of **Howard Hughes**, who had "discovered" him, he was widely rumored to have been blackmailing him.

Till her dying day, according to Darwin, **Greta Keller** believed that Hughes had him killed.

The year she married him, Greta was appearing in *Reunion in France*, which starred Joan Crawford and John Wayne. Greta and Joan launched a lesbian affair, Joan taking the opportunity to dish her co-star with statements that included "Get Wayne out of the saddle, and you've got nothing."

Meanwhile, Greta's husband, David Bacon, had inaugurated a homosexual affair of his own with the billionaire aviator and movie producer Howard Hughes, who had cast him in his latest film, *The Outlaw*, eventually released after endless delays and complications, and with a different male lead, in 1943.

[After the war, Greta became known as "The Great Lady of Chanson," appearing in Manhattan frequently at the Waldorf Astoria and later at its competitor, the Stanhope Hotel. In time, she always included Paul Anka's "My Way" in her repertoire of songs.

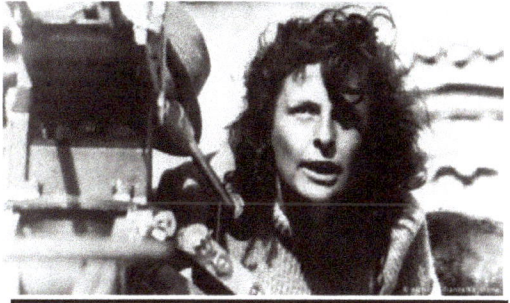

Depicted above is **Leni Riefenstahl**, propaganda assistant and filmmaker for the Third Reich. Two of the films she directed, *Triumph of the Will* (1935) and *Olympia* (1938), are widely considered two of the most effective and technically innovative propaganda films ever made. Her involvement in crafting them, and her "cordial" relationship with Adolf Hitler during their filming, greatly damaged her reputation after World War II.

In the mid-1990s, long after the passions of World War II had at least simmered down, **Greta Keller** invited **Darwin Porter** to join her for an intimate dinner at a game restaurant in Austria at which Leni, entirely clad in leather, was present.

That repertoire also included songs by Noël Coward and Cole Porter. She delivered a tender rendition of Jacques Brel's "Ne me Quitte Pas."

In the movie, Cabaret (1972), starring Liza Minnelli, Greta's by-then aged and cracking voice is heard in her rendition of the song "Heirat" ("Married).]

THE SAD AND SORRY SAGA OF DAVID BACON

Having recently hired publicist Russell Birdwell, the sinister Howard Hughes summoned him to his spooky estate, Muirfield, for a meeting at two o'clock in the morning, standard procedure for Howard, but "bizarre" in Birdwell's view. From the very beginning of their association, the former publicist for *Gone With the Wind* had understood that he was working for an eccentric millionaire. But the pay was good. So if his boss had no regard for the time of day, so what?

Howard revealed to Birdwell that he wanted to make a western based on the private life of Billy the Kid.

Through Birdwell, Howard painfully learned that Louis B. Mayer had already launched production on a competing film, also entitled *Billy the Kid.* Howard's sometimes lover, Robert Taylor, had been cast as Billy.

Howard was furious, feeling he'd been betrayed by both Taylor and Mayer. He vowed never to speak to Robert again—he would later rescind that—and to threaten the MGM boss with a lawsuit.

Birdwell responded by warning Howard about what should have been obvious: The saga of Billy the Kid was in the public domain. He also reminded Howard that MGM had previously cast cowboy star Johnny Mack Brown (another of Howard's former lovers) as Billy in an earlier film, and Robert Taylor's most recent version was a remake of the studio's previous picture. Birdwell also pointed out another obvious fact: the character of Billy the Kid was a standard fixture, an oft-repeated theme in dozens of Grade B westerns, called "oaters."

Growing impatient with Birdwell, Howard stood up. "You don't understand. My Billy the Kid is going to become the first sex western."

"But, Howard," Birdwell protested, "in westerns men ride off into the sunset with their horses—not the girl. They don't even kiss the girl."

"They'll do more than kiss in my picture," Howard predicted. "Billy the Kid will actually fuck Rio."

"Who's Rio?"

"The gal. And what a gal! The screen will never have seen anything like her."

"Who's the lucky star?" Birdwell asked. "I know them all."

"Some unknown. There's only one requirement. She doesn't even have to know how to act, but she's got to have the hottest-looking pair of knockers in the history of film. Your job is to launch the search to find her."

The Outlaw launched the career of big-bosomed Jane Russell, who ruled as "Sex Queen of Hollywood" until replaced by Marilyn Monroe.

* * *

The next day, a sleepy Birdwell wasted no time in launching the search not only for an actress to be cast as Rio, but for some handsome young man to play Billy the Kid. Only hours before, Birdwell had said to his boss, "I understand what you're looking for in the gal. But what about the actor to play Billy the Kid?"

"I want him to look like he's carrying around a ten-inch cock between his legs," Howard said. "And we're talking soft."

The moment the campaign was launched, Howard's office at 7000 Romaine Street was deluged with glossy eight-by-ten photographs of every aspirant young actor or actress in Hollywood. Some were submissions from agents, others came directly from

Henry McCarty (1859 – 1881), *aka* **William H. Bonney,** *aka* **Billy the Kid,** was a gunfighter, outlaw and cattle thief linked to nine murders: four for which he was solely responsible, and five in which he may have played a role alongside others.

His notoriety grew in December 1880 when newspapers that included **The Sun** in New York City carried stories about his crimes. Pat Garret, a local sheriff captured Bonney in April 1881, after which he was sentenced to hang. He escaped from jail, killing two sheriff's deputies in the process. Two months later, Garrett shot and killed Bonney, by then aged 21, in Fort Sumner, New Mexico on July 14, 1881. Since then, Billy the Kid's life and likeness have been widely and frequently dramatized in American pop culture. He has been a feature of at least 50 movies and several television series.

An unknown, **Jane Russell,** became the reigning sex queen of Hollywood with the release of "The First Sex Western," Howard Hughes' *The Outlaw.* It was a compelling but offbeat story of Billy the Kid that concentrated mainly on Jane's big bosom.

the hopefuls themselves. "Every handsome gas jockey in Los Angeles, every beautiful gal, sent in their photographs," Birdwell said.

Three weeks later, Howard called Birdwell: "Call off the search for Billy the Kid!" Howard ordered. "I found him last night. Actually, he was sitting alone in the Cock & Bull bar having a drink and looking sad. I came up to him. He knew immediately who I was."

Howard said that the stranger asked him to have a drink with him, and "I accepted his invitation. When I found out he was an actor, I asked him if he'd submitted his photo for Billy the Kid. He told me that he didn't see himself playing in a western. He has a Brahmin accent. Very New England. I told him that I could hire a diction coach to work on his accent. I also told him that I was signing him to a three-year contract. Yeah, just like that. That's how I do business. I also told him that I was going to get you, Birdwell, to start the publicity campaign rolling for him. In his case, we're going to bill him as 'the handsomest man in Hollywood.'"

"Christ, he must really be good looking," Birdwell said.

"He's good looking," Howard said. "In a town known for its male beauties, he may not be the handsomest, but we'll bill him as the handsomest, and the movie-going suckers will fall for it because we said it's so."

"And who's this new guy who's about to become immortal?" Birdwell asked. "What's his name? Tell me because I know we'll have to change it. I bet it's Prescott Reginald Percy the Third?"

"Nothing like that," Howard said. "It's David Bacon. We'll keep his name. David will suggest Michelangelo's statue, and Bacon means pork. Not a bad symbol. Haven't you heard of feeding a gal the pork, as we say in Texas?"

***

It was September 13, 1943. The wind was blowing in heavily from the Pacific, signaling the end of summer. From that same Pacific came news that the war was going badly. The American soldiers and sailors were meeting a formidable opponent in the Empire of Japan.

Although seemingly a perfect physical specimen, actor David Bacon had used the influence of his politically connected family in Boston to escape the draft.

Back in 1915, he'd been born some 3,000 miles away from Venice, California, in the historic town of Barnstable on Cape Cod. Named Gaspar G. Bacon Jr., he grew up as the son of one of the most prominent and socially connected Brahmin families in all of Massachusetts.

"David's family made Kate Hepburn's family look like white trash," Birdwell later said. David's father, Gaspar G. Bacon Sr., sat on the board of Harvard University and would later be elected lieutenant governor of the state. Backed by the support of his close friend, J.P. Morgan, Bacon Sr. encouraged talk that he might one day make a run for the governorship—"even the White House," he told his son.

He never made it to the Oval Office, but he became Ambassador to France under William Howard Taft and Secretary of State under Theodore Roosevelt.

Young David had been a disappointment to his father. Instead of becoming an attorney as his father urged, David had "an insane desire" [his father's words] to go to Hollywood and become an actor.

David—or Gaspar Jr., as he was called

Here's billionaire aviator and film mogul **Howard Hughes**, entertaining film actress **Ava Gardner** during the course of their (short-lived) mutual fascination. It was around the time of his unhappy affair with Greta's bisexual husband, David Bacon.

> HERE'S A GOSSIPY "GRETA" STORY FROM THE DAYS OF THE WEIMAR REPUBLIC, AS TOLD TO DARWIN PORTER DURING HER RESIDENCY IN HIS HOME.
>
> One evening, a corpulent **Hermann Goering**, one of the most powerful and terrifying leaders of Nazi Germany, dined at the same restaurant as Greta Keller along Berlin's *Unter den Linden*.
>
> She was wearing a carefully tailored Loden coat, one vaguely influenced by the traditions of Styria, in Austria.
>
> Goering rose from his chair and approached her, asking what merchant had sold her the coat. So taken was he with it that he went the next day to order one from the same merchant.

Gaspar Bacon Jr. Wins First Role on Screen
By MAYME OBER PEAK

The high-society son of a powerful Boston Brahmin, **David Bacon** made hometown news with his firstr Hollywood casting success.

Later, the horrible events associated with his murder made him even more famous. Greta Keller was married to him at the time.

then—managed to irritate his father all the more when he became involved in a homosexual scandal at Harvard that almost got him expelled. David and his roommate were "auditioning" some of the best bodies on the football team when word of this reached the administration. Only through his powerful father's intervention was David allowed to stay on at Harvard and eventually to graduate. His father had promised the board that he would secure psychiatric help for David "to cure my son of certain anti-social tendencies."

In summer, David deserted his family's summer home and appeared on the stage in amateur productions at Woods Hole on the Cape. His first acting role came with the University Players in West Falmouth. He ingratiated himself with two far more talented young actors, James Stewart and Henry Fonda, and "bunked" with the two men for a time. The director, Josh Logan, who knew all three of the actors, once said "when not dating girls, Jimmy, Hank, and David enjoyed the considerable charms of each other." Logan himself was rumored at various times to have had affairs with all three actors.

After Harvard, young Gaspar Jr. became "David Bacon." Fleeing New England, he arrived in New York where he was financially "sponsored" by William Blair, a wealthy Britisher from a prominent family who was spending the war years in New York, fleeing some sort of scandal back in London. According to David, his family had asked William to leave England, promising to support him in "the New World."

Although David's own father had refused to give him even a stipend during his pursuit of a career in the theater, his patron, William, was most generous. The couple were seen at all the New York hot spots together. Although he'd arrived there with only two hundred dollars in his wallet, David was soon wearing expensive jewelry and appearing at clubs in bespoke tailored suits.

Two views of **Jane Russell** with **Jack Buetel**, the actor who eventually nabbed the role promised to (and coveted by) David Bacon.

It is not known exactly what happened to end David's relationship with his sugar daddy. William was a bit corpulent, looking somewhat like a 1940s version of Oscar Wilde. In contrast, David was muscular and handsome, standing six feet tall. On the side, he specialized in equally handsome sailors. Apparently, William returned to his apartment one afternoon to find his pampered Brahmin in bed with one of the more well-endowed members of Uncle Sam's navy.

Within the next two weeks David had taken an overcrowded wartime train to Los Angeles to begin a new life.

A month later, he'd met and married Greta Keller.

Following her gig at the Algonquin and hoping to break into films on the West Coast, Greta migrated to Hollywood. There she renewed her affair with Pola Negri. At a party at Pola's house, Greta encountered "a lost and lonely boy," David himself. "He aroused a latent motherly instinct in me," Greta later said. "Even though I knew he had homosexual tendencies, we began to date. Dating led to a quick marriage. I took him under my wing. It was sort of like Barbara Stanwyck's marriage to Robert Taylor. We were beards for each other and didn't ask each other a lot of questions about private matters. David was bisexual. We were very much in love when I was with him."

Greta had an "understanding" with David, who allowed her to indulge her taste not only in girlfriends but in other men. Some of her young men were shared on the side with David. "He especially liked military men, and there were plenty of those back in Los Angeles in those days," Greta told Darwin as she was dictating her memoirs to him at Magnolia House in the 1970s.

"Suddenly, Howard Hughes appeared on my doorstep," Greta recalled, referring to the mansion she'd rented in Santa Monica, containing nine bathrooms, twelve bedrooms, and a swimming pool on the second floor. "Without knowing any of the details, I was told that David had signed a three-year contract with Hughes. In addition to the Santa Monica mansion where he 'officially' lived with me, Howard had rented a bungalow in the Hollywood Hills as a love nest where David spent a lot of his time, always in the company of his new boss."

"Even though I didn't think the role of Billy the Kid was right for David, he went ahead with a screen test anyway," Greta said. "I saw the test. It was laughable. David should have been cast in bedroom farces and drawing room comedies like those made in Edwardian England. I could have played the merciless William Bonnie better than dear, sweet David. Even though Howard had a powerful crush on my husband, even Mr. Texas Oil had to admit that there was no way in hell that David could be convincing as Billy the Kid."

David's romance with Howard came to an abrupt end when Howard "fell big, and I mean big, for Jack Buetel," Greta said. "As you and everybody else knows, Jack was eventually signed to play Billy the Kid instead of David. Who wouldn't fall for Jack Buetel?

Although he was still under contract to Howard, David was offered no parts after his failed screen test.

In time, Howard would become infamous for luring actors (or actresses) into ironclad, "exclusive" long-term contracts and then, to their enormous frustration, letting them "stew" in their semi-enslavement, never offering them a role. That, in fact, became his specialty. Eventually, David did get some parts, playing a good-looking college kid in *Ten Gentlemen from West Point* in 1942. In 1943, he appeared in *Crash Dive* (uncredited), *Gals, Inc.*, and the lackluster *Someone to Remember*.

David's first big break came when he was cast as one of the leads in the serial, *The Masked Marvel*, being shot over at Republic Films. The film is sometimes shown as *Sakima and the Masked Marvel*. Accurately perceiving the degree to which his career had collapsed, and resentful of having to work for a "Poverty Row" studio, David grew increasingly furious at Howard and denounced him frequently.

In 1943, he began to write the story of his affair with Howard, knowing that no publisher at the time would touch the material.

As cited by the *L.A. Examiner* in 1943: **Mrs. Greta Keller Bacon,** former Austrian singer and wife of David Bacon, is shown at home near collapse at news of her husband's slaying. Mrs. Bacon is an expectant mother.

"I urged David not to do it," Greta claimed. "But he sat at a typewriter and pounded out almost ten pages a day. I saw some of it. It was very pornographic. There was one very explicit scene where David described in graphic detail just how far Howard would go with him orally."

"My husband never actually planned to offer his manuscript to a publisher," Greta said. "Instead he wanted to show a typewritten copy to Howard Hughes. He said that he was going to demand that his former lover part with forty thousand dollars, which would give Hughes the rights to the manuscript. Of course, Hughes would then burn it."

Through Noah Dietrich, whom David knew, he had what was tantamount to a blackmail threat being delivered directly to Howard. A meeting was arranged between Howard and David.

"I warned David that he was playing with dynamite, making threats to a man as powerful as Howard Hughes," Greta claimed. "But my husband was very stubborn and wouldn't listen. Three days later, he walked out of our house in a white bathing suit and claimed that he was going swimming at Santa Monica beach. I often knew he met his boyfriends there, but nothing was said between us. I knew that he was getting something outside the home that I couldn't give him. He didn't say for certain, but I believed he was meeting Hughes."

Four hours later, a maroon-colored British-made sports car—a gift to David from Howard—was seen moving along Washington Boulevard in Venice. It was a Sunday. The driver was manning the wheel like he'd had two bottles of whiskey. Fortunately, there were no other cars on the road or else he would surely have crashed in a head-on collision.

Suddenly, the driver slammed on the brakes of the small car and rolled to a stop, jumping the curb. Sheila Belkstein was walking her German shepherd that day and later reported what she'd seen to the police. "I was walking my dog near a field of cabbage. At the sound of brakes, I spun around. My dog barked hysterically. From the car emerged a man wearing only a pair of white bathing trunks which showed blood stains. Across the street was a gas station. The attendant there must have seen the man. He called the police, I learned later. I was a little afraid at first, and I was having a hard time restraining my dog. I moved toward the man. I'll always remember the sunken look of despair on his face. 'Help me!' he said in a very plaintive voice. 'Oh, God, please help me. Please help me!' That was all he managed to say. His eyes rolled back in his head, which seemed to loll to the side like it was separating from his body. Then he fell to the ground. A stiletto was lodged in his back."

A coroner later confirmed that the stiletto had pierced his lung, and that David had bled to death. A thorough examination of his body revealed no bruises, no signs of struggle.

CELEBRITY AND THE IRONIES OF FAME (No One Understood Them Better than Greta)

For two years, deep into her eighties, preoccupied with the memories generated by her star-studded life, and just before returning to Vienna to die, **Greta Keller** occupied this bedroom at Magnolia House under the care, supervision, and patronage of her friend, Darwin Porter.

Police surmised that David had known his assailant, and that he had driven the car in a position hunched over the steering wheel.

For weeks to come, his death was the talk of Hollywood. Several years later, the youngest-ever editor of *The Saturday Evening Post*, Cleveland Amory, listed the David Bacon murder among the Top Ten Unsolved Murders in the History of Hollywood.

Police discovered a leather wallet, soaked with blood, in the pocket of David's bathing trunks. The wallet contained one hundred and fifty dollars, which was remarkable for the time, as few men carried around so much money, especially on a trip to the beach. In the sports car, the police discovered a camera containing a roll of film. The roll was developed by the police. Only one picture had been taken. It depicted David standing happily on a beach completely nude, his white bathing trunks not shown anywhere within the frame. From this, police concluded that David knew the mystery man who stabbed him, and that he had deliberately posed for his murderer.

After the investigation, the nude photograph and the still blood-stained wallet were returned to Greta, although the case was never officially closed. Today, the wallet and the photograph are the property of Darwin.

Greta Keller died in Vienna in 1977, a nostalgic, esoteric, and glamorous figure from a faded golden age. Until the end of her life, she maintained to anyone interested that she knew who stabbed her husband. "I can't prove it, but Howard Hughes murdered David."

WHEN DIVAS CLASH

**The fight over ROBERT TAYLOR when TAMARA GEVA
(the Great Russian Ballerina and ex-wife of George Balanchine)
Is Assaulted by BARBARA STANWYCK.**

**PLUS the Tormented Sexual Meddlings of
HOWARD HUGHES**

Megastars **Barbara Stanwyck** with **Robert Taylor**

Gossips at the time labeled their union "a lavender marriage."

Born in 1907 in St. Petersburg, Russia, the great ballerina and choreographer, Tamara Geva, was Darwin's frequent houseguest at Magnolia House in the 1970s.

As a little girl, she grew up in a house that was constructed in the 1700s with its own small theater and a museum of Russian theatrical memorabilia.

As a teenager, she attended the Kirov School of Ballet in Leningrad. After the Csar was overthrown during the Revolution, she was enrolled at the Theater School of Soviet Ballet. Here, she met a dancer and later choreographer, George Balanchine, who at the time was teaching classes in ballroom dancing.

He fell madly in love with her, marrying her in 1923 when she was only fifteen years old. Their union survived until 1926.

In today's dance world, Balanchine (1904-1983) remains a legend, hailed as the father of American ballet. He co-founded the New York City Ballet and remained its artistic director for thirty-five years.

He was said to have ruled the City Ballet as a feifdom, with a *droit du seigneur* among his privileges. The older he became, the more consuming his love affairs with young ballerinas.

After his divorce from Tamara, he married three more times, always with dancers: Vera Zorina (1938-1946), Maria Tallchief (1946-1952), and Tanaquil LeClercq (1952-1969). So far as it is known, he never fathered any children in spite of his numerous affairs.

When he died on April 30, 1983, writer Clement Crisp eulogized Balanchine: "He created 465 works and extended the traditions of classical ballet. His teaching technique is still in use today. He is one of the 20th Century's best-known choreographers, and his style and vision of ballet may remain for many generations to come."

Two more husbands and numerous affairs with both men and women loomed in Tamara's future. After her divorce from Balanchine in 1926, Tamara married Kapa Davidoff, an actor and fashion designer born in 1897. He had previously been married to the enigmatic Russian-born Lucia Davidova.

Lucia became intimate friends with her ex-husband's new bride, and the two of them, former and present wives, were seen

Four views of the Russian-American actress/ballerina **Tamara Geva**, a mother-lode of celebrity insight for Darwin Porter. *Upper left*, in 1923, dancing onstage in the Soviet Union with her first husband, the world-renowned choreographer, **George Balanchine**

photos left and right: Productions stills from the early heyday of Serge Diaghilev's **Ballets Russes. Tamara Geva**, the child bride of **George Balanchine**, was a prominent player and dancer in their midst during the organization's ideological purges and survival struggles.

everywhere with Davidoff. Rumors spread that they were a *ménage à trois.*

Ironically, Lucia Davidova was described as Balanchine's "best platonic woman friend," a relationship that lasted for half a century. She was present at every one of his performances. She was also a close friend of Igor Stravinsky, the Russian-born composer who immodestly identified himself as "the inventor of music."

As a teenager, Tamara became a professional ballet dancer, appearing in concerts and dance recitals throughout the Soviet Union. During a tour through Germany, Diaghilev approached Balanchine and Tamara and asked them to join his Ballets Russes. Together, they made the life-changing decision to defect from the Soviet Union. They remained with the Ballets Russes in Monte Carlo until 1926.

After a visit to America, Tamara decided this country would be her future home. In 1927, although divorced by then from Balanchine, she introduced his choreography to New York City.

Work as a dancer on Broadway followed, and she was featured in such musicals as *Three's a Crowd* (1930), *Flying Colors* (1932), and *Whoopee* (1934).

She and Balanchine remained friends, and by 1935, she was performing with American Ballet, the predecessor to the American Ballet Theater, in Manhattan.

Tamara eventually evolved into an actress, appearing in plays by George Bernard Shaw and Jean-Paul Sartre, delivering a magnificent performance in London opposite Raymond Massey in Robert Sherwood's anti-war play, *Idiot's Delight*.

On Broadway, her most notable role in 1932 paired her with Ray Bolger in *On Your Toes* by Rodgers and Hart. Bolger today is known for playing the scarecrow in *The Wizard of Oz* (1939) opposite Judy Garland.

It was in *On Your Toes* that she danced one of the most famous dance sequences of all time. Called *Slaughter on Tenth Avenue*, it was a balletic parody that won rave reviews in *The New York Times*.

She also starred in several films during the late 1930s and throughout the war years. Her movies are largely forgotten today, except by Darwin, who cited his favorite role when she played the Countess Olga Karagin in *Night Plane from Chungking* (1942). Starring Robert Preston and Ellen Drew, it was a remake of *Shanghai Express* (1932) with Marlene Dietrich. "Our cast and director found Dietrich a tough act to follow," Tamara said. "If I recall, the character I played was caught spying."

Before that, she'd been cast as Madam "Charlie" Charlizzini in *Manhattan Merry-Go-Round* (1937), a musical starring Phil Regan, Leo Carrillo, and Ann Dvorak. In supporting roles were Cab Calloway and his Cotton Club Orchestra and baseball great, Joe DiMaggio as himself.

In 1941, she starred in Euripides *The Trojan Women*. In 1947, she flew to Los Angeles to perform in Jean-Paul Sartre's *No Exit*. In one of her most unusual roles, she played the character of a sarcastic acrobat in the Manhattan revival of George Bernard Shaw's *Misalliance*, co-starring with Roddy McDowall and Richard Kiley.

In the 1940s and '50s, Tamara was offered a number of film roles, most of them mere fluff and unworthy of her remarkable talent. *Orchestra Wives*, a 1942 musical for Fox, starred George Montgomery, Ann Rutherford (Scarlett O'Hara's sister), Lynn Bari, Carole Landis, Cesar Romero, and Tamara. The movie was the last to feature the Glenn Miller Orchestra.

While making that film, she fell madly in love with its star, "the rugged, handsomely masculine" George Montgomery, who was both a boxer and an interior decorator, an unusual combination.

She met him right after he'd co-starred with Ginger Rogers in *Rosie Hart,* and right before he appeared with Betty Grable in *Coney Island* (1943).

Montgomery was one of fifteen children born to immigrant parents from Ukraine. Arriving in Hollywood, he found immediate work as a stuntman in Greta Garbo's *Conquest* (1937).

George Balanchine, the Father of American Ballet" in 1942

Tamara Geva with **Ray Bolger** on Broadway in the then *ultra-avant-garde* **Slaughterhouse on Tenth Avenue** (1936), a sudivision of **On Your Toes.**

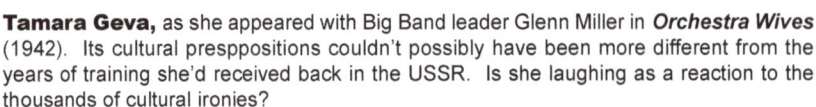

Tamara Geva, as she appeared with Big Band leader Glenn Miller in **Orchestra Wives** (1942). Its cultural presppositions couldn't possibly have been more different from the years of training she'd received back in the USSR. Is she laughing as a reaction to the thousands of cultural ironies?

When Montana-born Montgomery was having an affair with Tamara, he was seeing Hedy Lamarr every other night. At the time, Hedy was being hailed as "the world's most beautiful woman." Lana Turner had also staked him out.

"If you wanted George in your bed, you had to stand in line," Tamara lamented. Ultimately, he would ditch all these glamour queens and marry singer Dinah Shore in 1943, a union that lasted for two decades.

***

Tamara met and fell in love with another actor, John Emery, who was known on Broadway as "the poor man's John Barrymore." At the time she met him, he was still married to the formidable Tallulah Bankhead, her one and only marriage. "Once is enough, *dah-ling*.

Emery had a long theatrical background. His grandfather, Sam Emery, was said to have been the first interpreter of Charles Dickens on the English stage. His mother had played Little Eva in *Uncle Tom's Cabin*.

At the age of eleven, he was more or less "adopted" by John Barrymore and his then wife, Katherine Harris. There were rumors that the boy was Barrymore's illegitimate son.

Tallulah and Emery had married on the last day of August in 1937, a union that almost from the beginning was destined to fail. The following day, Tallulah announced that David O. Selznick had agreed to cast her as Scarlett O'Hara in *Gone With the Wind* (1939). Obviously, he changed his mind.

When Tamara became involved with Emery, he was still married to Tallulah, although they were no longer living together. He told Tamara that during their marriage, she often insisted that a man or woman join them in bed together.

Bright Lights, Big City

Here's **Tamara Geva,** evoking the langour of **Garbo,** with handsome **Phil Regan** in *Manhattan Merry-Go-Round* (1937).

Regan, incidentally, went on to perform the National Anthem at the 1949 inauguration of President Harry S Truman.

Tamara and Emery began living together during the final months of his marriage to Tallulah. Their divorce did not come through until 1941. Tallulah made Emery agree not to marry Tamara until a year had passed. "It would wreck my career, *dah-ling*, if word got out that I was dumped for another woman." He agreed to her terms.

A reporter for *Time* magazine asked Emery what married life was like with Tallulah. "Like the rise, decline, and fall of the Roman Empire," he answered.

Tallulah Bankhead with her then-husband, **John Emery.** She pointed out the size of his genitalia to anyone who would listen.

A year later, he married Tamara. Days before the marriage, Tallulah phoned Tamara: "*Dah-ling*, I must warn you that the weapon may be of admirable proportions, but the shot is indescribably weak."

"Maybe with you, dear one," Tamara answered. "But not with me. It's like a blast-off to the moon."

One night when Darwin and Tamara were dining together at the Algonquin Hotel in Manhattan, she told him of a party she'd attended at Tallulah's apartment.

"We both arrived and Tallulah opened the door," Tamara said. "She gave us each deep French kisses, with tongue, and invited us in. A bevy of Broadway performers were there, including Estelle Winwood, Ethel Barrymore, Mildred Dunnock, Donald Cook, Robert Ryan, and Florence Eldridge—even Elia Kazan and Fredric March."

Tallulah had been drinking heavily,

Tamara Geva with her then-husband **John Emery,** with a poster of the romantic comedy in which they starred together.

As **Tamara Geva** confessed to Darwin Porter one emotional, alcohol-soaked night, she once sustained a fling with **George Montgomery.** He's depicted here with Finnish-born **Taina Elg** in *Watusi* (1959).

Montgomery sometimes displayed a fascination for sophisticated European women. When he wasn't emoting with Tamara, he was *schtupping* Hedy Lamarr, before finding marital happiness with **"See the USA in a Chevrolet,"** Dinah Shore.

and about an hour into the party, as she was standing beside John, she suddenly unzipped his trousers and removed his penis. "*DAH-LINGS!*" she shouted at the room, filled at the time with her stunned guests. "Take a real good look. It's a two-hander that grows a foot."

During the final years of Tamara's marriage to Emery, the couple were estranged and lived apart. She divorced him in 1963.

From 1961 to 1964, Emery was romantically involved with the sultry brunette movie star, Joan Bennett. She cared for him during the final days of his illness, which led to his death in New York City at the age of 59 on November 16, 1964.

"The Only Man I Ever Loved Was Robert Taylor"
—Tamara Geva

A portrait of **Joan Bennett,** painted as part of the set decor for her appearance in the 1945 *film noir*, **Scarlet Street**.

One November night at Magnolia House, as the cold winds blew outside, Tamara Geva sat with Darwin beside one of the fireplaces and spoke lovingly of her on-again, off-again affair with matinee idol **Robert Taylor**. It had endured for more than fifteen years.

"We were hardly faithful to each other because we were married to other people during much of our love affair," Tamara confessed. "But he turned to me because I was more than a lover. I was also, at least in my view, a substitute mother and a psychologist. He feared he might be a homosexual, and indeed, he'd had a number of affairs with men."

"I was one of the few women with whom he could talk about his desires for men, knowing that I would understand, never condemn, and that I would protect his image and career. Bob had to live a private life in secret, using his marriage to Barbara Stanwyck as a cover. Of course, she had a lot in her own life to cover up as well, including her lesbianism."

Robert Taylor, the Pretty Boy who made thousands swoon.

Strikingly handsome, Taylor was destined to join that pantheon of movie idols that blossomed in the late 1930s and '40s. They included not only Taylor, but Clark Gable, Errol Flynn, and Tyrone Power.

Three of these men were bisexuals, all except Gable who in his early days was more "gay for pay," advancing his screen career by sleeping with director George Cukor and William Haines, about the biggest box office draw in America in 1930.

Taylor had been a drama student at Pamona College in Claremont, California. In the school production of *Journey's End*, on December 2, 1932, Taylor appeared in the pivotal role of Captain Stanhope set during World War I. A talent scout for MGM was in the audience and he held out the possibility of a studio contract.

Once in Hollywood, Taylor was launched on the road to screen glory, becoming one of the biggest stars in the MGM stable, a position he held for twenty-five years.

John Gilbert with **Greta Garbo,** engaged together in a torrid romance that helped destroy his matinee idol career.

He performed in such classics as *Magnificent Obsession* (1935), *Camille* (1937), *A Yank at Oxford* (1938), *Waterloo Bridge* (1940), *Johnny Eager* (1942), *Quo Vadis?* (1951), and *Ivanhoe* (1952).

Over the years, he worked with a stunning roster of leading ladies: Irene Dunne, Janet Gaynor, Loretta Young, Barbara Stanwyck, Joan Crawford, Greta Garbo, Jean Harlow, Eleanor Powell, Vivien Leigh, Margaret Sullavan, Myrna Loy, Hedy Lamarr, Greer Garson, Norma Shearer, Lana Turner, Katharine Hepburn, Ava Gardner, Arlene Dahl, Elizabeth Taylor, Deborah Kerr, Joan Fontaine, Eleanor Parker, Ann Blyth, Janet Leigh, Dorothy Malone, Julie London, Cyd Charisse, Shelley Winters, Anita Ekberg, and Rosalind Russell, plus many, many others—an array of female co-stars almost unmatched in the history of Hollywood.

The year of 1936 was pivotal in the life of Taylor, because his first male lover, the silent screen star, John Gilbert, had died. At one time, Gilbert was having affairs with Greta Garbo, Marlene Dietrich, and with Taylor himself. Hollywood biographer Mart Martin wrote, "Gilbert often attended gay parties where he danced with men, frequently in the company of Robert Taylor."

Except for Taylor, nearly all of Gilbert's affairs were with women, often famous ones, such as Mary Pickford, Clara Bow, Jeanne Eagels, Miriam Hopkins, Barbara La Marr, Carole Lombard, and Lupe Velez.

Gilbert at one time had hoped to marry Garbo, but she stood him up. Ironically, Taylor had a brief fling with

Garbo when they co-starred in *Camille* (1936). She later said, "He was so beautiful—and so dumb."

He had a different spin: "Working with her was a magnificent experience. I was just a scared kid of twenty-five, and she was thirty-one—and in full bloom, already a fantastic legend."

Privately, Taylor told Tamara, "George Cukor was about the best director who ever guided me through a film. He brought out the best in both Garbo and me. What I didn't like was his daily visits to my dressing room, where I had to put out for him. He certainly wasn't my type—give me Tyrone Power any day."

Director **George Cukor** put Robert Taylor on the casting couch.

According to Tamara, "I met Bob in the late 1930s, and we hit it off at once. It was the beginning of a long affair, although there would be long spells where we never saw each other. My affair with him lasted about as long as his marriage to Stanwyck. They finally divorced in 1952. Bob was a great shield for her, covering up her romances with Joan Crawford, her great love, and Marlene Dietrich."

"I had never seen Bob's picture with Joan Crawford, *The Gorgeous Hussy* (1936), Tamara said. "One night he set up a screening, and I got to see them emote. The press later asked, 'Which one of them does the title infer?'"

"During Crawford's ill-fated marriage to actor Phillip Terry, I think Bob spent more time in bed with her husband than Crawford herself did," Tamara claimed.

When Taylor and Stanwyck starred in *His Brother's Wife* (1936), their romance was in full swing. He told a reporter "Miss Stanwyck is not the kind of woman a boy would meet in Nebraska."

Stanwyck told the press, "I will never marry Robert Taylor. Got that? **NEVER!** And I'm a woman of my word."

Obviously, by 1939, when the couple got married, she'd changed her mind. According to the Hollywood grapevine, it was a "lavender marriage."

Taylor often shared with Tamara the conflicts in his marriage to Stanwyck. "In many ways, she reminds me of my mother, Ruth, a neurotic hypochondriac who tried to run my life…make that ruin. She wanted me to be at her side and never have anything to do with another woman."

Views of Robert Taylor and **Joan Crawford** in *The Gorgeous Hussy*. When Crawford saw the rushes, she vowed to never again act in a costume drama, citing the frumpiness of the 1830s.

"Even though Barbara did not sexually desire me, and was also disparaging the size of my penis, she didn't want me to get it elsewhere," Taylor told Tamara. "After a few years with her, and even though we still stayed married in name only, my penis got tired of hearing put-downs from Barbara—and never rose to the occasion again."

Tamara also revealed that Taylor always lived in fear of his "pretty boy" reputation, thinking that it might backfire and cause speculation that would end his career. As Tamara recalled, "He grew a mustache to make himself look more manly."

Once, when Stanwyck was on location, Taylor invited Tamara to his home. "I wasn't surprised when I found out those two slept in separate bedrooms. At that time, Bob had to work me in between his affair with Lana Turner when they were co-starring in *Johnny Eager* (1941)."

Robert Taylor with **Lana Turner** in *Johnny Eager* (1941)

Once, when Taylor was making *The Bribe* (1949), he slipped away with Tamara for a rendezvous in a bungalow in the rear of the Beverly Hills Hotel.

"He told me of his affair with the luscious Ava Gardner," Tamara said. "To keep our affair secret," he said, " I conducted it in the home of my mother, Ruth."

Taylor confessed "I viewed it as a 'safe house.'"

Gardner's biographer, Lee Server, said that one night, post-coital, "Taylor slipped out of bed and ran straight into his mother, who had words with him. Ava, wrapped in a sheet, heard Taylor pleading, 'Mother, would you rather I go to a cheap hotel?'"

The next time Taylor met with Tamara "for a roll in the hay" (as they called it in his native Nebraska), he said,

Bisexual rage on the set of *East Side, West Side*:

We're talking about **Ava Gardner** vs **Barbara Stanwyck**. Tamara Geva saw it all, and relayed most of it to Darwin.

"irony of ironies, Ava and Barbara starred in the same movie together, *East Side, West Side* (1949). Their co-star, James Mason, who is bisexual, told me that Barbara at first was very attracted to Ava, even suggesting that they share the same dressing room. But word soon leaked to her that Ava had an affair with me. Mason told me that Ava is now on Stanwyck's murderous list forever. Ava was gone from my life soon after she'd entered it. There was Robert Walker, there was Howard Duff, plus a fling with Gregory Peck during the time they co-starred in *The Gambler* (1948)."

"One of the last times I saw this divine man, Bob was making *The Conspirator* (1950) with a very young Elizabeth Taylor," Tamara said. "He told me that in love scenes with her, he always got an erection, and he had to ask the cameraman to photograph him only from the waist up."

"By this time, I knew it was time for me to move on, and I never saw Bob again. But we had some good memories," Tamara confessed. "The next thing I heard, he was dating actress Ursula Theiss, which led to marriage and two children. From what I hear, he's found contentment at last, at least I hope so."

OLD WOUNDS NEVER HEAL
TAMARA GEVA vs. "BLOODY BABS" STANWYCK

That's **"Bloody Babs" Stanwyck,** in *The Furies* (a noir Freudian Western released in 1950) evoking rage and about to attack: The way she did in the lobby of Lincoln Center when she assaulted Tamara Geva for a romantic infraction of yesteryear. HINT: It involved her then-husband, **Robert Taylor**

One of Darwin's all-time favorite actresses was Barbara Stanwyck. He escorted Tamara to Manhattan's Lincoln Center to see Stanwyck onstage at a Lifetime Achievement Gala. Naïvely, before they made their way backstage, Tamara assured him that she had arranged to introduce him to the screen goddess, whom she said she knew well "from long ago."

Their reunion didn't go well.

When Miss Stanwyck saw Tamara in the lobby of Lincoln Center and in front of dozens of embarrassed witnesses, she slapped her face. Stanwyck had apparently never forgiven her for sustaining a long affair with her former husband, matinee idol Robert Taylor. Darwin's hoped-for introduction to Stanwyck instantly "vaporized," ending disastrously in a morass of resentment.

TAMARA GEVA: A POSTSCRIPT

On December 9, 1997, Tamara Geva, aged 90, died in her Manhattan apartment from natural causes, leaving an indelible imprint on memories at Magnolia House. She was 90 years old. In 1972, she had published her highly sanitized autobiography, *Split Seconds*.

Darwin may have been among her last visitors. By her bedside was a copy of a novel he had written in 1977, *Marika,* a *roman-à-clef* loosely inspired by the lives of **Marlene Dietrich, Tamara Geva, Hedy Lamarr,** and **Pola Negri**.

"Your characterization of your heroine, Marika Kreisler, reminded me of my long life," Tamara said. "So much pain and sorrow always accompany moments of love and triumph. I've had all four in full measure, but one grows weary after a time."

Darwin Porter made it a point to NEVER mention, in her presence, **Hedy Lamarr's** starring role as a nubile "forest nymph' in an *avant-garde*, low-budget film experiment from the 1930s.

"She was mortified by it throughout the remainder of her life," he said.

HEDY LAMARR

The Bizarre Story of the Political Loyalties and Censorship Problems Whirling Around the Most Beautiful Woman in the World

As the years went by, and from all reports, **Howard Hughes**, the aviator and producer, didn't bring many women to orgasm. Starlets, call girls, and Las Vegas chorines reported the same sad story. But in 1939 Hughes met "the queen of orgasms," as she was called—based on the plot of her first movie—in Hollywood.

In one of her first films, Gustav Machaty's *Extase*, filmed in 1932, Hedy was billed as Hedy Kiesler. *[Just before the launch of her film career in Hollywood, she was renamed by Louis B. Mayer as Hedy Lamarr in honor of Barbara LaMarr, one of Hughes' early girlfriends, and an actress who seems to have elicited genuine sorrow from Mayer at the time of her early death.]*

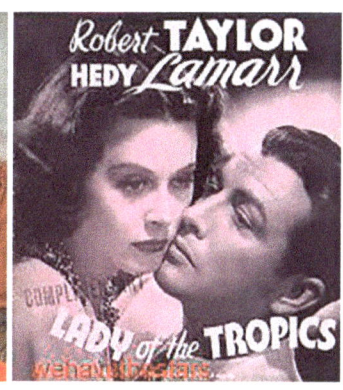

Released in America as *Ecstasy*, the movie had made Hedy a notorious figure in cinema. Hughes had screened it ten times and had been fascinated by the scene that depicted her swimming, then running through the woods in the nude. The director had also asked the actress to play a scene in the film in which she simulated orgasm. In real life, Hedy didn't have to fake such passion. It was genuine.

Hughes was savvy enough to know that Hedy had little talent as an actress. But she was one of the world's true beauties. "Even if she can't act," he told Noah Dietrich, his chief aide. "I can always look at her."

In *Lady of the Tropics*, **Robert Taylor** was cast as an American playboy who falls in love with an Eurasian beauty **(Hedy Lamarr)**. There was almost no chemistry between them.

Taylor would soon run off and marry Barbara Stanwyck, and Howard Hughes would, shortly after that, seduce Hedy.

On a visit to the set of *Lady of the Tropics* (1939), being filmed at Metro-Goldwyn-Mayer, Hughes encountered Hedy after she'd just finished playing a love scene with his sometimes boyfriend, Robert Taylor. They shook hands and looked into each other's eyes before the actress retreated to her dressing room.

Later, when they were alone, Taylor revealed to Hughes that he was going to marry Barbara Stanwyck sometime in the very near future. He wanted to know if Hughes had any objections to his wedding the bisexual star.

Hughes urged marriage onto the beautiful young man, claiming it would end speculation in Hollywood about Robert's homosexuality. Even though Hughes had rejected the possibility of a "lavender marriage" with Katharine Hepburn, he thought it would be right for his friend. "Stanwyck will throw the bloodhounds off your trail," he told Robert. "Fan magazines will be writing about the great Taylor/Stanwyck romance and quit concentrating on what you might really be up to. Besides, it'll take the heat off me."

Before leaving the set that day, Hughes knocked on Hedy's door and handed her his private phone number at his home, Muirfield. "Give me a call some night," he suggested to her.

"Mr. Hughes, in Austria, where I come from, it is the gentleman who calls the lady."

"You're in America now," he warned her, "and we have different customs here, especially if we reside in Hollywood." He tipped his fedora to her and walked away.

A lunatic bisexual obsessive, with tons of money and occasional flashes of genius

Howard Hughes

Later, before its release, he had a copy of *Lady of the Tropics* sent to Muirfield where he screened it in private. He later told Ben Hecht, writer of its screenplay, "Beautiful fuckable Taylor. Beautiful fuckable Lamarr. Beautiful costumes. Exotic story. Lousy picture. But just watching those two on screen will give you something to jerk off to."

In 1966 in New York, Darwin's literary/theatrical agent **Jay Garon**, director of the Garon/Brooks Agency, hosted a party for Hedy, celebrating the release of her ghostwritten tell-all autobiography, *Ecstasy and Me*. At the party, she spoke candidly about her aborted affair with Howard. But, first, she showed Darwin the results of a recent "elbow lift." After she introduced him to her latest boyfriend—"he's in porno, darling"—she launched into gossip about Hughes, goaded on with an extra dry gin martini.

"I made a man out of Howard Hughes," she said, startling her attentive audience. "I met him on the set of *Lady of the Tropics* in which I was appearing with one of his boyfriends. I forget his name."

"Robert Taylor," Garon butted in.

"Yes, that one. Remember how Greta Garbo devoured him in *Camille*?"

She leaned back on the sofa and asked her porno star to take off her high heels and massage her feet. "At first I was angry when Howard asked me to call him instead of him calling me. But he was handsome, a little bit sexy, and very, very rich. I finally broke down and made the call. I don't know why. At the time I could have had any other man in Hollywood. All the big stars. Gable. Tracy, James Stewart—they were calling me." She looked with contempt at the young man massaging her shapely feet. "In those days I didn't have to pay for it."

When she reached Hughes by phone that long-ago night at Muirfield, he invited her to come over right away. "I had pictured him inviting me to The Cocoanut Grove and arriving in a big, fat limousine, with sprays of orchids. Nothing like that happened. I put on a simple dirndl I'd purchased in Vienna and drove over to see him. In that garb, I looked like a fourteen-year-old. I'd heard that Howard liked them young. At his home, his housekeeper showed me into his living room. The devil didn't even bother to get up. He was wearing a ratty old bathrobe and some shoddy bedroom slippers. Later that night, I found out he didn't even have on a pair of pajamas under that robe. What a very casual way to receive a lady, I thought."

"He just sat there looking at me," she said. "Didn't even offer me a cocktail. I sat across from him, and we chatted about my life in Austria, my career at MGM. At some point the conversation got personal. I told him that Louis B. Mayer had exposed himself to me in his office and had asked me to perform oral sex on him."

She related that Hughes had given her some career advice. "He told me that a big war was coming, and that Hollywood would soon be churning out one war movie after another. He said that I should tell the studio to cast me only as beautiful Nazi spies. He thought I'd gain international fame if I stuck to playing Nazi spies. Later, I would play spies. But that night I thought that Howard was assuming I might have Nazi leanings, because my country was now controlled by Hitler. I informed him that I was a loyal American."

Austrian Nazi and munitions magnate **Fritz Mandl** *(left)* with his unhappy bride, **Hedy Keisler** *(right)* the *avant-garde* actress who morphed herself, thanks to the image-makers of Hollywood, into "the most beautiful woman in the world," **Hedy Lamarr.**

In reference to Hedy, cynics quipped that after her "handling" of the bigwigs of the Third Reich, the moguls of Hollywood were easy.

She did admit that at a party she and her husband, munitions king **Fritz Mandl**, had hosted back in Austria before the war, **Adolf Hitler** had kissed her hand. "Obviously he didn't know I was a Jewess."

"Howard seemed eager to learn about my background as Lady Mandl," she claimed. "I told him that I had two bodyguards and twenty servants in those days. Fritz gave me everything. All the jewelry in the world, beautiful gowns, eight cars. But he kept me a virtual prisoner and had me guarded day and night. He loved power and beautiful women. It was said that whenever he wanted to drum up some business for his munitions sales, he'd merely start a war somewhere."

"Considering that Howard was practically ready for bed when he greeted me, I just assumed at one point he'd make a pass at me," she said. "It was growing later and later. He made no move to seduce me. Finally, he asked me rather bluntly, 'Would you like to make ten thousand dollars in cash?'"

"I was insulted," she said. "I informed him that a prominent member of the Krupp family in Germany had once offered to give me half a million dollars in diamonds, emeralds, and rubies for 'one night of ecstasy' with me. I refused him."

"Sensing that he'd insulted me, Howard apologized," she claimed. "He said I had misunderstood him. For the ten thousand dollars, he wanted me to pose nude for him. From that photograph, he was going to instruct his engineers—if that's what they were—to make a life-sized replica of me in rubber. Realistic down to the last detail. He even wanted my vagina molded from life so that my dummy would have an exact duplicate of my sexual organs. I was horrified at the suggestion."

"He said that the reason for the dummy was that he didn't feel worthy of taking the real me," she claimed. 'You're too much of a goddess,' he told me."

At that point in her recitation, Hedy's porn-stud boyfriend mocked Howard's comment. "I'll have to use that line on some chick some night. It's a great seduction technique."

Hedy scolded him for being "a naughty boy," then continued. "I got up from the sofa and stood before Howard. 'You're worthy,' I told him."

"I kneeled down on the carpet and opened his bathrobe," she said. "I told him 'why bother with some stupid rubber dummy when he could have the real thing?' I performed oral sex. He took me into his library, and we made love all night. Don't believe all those stories that jealous women spread about Howard being impotent. He was very virile with me."

"Howard bedded me that night, and I think it was more thrilling for him than it was for me," she claimed, "even though I experienced multiple orgasms. He seemed to view this as the greatest accomplishment of his career. I think he considered himself lucky if he gave a woman one orgasm. What he didn't know was that I experienced frequent orgasms when having sex with most men. With some men, I had uncountable orgasms."

Hedy was perhaps the only movie star memoirist who ever wrote publicly about her tendency for multiple orgasms.

On another note, she added, "Men have told me that they can get an orgasm just by looking at me on the screen. I know for a fact that men attended my movies and masturbated under their jackets."

After the night of the orgasms, Hedy claimed that Howard "fell madly in love with me and sent me flowers every day, but our affair lasted for just a few short weeks."

"What went wrong?" she was asked.

"He wanted to marry me and make a prisoner of me," she said. "I wasn't ready for that. I had been married to Fritz when I became Lady Mandl in Austria, and he kept me under guard all the time, not wanting another man to look at me. I couldn't go through an experience like that ever again."

She was asked what the jealous Mandl thought of her nudity on the screen in *Ecstasy*. "He tried to purchase all the prints, but never succeeded because of bootleg copies. Benito Mussolini refused to sell Fritz his copy, and I know for a fact that Hitler watched the film several times."

"There was no way I could escape from Fritz and plunge into a marriage with yet another man who wanted to imprison me," she said. "Of course, Howard was very rich, like Fritz, and I tend to like very rich men. But on my own, I made thirty million dollars. Regrettably, I wasted it all and made many bad decisions. I stupidly turned down the starring role in *Casablanca*, fearing it might be too similar to my role in *Algiers*. That Swedish peasant, **Ingrid Bergman**, got it instead. I also turned down *Gaslight* which the bitch also took. I finally told Howard I didn't need him. Later in life, I would need him, but by then it was too late."

She claimed that she repeatedly warned him not to fall in love with her, as so many other unfortunate men had done. She cited the case of **Ritter Franz von Hochstatten**, who came from one of Germany's most distinguished families. "I wouldn't give up my career to marry him, and he hung himself. I didn't want that to happen to Howard, but I feared he'd do something drastic when I turned him down."

"Had I married Howard," she said, "he would never have had any need for another woman. When you have the world's most beautiful woman in your bed, there is no need for any other."

Before the end of that long-ago party in 1966, the agent, **Jay Garon**, Hedy's porno boyfriend, and **Darwin** each assured Hedy that she was the most spectacular creature since God created Eve—and that she ranked up there with Helen of Troy. Even Agnès Sorel in the Middle Ages did not equal her beauty.

"Why else would Cecil B. De Mille cast me as Delilah?" she asked. "The temptress of the ages."

"Because you knew how to deliver a mean haircut," Garon quipped.

Two views of Hedy Lamarr with top box office leading men of her era

Upper photo with **Charles Boyer** in *Algiers* (1938).

Lower photo with **Clark Gable** in *Boom Town* (1940).

***

Hedy was driven to Darwin's **Magnolia House** on Staten Island on two separate occasions, Darwin also escorted her to social events in New York and visited her in later years in Florida. She told him fascinating stories about her life.

Her story began in Vienna in 1914 when she was born on the eve of World War I, whose aftermath included the collapse of the Austro-Hungarian Empire. She had always wanted to be an actress, and by 1933, she appeared in Gustav Machaty's notorious film, *Ecstasy*, in which she was seen running nude in the woods. In that controversial, *avant-garde* film, she was also depicted in the throes of orgasm. *[Machaty achieved the desired effect by sticking a pin into her.]*

She abandoned her career when she married **Fritz Mandl,** an Austrian arms merchant selling munitions to fuel the Nazi war machine. Ironically, both the sadistic Mandl and Hedy were Jewish.

During that loveless marriage, she entertained, and was entertained by, the elite hierarchies of the Fascist world. She found Hitler "an arrogant, dangerous *poseur*," and Mussolini "a pompous ass."

On a hunt for new talent in Europe, Louis B. Mayer discovered the divorced actress and signed her to an MGM contract, hoping to replace Greta Garbo, who would soon retire.

She became an overnight sensation upon the release of *Algiers* (1938), starring Charles Boyer. Luminous, she was forever after associated with praise for her porcelain skin, her large, marbly eyes, her lilting Viennese accent, her Mona Lisa smile, and her aura of mystery. Throughout the course of the 1940s (the heyday of her film career), she seemed more like a celluloid mannequin than a natural woman.

Some of the era's most famous movie stars seduced her, including Errol Flynn, Charlie Chaplin, James Stewart, Stewart Granger, Victor Mature, William Powell, and John Garfield.

Along the way, she picked up five more husbands and had an affair with a young naval hero, who had recently returned from the war in the Pacific. "John F. Kennedy was charming, handsome, charismatic, and a real heartbreaker," she told Darwin.

As the years wore on, Hedy tried, unsuccessfully, to rescue her fading beauty with cosmetic surgeries.

Often dazed and confused, she became involved in two shoplifting incidents. The first was in June of 1961 at the May Company Department Store in Los Angeles, where she walked out with gold slippers and various sundries. At the time, her purse contained $14,000 of undeposited checks.

The second shoplifting incident transpired in August of 1991 in Casselberry, Florida. Once again, she walked out with unpaid merchandise—in this case, $21.48 worth of laxative tablets and eyedrops. Eventually, both charges were dropped.

"She was a dear, tormented soul, obsessively sharing memories of a fabled life," Darwin said.

She died on January 19, 2000, age 85, in Altamonte Springs, Florida. Her son, Anthony Loder, flew with her ashes to Austria and tossed them into the winds rustling through the Vienna Woods. She left a $3.5 million estate.

JACK DEMPSEY
The World's Heavyweight Boxing Champion

And his Widely Publicized Dalliance with the Sex Vamp
MAE WEST

"I was a pretty good fighter. But it was the writers who made me great."

—Jack Dempsey

Jack Dempsey with **Mae West:** She liked boxers, either black or white. Her favorite was "The Champ," Jack Dempsey. For years, she kept a frontal nude photo of him over her toilet.

According to Darwin, "It never occurred to me that I would one day meet Jack Dempsey, the former Heavyweight Boxing Champion (1919-1926) of the world. He entered my world late in his own life, and we became friends. He rarely discussed boxing with me."

"He knew I was a Hollywood writer, and he liked sharing a dream that never came true. Instead of a star in the ring, he wanted to be a star on the screen."

Darwin's meeting came about through an unlikely source. To get a fine arts insurance policy covering Magnolia House and its contents, he had to hire an appraiser. He was led to an art and antiques specialist who was credited as "the best in the business." Darwin was warned in advance that the candidate "is an effeminate flamer."

Stanley Cranston pranced into his life and spent most of his first day at Magnolia House close examining, and making notes about, its contents. At twilight, Darwin agreed to drive him back to Manhattan, where Cranston had scheduled dinner with a client and his wife.

Cranston had been told that he could bring a guest to the dinner, and consequently, Darwin was included in the gathering. To his amazement, it included **Jack Dempsey** and his fourth wife, the former Deanna Piatelli.

"I liked Jack, a kind and generous man," Darwin said. "He was not the super macho thug I had in mind, that of a boxer who rose to fame clobbering other boxers in the ring."

"We shared a mutual interest in Hollywood. It seemed that Jack had never really wanted to be a boxer, but a movie star like John Wayne and Gary Cooper, a leading man to the sex goddess, Mae West."

"Before my second dinner with Jack, I read up on his career," Darwin said.

[Subsequent generations might be unaware of this, but at one time in the Roaring Twenties, during his reign as the heavyweight boxing champion of the world, Jack Dempsey was the most famous man on the planet.]

Born in 1895 to an impoverished family in Colorado, he was of Irish, Cherokee, and Jewish ancestry. As a boy, he attended the Mormon Church.

Restless and wanting to be on his own, he ran away at the age of sixteen and survived riding the rails and sleeping in hobo camps. As he told Darwin, "I think I learned to use my fists by beating the hell out of those boy molesters I came across."

As he grew older and needed money, he would barge into a seedy tavern and issue a challenge. "I can't sing. I can't dance. But I can lick any SOB in here. Wanna take me on?"

He always found a challenger, and betting was high. As the victor, he made off with his share. By the time he hit Salt Lake City, he was billing himself as "Kid Blackie."

"One night in this mining town, a group of guys—I think all of them were homosexuals—offered a $500 purse if I'd enter the ring with their local stud. I'd get the money if I won, but only if I'd box without my trunks. Same for the kid. I won."

During World War I, he worked in a shipyard and kept up with his boxing bouts. He was nonetheless defined as a "slacker" for not enlisting in the U.S. Army. *[He had tried to enlist, but was classified as 4-F.]*

A game-changing prizefight: **Jack Dempsey vs. Georges Carpentier,** July 2, 1921 in Jersey City, NJ.

After Dempsey won, his life changed forever.

On the night of July 4, 1919, Dempsey came into world prominence by defeating heavyweight champ Jess Willard in Toledo, Ohio. Nicknamed "the Pottawatmie Giant," Willard stood 6'7" and weighed 245 pounds, in contrast to Dempsey, who stood 6'1" and weighed 187. He KO'd Willard seven times, leaving him with broken ribs, broken teeth, a broken jaw, and deep fractures to the bones and muscles of his face.

After winning the title, Dempsey toured America, performing at circuses and staging exhibitions. He also got to work in boxing scenes in low-budget silent films.

One of the most highly touted of his matches was his fight against the French World War I hero, Georges Carpentier. George Bernard Shaw had hailed him as "The Greatest Boxer in the World."

The Dempsey/Carpentier fight took place on July 2, 1921 in Jersey City, the first million-dollar gate in boxing history.

Before 91,000 fans in the auditorium, and broadcast to a radio audience of millions, it was "The Fight of the Century." Carpentier broke his left thumb in the first round but soldiered on to lose.

***

Dempsey first met **Mae West** when he attended her stage play (*The Music World of 1921*) in Manhattan. As he claimed, "I laughed louder than anybody else in the audience, and thought Mae West was one hot number. She even called me onstage to referee a mock boxing match. At the end, she whispered to me to come to her dressing room after the curtain fell. It was the beginning of a torrid affair."

"I didn't leave her hotel suite until Monday morning," he said. "Mae brought in a photographer friend of hers to photograph me in the nude. It seemed that she had a thing for boxers, both black and white. She said that you couldn't say a lot about them until they removed their boxing trunks."

He was at her apartment when the reviews of her show arrived.

Variety wrote that in her act "she left nothing undone. In her skin-tight clothes, she cooched and wiggled and took falls and vamped. She was pretty

---

The Queen of Camp's Last Hurrah

It was **Sextette** (1978), a self-indulgent parody of the campy glamour of "Marvelous Mae." Aged 83 at the time, she played Marlo Manners (aka Lady Barrington). Her "desperate to consummate their marriage" groom was the "impossibly wealthy" Lord Barrington, as portrayed by the impossibly handsome **Timothy Dalton**.

Sextette devolved into a campy, disorganized parody that hung on the premise that Lady Barrington's sexual allure is driving every man in the film into a frenzy, and that world peace hangs in the balance unless she fulfills at least some of their needs.

Although fans of Mae West remember *Sextette* with nostalgia and affection, it morphed into an embarrasing box office failure, grossing just $50,000 against an estimated budget of $4–8 million.

As reviewed by the **Montreal Star**, "It was about four o'clock yesterday afternoon and there I was alone—in a dark room—with Mae West. It was not a triumph! First of all, she was on the screen, and I was in an empty theatre, and secondly, she was appearing in what I pray is her final picture, *Sextette*. It looked as though the whole movie had been shot through a nylon stocking—the heel of a nylon stocking. The lady seemed out to prove that there is life after death and looked positively embalmed. The picture comes under the heading of 'must miss' movies."

snappy."

The New York World likened her shimmy to a woman "trying to get out of a strait jacket without the use of her hands."

As Dempsey heard years later, West didn't limit access to her all-white boudoir, with its mirrored ceiling, just to boxers and wrestlers. Coming and going were the likes of Duke Ellington, too.

She also went after movie stars known for their endowments, including Forrest Tucker (he referred to his penis as "The Chief"); George Raft (Mae named his "Black Snake"); Steve Cochran (he celebrated his as "The Schvantz"); Gary Cooper ("The Montana Mule"), David Niven ("The Beer Can"); and Cary Grant ("who doesn't measure up").

She also went for gangsters, notably Owney Madden and Bugsy Siegel.

At one point, Dempsey amused West by proposing that the two of them, as a romantic duo, become lovers on the screen.

As the world knows, that didn't happen, the honor going instead to George Raft, Cary Grant or his lover, Randolph Scott, brutish Victor McLaglen, handsome Johnny Mack Brown, gay Edmund Lowe, and even W.C. Fields.

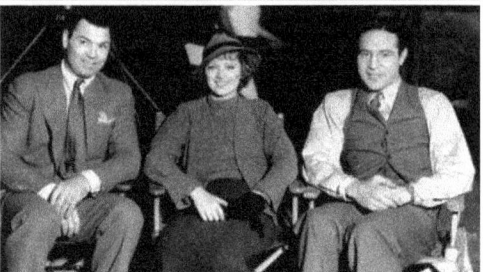

LOVE ON THE ROPES

Photo left: **Myrna Loy** as the featured star of the emotionally murky slugfest drama, *The Prizefighter and the Lady* (1933).

Photo upper right: **Jack Dempsey** looking "movie star handsome" during his fighting heyday. To his chagrin, he wasn't cast in the film as the prize-fighting male lead

Photo lower right, left to right ALLSTAR LINEUP: **Jack Dempsey, Myrna Loy,** and "bigtime boxer then in his prime" **Max Baer,** whose billing was more prominently featured than Dempsey's, and who had emerged as ""the winner" in the battle for Mae West.

Mae's career ended in *Sextette* (1976), where she co-starred (and sometimes feuded) with Ringo Star, Tony Curtis, Timothy Dalton, George Hamilton, and Dom DeLuise. Even Walter Pidgeon got in on the act.

***

As was inevitable, Dempsey in time lost his title. This came in September of 1926 when he boxed Gene Tunney, a former U.S. Marine, in Philadelphia. After a grueling ten rounds, Tunney was declared the victor.

As Dempsey explained to his then wife, Estelle Taylor, "I forgot to duck, honey."

[Years later, then-President Ronald Reagan would use Dempsey's exact words when, in the aftermath of an assassination attempt, he told Nancy the same thing.]

Dempsey still clung to his dream of becoming a Hollywood leading man, and he was elated when director W.S. Van Dyke from MGM called him about appearing in his latest movie, *The Prizefighter and the Lady* (1933).

Darwin learned about what went on behind the scenes during the making of that early talkie years later from Myrna Loy in Florida. At the time, she was touring onstage in Tampa and St. Petersburg with a friend of his in a play called *Relatively Speaking*.

"Van Dyke didn't make it clear to Dempsey," she said, "and he was horribly disappointed when he arrived on the set to find he was not playing the boxer, but himself as the referee in a bout between Max Baer and the then-heavyweight champ, Primo Carnera. Dempsey was humiliated. Not only was Baer a bigtime boxer and in his prime, but he was a rival for the affections of Mae West."

Myrna told Darwin that originally, under the direction of Howard Hawks, The *Prizefighter and the Lady* was to have been a vehicle for Clark Gable and Norma Shearer. After Shearer dropped out, the role went to Jean Harlow, which was convenient, since she was engaged in an affair with Gable at the time.

"We teased each other a lot on the set, playing dirty tricks on each other," Myrna said. "When I heard that Baer was terrified of mice, I released a toy mouse into the ring while the boxing match was being shot. Baer jumped into the arms of Carnera!"

"Max was not only afraid of that little toy," Myrna continued, " but Van Dyke told me he was nervous as hell during a kissing scene with me. He had seen me in other films onscreen, and thought I was a grand lady—and that made him scared. I was cast as Belle Mercer, who had this thing for boxers, evoking Mae West in her private life. When Max kissed me, I could feel him shaking. His smooch was like that of a high school boy on his first date. Imagine this timidity from a giant boxer who had once killed a man in the ring."

Dempsey never became a movie star but morphed, nonetheless, into an icon of the 20th Century. Sports writers praised his exceptional punching power and aggressive fighting. By 1950, the Associated Press named him the greatest boxer of the previous fifty years.

In Manhattan on May 31, 1983, at the age of 87, Dempsey suffered a heart attack and died. He was buried in Southampton on Long Island.

The time he spent at Magnolia House was memorialized with the installation of two garden plaques, depicted here, salvaged from The Bahamas estate of the British press magnate, Lord Beaverbrook. They were installed on one of its terraces, in his memory, shortly after his death.

His widow, Deanna, lived until 2003.

R.I.P Jack Dempsey

"A Champion is someone who gets up when he can't"

MAE WEST
Size Mattered

Born in 1893, The Little Chickadee wasn't so little. Looking her up and down, Adolph Zukor, Paramount honcho, said, "When I look at that dame's tits, I know what lusty means." Costume designer Edith Head said, "I've seen Mae West without a stitch and she's all woman. No hermaphrodite could have bosoms, well, like two large melons."

West loved boxers, black or white, including Jack Dempsey. For years she kept a nude picture of him over her toilet. She also liked wrestlers and especially men with well-built physiques and endowments. That's why she hired Mickey Hargitay (Mr. Universe) and Steve Cochran for her stage act. She wasn't opposed to what she called "The Music Men" either, namely, Duke Ellington and Oscar Hammerstein II. Of the magician, Harry Houdini, she said, "He didn't escape my trap."

She dated George Raft but finally concluded that, "He liked a boy's rosebud more than my bush." Gangsters gave her a special thrill, especially Benjamin "Bugsy" Siegel. "That mobster knew how to shoot in more ways than one."

When she appeared with Cary Grant, she claimed, "I knew he was a homosexual before he did." She failed to seduce another homosexual, Rock Hudson.

Later, in references to her, Hudson said, "She was just plain and simply a sweet old lady who told me marvelous stories about her life. She even told him what she said to Marlene Dietrich when the Kraut tried to seduce her: 'I go for men, and then only if they're hung like Anthony Quinn.'"

Mickey Hargitay with **Jayne Mansfield.** The busty blonde stole Mr. Universe from Mae West's boudoir.

Mae West claimed that "**Steve Cochran** was chosen by me for my stage act after I asked him to strip off his jockey shorts."

Bugsy Siegel was, according to West, "the best-hung gangster on the East or West Coasts."

"**Harry Houdini,**" said West, "could get out of any trap except my honeypot."

"**Duke Ellington** lived ip to the legend of black men," according to West.

HOW HENRY WILLSON,
Hollywood's Gay Svengali, Created the Beefcake Craze of the 1950s

He Renames Them and Morphs Truck Drivers or Mechanics into Heartthrobs
ROCK! TAB! GUY! CLINT! DACK! TY! KERWIN! NICK! TROY! CHAD!
He also Discovers LANA TURNER

In the history of Hollywood, **Henry Willson** (1911-1978) is known mainly for popularizing the beefcake craze of the 1950s. He is also known for being "The Man Who Invented Rock Hudson."

Willson was born into a show-biz family. He grew up meeting Broadway and vaudeville stars, including such legends as Will Rogers and Fanny Brice.

When he finished his education in the East, he embarked on "a long road to California," boarding a steamship that passed through the Panama Canal before continuing on to Los Angeles. On board, he met Dixie Lee, the Tennessee-born actress, dancer, and singer who also happened to be the first wife of Bing Crosby. They struck up a friendship. *[Willson would later write an article celebrating the birth of that couple's son, Gary Crosby.]*

Willson began to write interviews which appeared in, among others, the *Hollywood Reporter* and *New Movie Magazine*.

Stanley Mills Haggart, Darwin's future mentor, met Willson in 1940 when Haggart was a "leg man" for Hedda Hopper. The pair formed an enduring friendship.

According to Haggart, "I liked Henry as a friend, and I was richly rewarded. He let me in on some shocking secrets about Hollywood. Of course, many could not be printed, but I recorded them in my notebooks. Eventually, I gave those notebooks to Darwin and introduced him to Henry, who, in turn, introduced him to a lot of the movie stars or minor actors of the 1950s and beyond."

Willson eventually abandoned his dream of becoming a Hollywood features writer and opted instead to become a talent agent and scout. With that in mind, he began rounding up "handsome hunks," most of whom he would seduce, even though a lot of them were (nominally) straight. He soon learned that whether straight or gay, if an actor wanted to become a movie star, he would "put out."

As columnist Mike Connolly said, "Henry virtually invented the casting couch...for men, that is. Casting couches for gals have been around since the 1920s. Just ask Louis B. Mayer, Darryl F. Zanuck, or Jack Warner, to name a few."

For years after Willson's association with Hollywood's Zeppo Marx agency, he claimed that he discovered Jon Hall. So far as it is known, Hall became Henry's first seduction of a movie star.

Hall (1915-1979) zoomed to stardom when Samuel Goldwyn cast him in *The Hurricane* (1937) opposite sultry Dorothy Lamour, known for her long dark hair, full lips, sleepy, seductive eyes, and for how good she looked in a sarong.

A critic at the time wrote, "Jon Hall is handsome, well-built, slightly awkward, and not terribly charismatic. He nonetheless managed to become a leading man, half the time in A-list pictures, which isn't too bad for someone who cannot really act."

Three Frenemies in Frantic Pursuit of a Scoop

(left to right), **Stanley Haggart,** who learned part of his craft from gossip columnist **Hedda Hopper** *(center photo)*, his employer; and *(photo right)*, talent scout in search of male flesh and Hollywood's next Y-chromosome star, **Henry Willson.**

Jon Hall co-starring with **Dorothy Lamour** in *Aloma of the South Seas* (1941)

He starred with such leading ladies as Maria Montez, that cinematic mistress of high camp from the Dominican Republic.

From 1934 to 1955, Hall was married to singer Frances Langford.

On December 13, 1979, he committed suicide.

***

Once in a while, during his "research" of suitable *wannabes*, Willson actually "discovered" a female. An example included a sultry blonde named Julie Turner, whose name he changed to Lana Turner. When he introduced her to director Mervyn LeRoy, "The Sweater Girl" was born and a glittering cinematic career ensued for the woman who emerged as one of the most visible Love Goddesses of the 1940s.

Darwin's 600-page biography of Lana Turner (entitled *Hearts and Diamonds Take All* and published in 2017) was the most extensive and revealing ever written about her.

In 1943, Willson was hired by David O. Selznick as director of the talent division of his newly formed Vanguard Pictures. One of his first assignments involved finding and hiring three young men who could be convincingly appropriate as minor characters in the now classic World War II drama, *Since You Went Away* (1944), starring Claudette Colbert, Jennifer Jones, and Shirley Temple.

[The trio of young men Willson discovered for minor roles in Since You Went Away *morphed into movie stars, namely Craig Stevens, Guy Madison, and John Derek.]*

As an actors' agent, some of his clients were homosexuals; others were not. It didn't matter. Willson soon learned that if a young man wanted to be a movie star—and Willson could help him get roles—he was willing to lie on that overworked casting couch. "All I had to do was promise to make him a movie star."

***

Robert Ozell Mosely (1922-1996) was born in Pumpkin Center, California. Henry would "re-brand" him as Guy Madison, later claiming him as "one of my all-time best discoveries."

In 1944, during World War II, he was visiting Hollywood on leave from the U.S. Navy. Coming on strong, Willson told him he could get him the role of a sailor in *Since You Went Away*. "I want to rename you Guy Dunhill. No...not that." Then he looked across the street at the Dolly Madison Bakery. "No…Guy Madison."

The newcomer appeared on the screen as a sailor in that film for only three minutes. Nonetheless, the studio received thousands of letters demanding to know who he was. Everyone seemed to want a picture of him.

After he completed his tour of duty with the Navy, he moved to Hollywood, where Willson got him a starring role in the RKO drama, *Till the End of Time* (1946). In it, he played the love of Dorothy McGuire. Robert Mitchum was the star of the picture.

After that, Madison's film career more or less stalled until he was rescued in 1951 and cast in the hit television series *The Adventures of Wild Bill Hickok* (1951-58), co-starring Andy Devine as his pal, Jingles Jones.

Madison continued in film roles until 1989.

From 1949 to 1954, he was married to the actress Gail Russell, who cheated on him when she co-starred with John Wayne in *Angel and the Badman* (1947).

Before that, Wayne had seduced, among others, Joan Crawford, Clara Bow, Paulette Goddard, Carmen Miranda, and Marlene Dietrich. Despite his "successes," Wayne confessed, "Women scare the hell out of me. I've always been afraid of them."

Then-unknown 16-year-old **Lana Turner** *(aka "The Sweater Girl")* as "discovered" by Henry Willson and later cast in a brief but pivotal role in *They Won't Forget* (1937).

Two views of **Guy Madison.** *Upper photo*, with **Dorothy McGuire** in *Till the End of Time* (1946), and *lower photo* as *"Dream Beau of the Month"* in 1949.

Over the years, Darwin and Madison—having met at one of Willson's parties—became friends. On one occasion, Darwin visited him at his ranch house in the arid Morongo Valley, inland and west of Los Angeles. There was talk of Darwin "ghost writing" Madison's biography.

According to Darwin, "Guy finally decided that many of the details of his career rise should be kept secret. He didn't want to surprise or disappoint his dwindling fan base."

John Derek in (left photo) Rogues of Sherwood Forest (1950) and (right photo) The Ten Commandments (1956).

***

When Willson first met **Derek Delevan Harris** (1926-1998), the future John Derek, in a night club, he used the old line, "You ought to be in pictures."

"I found him the most beautiful male animal since Guy Madison," Willson once told Darwin. "Before I got him work, I asked him if he'd share some of his goodies with me. He didn't put up a fuss. Instead of putting up, he put out."

Henry came through for him, getting him cast in two small roles in Selznick pictures, not only *Since You Went Away*, but *I'll Be Seeing You*, both released in 1944.

"Then he told me the bad news," Willson said. "He'd been drafted into the U.S. Army to fight in the Philippines during the final days of World War II."

"Those atomic bombs saved me from having to invade Japan," Derek said.

Back from the Pacific, Derek arranged a rendezvous with Willson. It led to his getting cast as "Pretty Boy Romano," an unrepentant killer in *Knock on Any Door* (1949), starring Humphrey Bogart in a socially conscious melodrama. Its director was Nicolas Ray, who held his own private auditions with Derek.

John Derek as "Pretty Boy Romano' with **Humphrey Bogart** in *Knock on Any Door* (1949).

In the years to come, the handsome, dashing Derek would play swashbucklers (including Robin Hood); a college football player, and characters in war movies, *films noir,* and Westerns. In *Prince of Players* (1955), he was even cast as John Wilkes Booth, the assassin of Abraham Lincoln.

Derek married a Russian *prima ballerina*, Pati Behrs, in 1948. But it would be his next three marriages, each to stunning, media-savvy beauties, that morphed him into tabloid fodder. They included Ursula Andress, Linda Evans, and Bo Derek, his final wife, whom he wed in 1976.

Derek didn't mind showing off Bo's body to the world as viewers of *10* could clearly see. That was followed by *Tarzan, the Ape Man* (1981), in which she co-starred with Miles O'Keefe.

Critics denounced the movie as "the worst Tarzan picture of all time." However, fans of Bo and/or O'Keefe flocked to see it.

A promotional photo from MGM's *Tarzan, the Ape Man* (1981). Directed by **John Derek**, it showcasesd his wife, **Bo Derek**, and the Tennessee-born football hero **Miles O'Keefe**, whose role was mostly non-speaking.

***

For the third (and relatively minor) male role in *Since You Went Away,* Willson cast Craig Stevens, a handsome young actor he'd known since their days working with the Harpo Marx Agency. A son of Missouri, Stevens (1918-2000) had planned a career as a dentist until he enrolled in the drama club at the University of Kansas at Lawrence.

It convinced him to migrate to Hollywood as an actor. Eventually, he appeared in such films as a sailor in *Coast Guard* (1939), and in secondary roles in classics that included *Mr. Smith Goes to Washington* (1939).

During World War II, Stevens served in the U.S. Army Air Corps' First Motion Picture Unit based in Culver City, California. Its members, nicknamed "The Culver City Commandos," turned out government-sponsored propaganda and training films.

After *Since You Went Away*, Stevens worked steadily, but it wasn't until 1958 that he rose to national prominence when he starred as a private detective on the hit TV series *Peter Gunn*. It aired on NBC from 1958 to 1960, later moving to ABC for a year.

To conceal rumors of his homosexuality, Willson recommended that Stevens marry actress Alexis Smith. It was known as a lavender marriage, i.e., a legal union of a couple whose members hope will camouflage their mutual same-sex preferences. Amazingly, their marriage lasted for 49 years until her death in 1993. They had no children.

***

Over the course of many years, Darwin's friendship with Willson endured. He was invited to many of his parties. There, he got to know, and often became friends with, a new breed of actors, most of whom rose out of the 1950s. He interviewed each of the ones previewed below and became friends with a select few.

Actually, Darwin had another motive in mind: He wanted to write a book about Willson's collective discoveries with the intention of tracking both their careers and their personal lives. The working title he assigned it was *Pretty Boys: The Hollywood Discoveries of Henry Willson*. Regrettably, he had too many other contracts to fulfill and never got around to it.

In 2005, Darwin ruefully learned that author Robert Hofler had had the same idea and published *The Man Who Invented Rock Hudson*. It was subtitled *The Pretty Boys and Dirty Deals of Henry Willson*.

Upper photo: **Craig Stevens** with **Alix Talton** in *The Deadly Mantis* (1957) and *lower photo*, with his wife, **Alexis Smith**, in *The Windfall* (1971).

Darwin quickly recouped, focusing instead, in 2017, in collaboration with me (Danforth Prince) the redaction and publication of what became a Blood Moon bestseller, *Rock Hudson, Erotic Fire*. It was the most complete survey of Hudson's private life ever written.

In an interview, Darwin said, "Rock Hudson repeatedly beat out all of 'the bubblegum boys,' including blonde Tab Hunter or the blonder Troy Donahue, at the box office. Not just in the United States, but around the world. For terms of raw masculinity, Rock was an intensely photogenic, walking mass of testosterone."

What follows is a brief preview of the actors Darwin either interviewed or befriended during the gestation period of the above-mentioned book (*Pretty Boys*) he never completed.

***

When Willson met Orison Whipple Hungerford Jr., and signed him as a client, he immediately demanded that he change his name to the most *marquee*-friendly Ty Hardin. "I want your name to be as sexy as an erection."

"Ty, as I now called him, had been the nickname of Tyrone Power, but what the hell? The younger, newly christened Ty evoked a raw hunk of gorgeous flesh from Texas." *[He'd actually been born in New York City but reared in Texas.]*

A football scholarship had preceded Ty's entry into the U.S. Army during the Korean War. As a pilot, he eventually rose to the rank of lieutenant.

When he made his way to Hollywood, he was steered, through recommendations, in Willson's direction. Willson eventually managed to arrange a contract for him with Paramount.

John Wayne later disputed Henry's claim that he discovered Ty. "I met him and was impressed and introduced him to Howard Hawks and William T. Orr at Warners. Willson later became his agent."

Ty's big break came when Clint Walker walked out of his hit ABC TV series *Cheyenne* in 1958. For the remainder of the season, Ty was hired as his replacement. Jack Warner saw him on TV and was impressed, later casting him in his own series, *Bronco* (1958-1962).

As time went by, Ty moved for a while to Italy to make spaghetti Westerns.

Orison Whipple Hungerford Jr. *aka*

Ty Hardin

After his return to Hollywood, he co-starred with Joan Crawford in *Berserk!* (1967), which she considered "the worst picture I ever made." Hardin, instead of landing on Willson's casting couch, ended up on Crawford's.

Later, he worked in films in Australia and Europe.

In 1974, in Spain, he was arrested and sent to prison for drug trafficking.

Harding went in and out of marriages, his most notable being his 1961 wedding to Miss Universe, the German beauty queen, Marlene Schmidt. He told Darwin, "I wanted to have more marriages than Lana Turner or Elizabeth Taylor."

He also said, "Sometimes I got to work with a name actor—say, Henry Fonda, Jane Fonda, Kirk Douglas, Anthony Quinn. I was in *PT 109*, where Cliff Robertson portrayed John F. Kennedy after the President rejected Paul Newman as 'too Jewish.'"

"Other than Crawford, another star seduced me, and that was the bisexual actor Robert Taylor, when we made *Savage Pampas* in 1965," he said. [*Its plot? In the late 1800s, an army captain tries to tame the open plains of Argentina.*]

The last time Darwin ever saw him, Hardin said, "Every day, I think God for making me the most beautiful man on the planet."

Ty Hardin romancing **Joan Crawford** in *Berserk!* (1967)

An aging **Robert Taylor** in *Savage Pampas* (1965). In the 1930s, he'd been the original "Pretty Boy."

***

Kerwin Mathews (1926-2007) was another Willson discovery, one of his lesser-known actors. Born in Seattle, he and his divorced mother later moved to Wisconsin. During high school, he claimed that a drama teacher changed his life when she cast him as the lead in a school play. From that day forth, he wanted to be an actor. But first came World War II, during which he was a pilot for the U.S. Army Air Force.

In 1954, he moved to Hollywood, where he acted at the Pasadena Playhouse. The night he performed in Shakespeare's *The Comedy of Errors*, Willson was in the audience and made it a point to meet him backstage. After being subjected to Willson's by-now-regularized routine, Mathews was awarded a seven-year contract at Columbia.

His first credited part, in *5 Against the House* (1955), was also an early opportunity for Kim Novak, who soon was to become Columbia's answer to Marilyn Monroe.

"The biggest disappointment of my life," Mathews claimed, came when he was set to play the title role of *Joseph and His Brothers* with Rita Hayworth. A week before shooting had been scheduled to begin, the movie was canceled.

His first sizable role was in *The Garment District* (1957), in which he was cast as the idealistic son of Lee J. Cobb.

At long last, his break came when producer Charles Schneer cast him in what became a a big hit, *The 7th Voyage of Sinbad* (1958). This led to two other hits, *The Three Worlds of Gulliver* (1960) and *Jack the Giant Killer* (1962).

That was followed by one more film—this one relatively prestigious—when he was cast in *The Devil at Four O'Clock* (1961), in which he played the third lead opposite Spencer Tracy and Frank Sinatra.

After a series of disappointing low-budget films, Mathews retired from acting and moved to San Francisco, where he opened a chic cloth-

Kerwin Mathews in *(left photo) Tarawa Beachhead* (1958) and *(right photo)* in *The 7th Voyage of Sinbad* (also 1958)

ing boutique and an antique store.

While writing, researching, and updating the shopping section of *Frommer's San Francisco,* Darwin visited Mathews' store and bought two suits, promising to give the outlet a writeup. Mathews "reciprocated," inviting Darwin to dinner that night, with the understanding that they'd be joined by Mathews' long-time companion, Tom Nicoll, the display manager of the San Francisco branch of the British department store chain, Harvey Nichols. The couple had met in 1961, and were still together when Mathews died at the age of 81 in 2007.

Over dinner, Mathews didn't really want to talk about Willson. "For a while, at least, he was a real starmaker, both powerful and notorious. I have no good memories of him."

***

Manhattan-born **Yale Summers** (1933-2021) was convinced that Willson could make him a matinee idol. "He had the looks and quite a bit of talent," Willson had said about him, "but I can't win them all."

His screen debut—an uncredited role in the 1920s gangland drama *Mad Dog Coll* (1961)—was hardly noticed. *[Ironically, It marked the screen debuts of both Gene Hackman and Telly Savalas.]*

From there, Summers drifted into television, finding it a more welcoming medium. He appeared in a recurring role in the ABC soap opera, *General Hospital* as Dr. Bob Ayres for a year (1964) of its rambling history. *[Surpassed only by* Guiding Light, General Hospital *is cited as the second-longest-running daytime TV soap opera in television history.]*

Summers became even better known to TV audiences when he was cast as Jack Dane in *Daktari,* a family-friendly TV series about a veterinarian who protects animals from poachers at an East African game reserve. It aired for two years beginning in 1966.

He got the most fan mail when he starred as Rodney Harrington in the hit NBC TV daytime series *Return to Peyton Place.* He replaced actor Al Lawrence Casey.

In Hollywood, he was best known for his associations with SAG and AFTRA. He was the co-founder and producer of the Screen Actors Guild Awards (1995-2009). Later, he was active in the American Federation of Television and Radio Artists.

Yale Summers from an episode of ***Daktari*** *(*1966)

***

Broad-shouldered **Clint Walker** (1927-2018) was another Willson discovery. After service in the U.S. Merchant Marine Corps from the age of 17, he did odd jobs in Texas, working his way to Las Vegas and then to Los Angeles. He was everything from a garbage collector to a doorman at the Sands Hotel in Las Vegas during its early years.

Willson was impressed with not only his handsome face, but his imposing physique. He stood 6 feet 6 inches tall with a 48-inch chest and a 32-inch waist. Every morning, he spent two hours in a gym.

His big break came when he was cast as the male lead in the long-running TV series *Cheyenne* (1955-1963) as Cheyenne Bodie, a roaming cowboy in the years immediately following the Civil War.

The series was broadcast on ABC/Warner Brothers. Whenever possible its directors photographed him bare-chested. To their delight, they quickly learned that he could also sing.

Walker also starred in the Western feature film *Fort Dobbs* (1958). Film critic Howard Thompson described him as "the biggest, finest-looking Western hero ever to sag a horse, with a pair of shoulders rivaling that of King Kong."

A contract dispute led to him leaving the series. In an interview, he told

Clint Walker *(left photo)* in ***Cheyenne*** and *(right photo)* with **Sonia Sahni** in ***Maya*** *(1966)*

Darwin, "My god, the bastards had me working a 12-hour day and were stingy with my paycheck."

After leaving TV, Walker worked with Rock Hudson and Doris Day in *Send Me No Flowers* (1964) and in the war drama *None but the Brave* (1965) starring Frank Sinatra.

His biggest feature film hit was as a male convict in the war drama *The Dirty Dozen* (1967).

Walker also told Darwin, "I can't believe I'm still alive. Once, after a ski accident, I was rushed to the hospital and pronounced dead, until a young medic saw a bit of life still left in me. I was rushed into surgery."

He was referring to an accident that occurred in May of 1971 on Mammoth Mountain in the central part of eastern California. While following the contours of the twisting, irregular terrain, he began tumbling out of control before coming to an abrupt stop after being pierced through the heart with a ski pole.

"As for your friend, Henry Willson," he told Darwin, "I think he was a jerk. When I first came into his office, he looked me over from toe to head, lingering below the belt. Then he asked me if I were big all over."

Walker was married three times, each union lasting some twenty years.

***

Dack Rambo (1941-1994) was born an identical twin. His brother was named Dirk, and collectively, they were called "Dack & Dirk" throughout most of their lives.

"At the age of 20, the twins were discovered by Loretta Young, who cast the then-teenagers in her hit TV series, *The New Loretta Young Show* (1962-1963). Tragically, Dirk was killed in 1967 in a road accident when he was only 25.

One of Rambo's best-known roles was when he was cast as the grandson of crusty old Walter Brennan in *The Guns of Will Sonnett* in 1967.

During the 1970s and '80s, he was frequently seen on television in series that included *Charlie's Angles* and *Murder, She Wrote*. He went on to play Jack Ewing in 51 episodes of *Dallas* from 1965 to 1987.

In the summer of 1991, his doctor told him that he had tested positive for HIV. He admitted that he'd had numerous sexual encounters with both men and women for years. "I liked a spicy sex life," he confessed, "and I never practiced safe sex."

He died at the age of 52.

Dack Rambo, the twin who survived until the debut of AIDS.

***

Brooklyn-born **John Saxon** (1936-2020), another of Willson's discoveries, appeared in more film and TV projects than any other actor he discovered.

Willson first saw Saxon's handsome face in *True Story* magazine. "I fell in love with the boy the moment I saw that picture," Willson confessed to Darwin. "The very next day, I tracked him down and visited his parents, Mr. and Mrs. Orrico. He was a dockworker, and she was a recent immigrant from Calabria. In just one afternoon, I convinced them to let me take this 17-year-old hunk on a plane with me to Los Angeles. He would be well taken care of and fed a healthy diet. Of course, he would sleep in great comfort with me in my luxurious bed, where a teenager's sexual needs could be well satisfied."

Saxon also won the approval of Willson's assistant, Pat Colby. "To me, he looked like the son of Sophia Loren."

After subjecting Saxon to nightly "auditions," he was on his way, getting cast as a juvenile delinquent in *Running Wild* (1955). His co-star was Mamie Van Doren. Years later at a party in Hollywood, Saxon told Darwin, "I think Mamie was far sexier than Marilyn Monroe."

His first major role was when cast as the stalker of Esther Williams in *The Unguarded Mo-*

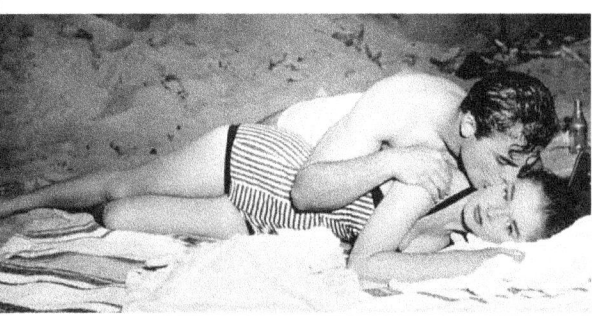

Two views of **John Saxon.** *Right photo*, with **Luana Patten** in *Rock Pretty Baby* (1957)

ment (1956). But it was the film, *Rock, Pretty Baby* (1956) that turned Saxon into a teen idol.

He often played detectives or police officers, as well as Western and horror films, even Italian movies until 2017, the year he retired, three years before his death at the age of 83.

A wide range of stars and directors had moved through his life—Sandra Dee, Blake Edwards, Debbie Reynolds, Vincente Minnelli, Rex Harrison, Kay Kendall, Frank Borzage, Howard Keel, Jane Fonda, John Huston, Burt Lancaster, Audrey Hepburn, Lana Turner, Anthony Quinn, Audie Murphy, Dick Powell, Otto Preminger, Marlon Brando, and Robert Redford.

He had three wives—one a screen writer, another an investment banker, and the last, a model.

***

Although **Doug McClure** (1935-1995) did not turn out to be the superstar that Willson had envisioned, the actor found steady work until the year of his death at the age of 59.

His best-known role was as the cowboy Trampas in *The Virginian*, which was an NBC telecast in 1962. *[This drama had the same name as the 1929 Gary Cooper classic from Paramount, but the scripts were different.]*

One of his A-list movies was released in 1955 when he starred opposite James Stewart in *Shenandoah*. McClure went on to star alongside such veterans as Lee J. Cobb and John McIntire.

The biggest star McClure ever worked with was Bette Davis when they made the TV movie, *The Judge and Jake Wyler* in 1972.

McClure was also seen in such sci-fi films as *The Land that Time Forgot*.

He told Darwin, "In spite of all the movies I've made, it seems more people have seen me hawking Hamms Beer, a gig I've had on TV for years beginning in the 1970s."

"Wanna know the worst jerk I've ever worked with?" he asked. "William Shatner. What a bastard!"

Doug McClure: "My goal was to become the next Gary Cooper."

***

As he often did with many handsome male actors he signed, Henry told a young actor who had been raised in Dearborn, Michigan, that he'd have to submit to a name change. So Raymon Lee Cramton (1937-2012) morphed into **Chad Everett**.

The son of a racecar driver, Everett had been a quarterback on his university football team, but he also appeared in school stage plays. . "I went into acting because I was easily bored. Acting seemed to give vent to a lot of different feelings."

He later told Darwin, "Henry Willson and I got off to a bad start. I was very religious, and had been taught that homosexuality was evil, against the teachings of the Bible. Right from the beginning, I felt Willson was a queer."

Willson later confirmed that he never seduced Everett: "On a boat trip to Catalina Island, I came into his cabin as he was changing into a bathing suit. Like Monty Clift, he was Princess Tiny Meat. Not for me!"

It seems ironic that MGM, the studio that in the 1930s boasted that it had "More Stars than there are in Heaven," had only one actor under contract in 1968: Chad Everett.

Chad Everett as Dr. Joe Gannon on *Medical Center* (1969-76)

In all, Everett would star in 40 films and TV series, including appearances in *The Singing Nun, Airplane II, The Nanny,* and *Murder, She Wrote.* He achieved his greatest exposure in that TV drama *Medical Center*, which ran from 1969 to 1976.

The actor struggled with alcoholism, finally overcoming his addiction in 1986.

In all, his career lasted from 1966 to 2011, a year before he died at the age of 75 of lung cancer.

***

Mike Connally built a career as a gossip columnist for the *Hollywood Reporter* from 1951 to 1966, the year of his death at the age of 53.

Newsweek once hailed him as "the most influential columnist inside the movie colony." We consider that hyperbole. Had that writer never heard of Louella Parsons and Hedda Hopper?

Darwin first met Connally at one of Henry Willson's Saturday afternoon pool parties. "Mike was fascinating," Darwin said, "filled with genuinely shocking stories. Whereas back then, I had already picked up a lot of Hollywood dirt, he knew wheelbarrows of it, most of which, for legal reasons, he couldn't publish."

At the time of his meeting with Darwin, the *Hollywood Reporter's* columnist was working on an article about an actor with an roughly equivalent name: **Mike Connors**. According to Connally (the columnist), "Connors told me that Henry Willson never made a pass at him. He also told me that Joan Crawford did not bed him when he had a role in her picture, *Sudden Fear*."

Connally, however, quickly added, "But anyone who believes that Connors was telling the truth also believes in the tooth fairy, that the world is flat, and that Hitler loved Jews."

The first mention of Mike Connors in a column by Connelly had this line: "Touch Connors is a he-man who'll put all Hollywood sissy actors to shame."

It was Willson who invented the actor's (later revised) name of "Touch Connors" shortly after discovering him. Connors had been born in 1925 into a family from Armenia who had christened him Krekor Ohanian. When he'd played basketball in school, his teammates nicknamed him "Touch," a moniker seized upon and reinforced by Willson. But after being identified by that name in about a dozen early movies, the actor himself changed it to "Mike Connors."

Two views of **Mike Connors** as *Mannix* (1967-1975). *Right photo* with **Gail Fisher** as his secretary.

A native of Fresno, California, he worked steadily from 1952 to 2007, ten years before his death.

"I pitched Connor's manly charms to Crawford when she was starring in the psychological drama/thriller, *Sudden Fear* (1952)," Willson said to Darwin. "To her, I emphasized his allure below the belt."

"She often seduced her leading men, most notoriously Clark Gable. She detested her leading man (Jack Palance) in that film. And she was immediately intrigued by (and signed) Conners into one of that film's secondary roles."

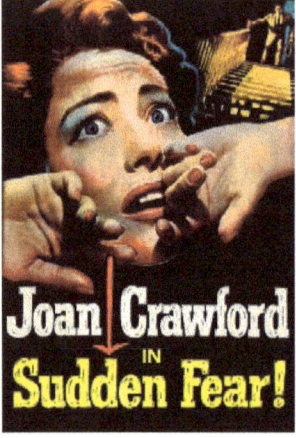

Mike Connors in *Sudden Fear* (1952). Whereas in the publicity photo, above,, he's romancing **Gloria Grahame**, behind the scenes, his ardor was aimed at the movie's star, **Joan Crawford**.

"When I made *Sudden Fear* with Connors, he was billed as "Touch" Connors. Believe me, he does more than touch," Crawford claimed.

After that, Connors was cast alongside John Wayne in *Island in the Sky* (1953). In it, he played a crewman aboard a search-and-rescue plane.

Three years later, Connors was cast as an Amalekite herder in Cecil B. De Mille's *The Ten Commandments* (1956).

One of Connors' highest-profile roles was as the leading man to Bette Davis and Susan Hayward in *Where Love Has Gone* (1964).

He also co-starred with Robert Redford in one of his early films, a World War II black comedy, *Situation Hopeless, but Not Serious* (1965). Redford and Connors played American soldiers taken prisoner by a German villager (Alec Guinness). Later, Connors played a card sharp in the remake of *Stagecoach* (1966), which in 1939 had shot John Wayne ("The Duke") to stardom.

Connors' dream of stardom came true when he was cast as the tough but charming private eye in the hit CBS TV series *Mannix* (1967-1975). That role earned him a Golden Globe Award in 1970, as well as four consecutive Emmy nominations he received between 1970 and 1973.

Mannix had originally been produced by Desilu Productions when its then-President, Lucille Ball, was the most powerful female executive in Hollywood. A rumor was spread that Connors ended up on her casting couch, but that was never confirmed. All Connors had to say about his boss was, "She wasn't Lucy Ricardo."

As for the rest of his post-*Mannix* career, Connors confessed, "I made a series of pictures just to pay the rent."

***

One of the many biographies Darwin conceived and researched but never wrote because of other commitments was the dramatic saga of actor **Rory Calhoun**.

Darwin met him at a party hosted by Henry Willson, and encountered him again on several other occasions over the years. "The more I learned about him, the more I felt that his life should not only become the subject of a biography, but perhaps a movie, too."

Born Francis Timothy McCown in Los Angeles in 1922, the future Rory Calhoun worked in motion pictures from 1941 to 1993.

His boyhood read like a horror story. A wild youth on the rampage, he stole a revolver and bullets and went on a shooting spree. That led to his being sent to a juvenile reform school.

After his release, he discovered that his mother had married a brutal sadist. His new stepfather beat him almost daily.

At the age of 17, he ran away from home and began hot-wiring cars. He also broke the window displays of five jewelry stores. When crossing state lines in a stolen vehicle, he was apprehended and sent to a Federal prison in Springfield, Missouri. There, because of his youth and male beauty, he was held down and repeatedly raped.

Two views of **Rory Calhoun.** "I seduced both Lana Turner and Marilyn Monroe. Of the two, I preferred Lana."

He was paroled right before his 21st birthday. This began a relatively undocumented chapter in his life as he drifted from job to job: a forest firefighter, a logger in the California redwoods, a mechanic in a garage, a cowboy in Arizona, a truck driver, a crane operator, and a hard-rock miner in Nevada.

While horseback riding in the Hollywood Hills early in 1944, he met the bisexual actor Alan Ladd, an already an established movie star, Ladd was immediately attracted to Calhoun and invited him to a cabin he owned two miles away in the mountains. There, he gave him a hundred dollars and seduced him.

He also invited the handsome young man to meet his wife, Sue Carol, a talent agent, who suggested that he might be groomed for stardom.

Rory Calhoun with **Marilyn Monroe** in *River of No Return*. "During the shoot, my competition for Monroe was Robert Mitchum."

To Calhoun, in reference to her husband, she said, "The first time I saw Alan, I thought he looked like a Greek God and had the potential of becoming a big star. The only problem was that he stood only 5 feet, 3 inches tall. You don't have that problem, I see."

During the remaining years of World War II, she got Calhoun some minor roles. It was Willson, not Sue Carol, who launched him (after many dalliances on his casting couch) on his road to stardom. Eventually he got Calhoun signed with Vanguard, the studio owned and managed by David O. Selznick. Willson also concocted the budding studmuffin's revised name: **Rory Calhoun**.

As part of publicity campaign, Willson arranged a date for Calhoun with another of his clients, the sultry and sexy bombshell, **Lana Turner**. They were heavily photographed, and looking gorgeous, at the première of Alfred Hitchcock's *Spellbound* (1945), a Selznick production. Their images were widely circulated, and calls came in from casting directors.

Rory Calhoun, ready to rumble, in *Colossos of Rhodes*.

Calhoun was on his way to stardom. Nonetheless, although reluctantly, he continued his visits to Willson's casting couch, becoming "a regular."

"I knew Rory would go over big with Lana," Willson told Darwin. "She and I like to devour well-hung young men."

Calhoun's publicity stunt with Lana paid off. The next day, Willson phoned Louella Parsons, predicting that Rory Calhoun would become "the next Clark Gable."

Calhoun began to work steadily, appearing in such films as *That Hagen Girl* (1947) with Ronald Reagan and Shirley Temple. For Monogram, he was cast opposite Guy Madison in *Massacre River* (1949). The men formed a strong emotional bond that lasted for years. Calhoun was a known womanizer, but Madison managed to lure him from the straight and narrow path.

One stormy night in front of his house, Willson found them together in the back seat of a car. "Rory was sodomizing Guy," Willson said, "and I was jealous. But I forgave them."

In the weeks that followed, Willson was often seen about town with both actors, patronizing such restaurants as Chasen's and Romanoff's.

Rory soon embarked on an affair with the French actress Corinne Calvet. It marked a high point of his reputation as a stud. "Word got around," he told Darwin. "Now, whenever I meet a woman, she starts taking off her panties."

From 1950 to 1954, Calhoun worked for Fox, where he was cast in such pictures as *A Ticket for Tomahawk* (1950). At Fox, he met and seduced a young, fast-rising starlet named Marilyn Monroe.

A fiery redhead, Susan Hayward, was added to Calhoun's list of conquests during his gig as second male lead in *I'd Climb the Highest Mountain* (1951).

A studio shot of **Rory Calhoun (left)** with **Guy Madison,** snapped as an insight into how they'd relate. They did.

"I got to Susan after two U.S. Presidents did," Calhoun said. "Notably, Ronald Reagan and JFK." His affair with Hayward continued when they were cast together in *With a Song in My Heart* (1952).

After Hayward, Calhoun romanced Betty Grable [*the favorite pinup girl of G.I.s during World War II*], during their filming of *Meet Me After the Show* (1951). "She and I would tangle again in the future. So would Marilyn and me."

On the set of *How to Marry a Millionaire* (1953), Calhoun wandered back and forth between the beds of Monroe and Grable.

"When I made *River of No Return* (1954), it was Marilyn who went from bed to bed between Robert Mitchum and me," Calhoun said. "She managed to keep both of us satisfied."

Calhoun was married three times— first to Lita Baron (1948-1970); and then twice (1971-1979 and again from 1982-1999) to Sue Rhodes.

Calhoun with **Betty Grable** in *How to Marry a Millionaire.* "Off screen, I had to keep two blondes sastified," Calhoun boasted.

Calhoun with **Susan Hayward** in *With a Song in My Heart.* "Her hair was not the only thing fiery about her," Calhoun claimed.

When Baron divorced him, she charged, in court, that he'd had an adulterous affair with Betty Grable and with 79 other women.

As Calhoun later said, "She didn't know the half of it. I'm sure I seduced at least twice that many broads."

In reference to his career, he said, "I don't know how I'll fare with future historians. Maybe a footnote."

***

As a teenager growing up in Miami, Darwin was an active member of a group of high school and college students who were dedicated movie fans—about 50 in all. Each was a devoted fan of, among others, Joan Crawford, Gary Cooper, Bette Davis, Clark Gable, Irene Dunne, Claudette Colbert, Humphrey Bogart, Marlene Dietrich, and Greta Garbo.

Fortunately, there were at least four theaters (scattered between downtown Miami and Miami Beach) that screened classic films from the Golden Age long became they became available on television or streaming through the web.

Club members did not live exclusively in the past, as they also developed favorites among stars that had emerged in the 1950s: Marlon Brando, James Dean, Tab Hunter, Robert Wagner, Paul Newman, Natalie Wood, and Marilyn Monroe.

At the time, *Confidential* was the leading scandal rag in America. In 1955, it featured an article stating that Tab Hunter had been arrested at a "limp-wrist pajama party" after it was raided by the police.

Warner's feared that revelations about Hunter being gay would destroy what had become its No. 1 star. A decision was made to involve him in a publicity tour through strategic markets in South Florida to test audience reactions to his personality and style. Warner's greatest fear involved the possibility that members of any audience might shout "faggot" or "queer" at him.

A key stop on the tour was the University of Miami, whose demographics included a diverse student population hailing from both the Northeast and the South.

Since Darwin Porter was the Editor-in-Chief of the University's newspaper, and since he'd seen every Tab Hunter movie ever made [*including The Island of Desire; 1952, in which he'd co-starred with Linda Darnell*] he was selected to introduce him and interview him in front of the student body.

"Tab was treated with great respect and received thunderous applause at the end of his talk," Darwin said. "It was filled with anecdotes—charming ones—about movie-making in Hollywood."

Blonde, square-jawed, and dazzlingly handsome Hunter was born in Manhattan in 1931, the son of a Jewish father and a mother who was a devout Catholic of German origin. He was "discovered" cheerfully shoveling manure in a Los Angeles stable.

Henry Willson renamed him Tab Hunter and took him out on a date to the Mocambo. "There were little nudges under the table, and his fingers lingered too long on my hand," Hunter recalled. "I knew what would be in store for me later."

Hunter's first major hit was his appearance in the World War II drama, *Battle Cry* (1955), in which he played Danny Forrester. For that coveted part, he beat out both James Dean and Paul Newman.

In an amazing breakthrough as a vocalist, he knocked Elvis Presley off the pop charts when he recorded "Young Love," a charming ballad that sold millions of copies.

Another big Tab Hunter success was his portrayal of Joe Hardy in the movie musical *Damn Yankees* (1958) opposite Gwen Verdon.

In time, Hunter would fire Willson and move on to another agent. He enjoyed great success. Darwin remembered that once he saw pictures of the actor on the covers of six different movie magazines, each displayed side-by-side at the same newsstand.

Hunter made "the business mistake of my life" when he bought out his contract at Warners, hoping that freelancing as an actor would garner more inspiring roles. That did not happen. Instead, Warners quickly (some said "with ruthless efficiently") replaced him with another blonde Adonis, Troy Donahue.

As part of ongoing attempts to camouflage his homosexuality, Hunter had gone out on some high-profile dates arranged by the studio, most notably with Natalie Wood. Gossipy competitors in Hollywood joked, "Natalie Wood, Tab wouldn't."

At the time, Tab was involved in a long-term relationship with Anthony Perkins, who later immortalized himself in Alfred Hitchcock's *Psycho* (1960). After their breakup, Hunter sustained a number of other gay affairs, the most famous being with the Russian ballet dancer, Rudolf Nureyev.

Eventually, Hunter found the love of his life, film producer Allan Glaser, with whom he remained for the rest of his life, dying in 2018 at the age of 86.

Darwin saw a lot of Hunter when he moved to Manhattan after Tony Richardson cast him in the Tennessee Williams' play, *The Milk Train Doesn't Stop Here Anymore*. Darwin, of course, was a close friend of Tennessee, and also of the production's star, Tallulah Bankhead. [*He was also a friend and frequent escort of its co-star, Marian Seldes.*]

Whereas Tallulah made the choice to descend, during her performances, into elaborately high camp, Hunter took his role seriously, even earnestly, craving critical approval as a "serious" dramatic actor. Both Hunter and

Tab Hunter, from the era Darwin Porter hosted him at the U. of Miami. "In my early films, directors always wanted to have me take off my shirt," Hunter said. "I became the beefcake darling to millions of fans. But all too soon, they were *Gone With the Winds* as my career declined."

Tab Hunter in 1959 with **Tuesday Weld.** "We'd be together as part of a studio-arranged date until 11PM," Hunter said. "Then we'd say goodbye to hook up with our real lovers."

Anthony Perkins *(left)* **and Tab Hunter** *(right)* were secret lovers. "He wasn't exactly Norman Bates, but he was a bit kinky. He liked to be pissed on. He also liked me to tie him up, go outside, and climb through a window into his bedroom to rape him."

An "Odd Couple" co-starring together on Broadway, **Tab Hunter** and **Tallulah Bankhead**, in Tennessee Williams' *The Milk Train Doesn't Stop Here Anymore.* She told its director, Tony Richardson, "I'm sure that Tab boy and I will get along like spitting cats."

When she was first introduced to Hunter, she extended a weak handshake: "I suspect I don't have the right equipment for you, *dahling.*"

Tab Hunter always displayed an ability to self-satirize. Here, he appears with the world-famous drag queen, **Divine**, in John Waters' satirical comedy, *Polyester* (1981).

Bankhead were long past their glory days. Offstage, during interviews with the press, Tallulah was naughty, provocative, and—insofar as Hunter was concerned—embarrassing: *"I don't know if Tab Hunter is gay or not… He's never gone down on ME, dahling."*

Less than five weeks after the assassination of JFK, on New Year's Night, 1964, the Tallulah Bankhead/Tab Hunter collaboration opened on Broadway. A sophisticated exploration of an over-the-hill diva purchasing love and lust from an emotionally conflicted young man, it received scathing reviews and flopped. Playing to sparse audiences consisting mostly of gay men, it closed after only three performances.

[*As an unexpected dénouement, three years later, in 1967, Elizabeth Taylor and Richard Burton brought that Tennessee Williams play to the screen, re-titling it Boom! Adding to the über-campy context, Noël Coward was imported as a new character they introduced as "The Witch of Capri."*]

During one of the nadirs of his career, Hunter was cast by the notoriously campy director, John Waters, in *Polyester* (1981) starring as the love interest of the cross-dressing Divine. Before he signed his contract, Waters asked Hunter if he could kiss a 300-pound transvestite.

With self-deprecating charm, Hunter ruefully replied, "I've kissed a helluva lot worse."

**Rest in Peace
TAB HUNTER**
(1931-2018)

Troy Donahue
Pin-up Boy of Pop Culture

Troy Donahue personified the blonde-haired pretty boy of the late 1950s and early 1960s. Known for his pin-up image, he became an icon of pop culture.

Born as Merle Johnson, Jr. (1936-2001) in New York City, he grew up wanting to become an actor. Unfortunately, he started drinking in the seventh grade, later becoming an alcoholic and heavy user of recreational drugs.

From Day One, he always wanted to be an actor, coming as he had, from a theatrical family. Early in his life, he met Gertrude Lawrence, who was appearing at the time in a local stage production of *The King and I*.

After migrating to Hollywood, he was signed to a six-month contract at Universal, mainly because of his good looks. That seemed to go nowhere. When his $125-a-week contract expired, it wasn't renewed.

Troy Donahue was known for his pin-up image in the pop culture of the late 1950s and early 60s.

In 1961, Darwin met Donahue at a party hosted by Henry Willson, who had signed the actor after a casting couch interview. The party included many of Willson's actor clients, some members of the press, and both Lana Turner and Rhonda Fleming.

From the beginning, Donahue's heavy drinking got him into serious trouble. In 1956, while driving drunk, he had a terrible car accident, plunging his car 50 feet into a canyon off Malibu Canyon Road. He barely survived, suffering a bruised spinal cord, a cracked kneecap, a crushed kidney, and two cracked ribs. He lost a tooth and suffered through 40 stitches.

Two years later, he was arrested for drunken driving, spending 15 days in the Los Angeles County Jail. Later, he claimed to have been sexually assaulted there every day.

Freely admitting to his alcohol addiction, he was known to have downed a pint—and sometimes a quart—of vodka a day. Later, he was known to have laced some of his vodka with codeine.

Two views of Troy Donahue's links to ABC-TV's detective drama series, *Surfside 6* (1960-1962). It was conspicuously located on Miami Beach, despite most of its episodes being filmed in Los Angeles Relatively "blonde," and relatively vanilla, and relentlessly wholesome by today's standards, it dovetailed neatly with the sexual revolution of the 60s.

After becoming one of Henry's clients and reclining on his casting couch, his name was changed to Troy Donahue. *[An earlier proposal—Paris Donahue—was rejected.]*

Stardom did not come easily. The night Darwin met him, he found that he was about to be evicted from his apartment because of back rent he owed. He had been paid for his film work, but had wasted his salary on drugs and other diversions.

Ironically, the apartment he occupied was owned by Gordon Howard, a close friend of Darwin's. Darwin intervened, paying the actor's overdue rent and persuading his mentor, Stanley Haggart, to hire Donahue as a "background actor" in an upcoming commercial being shot that week in Los Angeles.

Rock Hudson, Willson's biggest movie-star client, co-starred with Troy, filming *The Tarnished Angels* (1957. During a break in the shoot, Hudson summoned the young actor to his dressing room, where he seduced him.

The next day, Hudson reported his conquest to Willson: "Great cocksucker! Small dick!"

Willson replied, "Tell me something I don't already know."

At last a breakthrough role, though minor, emerged for

Troy Donahue (left figure, above) as "also ran, second-tier'" beefcake on the set of *the barnstorming drama*, Tarnished Angels ((1957). Here, he emotes, off-screen, with Rock Hudson, the A-list star of the film.

"Troy was cute, but didn't deliver under the sheets," Rock later told his co-star, Robert Stack. "Good looks are one thing, but a guy's got to deliver under the belt for me...or else out he goes."

Troy when he was cast in *Imitation of Life* (1959), starring Lana Turner, whom Donahue had met at one of Willson's parties. The character he'd play was unsympathetic. Cast as Frankie, he played the brutal boyfriend of a "passing-for-white" Susan Kohner, who was also dreaming of super stardom.

Finally, fame arrived in the form of Warners' casting him in *A Summer Place* (1959) opposite Sandra Dee. Critics were mixed in their reviews, but the film opened as the No. 1 box office champion nationwide. Its theme song ("A Summer Place") morphed into a nationwide hit, too.

Donahue won a Golden Globe award as "Most Promising Newcomer" and toured the country with press agents from Warners. From town to town, he was met with mobs of screaming teenage girls.

Soon, he was driving a new Porsche and moving into a more luxurious apartment. In time, he became famous for his open house parties, which often devolved into orgies "without any particular gender preference."

Imitating Tab Hunter's success, Donahue also recorded songs, but they did not go over well with the public. Wherever he went, he was often confused with "Tab" or "Mr. Hunter," and asked for autographs.

Troy Donahue as the crude and cruel boyfriend of the character played by **Susan Kohner** in the 1959 remake of *Imitation of Life*.

His greatest exposure came when he starred in the hit TV series *Surfside 6* (1960-1962). His face appeared on posters, lunch boxes, and board games.

"Sex sells," Willson told him. "Put on a bathing suit and head for the beach, where I'll arrange to have you photographed. After all, it's the era of beefcake. I practically invented it."

Troy's heavy drinking continued, and sometimes, he showed up for work intoxicated. Nonetheless, he had developed a fan base and that was what mattered to directors and producers. "Sober him up," a director might be ordered by the studios top brass—including Jack Warner himself.

Reporter Rick Du Brow wrote, "Troy Donahue is big and strong and has the rare ability to make the most glamorous and exciting events seem dull, colorless, and flat." In contrast, other critics hailed him "as the next James Dean."

Darwin came to know Donahue far better when he was cast in *Parrish* (1961), starring the great Claudette Colbert in a minor role. The featured female lead in that film was Connie Stevens.

At the time, Darwin was seeing a lot of Sylvia Miles, who had a minor role in the film, too. He visited the set several times during the shoot.

Sylvia, with Darwin, invited Donahue to "go out on the town" with them one night, visiting L.A.'s chic bars and clubs.

"It was obvious that he was really hitting the bottle," Darwin said, "but he was amusing. Sylvia liked him. And so did I."

Later, in New York, Darwin invited Donahue to a party he was hosting for business associates of Joseph Papp. *[Papp's Astor Place Theater, later renamed the Public Theater, was immediately across Lafayette Street from where Darwin was living at the time, a duplex on the top floor of the Astor Colonnade. Thanks to the convenient proximity of Darwin's apartment to the site of Papp's theatrical "experiments," both Papp and Darwin found such press and PR collaborations convenient and profitable.]*

Children of Divorced Parents, circa 1959: in Love and Partially Unclothed

Troy Donahue as the male lead, co-starring with **Sandra Dee**, in *A Summer Place*. By today's standards, its plot was corny and its male lead looked muscularly underdeveloped.

About thirty guests, at the bequest of Joseph Papp, showed up at Darwin's apartment. Among others, they included Sylvia, John Agar (famous as the ex-husband of Shirley Temple) and the TV producer, Brooks Clift (a client of Darwin's) with his current girlfriend, Broadway star Kim Stanley. Accompanying Clift and Kim Stanley was Brooks' brother, the enigmatic movie star, Montgomery Clift.

"The party, as many parties did in those days, degenerated into a competition about who could drink the most," Darwin said, "Monty or Troy."

Sometime after 2am, after most of the other guests had left, Donahue passed out. "Brooks helped me put him to bed," Darwin said.

The next morning, Donahue woke up and requested an old-fashioned breakfast of bacon and eggs with all the trimmings.

"It was a long time before I ever saw Troy again," Darwin said. "He was entering a career peak, receiving an estimated 7,500 fan letters a week, mostly from teenaged girls but also from a lot of gay men who found him alluring."

***

Donahue starred in *Susan Slade* (1961), a romantic drama in which his co-stars were Connie Stevens and the veteran, more seasoned actress, Dorothy McGuire. It was a hit.

That was followed with another success, *Rome Adventure* (1962), in which Donahue appeared opposite Suzanne Pleshette. They fell in love and were married in 1964 but divorced that same year. Obviously, his heavy drinking and drug abuse contributed to their breakup.

Pleshette was his first wife. He would marry three more times, each ending in divorce. At the time of his death, he was living with Zheng Cao, the operatic mezzo-soprano.

Donahue, late in life, blamed Jack Warner "for destroying my film career. The bastard must have called every studio mogul in Hollywood, claiming that I was a heavy drinker and couldn't be relied on to face the camera sober. After he got done destroying my reputation, all the crap I was offered after that was pure shit. I couldn't bear to sit through one of my pictures."

1964: **Suzanne Pleshette** with **Troy Donahue** at their wedding. The marriage was brutal and short-lived.

***

As the years went by, Donahue found work in B pictures, roles not worthy of him. In 1971, he starred in the blood-gushing shocker, *Street Savior,* in which he played a creepy sadist whom some viewers, years later, claimed was evocative of the demented cult leader, Charles Manson.

In 1973, Donahue showed up onscreen in the low-budget *South Sea Massacre.* Its story line included graphic depictions of rape, brutal beatings, machete slayings, shootings, decapitations, and lots of nudity.

In October of 1968, Donahue filed for bankruptcy, losing his home and the last of his savings. He was seen in and around Manhattan, and was rumored to be sleeping (as an increasingly unwanted guest) on the couches of some of his fans.

One day, he showed up at the Astor Colonnade, in which Darwin still maintained an apartment, even though his main residence was elsewhere.

[The Astor Colonnade, on Lafayette Street in Manhattan's NoHo neighborhood, is a landmarked, interconnected line of identical Greek Revival row houses built by John Jacob Astor in the 1830s. Of the original nine homes, four—long ago subdivided into private apartments—remain.]

Here's the lurid cover art for the German-language release of **South Seas Massacre** (1974). Gratuitously violent, and verging on the sadomasochistic, it starred, as his new low, **Troy Donahue,** a former darling of Henry Willson's "stable" of morally flexible young actors.

Marketers plugged the film as "hard, realistic, barbarous, and cruel."

"At first, I didn't recognize him," Darwin said. "He sure didn't look like the leading man of Connie Stevens or Sandra Dee. He was gaunt and unshaven, telling me that he'd spent the night sleeping under a bush in Central Park."

"I invited him in, arranging a big tub bath and a shave, along with new clothes, before I fed him a big meal. He claimed he hadn't eaten in a day or two."

Darwin was hours away from a departure for Europe, as dictated by his editors at The Frommer Guides. Inconveniently his duplex in the Astor Colonnade would not be available, since his mentor, Stanley Haggart, had already announced his intention of occupying it during the shooting of some upcoming commercials for TV Graphics.

Darwin hastily improvised a solution: Ray Hadley, an actor friend of Darwin's, was on the verge of touring nationwide as part of road show. He brokered a deal to sublet Hadley's apartment, then (with Hadley's permission) transferred the keys to Donahue with enough money—despite his fear that he'd squander it on drugs and liquor—for food and expenses.

When Darwin returned from Europe a few months later, Hadley told him that Donahue had departed unexpectedly without leaving a note. He never heard from him again.

In one of the last statements Donahue ever made to a reporter, he said, "You know that you're washed up in Hollywood when nobody returns your phone calls."

His final years were marred by drunken arrests, lawsuits, and cringe-inducing magazine *exposés*.

Death came to Troy Donahue in Santa Monica on September 2, 2002, at the age of 65.

***

STAR-CROSSED LOVERS

ROBERT WAGNER & NATALIE WOOD

During their Heyday, the Only Couple
More Famous Was "Jack and Jackie"

An Explanation (or Disclaimer) from Darwin Porter

"On at least eight occasions, I encountered Robert Wagner and Natalie Wood at parties and found both of them charming and easy to talk to. I never got to know them intimately.

"In contrast, I got to know their life stories by spending years researching their tangled personal lives, hearing tantalizing stories from those who did know them well.

"I was preparing for the day when I'd write a tell-all biography of the starry pair. That day never came. My publisher was not a fan of either Wagner or Wood and discouraged me from going forth with the project."

"What follows, therefore, is an insight into the fuller, more lavish treatment that might have been. It's presented here as a preview of a biography that never was."

***

Robert Wagner was born in 1930 to German parents in Detroit. His mother was a former telephone operator, his daddy a traveling salesman for the Ford Motor Company.

The Wagners moved to Bel Air, California, in 1937, where Wagner was schooled. As a teenager, he nurtured dreams of becoming a movie star, a fantasy shared by many of his schoolmates.

He began meeting movie stars when he worked as a caddy on a golf course. Here, he met Clark Gable and Bing Crosby, following them around the golf course as their caddy. Cary Grant, for whom he also caddied, showed an extreme interest in the good-looking teenager.

When he was 19, a chance encounter with starmaker Henry Willson occurred at a cocktail lounge called the Gourmet. Willson gave Wagner his business card and asked him to call him the next day.

Two views of **Robert Wagner:** *Left* As he appeared in *Under the 12-Mile Reef* (1953) and *right:* in 2013. When he started out, there was little suggestion that he'd be around in the next century.

Their meeting went well, with Willson telling him he'd be perfect cast as "the All-American Boy Next Door."

What happened during the next few days between Willson and Wagner will remain a secret that Wagner will take to his grave. They were seen making the rounds of various clubs. This led to Wagner getting a contract from Fox paying $150 a week.

His first film for Fox involved a minor role in *The Halls of Montezuma* (1951), a World War II drama starring Richard Widmark. He impressed the older actor by telling him how much he'd admired his screen roles. That led to Wagner getting cast with Widmark again in *The Frogmen* (1951).

On location for that film, he met an equally good-looking actor named Jeffrey Hunter. The two men bonded and became good friends.

"Jeff had the most piercing eyes I've ever seen on anybody," Wagner said. "That's probably why he was called upon to play Jesus Christ. I was completely devastated by his early death in 1969. He and I got to co-star in a crime thriller, *A Kiss Before Dying* in 1956."

A break came for Wagner in the form of a brief role as a shell-shocked soldier in *With a Song in My Heart* (1952), opposite Susan Hayward. His performance generated an avalanche of fan mail for Wagner from crazed teenaged girls.

Wagner was on his way to becoming a star, as Willson had promised. He appeared with prissy Clifton Webb (as John Philip Sousa) in *Stars and Stripes Forever* (1952). The older actor became "mad about the boy," a hopeless endeavor for him.

Darwin, on many an occasion, talked to Willson about his "creation" of "Natalie and Robert."

"At times," Darwin said, "I felt that he exaggerated his involvement in their respective careers, although Natalie seemed grateful to him for making her a star."

As time went by, Robert downplayed Henry's early role in his career, seeming to distance himself from the casting couch agent.

Wagner had his first big hit in *Beneath the Twelve Mile Reef* (1953), in which he co-starred with Gilbert Roland and sexy Terry Moore. There were rumors of an affair between Wagner and Moore.

Reviews were lackluster for *Beneath the Twelve-Mile Reef*, but it was a big hit, in part because it was the third film ever to be shot in CinemaScope.

In 1933, Wagner was cast in *Titanic* (1953), a saga about the sinking of the fabled British ocean liner. The lead was assigned to Clifton Webb, who still had a crush on Wagner. But instead of Webb, Wagner turned to that film's [older than him by 23 years] female star, Barbara Stanwyck, beginning a long affair which intensified after he moved in with her.

Wagner made a Western, *Broken Lance* (1954), in which he played the son of Spencer Tracy. The older (and bisexual) Tracy developed a crush on the handsome newcomer. When he made *The Mountain* (1956), the older actor again requested Wagner to co-star as his (obviously younger) brother.

Wagner disliked his role in the epic *Prince Valiant* (1954). "With that wig," he said, "I looked like Jane Wyman."

He struggled on, at times feeling that it might be hopeless for him to become a top-tier star. "I got cast as the lead in *Stopover Tokyo* (1957). It had been offered to John Wayne. Here I was, a smiling Joe Juvenile, in this dog of a picture."

Wagner met a rising young actress, Natalie Wood, and fell in love with her, marrying her in 1957, although he still adored the older Stanwyck. Nonetheless, he opted to leave her in favor of his new and younger love object, with whom he would forever be associated. Soonafter, MGM teamed "Wagner and Wood" in *All the Fine Young Cannibals* (1960).

The nuances of their love affair would fill a book, as indeed it did. They divorced in 1962 but a decade later, they remarried. In the meantime, he had met and married Marion Marshall, an actress with whom he produced a daughter.

In the aftermath of Natalie Wood's death, in 1990, Wagner married the actress Jill St. John. It was his longest-lasting union. He had known her since the 1950s, and they had been cast together in *How I Spent My Summer Vacation* (1966), a made-for-television film.

Wagner eventually became better known for his television roles than for his movies, which seemed increasingly lackluster as time marched on. As for film roles, he made "the mistake of my life" when he rejected the role of James Bond as offered by producer Albert Broccoli.

Wagner made his TV debut in *It Takes a Thief* (1968-1970) for ABC. His television career was at its peak when he starred in *The Switch* (1975-1978) on CBS-TV opposite Eddie Albert, who became his lifelong friend.

Following in the footsteps of Elizabeth Taylor and Paul Newman, Wagner and Wood starred together in a 1976 made-for-TV production of Tennessee Williams' *Cat on a Hot Tin Roof*. Laurence Olivier was cast as Big Daddy.

Wagner's third hit TV series was *Hart to Hart*, co-starring Stefanie Powers and telecast on ABC-TV from 1979 to 1984. He also starred opposite Audrey Hepburn in *Love Among Thieves* (1987), another made-for-TV movie.

His final role was as President John Garfield in

Robert Wagner, blowing his horn as a rookie under the tutelege of the bandmaster played by his mentor, Clifton Webb (who developed a crush on him again, and again, and again...) in *Stars and Stripes Forever* (1952)

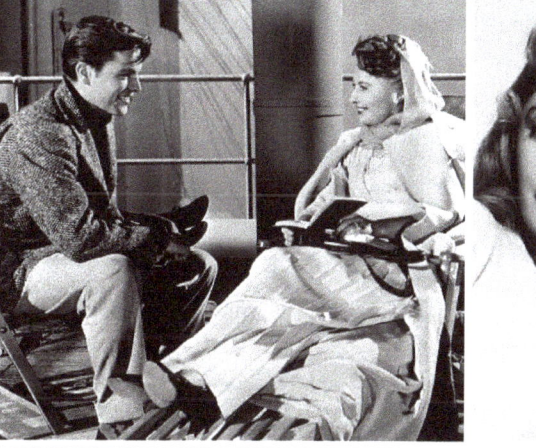

Mentoring (and falling in love with) a Younger Man

Two views of **"Bloody Babs" Stanwyck,** *left photo*, as she appeared with **Robert Wagner** in *Titanic* (1953) when he claimed to have "first fallen in love with her."

In the *right photo*, **Stanwyck** as she starred in that *film noir* classic, ***Double Indemnity*** (1944).

the comedy/horror flick, *Netherbeast Incorporated* (2007).

In his memoirs, Wagner admitted to affairs with Elizabeth Taylor, Anita Ekberg, Shirley Anne Field, Yvonne De Carlo, Lori Nelson, Joan Collins, and the man-devouring Joan Crawford.

To that glittery array might be added Linda Christian, Mona Freeman, Terry Moore, Jean Peters (his co-star in *Broken Lance;* 1954), Stephanie Powers, Debbie Reynolds, Tina Sinatra, Lana Turner, and Susan Zanuck, whose father was the head of Fox.

Throughout his career, Wagner was rumored to have homosexual affairs, but data on that is lacking. He always identified himself as straight. However, Lana Wood, an outspoken sister of Natalie, alleged that Natalie had caught her then-husband making love to another man, an event that led to their first divorce.

Summing up his love affairs, he said, "My life with Natalie never really ended. It was just interrupted. We had each other in our youth, and now we have each other in our prime."

Robert Wagner with **Natalie Wood** in 1972 at the Dorchester Hotel in London. Love is so much better the second time around.

***

At a Hollywood party, a slightly intoxicated Natalie Wood amused a group of guests who included Darwin Porter, Roddy McDowall, Tony Curtis, Celeste Holm, and Arlene Dahl. She was recalling how Henry Willson helped her transition from a child star into a teenaged siren.

"He didn't put me on his fabled casting couch like he did dozens of hopeful actors. I wasn't his type. I don't know if he put my darling husband, Robert Wagner, on that couch. I know for a fact that he drained Rock Hudson dry when he discovered him as a truck driver."

"When I worked with Jimmy Dean on *Rebel Without a Cause* (1955)," she continued, "he claimed that Henry went after him bigtime, but Jimmy escaped his clutches. He told me, 'I detested the ugly son of a bitch.'"

"There was never any pretense," Darwin said, "about Natalie. She spoke her mind about the peaks and valleys of a movie star life."

James Dean with **Natalie Wood** in *Rebel Without a Cause.* Live fast, die young.

"Half the time, I didn't know who I was," she claimed. "I was whoever they wanted me to be. 'They' being agents, producers, directors, or whomever I was trying to please at the time."

Natalie (1938-1981) was born in San Francisco to parents who were of Russian and Ukrainian descent. Her mother, whom Natalie nicknamed "Mud," always claimed, perhaps falsely, that she was descended from the Romanov dynasty.

Her father was a carpenter. Her parents married in February of 1938, five months before the birth of their daughter.

"God created the future Natalie Wood, but I was the one who invented her," Mud claimed. "The first time I looked into the eyes of my newborn, I saw them glittering with stardust. I just knew at that moment that I was looking at the newly emerged face from my womb that would one day, sooner than later, become a world famous movie star. I knew that even when I changed her shitty diapers."

Starlet **Natalie Wood** *(right)* with her mother, **Maria Zaklhjarenko** (aka **Maria Gurdin**). Nicknamed "Mud," she was a stage mother from hell.

Mud's words were prophetic. At the age of four, Natalie, whose birth name was Natalia Nikolaevna Zakharenko, was cast in *The Moon Is Down,* based on the John Steinbeck novel of the same name. A series of bit parts awaited her until, at the age of seven, she was cast as a post-World-War II German orphan in *Tomorrow is Forever* (1946). Its adult stars were Orson Welles and Claudette Colbert.

One scene called for her to cry on cue, and Mud saw that her daughter would, indeed, pull that off successfully. Natalie adored butterflies and was thrilled to watch them fly through the air with their beautiful wings. Mud brought some of them, alive, to the set. There, young Natalie watched, horrified, as Mud plucked off their wings. The brutality of that act caused her to cry, on camera, and on schedule.

As a child actress, Natalie faced her big break when cast in that classic Christmas movie, *Miracle on 34th Street* (1947), starring Maureen O'Hara and John Payne. Natalie played a cynical little girl who comes to believe that a kindly department store holiday season employee portrayed by Edmund Gwenn is the real Santa Claus.

Child actress **Natalie Wood** in *Miracle on 34th Street* (1947). "Move over, Margaret O'Brien."

One role followed another as she competed with Margaret O'Brien for the title of best child actress in Hollywood. In roles to come, she worked with such stars as Fred MacMurray, James Stewart, Joan Blondell, and Bette Davis during their filming together of *The Star* (1952).

At last, Natalie went from pigtails to roles suitable for a teenaged *ingénue*. At the age of 16, she co-starred with James Dean and Sal Mineo in *Rebel Without a Cause* (1955), a Nicholas Ray film that focused on teenage alienation. She was nominated for an Oscar as Best Supporting Actress, losing to Jo Van Fleet for her performance in *East of Eden* as the long-absent mother of the character played by Dean, morphed into the shrewd manager of a local whorehouse.

Natalie was not a virgin at the time. Mud had seen to that. She began dating fellow actor Nick Adams when she was only 14. Mud asked the young man if he would teach her daughter "the ways of the world."

"I wanted him to be the first to deflower my daughter because I trusted him to be gentle. Many men are brutal to teenage girls, some of whom in the old country were taken as brides at the age of 13."

***

Playwright William Inge had developed a powerful crush on the rising young actor named Warren Beatty. Darwin's best friend, the novelist James Leo Herlihy, had written a novel entitled *All Fall Down*. Inge adapted it for the screen in a production that starred Beatty with Angela Lansbury, Eva Marie Saint, and Karl Malden.

According to Darwin, "Self-absorption, rebellion against convention, narcissism—all these qualities joined with Beatty's own psyche and enabled him to summon up a passable performance."

In Key West, Darwin and Herlihy visited the set of *All Fall Down* during filming, and that became Darwin's first meeting with the soon-to-be-world-famous movie star, whom he would write about frequently in the future.

Beatty, along with his sister, Shirley MacClaine, became fodder for a future brother/sister bio that Darwin contemplated for decades but never got to write because of conflicting contracts.

The sexual brutality that Mud feared for her daughter actually came true when she was only 16. Suzanne Finstad's 2001 biography of Natalie alleged that the girl was brutally raped by one of the most famous actors at the time in Hollywood. She did not name the assailant.

"This married man tricked Natalie into coming to his room to act out a scene in an upcoming picture, a sort of private screen test, as he promised. However, when she got there, he ripped off her dress, held her down, and raped her."

Before that awful afternoon, he'd been a screen favorite of hers. After that, she could not bear even mentioning his name. To the public at large, his identity remained an awful secret."

In July of 2018, Natalie's sister, Ana, asserted that that brutal assault occurred at the Château Marmont "and went on for hours. He was insatiable."

It wasn't until 2020 that the name of the rapist movie star was revealed. In a memoir, Lana Wood revealed that the assailant was Kirk Douglas.

Darwin was a close friend (and former landlord) of Inge. After adapting James Herlihy's novel *All Fall Down* into a screenplay for Warren Beatty, the older playwright went on to craft another (also aimed at Beatty) entitled *Splendor in the Grass* (1962).

The director of *Splendor in the Grass* was Elia Kazan. It starred Beatty with Natalie Wood. "It was obvious that Inge had fallen for Warren," Darwin said. "It was so hopeless that I felt sorry for him. Inge was a shy, chubby, middle-aged Midwesterner with thinning hair. He looked like a god damn insurance salesman in an ill-fitting suit that needed to be sent to the cleaners. Even so, he became Beatty's endlessly forgiving 'fairy godmother.' Beatty was kind

Nick Adams as the star of the ABC-TC Western series *The Rebel* (1959-1961). After de-flowering Natalie Wood, at the request of her mother, he was mysteriously murdered, probably in conjunction with attempts to blackmail Elvis Presley.

Two manifestations of the book and film project that made waves when they happened: *Left photo*: the cover of a novel by Darwin Porter's close friend, **James Leo Herlihy**; and *right photo*, a poster for its film adaptation starring **Warren Beatty**

Who adapted Herlihy's novel into a screenplay? It was **William Inge**, then one of the leading playwrights in America, who crafted the screenplay specifically for "the object of his affection," Warren himself.

Kirk Douglas in one of his most memorable roles. Years later, it was revealed he was the actor who raped a teenage Natalie Wood.

to Inge, but that was all. He soon moved on to greater glory, leaving the lovesick playwright 'in the dust' without any of the splendor."

Natalie's first marriage to Robert Wagner was coming to an end when she began her torrid romance with Beatty.

Splendor revived Natalie's sagging career.

Natalie Wood with Warren Beatty in the film adaptation of William Inge's *Splendor in the Grass* (1962). The playwright fell hopelessly in love with Beatty. So did Natalie.

***

Natalie's affair with Beatty, the great womanizer of Hollywood, ended on a cruel note. He'd invited her for dinner at the chic restaurant, Chasen's, which had a heavy patronage of movie stars.

After the first course was served, Beatty rose from the table and excused himself for a visit to the men's toilet. *En route*, he met a blonde and beautiful cloakroom attendant. He invited her to abandon her post and to disappear with him into the night.

Alone at table Natalie waited and waited for his return. Eventually, she was informed that he had left the building and was handed the check.

She would endure another encounter with Beatty, by then, her ex-lover. She pleaded with him to use his influence to get her cast as his co-star in the upcoming crime drama *Bonnie and Clyde* (1967). He rejected her, preferring Jane Fonda. When Fonda was offered (and rejected) the role, it went to Faye Dunaway.

After losing the part, Natalie was despondent, claiming, "I don't want to live anymore." That night, she overdosed on sleeping pills. Her unresponsive body was discovered by an employee in her household and rushed, just in time, to the hospital.

***

In addition to Wagner and Beatty, Natalie, throughout her life, didn't lack for lovers. She even managed to seduce two gay actors, Tab Hunter and Raymond Burr of *Perry Mason* TV fame.

One of her biggest conquests was Elvis Presley. ("He was a lousy lover.")

Director Nicholas Ray seduced her, as did Dennis Hopper and James Dean.

Heavy-hung John Ireland also seduced her ("too big"), as did Audie Murphy ("He might have been a World War II hero, but not for his achievements in bed.")

Frank Sinatra was added to her list when they co-starred in *Kings Go Forth* (1958). She even had an affair with Jerry Brown, the governor of California.

FBI agent Donald C. Wilson claimed in 2015 that he had a four-year affair on and off with her that began in 1973.

Between her two marriages to Wagner, she wed Richard Gregson, the British producer and agent. He had little to say about the union: "She was very unwilling to be told that she was wrong about anything."

Her reaction to Gregson after she divorced him? "I've had better, lots and lots of better."

When researching his tell-all bio of actor *Steve McQueen—King of Cool, Tales of a Lurid Life*—Darwin learned of the actor's affair with Natalie. They came together when they co-starred in *Love With a Proper Stranger* in 1963.

"It wasn't at all memorable," McQueen later said. "There were certain things, which I want done, that she wouldn't do. Give me Ann-Margret, Sharon Tate, or Lee Remick any day."

One of Natalie's all-time hits was *West Side Story* (1961) in which she played a restless Puerto Rican girl on the West Side of Manhattan. It was based on the stage musical of Jerome Robbins and Robert Wise. Critics hailed it as a modern version of *Romeo and Juliet*. Her singing voice in the movie was dubbed by Marni Nixon.

Another big hit for Natalie was *Gypsy* (1962), based on the life of Gypsy Rose Lee, America's most famous stripper. Rosalind Russell played her domineering mother.

At the time, many critics rated Natalie as one of the three greatest box office stars

Left to right: Natalie Wood in her not-particularly-successful screen dynamic with Steve McQueen; Steve McQueen as *Bullitt*; and the front cover of Darwin Porter's brutally frank biography, *Steve McQueen, King of Cool, Tales of a Lurid Life*.

in Hollywood, ranking up there with Elizabeth Taylor and Audrey Hepburn.

With Robert Redford as her co-star, Natalie made two movies with him: *Inside Daisy Clover* (1965), in which he played a homosexual; and *This Property is Condemned* (1966), based on a play by Tennessee Williams.

That same year, she showed what a good sport she was by showing up to accept the Harvard Lampoon Award for being "The Worst Actress of Last Year, This Year, and Next Year."

After a three-year hiatus from films, Natalie returned to film the controversial *Bob & Carol & Ted &Alice* in 1969, a comedy about sexual liberation. It was a signature film of Paul Mazursky and became both a critical and commercial success, the sixth highest-grossing film of 1969.

Turning to television, Natalie had success in the 1979 remake of the classic *From Here to Eternity*, co-starring with Kim Basinger and William Devante.

Critics have suggested that Natalie's film career evokes a portrait of modern American women in transition, as she was one of the few to take on both child and middle-aged characters.

An extra-marital, Esalen-inspired romp, starring *(left to right)* **Elliott Gould, Natalie Wood, Robert Culp,** and **Dyan Cannon.**

As an answer to the sexual revolution of the 60s and 70s, **Bob & Carol & Ted & Alice**, released in 1969, was a smashing success, winning four Academy Award nominations.

NATALIE WOOD vs. JAMES DEAN

Darwin Porter had long been an avid fan of James Dean. As a teenager in 1952, during a visit to New York, his stepfather (by then divorced from his mother) had taken him to watch *See the Jaguar* at the Cort Theatre. Together, they attended, on its third night, a play that ran for only five performances. It co-starred Arthur Kennedy

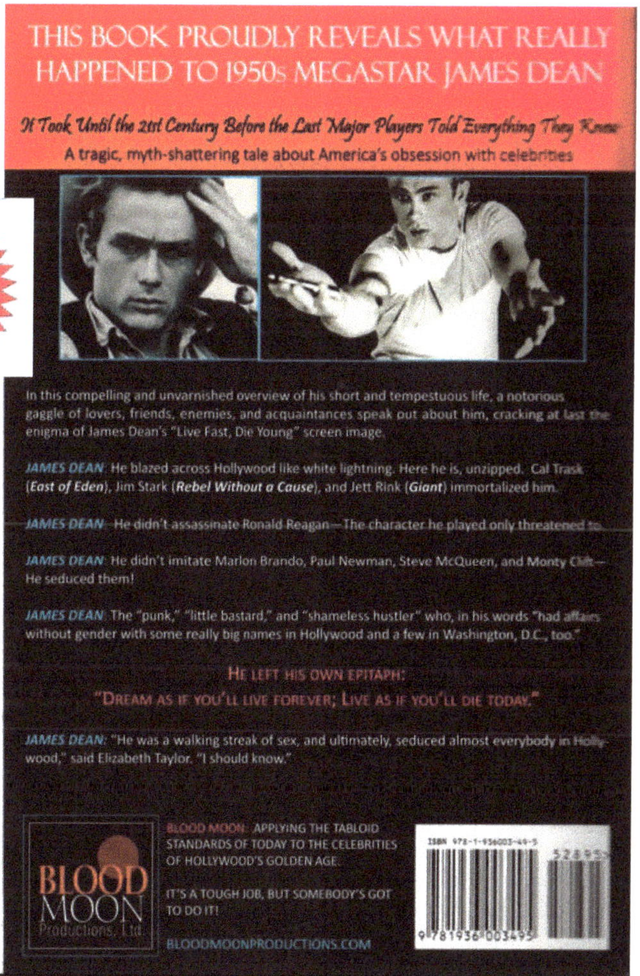

Since childhood, **Darwin Porter** was, to some degree, and in his own words, "obsessed" with the legacy of **James Dean.** At least some of this special feature on Natalie Wood derives from information that appeared within his 2016 biography of the mighty *Rebel Without a Cause.*

and Constance Ford. Dean played a 17-year-old, Wally Wilkins, a tortured and captive innocent, defenseless in the face of a brutal society.

Once again, in February of 1954, at the Royale Theatre in Manhattan, Darwin saw Dean perform onstage in *The Immoralist,* based on an early 20th-Century novel by André Gide. *[Edward Saïd, a literary critic, cited it as an overview of the complicated relations between the citizens of French Algeria and colonial France.]* This time, Dean's co-stars were Geraldine Page and Louis Jourdan.

As for James Dean's movies, Darwin saw the famous trio of Dean films three times each during the respective years they were released: *East of Eden* (1954) was adapted from the novel by John Steinbeck and co-starred Julie Harris, Raymond Massey, Burl Ives, Dick Davalos, and Jo Van Fleet.

That was followed by *Rebel Without a Cause* (1955). *[It had originally been slated, in 1945, as a vehicle for Marlon Brando.]* Dean co-starred in it with Sal Mineo, Natalie Wood, and Dennis Hopper. The notorious Nick Adams had a small role in it, too. *[As it turned out, Adams would play an enormous role in Dean's short, tragic life.]*

After Dean's death, Darwin was thrilled to see Dean in *Giant* (1956), released after his fatal car crash. Directed by George Stevens, it co-starred Rock Hudson and Elizabeth Taylor, who jointly spearheaded a remarkable cast of other talented actors. Shortly before he died, Dean said, "The part I played, Jett Rink…That's me!"

At the age of 22, young Darwin resigned his position as Bureau Chief of *The Miami Herald* in Key West and relocated to Manhattan. He'd been offered the vice presidency of Haggart Associates, making him the youngest executive on Madison Avenue.

By coincidence, the men he first worked with, Rodgers Brackett, a TV producer, and Stanley Mills Haggart, an art director, had been intimate friends of the late actor. In fact, Brackett is credited as the man who discovered and seduced Dean after they met in a parking lot in Los Angeles.

Brackett later introduced Dean to Haggart, who became his friend, too. At the time, Haggart rented four side-by-side apartments, none of them interconnected, on the top floor of a building on East 74th Street in Manhattan. Each had a separate entrance opening onto a hallway and stairs leading down to the street. Haggart offered the use of one of the apartments to Dean, rent free. The aspiring actor could come and go as he pleased without encountering anyone.

In the years that followed, Darwin continued encountering people who had known Dean. He became friends with Geraldine Page, whom he met through an introduction from Tennessee Williams. Page shared memories of working with Dean onstage.

Alex Wilder, the composer, became a friend of Darwin, as he had been of Dean.

In Key West, during the film adaptation of Darwin's bestselling novel, *Butterflies in Heat,* Darwin met and befriended the actress/singer Eartha Kitt. *[She had been cast as Lola La Mour, a character that Darwin had originally crafted as a transsexual in the original novel on which the film—entitled* The Last Resort*—was based.]* Darwin spent several evenings with her, during which she relayed her own convoluted involvements with Dean.

And so it went as the years went by Darwin collected more and more data without ever getting any time off to write his James Dean epic.

Then, during Darwin's composition of the first edition of *Frommer's Los Angeles,* he met even more actors and technicians who had worked with (or interacted with) Dean. They included some who had been slated to appear in *Rebel Without a Cause* but weren't cast.

At one point, Jay Garon, owner and founder of the Garon/Brooke Agency, wanted Darwin to ghost-write the memoirs of Sal Mineo, but that actor later retreated, refusing to "come clean" about his many affairs, male and female, especially male.

It wasn't until I (Danforth Prince) began tackling the massive amounts of data that Darwin had accumulated about James Dean, that we jointly co-authored the most definitive statement ever published on the fabled actor. Entitled *James Dean, Tomorrow Never Comes,* it was released, to wide acclaim, in 2016.

Since then, three different producers have taken options on it for adaptation into a motion picture or TV series. Regrettably, all of them failed to raise enough financing.

Our biography's front cover was designed by a San Francisco-based artist named Richard Leeds. It included two photos of Dean threatening then-actor Ronald Reagan with a gun. Letters of protest came in, readers asserting that the images had been "PhotoShopped," in a darkroom. Actually, each of them was authentic replication of photos within a clip, culled from a 1954 episode ("The Dark, Dark Hour") from the General Electric Theater, whose eclectic dramas were broadcast by CBS-TV beginning in 1953. In it, the character played by then-actor Ronald Reagan (who was the host of the show) is threatened by a juvenile delinquent played by Dean.

What follows is an excerpt from *Tomorrow Never Dies.* It reveals many behind-the-scenes details about the making of *Rebel Without a Cause,* a classic *noir* still frequently streamed or broadcast on TV.

REBEL WITHOUT A CAUSE
"You're Tearing Me Apart!" Jimmy Screams, Igniting the Angst of Teenagers Everywhere

LIVE FAST, DIE YOUNG AND VIOLENTLY

The Jinxed Curse of Rebel:
Nick Adams, Sal Mineo, & Natalie Wood: "Who's Sleeping with Jimmy Tonight?"

Long before he met Jimmy, director Nicholas Ray had filmed *They Live by Night* (1949), co-starring Farley Granger and Cathy O'Donnell, a *film noir* story of teenage lovers fleeing from the law.

Since then, he had wanted to create another "youth-in-angst" saga. Originally entitled *The Blind Run*, it was later renamed *Rebel Without a Cause*.

In the late 1940s, he'd screen tested Marlon Brando for the role, but never got a green light to film a script inspired by a case study researched and written by Dr. Robert Lindner, *Rebel Without A Cause: The Hypnoanalysis Of A Criminal Psychopath*. It had been researched during Lindner's stint as a staff psychiatrist at the Federal Penitentiary in Lewisberg, Pennsylvania. Warners had acquired the film rights to Lindner's book back in 1943, but the property languished until it was reactivated in 1954, an era when juvenile delinquency was making headlines across the country.

Ray had recently directed what became one of the most notorious westerns of all time, *Johnny Guitar* (1954), co-starring Joan Crawford and Mercedes McCambridge. "I fucked Crawford and got to suck off Scott Brady, who is very well hung," Ray later told Jimmy Dean shortly after they met. "I got to see Sterling Hayden, a Viking god, in the nude, and what a whopper, but he made it clear to me he was off limits."

In his development of *Rebel Without a Cause*, Ray went through two distinguished writers, Leon Uris and Irving Shulman, rejecting each of their scripts.

Ray finally hired Stewart Stern, the cousin of Jimmy's lover, Arthur Loew, Jr. He'd written the script for Pier Angeli's debut film, *Teresa* (1951). In Stern's version of the script, seventeen-year-old Jim Stark is the new kid on the block, arriving at Dawson High, where he is immediately menaced by a tough gang.

"We get going with a bang," Ray said. "Stark gets into trouble with the cops, the girl next door snubs him, and a young homosexual develops a crush on him."

It was his screening in New York of *East of Eden* that had convinced Ray that Jimmy would make the ideal Jim Stark. He immediately got in touch with Jimmy's New York agent, Jane Deacy, and a meeting was scheduled.

The two men bonded almost from the first. Although Jimmy had already turned twenty-four, Ray thought he looked young enough to pass for a teenager.

"Jim Stark and Jimmy shared one thing in common," Ray said. "Both of them wanted to belong yet feared belonging. Dean understood the character, and Stark's conflict of violent eagerness and mistrust, the intensity of his desires, his fear, all of which could make him at times arrogant and egocentric. I felt Dean could capture the character behind all this and depict Stark's desperate vulnerability."

Ray spent two weeks in New York with Jimmy, concluding that he encapsulated many of Jim Stark's characteristics, as laid out in the script. "He was both the boy and the man, the gay and the straight, the tender and the violent."

Ray told Elia Kazan, "I lived for a while with Jimmy in that little apartment of his, cluttered with books and other junk, including a matador's cape on the wall. We went to a lot of movies. We got drunk a lot. Jimmy let me fuck him…

Rebel Without a Cause originated as a scholastic dissertation by **Dr. Robert Lindner**: the case study of a criminal and imprisoned teenage psychopath.

It was later developed into a storyline synopsis by director Nicholas Ray and subsequently adapted into the classic 1955 film starring James Dean.

Nicholas Ray had already addressed juvenile delinquency and teen-aged anguish in *They Lived by Night* (1949) starring **Cathy O'Donnell** and **Farley Granger.**

With a storyline that included bank heists, murders of police officers, and "love on the run," it prefaced the 1954 release of *Rebel Without a Cause* by six years. But unlike the version with James Dean and his "team," it bombed at the box office.

a lot. He was better than my former wife, that whore, Gloria Grahame."

"Actually, I needed Dean to help me flesh in Stark's character and bring him to life on the screen. The script had not been fully developed. I wanted Dean to probe his own experiences in life and apply them when needed."

As Ray told Kazan, who had helmed Jimmy in *East of Eden*, "You know I walk on both sides of the sidewalk. I not only screwed Jimmy in New York, and I plan to take director's privilege and keep plugging him as long as we're making *Rebel*. I'm looking forward to it."

"I'd rather fuck Marilyn Monroe, which I do," Kazan said.

After returning to Los Angeles, Jimmy hit some of the rougher streets, hanging out with alienated young men and often with their "gang molls," as he called their girlfriends. "They wore leather jackets and roamed the streets at night, looking for a faggot to beat up. Not all of them were poor. Some were from rich families. Boy, those guys scared me. One night, I got gang raped by three guys. But I'm not going to go into that." *[He made this revelation to Ray, who had already flown back to Hollywood.]*

Jimmy signed on to the film shortly before Christmas of 1954. At the time, he had serious reservations about it, interpreting it as a Grade B movie typical of the type being cranked out by producer Roger Corman.

Originally, Stern had told Jimmy that he envisioned *Rebel* "as a modern version of *Peter Pan*, three troubled kids inventing a world of their own. I want to say something about the nature of loneliness."

"I set for myself a big goal," Stern said. "Within a period of only twenty-four hours, I wanted to tell the story of a young generation coming into maturity."

Stern later said, "It was obvious to me that Jimmy did not want to play the role I wrote. He wanted to play himself."

Before shooting began, Ray asked Jimmy about his draft status. He replied, "I was rejected for bad eyes, flat feet, and butt plugging."

For his work on the film, Jimmy would receive only $12,500.

[That compared with 20th Century Fox giving Marilyn Monroe $15,000 for her co-starring role in Gentlemen Prefer Blondes *(1953).]*

[The James Dean Foundation takes in $6 million annually, including licensing agreements for such products as jogging suits, T-shirts, pillowcases, and sunglasses. In Japan, a customer can buy a life-size mannequin of Dean to take to bed for whatever pleasure one desires.]

***

Author Gore Vidal was living at the Château Marmont with his longtime companion, Howard Austen. His friend, Paul Newman, had turned him onto the place. Grace Kelly occupied one of its bungalows, as did Nicholas Ray. One Sunday, Vidal met Ray by the pool, where he introduced himself, thinking that perhaps he might buy one of the film scripts he was writing at the time.

Within thirty minutes, Vidal and Ray argued, Vidal maintaining that the scriptwriter was more vital to the film than its director. Ray responded with, "If it's all in the script, why film it?"

Despite their disagreement, Ray invited Vidal to a party that he was hosting later in his bungalow. He told Vidal that he was casting a film called *The Blind Run* about juvenile delinquents and starring James Dean.

"I've seen Dean before," Vidal said. "At the Actors Studio. He's always hanging around sucking up to Tennessee Williams, hoping he'll write another great part like he did for Brando."

Vidal attended the party with every intention of "putting the make on Dean." But it didn't work out that way. "I found him arrogant and insulting to me. What a prick he was. We hated each other on sight."

Vidal later described his negative impression of Dean to Ray: "The first thing he said to me was, 'I never heard of you.' He knew damn well who I was. I should have told him, 'I never heard of you, either, punk.'"

"Since you and Dean didn't hit it off, I'll introduce you to Dennis Hopper," Ray said. "He's just getting started as an actor. And he's available—that is, if you're not a size queen."

SEARCHING FOR JUDY
How Its Outcome Was Decided on Ray's Casting Couch

After Jimmy's casting as the male lead was finalized, Ray set about hiring the rest of the ensemble. The film's other most important role was that of Judy.

As a juvenile delinquent, she comes from a cold home and perhaps is in

Articulate, witty, caustic, brilliant, with an enemies list of genuinely scary politicians and public figures: **Gore Vidal**

love with her father, who can't stand for her to kiss him. Her character yearns for a utopian family that includes Jim and herself as central figures.

Jimmy's friend, Lew Bracker, left the impression in a memoir that starlet Lori Nelson had not made a favorable impression on Jimmy when they dated briefly. Actually, Jimmy may have been more impressed with her than Bracker thought. He recommended that Ray consider Lori for the role of Judy. His recommendation was backed up by an onslaught of letters from the Lori Nelson Fan Club, pleading with Ray to cast their favorite star as Judy.

For a very brief period, Ray considered Margaret O'Brien, the former child actress of the 1940s, for the role. As a child, she had enthralled audiences of the World War II era, eventually replacing the fast- maturing (and increasingly syrupy) Shirley Temple as America's favorite pre-adolescent. After MGM let her go after she turned twelve, she complained to the press, "The public can't accept me with a bosom."

Jimmy had seen O'Brien in only one film. When she was seven, she had played Judy Garland's sister, Tootie, in *Meet Me in St. Louis* (1944).

When Ray auditioned Margaret, he asked her what she thought of her parents. "I love them," she answered. That was not the response he wanted. "Judy is alienated from her parents," Ray said.

Jimmy told him, "I can't emote with Little Tootie. Instead of Margaret, why not Shirley Temple?" he asked sarcastically. "Seriously, perhaps you'll consider Carroll Baker."

Margaret O'Brien was out the door.

Jimmy pursued Baker, whom he knew from the Actors Studio. When she was contemplating a role in *Giant*, he approached her. "I'm going to do another film before *Giant*. The script is crap, but the characters are good. I think you'd be perfect in the female lead of Judy. The director, Nick Ray, is a good guy. I'll take you to him, I bet his tongue is hanging out at the prospect of getting you. I've already pitched you for the lead."

Baker, however, was also rejected by Ray.

Ray told Jimmy that MGM "is trying to push Debbie Reynolds onto me. I guess they don't have anything for her to do. If it's a musical, she'd have been perfect."

In reference to Reynolds, "I've met her," Jimmy said. "She's the least likely juvenile delinquent in Hollywood. Maybe you could recycle 'Abba-Daba Honeymoon.'"

[Relentlessly cheerful, and written and first recorded in 1914, "Aba-Daba Honeymoon" became a nationwide hit in 1950 when it was reprised in Two Weeks with Love *(1950) as a song-and-soft shoe dance by Debbie Reynolds, Carleton Carpenter, and a banjo-strumming ensemble of Edwardian-era singers and dancers.]*

During Nicholas Ray's casting of *Rebel's* turbulent female lead—a juvenile delinquent named Judy—other actresses auditioned and were rejected as "too goody-goody, too wholesome."

They included (top to bottom) **Lori Nelson, Margaret O'Brien,** and **Debbie Reynolds.**

The supremely talented Reynolds, who in time, proved her mettle as a bawdy *rouée* in many subsquent films, later regretted that she'd ever type-cast herself as such "a wholesome god-damned virgin."

JAYNE MANSFIELD

Jimmy Vs. the "Relentlessly Pink" Working Man's Marilyn Monroe

The next candidate for the role of Judy was Jayne Mansfield, whose widely publicized superstructure famously measured 40"-24"-36".

Jimmy said, "As Judy, she would be 'busting' out all over."

The studio was pushing Jayne onto Ray, who defined the idea of casting her as "the most outlandish suggestion of the decade."

Actually, Mansfield as Judy was not as outlandish as, in retrospect, it appears. *Rebel* had originally been conceived as a cheap and fast-produced black-and-white juvenile delinquent film of the genre so popular in the 1950s. Some of those featured Jayne's major rival at the time, Mamie Van Doren, whose quickie genre flicks later included *Untamed Youth* (1957)

As the script for *Rebel* had originally been conceived, the film would have opened with sixteen-year-old Judy being arrested for solicitation. That episode was later "tamed," rewritten to depict being disciplined at the police station for breaking curfew.

Ray was secretly dating Mansfield at the time, and over pillow talk, she was urging him to cast her as Judy.

She agreed to a screen test, but the director later confessed, "I didn't put any film in the camera. I knew at the time I was never going to use her."

Ray was also engaged at the time in "carnal adventures" with Shelley Winters, who recalled that his bungalow at the studio was "surrounded by night-blooming jasmine." Also seen coming and going from that bungalow were two other blondes, Marilyn Monroe and Judy Holliday.

When Jimmy learned that Ray was dropping Jayne, both as a girlfriend and as a candidate for the role of Judy, he said, "Wait one night before telling her. Give me her number. I want to call her and tell her that I'd like to test the chemistry between Jim Stark and Judy."

"Okay, buster," Ray responded. "But you'll owe me one. You'll get Jayne's ass, and I'll get yours."

Dubbed "The Working Man's Marilyn Monroe," Jayne seemed only too eager to welcome Jimmy into her home. She'd cleared the house of family members and servants so that she could entertain him in private.

He later reported to Ray, "As you know from banging Jayne, she's more of a cinematic sight gag than an actress, but she sure is bosomy and breathy. She *cooed* and *aaahed* her way through the night, especially when I plugged her. She greeted me at the door in an ivory-colored see-through *négligée*. She didn't walk toward me, she sashayed."

"I couldn't wait to sink my teeth into those pink nipples of hers. She served me dinner. All her décor is pink and heart-shaped. Cupids everywhere. She even dyes the mashed potatoes pink. Naturally, the drink was pink champagne."

"I detest the color pink," she told him. "But it's important for my image. Men want women pink, helpless, and to do a lot of deep breathing. When I was first told about how sex worked, I laughed and then I cried. I just couldn't see the point of it. Fortunately, I've changed."

"After our romp in her pink bed with its pink sheets, she told me that she just knew that she could play 'that trollop Judy, even though I'm a good girl.'"

"If you get the part, we'll have to change the title," he said. "Make it *Rebel With a Cause*."

"And what might that be?" she asked.

"To bang Suzi every night." *[She had already told him that she'd nicknamed her vagina Suzi.]*

After that encounter, Jimmy never saw Mansfield again and, needless to say, she didn't get the role of Judy.

"I'm Going to Marry James Dean"
—Natalie Wood

Ray might have gone for Carroll Baker had not a sixteen-year-old brunette, a ferociously competitive former child actress, entered the fray. Her name was Natalie Wood.

She had worked with Jimmy before in the teleplay, *I'm a Fool*, based on a plot by Sherwood Anderson, and more fully described in Chapter Eight of *Tomorrow Never Comes*. *I'm a Fool* was eventually broadcast in November of 1954 through television's General Electric Theater, hosted by Ronald Reagan.

After her first viewing of *East of Eden* (1955), Natalie exited from Hollywood's Egyptian Theater exclaiming to her girlfriend, "I'm going to marry that Jimmy Dean!"

"I felt an instant link to Judy," Natalie said. "I just had to take the role to express something inside of me. Up until *Rebel*, I had been a child actress, or else playing an ingénue. Judy was real, a gutsy character. The prospect of bringing her to the screen with Jimmy thrilled me."

As she admitted, she stalked Ray, trying to get the role. "Nick still saw me as a child actress in pigtails," she lamented. "I knew I had to convince him I was grown up. Actually, I was only sixteen, but I had the desires of a woman."

Live Fast, Die Young

Jayne Mansfield

The Tropicana Las Vegas launched **Jayne Mansfield's Striptease Revue** in 1958, a busty and athletic stage act that generated—in part because of her own self-deprecating humor--news coverage across the country. Lloyd's of London insured her for a million dollars in the event that she was injured as her then-husband, weightlifter **Mickey Hargitay,** whirled her around, onstage. Those stage revues, raised impressive funds for the **March of Dimes** and generated some of the biggest salaries (as much as $35,000 a week) of her career. Her wardrobe featured a gold mesh dress the press promoted as "Jayne Mansfield with a few sequins."

In an era less sensitive to body shaming and anti-feminist raunch, her breasts became lurid fodder for crude jokes nationwide. Nonetheless, her film and nightclub performances inspired films, documentaries, and a musical album entitled *Jayne Mansfield Busts Up Las Vegas* (1962). Later, she made personal appearances (drug store openings, supermarket promotions, etc.) priced at $10,000 per appearance ($105,000 in today's dollars).

Despite (or in part, because of) her gruesome death in 1967 when she was 34, she remains one of the most-remembered sex symbols in the history of Hollywood.

"Then one night, I was involved in a car accident with Dennis Hopper, who would also get cast in *Rebel*. Ever since Nick Adams, who was also cast in the picture, took my virginity, I'd been carrying on with both of them. Dennis and I had this car accident, and I was rushed to the hospital, injured."

"I ordered the nurse to call Ray at once and get his ass over here," she said. "I wanted him to see me in my condition. He looked me over. I was a wild juvenile delinquent out speeding in a car with my lover. 'Now do I get the part?' I demanded of him. He thought about it a minute, and then said, 'You are our Judy.'"

"Ray not only gave me the part," she told Jimmy. "He's also fucking me. Is there a man who doesn't desire a sixteen-year-old girl?"

She revealed, "Nick took me to a tiny candlelit restaurant where the tablecloths were pink. We drank pink champagne. Jayne Mansfield had nothing on him when it comes to pink. Incidentally, pink is my favorite color."

Years before they famously filmed *Rebel Without a Cause*, **Natalie Wood** (left) had appeared with **James Dean** in a teleplay for the General Electric Theater. It was supervised and introduced, onscreen, by Ronald Reagan.

Here, they're together in a screen shot from *I'm a Fool*, first broadcast in 1954.

"He then took me back to his suite at the Château Marmont, where he seduced me. He told me, 'I want to make love to you.' That was so romantic. Most of you young guys tell a gal, 'I want to screw you. How about it?'"

"Nick might be an old man, but some guys are still sexy after forty," she said. "And he sure knows how to deliver the goods. "He's a thirty-minute man in the saddle. Poor Dennis seems to shoot off just as he's putting it in."

Later, she would tell her friends that she and Jimmy shared some of the same men: Arthur Loew, Jr., Nick Adams, Dennis Hopper, Steve McQueen, and Lance Reventlow. She included Tab Hunter in that list as well, although in his case, despite rumors, it's unclear whether he was actually involved with Jimmy.

Jack Simmons
"The Hawk" Glides Into Jimmy's Life

A former child actor born in Los Angeles in 1935, John Gilmore, the future author, became friends with James Dean in 1952. Years later, in the *Hollywood Star,* he published an article entitled "I Had Sex With James Dean." In it, he claimed that Jimmy liked to cuddle in bed, and that he preferred oral sex. According to Gilmore, "I came to feel I was his mother, brother, and lover."

One night, Gilmore encountered Jack Simmons, a wannabe actor who would become his chief rival for the lovemaking of James Dean.

Simmons had come to Hollywood to become a movie star, or at least a screen actor. Gilmore remembered his hook nose. "Everybody called him 'The Hawk.' He had a reputation as one of the most notorious faggots of Hollywood."

The first time Gilmore met Simmons, he was dancing with Rock Hudson at a gay bar in Santa Monica, the Tropical Village, and wearing a tight-fitting pink bikini. Gilmore wrote that Simmons was "a reject, a pitiful fringe-nut in Hollywood's substratum, who captured Jimmy's interest with his unwavering, doglike devotion." Jack would later claim that Jimmy was the only love of his life."

Author Donald Spoto wrote: "For years, the Dean-Simmons friendship was the subject of considerable pornographic imagination. Both men died without uttering a word about the specifics of their relationship, and, as the old maxim runs, no one held the lamp. Most people in the social circle saw the devotion as one-sided. It was a case of the adoring Jack, the acolyte to a diffident Jimmy, who made him a kind of hip valet."

Simmons is one of the most mysterious figures in the life of James Dean. The character of Plato in *Rebel* was said to have been based on him.

He hailed from Philadelphia and was 20 when he arrived in Hollywood. In December of 1954, he met Dean in a bar. Dean invited him back to the apartment where he'd been living for several months.

Dean went on to get him a role in an episode of *General Electric Theater*

Two views of actor/author **John Gilmore**, *left photo*, in 1961, *right photo*, from around the time he published **"I Had Sex With James Dean."**

entitled "The Dark, Dark Hour." Together, they appeared as foils to the character played by Ronald Reagan.

Faye Nuell Mayo, Natalie's stand-in on *Rebel*, claimed, "Simmons adored Jimmy, but how seriously Jimmy took him was really unclear to everybody."

Simmons was the best friend of Maila Nurmi (Vampira), and it had been through her that he had met Jimmy.

Biographer Paul Alexander wrote: "When Jimmy returned to Hollywood, he and Jack Simmons became romantically involved. More than likely, it was Jack who made himself available to Jimmy, for he had seen pictures of Jimmy in the newspapers and had gone to see *East of Eden*."

Jack told friends that he was going to pursue Jimmy, get him, then spend the rest of his life doing whatever Jimmy wanted him to do. Based on events that later unfolded, only the first two parts of Jack's plan came true.

Jimmy told William Bast that when they first met, he considered Simmons "a pest. He wants to have sex with me, but I keep turning him down. I'm not remotely attracted to the kid sexually. He keeps telling everybody that sooner or later, he's going to kiss me."

Simmons did not take Jimmy's rejection as his final word. He remained undaunted in his pursuit.

Jack Simmons *(left)* with **James Dean** on the set of *Rebel Without a Cause*.

Vampira learned and later talked about the intimate details of their relationship: "When Jimmy found out that Jack imposed no limits on what he would do sexually, Jimmy reappraised him. They had a lot of sex. Jack told me about it. But it wasn't the usual kind of sex."

"With Jack, Jimmy began to live out his darker fantasies. He was very abusive to Jack and put him through all sorts of hideous, disgusting scenes, things no human should do to another. And Jack took it."

"I don't want to go into the graphics, but surely, you can use your imagination. Bondage was the more vanilla stuff Jack went through."

Jimmy got Ray to agree to a screen test that would include Simmons and himself as a means of evaluating Simmons' suitability as Plato. It was a disaster.

Its venue was the stage set for *A Streetcar Named Desire*, which had not yet been dismantled. The stairway to the Kowalski apartment in New Orleans was still there. Jimmy couldn't resist running up those steps, bellowing like Brando did in both the stage and movie versions, "*STELLA-A-A-A-A!*"

"I couldn't believe what happened next," Ray said. "Suddenly, Simmons followed Jimmy up the steps, and the two men disappeared behind a screen. We heard them giggling, followed by two golden streams of urine raining down from one of the flat's windows. It turned out these jokers were having a pissing contest to see which stream could reach the greatest height. Jimmy said he won the contest, but how would I know?"

He later told Ray, "Jack was nervous, and I figured pissing might relax him before the test."

"The boy just couldn't act," Ray said. "But he was a real pisser."

Ray rejected Simmons for the role of Plato. According to Stewart Stern, "In my script, I wanted to present Jim Stark and Plato in gay overtones. But Simmons was a bit much. It would have made Plato's relationship with Jim Stark too obvious, just too much."

After Simmons was rejected as Plato, Jimmy managed to get him cast as Moose, one of the gang members.

During the filming of *Rebel*, Simmons lived with Jimmy at his apartment on Sunset Plaza Drive.

Although Simmons was absolutely devoted to and committed to Jimmy, he finally dropped him altogether.

Columnist Sidney Skolsky wrote: "Wherever Jimmy goes, Simmons was sure to follow. If Jimmy wants coffee, he gets it. A sandwich, Simmons gets it. He also runs interference for Jimmy, keeping people away if Jimmy doesn't want to see them."

Decades later, Simmons would break down and sob at the mention of Jimmy's name. He claimed that he had not only lost his "one true love," but his soul as well.

Goth and Scream Queen **Maila Nurmi** (aka **Vampira**) as she appeared on the cover of the July 17, 1954 edition of *TV Guide*.

In 1944, she'd been fired by Mae West from the cast of West's Broadway play, *Catherine Was Great*, because West feared she was being upstaged.

Sal Mineo
Makes Pornographic Love to Jimmy in Full View of Nick Ray as a Demonstration of their Onscreen Chemistry

More than Best Buddies

James Dean with **Sal Mineo** in a publicity photo from *Rebel Without a Cause*.

For weeks, Sal Mineo, in avid pursuit of the role of Plato, had pursued Ray.

Mineo was the veteran of two Broadway shows, including *The King and I* (during the course of which Yul Brynner had molested him backstage) and Tennessee Williams' *The Rose Tattoo*. Despite his status as a fifteen-year-old, he was nonetheless fully immersed in homosexuality. "I matured early in the Bronx, especially one part of me."

At the time, he was already a film industry veteran, having appeared in two movies, *Six Bridges to Cross*, and *The Private War of Major Benson*, both released in 1955.

Ray kept rejecting him as Plato, claiming, "I don't see any possible chemistry between you and Dean."

But finally, he relented, inviting both Jimmy and Mineo to his lodgings at the Château Marmont.

Mineo arrived wearing pegged pants, a skinny tie, and a jacket. Jimmy showed up in jeans and a T-shirt. "They were from different planets," Ray said.

Mineo later revealed what happened that late Sunday afternoon.

"At first, Jimmy and I were awkward, and I gave a bad first reading of the script. Perhaps Ray was right: We had no sexual chemistry. But I was determined to play Plato, and begged for a chance to do it over. Ray tried to get us to relax with each other. Instead of reading the script, we were told to improvise."

"Suddenly, Jimmy and I were talking to each other, and he was fascinated to learn I'd been a street kid from the Bronx. We relaxed—and how! He even started to wrestle me, which ended up in a long, passionate kiss. We stripped down to our underwear and continued to wrestle some more until both of us got erections. Off came our panties."

"Right in front of Ray, I came on to Jimmy like gangbusters. Ray was all eyes. Jimmy and I really went at it. When I looked over at our director, he'd whipped it out and was jerking off. I got the role of Plato, and I later got Ray. But by then, I was already in love with Jimmy."

Something happened during the making of *Rebel*, Mineo said. "It was as close as you could get to a spiritual experience. Jimmy was the focus of all of it. Everything that happened was a result of his presence."

During the first week of his involvement with *Rebel*, Jimmy told Mineo that he couldn't sleep and that he was overcome with a nervous anxiety. He went to three sessions with a psychiatrist. "This headshrinker told me to love my father. What a stupid assignment! I could have told him that fifteen years ago. The fucker should have tried to love my father himself."

"Whatever's inside me makes me what I am. Cut me open and take it out, and let in the light, and it might kill my acting talent. Tennessee Williams calls it 'creative malady.' Sometimes, it's the wackos who create the greatest art. Make them normal, and they may lose that neurosis that drives them to create in the first place."

Natalie's double on *Rebel*, Faye Nuell Mayo, also became aware of Jimmy's anxiety, and she thought she knew what might help to relieve his tension. She invited him to attend a class where Kenpō karate was taught.

He attended only one class and didn't like it. He told her, "Instead of a karate chop, I prefer to stick to my own kind of fighting. A finger with a sharp nail in the eyeball, and a castrating kick in the balls."

REBELLIOUS CASTING ISSUES

A Henpecked Husband, A Domineering Tarantula of a Mother, A Cardboard 1950 Sitcom Mom, & an Incestuous Father

After players for *Rebel's* three leading characters had been cast, Ray set about hiring actors for the secondary roles, including Jim Backus and Marsha Hunt.

[Marsha Hunt, hailing from Chicago, was known as "Hollywood's most unfortunate also-rans." Attractive, and with alluring eyes, she spent most of her career under contract for MGM, making B-list pictures, or as a supporting player in such movies as Pride and Prejudice *(1940) playing one of Greer Garson's sisters.*

Regrettably, during the early 1950s, she came under fire from Senator Joseph McCarthy, who claimed she was a com-

munist. When Ray cast her in 1955, she had not worked in three years because of her inclusion on the Red Channels list.

When she arrived on the set of Rebel, *she announced to Jimmy, "Here's what's left of Marsha Hunt after all those witch hunters in Washington finished with me."*

Ray, also a champion of left-wing positions, wanted her for the role of Jim Stark's henpecking mother until a phone call came in from Jack Warner, asking him to get rid of her and to cast Ann Doran instead.]

***

Marsha Hunt, a successful fashion model and a respected actress, appears on the cover of the March 6, 1950, edition of *Life* magazine for her performance on Broadway in *The Devil's Disciple*.

She was the first pick for the role of James Dean's domineering mother in ***Rebel Without a Cause***, until she was blacklisted during Joseph McCarthy's anti-Communist Witch Hunt.

Doran, once marketed as "The Yellow Rose of Amarillo, Texas," was cast as Jimmy's domineering mother. As a hard-core shrew and a major league emotional blackmailer, her character reminds Jim Stark that, "I almost died giving birth to you."

[In time, Doran, a genuine Hollywood workhorse, would appear in some five-hundred motion pictures.]

In an unlikely friendship, Jimmy bonded with her, although she claimed that he almost killed her after they'd first met. He had invited her for a ride on his motorcycle.

Jim Backus, cast as Jim Stark's father, warned her, "Jimmy Dean is opinionated, and he'll tell you how to act."

"Just let him try it!" she responded.

Backus was right. After his first rehearsal with Doran, Jimmy attempted to tell her how to play it.

"Listen, junior," she said, icily. "I've been around a long time, and you're new. Don't tell me how to do it. Let me make my own mistakes."

Despite their early confrontation, the two actors bonded, and soon he was referring to her as "Mom."

In her place was cast **Ann Doran,** who played **James Dean's** devouring mother in the age of "Momism" with deft (and devastating) destructiveness.

Prior to his casting as Jimmy's henpecked screen father, Jim Backus, beginning in 1949, had been known mainly as the voice of the cartoon character, "Mr. Magoo." Later, he was indelibly associated with his characterization of a wealthy, out-of-his-depth eccentric, Thurston Howell III, on the widely syndicated TV sitcom, *Gilligan's Island* (1964-1967)

He was astonished to see Jimmy directing the picture. "Never in the history of motion pictures had an inexperienced 24-year-old become, in essence, a co-director, especially with one as established as Nicholas Ray. He gave Jimmy full reign."

Judy's parents were to be played by William Hopper and Rochelle Hudson. Hopper had appeared in more than 80 feature films during the 1930s and 1940s, although he'd obtained his greatest fame as Paul Drake to Raymond Burr's *Perry Mason* in a TV series (1957-1966). Although married, Hopper pursed a closeted homosexual lifestyle. Stanley Haggart, Jimmy's friend, had known Hopper back in the 1930s.

"Bill appeared in more than ten films with Ronald Reagan," Haggart said. "He had a big crush on Reagan, but apparently, he never scored, even though they shared a bedroom together on location. He got to see Reagan in the nude—and that's about it."

"Alas," Hopper said. "Ronnie was saving it for Lana Turner or Susan Hayward."

In *Rebel*, Rochelle Hudson was hired to portray Natalie Wood's mother. A star in the 1930s, she'd begun making pictures when she was sixteen as an attractive ingénue. She'd already appeared in such films as *She Done Him Wrong* (1933) with Mae West and Cary Grant, and she had starred as Claudette Colbert's daughter in *Imitation of Life* (1934). Jimmy knew nothing of her movie career but wanted to hear about her espionage work for Naval intelligence when she was stationed in Central America during World War II.

For Hudson, a woman who'd starred in major movies, her role in *Rebel* wasn't much. One reviewer noted, "She is nothing but a cardboard cutout of a

Jim Backus, Dean's hapless father in *Rebel*, went on to sitcom success as Thurston Howell II in *Gilligan's Island*, a CBS sitcom that ran for three seasons (1964-1967) and whose reruns reached vast daytime audiences in the 70s and 80s. He appears here with **Natalie Schafer,** his pointlessly glam TV wife, one of the funniest characters on TV.

1950s sitcom mom."

As juvenile delinquents, Ray rounded up a cast that included Corey Allen, Beverly Long, Frank Mazzola, Steffi Sidney, Jack Simmons, and Dennis Hopper.

For a while, Steffi Sidney held out the hope that she might be cast as Judy. However, Ray decided instead to give her the lesser role of Millie, one of the "gang molls." Steffi was the daughter of the famous Hollywood columnist Sidney Skolsky, who had written extensively about Jimmy. His "office" was Schwab's Drugstore, where Jimmy often hung out.

According to Steffi, "My character always carried a hairbrush with her, and I was a very insecure girl who desperately wanted to belong to the gang."

Some of the other cast members resented her, charging nepotism, claiming that Steffi got the part only because of her influential father. The same charge was leveled against William Hopper, son of Hedda Hopper, who was cast as Natalie's angry father.

Steffi was disappointed with Rebel's final cut. "My scenes were eliminated. I was left with one line and a sneeze."

She said that the first time she saw Jimmy, which was during a wardrobe test, "He came up to me, and he just swaggered, and then he hit me real hard. I thought, 'Why in hell did he do that to me?' The next time he wandered over, I said, 'What, you're not going to hit me again?' He said, 'No, no, my name is Jimmy Dean.'"

More than a Bromance:
DENNIS HOPPER

Dennis Hopper in 1973. Rebelliousness as an (oft-repeated) art form. His big dream was "to become the next James Dean."

Of all the gang members, only Dennis Hopper was being groomed for stardom at Warners. "I tried to get to know Jimmy. I started by saying 'hello.' No answer. He wouldn't talk to people on the set. He would go into his dressing room. He would be into himself, into his thing. He'd lock himself away."

"Finally, about halfway through filming, during a break in the nighttime filming of 'the chickie run' scene, I grabbed him and threw him into the car. I said, 'Look, I want to be an actor, too, and I wanna know what you're doing, what your secret is.'"

Dennis uttered those words in a documentary released in *James Dean: The First American Teenager* (1976). After that interchange, the ice was broken, and they became intimate friends.

Cast as "Goon," Dennis was four years younger than Jimmy and looked even younger. Like Jimmy, he had grown up in the Middle West, in his case, Kansas. He told Jimmy, "When I was a kid, I used to get off sniffing gasoline from my grandfather's truck."

"There will never be another man like Dean," Dennis said after his friend died. "In a strange way, I had a closer friendship with him than most men have with each other. It wasn't the kind of friendship where you say, 'Let's go out and tear up the town.' Sometimes, we'd just have a quiet dinner together and share our darkest secrets. Also, Jimmy and I were into peyote and grass before anybody else caught on."

"I was with him almost every day for the last eight months of his life," Hopper claimed. "I was haunted by his death, which had been the greatest emotional shock of my life. When he died, I felt cheated. I had my dreams tied up with him. His death blew my mind."

When pressed about whether his relationship with Jimmy turned sexual, he said, "What in the fuck do you think? How much do I have to spell it out? Do you want a blow-by-blow description?"

Movie historian David Thomson wrote, "Dennis Hopper was an ardent young man fatally unlucky to cross the path of James Dean—in *Rebel Without a Cause* and *Giant*. He believed he was the heir to something. He knew he wanted to act, and he believed that rebellion was some proof of his artistic integrity. Much of Hollywood found Hopper a pain in the ass, strident, staring, and monotonous."

***

Corey Allen was cast as the gang's leader, "Buzz," who tangles with Jimmy in an ego-driven conflict that ends in a knife fight.

He claimed, "I was twenty, inexperienced, and I had a very high kind of voice. I felt unmasculine. I was awed to be working with Jimmy after seeing him in *East of Eden*. When I met him, we got off on a bad start. I came up to him where he was sitting, surrounded by a bunch of kids fawning over him. I told him I was going to be his adversary in *Rebel*. Without looking up, he said, 'Yeah, hi.' And then he turned back to chatting with those adoring kids."

Three years younger than Jimmy, Allen bore an amazing resemblance to a young Marlon Brando. "On the second day, when Jimmy talked to me and looked at me, I felt that instead of indifference, he was really turned on by me. He felt I looked like either Brando's son or else his younger brother. He brought that up time and time again."

Ray warned Allen not to get carried away and to try to imitate Jimmy's style.

To that, Allen responded, "Jimmy was like a kind of black hole, with magnetism so great that nothing can go in the other direction."

Ray recruited a real, "from the streets" gang leader, Frank Mazzola, to play "Crunch," a member of the gang in *Rebel*. As a child, he had worked on the Bogie film, *Casablanca*. At Hollywood High, he'd led the Athenians, the most infamous gang in the city.

"Our major activity was strolling the streets at night, trying to pick a fight with some punk," he said. "We were real tough guys, football players, boxers. One time, I punched this guy and threw him out of a second-story window. He survived, with a few broken bones."

"I played the right-hand man to Buzz, the leader of the pack, but I should have been the Big Cheese."

Mazzola got to know Jimmy and even took him shopping to show him how a contemporary teenager dressed. "Jimmy was allowed to attend secret meetings of the Athenians. Sometimes he'd spar with me, but mostly we just hung out. He was a good basketball player."

Beverly Long had been in the Pepsi Cola commercial that's acknowledged today as Jimmy's first appearance on TV, and was said to have dated him for a while.

Long was cast as Helen, a tough, pony-tailed blonde bimbo.

"You never knew what Jimmy's attitude would be," she said. "In the morning, he might speak to you, then again, he might not. He could look right through you like you didn't exist."

"I was easy prey for his off-color jokes. One time, in one scene, while he was repairing a slit tire that Buzz had slashed, Dean handed me the tire iron. 'Ever felt a thing so hard in your life?' he asked me. He could twist and turn anything into an off-color joke."

Dennis said, "Jimmy captured the moment of youth, that moment where we're desperately trying to find ourselves."

Mineo went a step farther: "Jimmy started the youth movement."

"Me Tarzan, You Jimmy"
—Johnny Weissmuller

Two weeks before actual shooting began on *Rebel*, Jimmy mysteriously disappeared. There were rumors that he'd been kidnapped by a gang of gay bikers, and that they were repeatedly sodomizing him at some remote desert outpost.

Jack Warner phoned Jimmy's West Coast agent, Dick Clayton, threatening him. "If that bastard kid doesn't show up in the next forty-eight hours, I'm firing him from the picture and replacing him with Robert Wagner, if he's available. If he's not, then maybe John Kerr."

Thinking he might not return, Ray considered recasting Dennis Hopper as Jim Stark.

"It would have been my first big break," Dennis reflected, years later. "Alas, it was not meant to be. Thank god that *Easy Rider* later came along."

Jimmy's mystery trip out of Hollywood may have had something to do with a casual chat he'd had with Stewart Stern, who was still revising the script. He wanted to signal to the world that Plato was gay, but not in any obvious way that would incite censors to cut it.

He came up with the idea of Plato opening his locker at school. Inside their own lockers, the other boys often attached publicity photographs of their favorite pinup queens.

"I wanted Plato to post a really handsome picture of his favorite hunk of beef. That will show viewers what turns him on."

Jimmy said that during his teenage years in Indiana, he had decorated the walls of his bedroom with pictures of screen Tarzan, Johnny Weiss-

After the success of his first major film, ***Tarzan the Ape Man*** (1932) **Johnny Weissmuller** *(right figure)* appears with an unknown associate in Palm Springs.

As a teenager, James Dean had "worshipped" Weissmuller as Tarzan, pinning up pictures of him in his bedroom. In addition to the "Man of the Jungle," he was an undefeated swimming and Olympic champion, a hero to millions of fans around the world.

"Jimmy was impressed by my measurements," the screen Tarzan confessed. "Height 6 feet, 3 inches; weight 190 pounds; chest (normal) 40 1/4 inches; forearm 12 1/4 inches; penis 10 inches."

muller.

"Why don't you call him?" Stern asked.

"Maybe he wouldn't even talk to me," Jimmy replied.

"Wise up, kid," Stern said. "You're now a god damn movie star. One of the privileges of being a hot-shot star is that you can get to meet almost anyone you want. As I said, ring him up. I bet he'd meet with you any time you wanted."

"Maybe I'll just do that," Jimmy said. "See if the real thing lives up to my schoolboy crush."

Jimmy's friend, Stanley Haggart, who had sometimes granted him access to one of his apartments in New York, and also to his guest cottage in Laurel Canyon for his sexual trysts, knew what Jimmy was up to.

According to Haggart, "Just out of the blue, Jimmy, in New York, phoned and asked if he could come by with a friend. I told him that would be fine. When he showed up with this mysterious friend, I was shocked. It was the film industry's most famous Tarzan, Johnny Weissmuller. If Jimmy was known for anything, it was for his 'odd couple' matings."

"He later explained that as a kid, he had long fantasized about Tarzan in his loincloth."

"I understand that," Haggart said. "I collected pictures of John Gilbert." He welcomed both of them, and even fed them a late night supper with champagne.

Jimmy claimed that he'd met his screen idol at his favorite restaurant, the Villa Capri. The owner had given the Austria-born former athlete permission to let out his ear-splitting jungle yell any time he came in for dinner. Weissmuller would thump his chest and bellow that maniacal yell.

"I tried to imitate that yell as a kid," Jimmy said. "But it never came out right."

As it turned out, Weissmuller was an amusing guest, not at all as inarticulate as Tarzan.

"Jimmy and I discovered we have something in common," he said. "We've both fucked Joan Crawford and Tallulah Bankhead. Tallulah once told me, 'Dahling! You are the kind of man a woman like me must shanghai and keep under lock and key until both of us are entirely spent. Prepare for a leave of at least ten days.'"

Weissmuller went on to relay other amusing stories based on his early days in Hollywood, some of them were spent traveling on promotional tours for the *Tarzan* series.

"In Texas, during World War II, I was at a bond rally. I was auctioned off, presumably to deliver the Tarzan yell in private. The highest bidder was willing to pay $50,000. Some sources say only $5,000. But it was $50,000 big ones. A rich Texas oilman was the highest bidder."

"He invited me for dinner in his hotel suite, and I went," Weissmuller said. "When I got there, a lobster and Texas steak dinner, with lots of champagne, was sent up."

"After dinner, my host told me, 'I don't give a damn about that Tarzan yell. I'm not going to pay that kind of money for some yell. I brought you up here to find out what's under that loincloth. Incidentally, you'll soon find out that I'm the best cocksucker in Texas.'"

"In case Johnny doesn't show it tonight," a drunken Jimmy said, "It's ten inches, but the final inch is pure foreskin."

"When I first arrived on the MGM lot," Weissmuller said, "I was sent for a costume fitting. This fucking sissy handed me a feathery-looking G-string and asked me if I knew how to climb a tree. He tried to fit this damn G-string on me. No way. I demanded a heavy duty jock strap."

"Johnny wasn't what I was expecting," Haggart said, later. "He was the last actor in Hollywood I thought Jimmy would hang out with. Most of Johnny's references were far more sophisticated that that 'Me Tarzan, you Jane' crap."

"As an art director on TV, I often had to fit stars into their outfits when the budget didn't allow for a wardrobe master (or mistress). Johnny spotted some old fashion magazines in my living room. Before he left, that night, he asked me if he could take some of my old editions of *Vogue*. I agreed, of course."

"He surprised me by telling me that *Vogue* was one of his favorite magazines. He also thanked me for my lavish dinner, telling me with meals like that, he was going to have to come up with new devices to cover his expanding waistline."

"Johnny wasn't the Tarzan that both Jimmy and I had once fantasized about from back in the late 1930s and '40s," Haggart said. "After all, he was born in 1904 and was older than I was. Even so, he was still the hot stud that no one in a gay bar would turn down."

[Johnny Weissmuller lived until 1984. His last screen appearance was in Won Ton Ton, the Dog Who Saved Hollywood *(1976).]*

***

In Los Angeles, Stewart Stern picked up his phone at about two o'clock in the morning. Jimmy was on the other end of the line, calling from New York, where he'd stashed himself away, without permission, from *Rebel*, its director, and its scheduling.

Stern warned him that if he didn't fly back to Los Angeles at once, Warner was going to replace him with another actor. "You'll be suspended. Without pay. Your career will be ruined."

"I want to come back, but I'm frightened," Jimmy said. He sounded drugged. "I don't think I can play Jim Stark—and I don't trust Nicholas Ray as a director."

Stern entreated him to return. "Jimmy, we're ready to begin shooting. I've tried to fashion all my rewrites around Jim Stark, based on you. You can do it. You haven't seen the final script. It's Jimmy Dean! God damn it, you can play yourself, can't you?"

Two days later, at around midnight, Jimmy showed up on Ray's doorstep at the Château Marmont. "He just walked in," the director said, "and had absolutely no excuse for his running away. He wanted to spend the weekend in bed with me, making love until I forgave him. The kid got his wish."

Jimmy Rages
Through Some of the Most Iconic Film Sequences
In the History of Cinema

James Dean, "poster boy" of unresolved teenaged *angst*, in a pivotal scene from *Rebel Without a Cause.*

At last, after almost a decade of delays, *Rebel Without a Cause* was set to go before the cameras. All sorts of problems had already been resolved, including censorship by Warners, casting problems, even Jimmy's mysterious disappearance.

Ray wanted a very dramatic opening, and both he and Jimmy worked together to create something unusual, even stunning, to launch their movie.

As the title and opening credits of *Rebel Without a Cause* are flashed across the screen, a drunken Jim Stark lies on the sidewalk intoxicated, whimsically playing with a toy monkey. The scene might not have worked, but Jimmy made it memorable. The toy monkey was his idea.

Within a week of shooting in black and white, Jack Warner halted the production after reading the acclaim that Jimmy's performance had generated for *East of Eden*. "We've got a star on our hands," he told Ray. "There's big box office here. We're going to shoot the damn picture in color."

Consequently, costume designer Moss Mabry scrambled to redesign Jimmy's wardrobe, replacing Jim Stark's original black leather jacket with a red nylon windbreaker. It became one of the most enduring costumes in film history, rivaled—among male stars, at least—by Charlie Chaplin's bowler and Humphrey Bogart's trenchcoat.

[Mabry dressed not only Jimmy and the other stars of Rebel, *but would go on to design Elizabeth Taylor's outfits in* Giant, *for which he received an Oscar nomination in 1956.]*

During the filming of *Rebel*, Jimmy's reputation from *East of Eden* grew rapidly, as did his fan base. Letters poured in from across America, including bags of mail from gay men. Many other handsome, well-built male stars, including Rock Hudson, also received gay fan letters, but none with the volume of what was sent to Jimmy.

As regards Jimmy's friends, journalist George Scullin noted some changes: "He collected a group of sycophants who performed what *gaucheries* they could think of—party crashing, drunken binges, drug excesses, and offending for the sake of offending. What a pack of bastards!"

Early in *Rebel*, three troubled teenagers, as portrayed by Jimmy, Natalie, and Sal Mineo meet, at random and for unrelated transgressions, at the local police station.

[In that scene, a drunken Jim Stark slams his fist into the side of a desk with a force greater than what the script had called for. When the scene was over, Jimmy was rushed to the hospital, since Ray feared he'd broken some bones. As it turned out, he was only badly bruised. "Too much Method acting," Ray told him.]

Plato (Mineo), a mentally disturbed youth, had been hauled into the station for killing a litter of puppies for reasons he cannot explain. Judy was there for having violated some unexplained curfew.

Later, all three encounter each other again on the first day of school. As the camera focuses on Plato, an object of derision and ridicule by his peers, Mineo opens his locker to reveal a handsome publicity photo of his movie idol, Alan Ladd. Based on this cinematic clue, whereas gays across America immediately recognized Plato as one of their own, straight audiences of that day hardly took notice of the signal being (discreetly) projected.

In Manhattan, years later, Jay Garon, a notoriously well-known literary and film rights agent, proposed that Mineo write a memoir, for which Mineo would receive an advance of $40,000. Garon designated his client, Darwin Porter, co-author of this book, as its ghost writer.

According to Mineo, as relayed to Porter, "Late one night, after *Rebel* was released, I got a call from Alan Ladd." Mineo said. "He sounded drunk.

Alan Ladd, uncharacteristically without one of his "Cowboy" uniforms, an idol to Plato.

"Thanks, kid," he said, "for using my picture as your dreamboat in that locker scene in *Rebel*. I need all the publicity I can get."

"They wanted me to use Burt Lancaster, but I went for you," Mineo said. "My all-time favorite."

"As a reward, I'd like any fantasy you might have to come true tonight. I'm home alone if you care to drop in."

"Did you accept the invitation?" Porter asked.

"What do you think?" Mineo replied. "I'll tell you this much. Alan was not short all over."

[Since the early 1940s, Hollywood insiders knew that Alan Ladd led a secret bisexual lifestyle.]

Mineo's autobiography collapsed when he refused to out himself as a homosexual. Without that revelation, no publisher wanted a "vanilla view" of his life.

"I just couldn't break all those female hearts, who sent me all those adoring letters in the 1950s," Mineo said. "The money would sure have been nice, though."

***

"The repressive censorship of films, originating in the 1930s, was on life support when *Rebel Without a Cause* was made," Ray said. "But it would have been an even more powerful film if the original script had been used."

He was referring to the underlying homosexual context of the dynamic between Plato and Jim Stark. "Homosexuality was still the love that dared no speak its name on the screen. And Judy was supposed to be a teenaged trollop. But we gave in to the demands of the censor, much to my regret."

"Jimmy wanted to do other, more daring scenes that were not in the script. In one episode, he wanted to be shown lying in bed on his belly, with his naked ass showing. Of course, in a few years to come, such a scene would be considered typical, but not in 1955. European films had already broken through most of these taboos, but Hollywood was slow to catch on."

"I watched Jimmy and Sal fall in love right on camera," Ray recalled. "Jimmy even issued a director's cue to Sal, telling him, 'Pretend you want to run your fingers through my hair, but you're too shy. Make believe you want to throw yourself in my arms and kiss me passionately. I want Nick to film us kissing and see what the blue noses say about that. They're all mother fuckers anyway. Art should not be censored. Neither should love. It's all right for films to depict men brutally killing each other. But to love a man? That's out!"

So spoke James Dean.

Rebel, in addition to same-sex attraction, contained very oblique references to yet another theme of forbidden love too—incest.

Stern's script called for William Hopper and Natalie's characters to suggest an undercurrent of incest. An early version had called for her to sit on his lap, as she'd done for years in her capacity as his adolescent daughter. Without getting embarrassingly graphic, Stern had hoped to portray Hopper becoming sexually aroused, with the understanding that when he ultimately rejected her, it would be as a punishment for his own sexual feelings toward her.

In a pivotal scene that made the final cut, when Judy repeatedly tries to kiss her father, Hopper, with barely concealed fury, rebuffs her, saying "You're getting too old for that kind of stuff, kiddo." In reaction, she kisses him anyway, receiving a vicious slap in response. As her mother passively (and naïvely) observes this dynamic, Judy, sobbing, storms out of the house.

***

Based on the rave reviews being generated for *East of Eden*, Jimmy felt entitled to direct the other actors. Consequently, he instructed Dennis Hopper, "Don't act like you're smoking a cigarette. Smoke it! When you know there's something more that should go into a character, and you're not sure what it is, you just have to go after it! Walk on a tightrope!"

Jim Backus, in his own words, was Jimmy's "henpecked father in an apron, mentally flabby and shillyshally."

"He was a self-deprecating weakling of a man whose wife had long ago cut off his balls," he claimed.

"I wish my character had been rewritten. I felt that, like my Mr. Magoo, Mr. Stark was also a cartoon character, not three-dimensional at all. I struggled to do the best I could, but the fault was with the script."

Two views of **William Hopper:** *Upper photo*, with **Natalie Wood** (Judy) in *Rebel Without a Cause*, and *lower photo*, as the private detective, Paul Drake, interacting with **Raymond Burr** in the weekly legal drama series, *Perry Mason* (1957-1966).

Hopper, incidentally, was the handsome son of Hollywood's most feared and loathed gossip columnist, Hedda Hopper.

"Actually, I never knew it would become such a legendary picture," Backus said. "We started out to make a sort of Ozzie and Harriet sitcom with venom until Dean suddenly became an overnight sensation on our hands."

***

Rebel's soon-to-be-famous knife fight (Jim Stark vs. Buzz) was shot at the Griffith Planetarium, high in the hills above the Hollywood Bowl. With Jimmy and Corey Allen, Ray attempted to film the scene eight times, but none of them looked realistic. Finally, the two young actors got it right, although at one point, Allen's switchblade slashed the skin of Jimmy's throat. Although it was a surface wound, the cut drew blood.

Genuinely alarmed, and in his capacity as the film's director, Ray yelled "cut" and frantically summoned the on-site nurse.

Bleeding from the throat, Jimmy denounced Ray for halting the action. "Just when we were getting real, you fucked it up, you bastard!"

The cast had rarely, if ever, heard an actor address his director like that.

The nurse bandaged Jimmy, and he didn't need to go to the hospital. After that, Ray instructed Rod Amate, a young stuntman, to double for Jimmy during the scene's final moments, with the understanding that his face would not be visible.

Amate would also double for Jimmy in his souped-up '46 Ford for the "chickie run" scene.

Days before the knife fight scene, Jimmy and Allen had each been carefully coached and rehearsed by "Mushy" Callahan, a former welterweight boxing champion, and a former street fighter.

***

Corey Allen was one of the longest-lived members of Rebel's cast, surviving many of film's other actors by decades, until his death in 2010. It took him years to be able to discuss the events that transpired between Jimmy and himself.

"Jimmy was practically directing the picture himself," Allen said in his last interview. "Late one afternoon, he asked me if I'd ride off with him for the weekend. I didn't want to, so I turned him down. He almost begged me to change my mind, and I finally gave in to him. I didn't want to antagonize him. He invited me to this rental home he had, which looked like a hunting lodge."

"I'd heard stories that he was gay, so I suspected what was coming. I was straight, and I felt that all I had to do was let him blow me. But after some weed and a few drinks, he made his request very explicit: 'I want you to ride me like you're Brando's son,' Jimmy said. 'Really fuck the hell out of me.' Believe it or not, I actually enjoyed it. Very tight. Great sex, I stayed all weekend, and he did things to me like no gal ever did. I don't want to get specific, but there are some things a whore might do, but in most cases, not a girlfriend."

"Before the end of the weekend, he told me what he really wanted from me as an actor during the final moments of the chickie run. He wanted me to convey that under different circumstances, instead of enemies, we might have been lovers. I understood that, and I tried my best to convey that on the night we shot the scene."

"The character I played turned to him and said, 'You know something? I like you.'"

"Why do we do this?" Jim Stark asks.

Allen, as Buzz, answers, "We gotta do something, don't we?"

"It was a tender moment between the two men, one of whom will careen in his car off the cliff, crashing to a fiery death onto the rocky beach below. "I get my jacket caught and can't escape from my car in time. Those were my final words to Jim Stark. My character has only moments to live."

When Jimmy jumps from his car before it plunges over the cliff, he was supposed to land on a mattress, with the understanding that as a prop and safety device, it would not be shown on camera. He ordered the prop man to take it away. "Okay, kid," the man said. "It's okay with me if you want to bust your nuts. But it's the same mattress Errol Flynn used to land on out of camera

Rebel Without a Cause.
The Chicken Game

Rebel's most hair-raising scene involved the infamous "chickie run." As a means of flaunting their nerves of steel (or their "yellow bellies," depending on the outcome) Buzz confronts and challenges Jim Stark to a deadly and motorized game of "chicken."

Each of them agrees to race (stolen) cars to the edge of a cliff. The "coward" will be defined as the one who loses his nerve and jumps out first.

The 1949 Mercury driven by James Dean in Rebel Without a Cause.

range in one of his swashbuckling movies. It came from Warner's prop department."

"I said to move the god damn thing!" Jimmy ordered.

Allen later said, "That scene became iconic. It was a classic, the underlying question of each generation. 'Here we are. What do we do?'"

After Buzz disappeared over the cliff and burst into flames on the beach, Judy (almost unbelievably and perhaps opportunistically) shifts the focus of her love away from the deceased gang leader and onto Jim Stark.

Another classic scene occurred after the death of Buzz, when Jimmy returns home to confront his parents, as played by Doran and Backus. He wants to go to the police and tell them the whole story.

Years after Jimmy's death Doran, with a sense of admiration for his raw, intuitive talent as an actor, noted how Jimmy prepared for one of his scenes: "He'd drop to the floor in a fetal position for the longest time, chin and knees together, but still on his feet. He'd get as close to the floor as he could without lying on it. Finally came this weak little whistle from him, and he stood up, ready to do the scene, which he'd do in a single take."

A big scene between Backus and Jimmy, with his mother looking on, occurs at the foot of a staircase. "A boy—a kid—was killed tonight!" Jim cries. He wants to report the incident to the police, but Mrs. Stark aggressively opposes that. "A foolish decision like that could wreck your whole life!"

In response, Jimmy pleads with his father: "Dad, stand up for me!"

At that point, Jimmy broke from the script and devised the action on his own. Backus wasn't prepared for what happened next: Jimmy leaped at him like a wild animal released from its cage. He grabbed the beefy actor by his lapels and dragged him down the stairs and across the living room. The violence continued at a whirlwind pace as he threw Backus onto a chair, which fell over backward. Jimmy then wrapped his hands around Backus' throat in a choke hold.

"He choked me until I thought I was a goner," Backus said.

Doran, as Mrs. Stark, screamed, "You're killing him! Do you want to kill your own father?"

The screenplay's author, Stern, said, "I didn't mean for the scene to be that violent. In my script, I expressed my own feelings about my own father. I wanted him wiped out, but I also wanted him saved."

As one critic wrote, "In that dramatic scene, James Dean channels a young generation's frustration and emotional claustrophobia."

***

Near the end of the film, a decaying mansion became the setting for the most evocative scene in the movie. It involved Jim Stark, Judy, and Plato in a kind of love triangle, with Jimmy as the object of the others' affections. It laid the groundwork for the film's tragic ending.

It was Stern who came up with the idea of renting it. Located at the intersection of Wilshire and Crenshaw Boulevards, and owned by J. Paul Getty, one of the era's richest oilmen, it was slated for demolition. Its cinematic fame had derived from its setting as the home of the demented movie queen, Norma Desmond, as portrayed by Gloria Swanson, in *Sunset Blvd.* (1950).

Desperately, Stern and Ray tried to contact the oil magnate so that they could film there. They finally reached him, and he agreed, charging them only $250 a day. "I bet that's what he pays for a lobster cocktail," Ray said.

Dating from the flapper age of the mid-1920s, the mansion, with its Mediterranean-style porticoes, pool, balustrades, and gardens, had been built by William O. Jenkins, the sugar magnate. Its swimming pool was especially famous, thanks to the fact that in *Sunset Blvd.*, William Holden's body had fallen into it after the abandoned egomaniac (Norma) fatally shot him.

It had been dubbed "The Phantom House," because for many years, no one had lived there.

After Getty granted his approval for the building's use as Ray's film set, the director said, "I'm ready to film our Walpurgis Night."

Walpurgisnacht

"All those kids in Rebel *were sleeping with each other. Gender didn't matter—and Nick Ray was sexually involved with most of them"*

—Ann Doran

In Germanic folklore, **Walpurgisnacht**, the night of April 30th (May Day's eve), is when witches congregate on the Brocken mountain in north-central Germany, and conduct sexual revels with their gods in anticipation of the arrival of Spring.

Natalie said that when she came together again with Jimmy in 1955, after having made a teleplay with him the year before, "I was older and more grown up, and I knew a lot more about sex than I did when we first met."

"I liked talking to him more than to anybody else I knew. My whole life seemed to change completely when he walked in. I was in incredible awe of him. I also thought he was the sexiest boy I'd ever met. Of course, I said the same thing about this guy named Robert Wagner."

One afternoon, Jimmy told Natalie that in the real world, each of them lived a variation of the alienation that was represented by the characters they were playing, Jim Stark and Judy.

Columnist Hedda Hopper wrote: "During the making of *Rebel Without a Cause*, Natalie Wood fell hard for James Dean."

Even though he stole scenes from her, Natalie claimed that, "Working with Jimmy is pulsating, as he generates a theatrical electricity. Anyone playing with him can't help but feel his tempo and drive. Even if he doesn't have a line to speak, I feel he's talking to me. I can tell by the way he looks, the movement of his hands, the slight motion of his facial muscles. I've never felt so excited with an actor as I do with him."

Left to right: **Sal Mineo, James Dean**, and **Natalie Wood** make a cuddlesome trio in *Rebel Without a Cause*—just the three of them against the world.

Off screen, although they didn't choreograph a *ménage à trois*, both Mineo and Wood had private sexual trysts with "that stick of dynamite" known as Dean.

"It's great working with her," Jimmy said. "Gone are the pigtails. No more bobbysox. She has pep, real vitality, and all the attributes of a powerful performer. I'm sure that in her future, she'll play such roles as a whore."

In reference to what happened over the course of the next few weeks, author Gore Vidal—who, like Ray, was living at the Château Marmont at the time—made several very clear assertions in his memoir, *Palimpsest*. "Nick Ray was openly having an affair with the adolescent Sal Mineo while the sallow James Dean skulked in and out, unrecognizable behind thick glasses that distorted myopic eyes. Ray would soon be embroiled in a different affair with a sixteen-year-old girl, Natalie Wood herself. He was forty-three at the time."

Beverly Long said, "Dennis Hopper was terribly in love with Natalie, too, and he was heartbroken when he found out that she was also sleeping with Ray and Jimmy."

Natalie said that it was Nick Adams who took her virginity at the suggestion of her mother. She approached Adams when he came over one evening to pick up her daughter. "Mud" told him, "I want you to teach Natalie the ways of the world. I'm afraid that if you don't, she might be broken in by that queer guy, Jimmy Dean. That fellow is weird. You're not. I trust you with my daughter."

In *Rebel*, Jimmy gave Natalie her first screen kiss. "We did a lot of practicing off screen so we'd be camera ready," she said, giggling.

"I played my first love scene with Jimmy," Natalie said. "He seemed like a great nonconformist, a great rebel, but really, he was only eccentric."

She also said that Jack Simmons was always trying to find out if Jimmy were having sex with her.

She was still curious to know if Simmons was also having sex with Jimmy. He told her, "I won't say no, and I won't say yes. I love and worship Jimmy."

During filming, Natalie developed this powerful crush on Jimmy and was always ready to accept his invitation to his dressing room any time he wanted to seduce her.

"After our lovemaking, he gave me advice as an actress, very good suggestions. He was very critical of his own work, and never satisfied with a performance he'd just given. He worried about how every scene would turn out. He also had the ability to make his co-stars look great, too."

***

Sal Mineo said, "During the filming of *Rebel Without a Cause*, I had a hot and heavy affair with Jimmy. In one scene, Ray had us kissing, but, in the uptight '50s,

Although **Sal Mineo** played a gawky, alienated adolescent in *Rebel Without a Cause*, he morphed into a tiger of an adult—confident, artistically driven, and very much a high-testosterone male. Here are three views of him from about a decade after playing Plato. Each was photographed by Ken Duncan and now reside within the archives of the New York Public Library.

when homosexuality couldn't even be mentioned on the screen, that segment was cut by the censors. The world wasn't ready to see two young men kissing."

Mineo told Darwin, "Natalie was real competition for me. I was madly in love with Jimmy and so was she. Before she was cast in *Rebel*, she told me that she must have seen *East of Eden* fifty times. Even if she were exaggerating, she'd seen it a hell of a lot."

[*Ray confronted Natalie years after Jimmy died. "You're telling the magazines and even friends that you and Jimmy did not have sex. Is that true?"*

"Come on, Nick," she said. "I can tell the innocents that, but not you. You know I've spent many nights with Jimmy. What did you think we did? Hold hands? Frankly, I much prefer Robert Wagner's cock to Jimmy's, but we did go at it more times than I can remember. Sometimes, Jimmy liked to hurt his partner, and be hurt, and I don't go in for that."]

"Both Natalie and I adored Jimmy," Mineo claimed. "If he didn't give me a warm embrace when we met on the set in the morning, I was a wreck for the day. Actually, I wanted to kiss him any time I was around him, but there were always people about. I waited for him to call me into the privacy of his dressing room. That guy was some swell kisser, among other attributes."

Jimmy's friend, John Gilmore, paid a visit to the set. Between takes, the two actors amused themselves by naming the producers and directors who had put the make on them.

During Gilmore's visit to the set, he became aware that Jimmy was having an affair with Mineo. "I knew something was going on. We headed for lunch in the commissary, and Mineo was walking ahead of us. Jimmy stepped up and pinched the right cheek of his ass. Mineo jumped. He was startled. But when he realized it was Jimmy, his big brown eyes lit up. His face flushed red, and he giggled, beaming in awe at his top."

Another friend of Jimmy's, William Bast, learned graphic details about Jimmy's affair with Mineo. "Sal may be just a kid, but he's got nine inches of Italian sausage that no butcher has ever tampered with," Jimmy claimed.

"The nights Jimmy could spare for me were the most delightful of my life," Mineo confessed. "I had never been penetrated before he did the job. Up to then, only oral sex. It hurt at first, but he made me take it, and I came to love it. He told me I had to endure the initial pain to prove my love for him. I did, and soon that pain turned into the greatest sexual thrill of my life."

Mineo also confessed that, off screen, Jimmy experimented with S&M, and that, on occasion, urged lovers to crush out their cigarette butts on his ass. He wanted to keep his chest and back free from burn marks in the event that he had to strip before the camera. "Jimmy wanted some kinky stuff, but I told him to get it elsewhere," Mineo said. "I wasn't into doing stuff like that. I just liked regular gay sex."

In the wake of Jimmy's fatal crash, a coroner examined his body, inch by inch, making a note of the "constellation of kerotoid scars" he discovered.

Mineo described a bizarre and heretofore unreported event that happened to Jimmy and himself during the making of *Rebel*: Before the beginning of filming, Jimmy had hung out with a street gang from the south side of Los Angeles, hoping to absorb enough atmosphere to convincingly portray Jim Stark.

At one point, Mineo and Jimmy were abducted and taken to an abandoned warehouse in South Los Angeles. One biker accused Jimmy of not only giving him crabs, but a venereal disease too.

"We were saved by a miracle," Mineo said. "Jimmy was allowed to call this doctor friend who agreed to cure the biker of both afflictions. Of course, getting rid of crabs was a lot easier than VD."

Jimmy also made a $5,000 payment to the bikers. Mineo believed that "If he hadn't done that, I expect that both of us might have gotten a switchblade embedded in our guts."

[*Nightly in that part of L.A., bikers and members of their gangs were routinely murdered, especially during their turf wars.*]

Shortly before Mineo was murdered in 1976, he told Darwin that "I'm the father of a child somewhere, but I don't know where he is today."

Jimmy's on-again, off-again affair with Mineo would continue after both of them were cast in *Giant*. "Instead of Natalie and Nick Adams, I had to compete with Elizabeth Taylor and Rock Hudson, at least in the beginning. Elizabeth continued to adore Jimmy until the end of his short life, but by the end of filming, Rock hated him and turned to me for sexual relief."

"Mineo denied that he and Jimmy were lovers, at least at first," Ray said. "Why not? It would have ruined his career. But his comments were hogwash. I'd seen them make love in my suite. They were great at it."

In the years that followed his filming of **Rebel Without a Cause**, **Sal Mineo** became more willing to promote the fluid sexuality for which he had become known.

Here's the front cover of his Los Angeles production of **Fortune and Men's Eyes**, a 1967 play (and 1971 film) written by John Herbert about a young man's experience in prison, exploring themes of homosexuality and sexual slavery.

The press and PR photo, featured on the program's cover, depicts Mineo graphically raping another inmate—in this case a young **Don Johnson** before the spectacular fame he generated in **Miami Vice**.

***

As the years went by, Mineo became more open about his sexuality. During one of his last interviews, he told *The New York Times,* "I was in incredible awe of James Dean. I was fascinated by him. I think it was sexual to some extent, but I had no understanding of affection between men. I really gave him hero worship, and I recognized later what it was, but the feeling then was that I couldn't wait just to get near him. It was only years later that I understood I was incredibly in love with him."

Mineo recalled his death scene toward the end of *Rebel,* when he is shot by a policeman after he ran out of the Planetarium with a gun. It was not loaded. Jim Stark had removed the bullets.

"I wanted to do the scene over and over because he was grieving over losing me, and I was thrilled to be loved like that by someone. If you watch the scene, you realize he seemed genuinely moved, and I felt loved. After that, he was very protective of me. For the rest of the time, he didn't want me out of his sight. He was always there for me. Alas, it didn't last."

***

Dennis Hopper, on the set of *Giant,* bragged to Jimmy about the conquests he had made, even at a young age. "I don't think there's a starlet walking that I can't screw," he boasted. "Actually, I prefer to give head to a beautiful woman rather than fuck her."

In time, Dennis would have A-list conquests such as Ursula Andress, Jimmy's former girlfriend, and Joan Collins. But when Jimmy met him, he was involved in an affair with Natalie.

He later confided to Jimmy, "A day after I met Natalie—Ray introduced us—the little bitch phoned and asked if I'd go out with her. She told me I was very good looking, and that she wanted me to fuck her. I found out that Nick Adams had broken her in. Back in Kansas, women weren't this aggressive. The following night, we drove up to Mulholland Drive and made love. I think she wanted to get into her character of Judy, who in the first script, was sexually promiscuous."

"I got into terrible problems with Ray," Dennis said, "because we were both fucking Natalie. Her parents were starting to figure that out. Nick snitched on me to them. I was furious at the bastard."

Perhaps to get back at Dennis for his pursuit of Natalie, Ray decided to set him up with his neighbor at the Château Marmont, author Gore Vidal. As a means of engineering the hookup, Ray lied to Dennis, telling him that Vidal was writing the script for a major motion picture that might contain an Oscar-winning lead role for him.

"Hopper went for it," Vidal later told Tennessee Williams and others.

"He arrived all innocent and wide-eyed, dewey eyed, really," Vidal said. "For dinner, he drove me to his favorite pizza joint in his new red Austin convertible he purchased with money he'd made in the movies."

"When I got him home, he objected to getting fucked, but he endured it anyway," Vidal said. "I told him to think of God, country, and the lead role in the hottest new movie property coming up. He endured it, but then wanted me to blow him. I told him I'd owe him one."

"There was no movie contract," Vidal said. "The kid had to learn that you don't trust people like Gore Vidal or Nicholas Ray."

***

Despite his sexual involvements with a number of men—namely Simmons, Ray, Dennis Hopper, and Mineo—Jimmy continued his dating of women. Once, he invited the Swedish starlet, Lilli Kardell, to the set of *Rebel* to watch a scene being shot.

Natalie seemed jealous of her, especially when Kardell informed her that Jimmy had escorted her to the bullfights in Tijuana the previous weekend. "Later, in our hotel, he stripped naked at the foot of the bed and told me to pretend that I was the bull. Then he got an erection and jumped on top of me, plunging his sword deep into the gut of the 'bull.'"

Nick Adams *(above)* first met James Dean when they were hired to appear in a commercial hyping Pepsi-Cola. They became instant friends—also lovers—and moved in together. Money was short, and they were forced to hustle "johns" along Santa Monica Boulevard.

***

Beverly Long, cast as Helen, one of *Rebel*'s "gang molls," noted how "Nick Adams was always sucking up to Jimmy, desperately trying to be his best friend. They had been roomies."

Adams had serious competition from Jack Simmons. He was ready to hop into Jimmy's bed, or Natalie's bed, whoever summoned him. Sometimes, it was Ray himself.

"I had the feeling that Jimmy knew that Adams was sucking up to him," Long said.

At the time of filming, Adams was rooming with Dennis Hopper. Jimmy with a certain derision referred to them as "Big Dick and Little Dick." [The chronically indiscreet shock jock, radio star Howard Stern, once asserted, on the air, that "Dennis Hopper's got one the size of an elevator button."]

One day at lunch, Adams was dining with Jimmy in the commissary. Jimmy looked up and saw that a publicity picture of himself had been on the wall where an equivalent likeness of Dennis Morgan had once hung.

"Morgan out, Dean in," he told Adams. "I can't stand publicity." He jumped up, grabbed the photo from the wall, and smashed its protective glass by hurling it to the floor. Then he stormed out of the dining room.

Ironically, George Stevens, who later directed Jimmy in *Giant*, summoned Adams to a recording studio after Jimmy's death. When Jimmy played Jett Rink, an old man in a drunken banquet scene, his voice had not recorded properly. Nick Adams was the best imitator.

"I stuffed my cheeks with chewing gum to produce Jimmy's exact sound," Adams later explained.

Natalie claimed that "Nick Adams wanted to be my lover, Jimmy's lover, and Ray's lover, but what he really wanted was to become Jimmy's replacement, adored by millions. Alas, dreams often are only to be dreamed."

***

One night in his apartment, Jimmy told Jack Simmons, "I really like Natalie, and I want to be friends with her, perhaps star in another movie with her. But I'm growing bored with her schoolgirl crush on me—in fact, I find it intolerable. I have this plan. It's inspired by something really shitty that Marlon Brando did to Pier Angeli to break off their affair."

Independently, and as confirmation of that, Natalie also discussed some of the shocking provocations that ended her romantic fantasies about Jimmy.

As they moved deeper into their relationship, he began to taunt and tease her. One day, when she was studying her lines from a script, he walked over to her, whipped out his penis, and urinated on her pages.

At first, she was forgiving, dismissing it with, "He's just a Method actor trying to work himself up to play Jim Stark before the camera. That act was something that Stark, an alienated outsider, might do."

His provocations of her continued: Almost daily, Jimmy began to chastise Natalie for being "too Hollywood," accusing her of coveting the trappings of stardom and longing to become as famous as Marilyn Monroe.

As part of this ongoing campaign, Jimmy invited Natalie to visit his rented home—the one that resembled a Bavarian hunting lodge. "I'll be upstairs on the balcony—just call up to me and come in. The door will be unlocked."

That night, however, he wasn't waiting for her on his balcony, but downstairs on the ground floor, entertaining Mineo. Shortly before her scheduled arrival, Jimmy stripped off his clothes and ordered Mineo to do the same. They were kissing and fondling each other when Natalie's car drove up. Mineo was ready to reach for his clothes, but Jimmy held him down and forcibly penetrated him, imprisoning him.

From the driveway, Natalie called up to the (otherwise empty) balcony and, as instructed, opened the front door without knocking. She screamed in horror at the sight of her (naked) lover sodomizing Mineo. In tears, she fled from the scene.

The next day on the set, Jimmy approached her. "Stop your dreaming about me. I'll never marry you."

Holding back her tears, she ran toward her dressing room.

***

In years to come, usually during conversations with a girlfriend, Natalie would become very graphic during discussions of the various merits (or lack thereof) of her lovers and their respective endowments.

"Nick (Adams) had the biggest, Dennis (Hopper) had the smallest, and Jimmy was somewhere in between. Nick Ray was far more than average. When it came to kissing, Jimmy sure beat Elvis Presley. Nicky Hilton was a beer can. I don't know why Elizabeth (Taylor) divorced him. Steve McQueen was a dud in bed, but he told friends I was lousy in bed, too. Frankly, he just didn't inspire me. When it comes to giving out a prize the length of Oscar, the Academy should present a statuette to John Ireland. What a man! Oh, and Frank Sinatra should at least get a Supporting Player award."

Natalie had this X-rated conversation with gossipy Shelley Winters, who had also seduced both Jimmy Dean and John Ireland.

If **Nicholas Ray** behaved (and promoted sex) with actors he directed in a film today, like he did in *Rebel Without a Cause*, he'd probably be sued and/or arrested and been drummed out of the industry.

***

Jimmy dreaded the end of shooting of *Rebel Without a Cause*. After his involvement in its filming ended, he lingered on the set for a conversation with Ray, telling him, "Never has an acting job taken so much out of me. I put everything I had into that film."

"Jimmy and I were alone," Ray said. "We wandered about and didn't want to admit it, but it was all over. Finally, I said to him, "Let's go. We've got nothing more to do here."

"We kissed each other passionately. Then he climbed onto his motorcycle, and I got behind the wheel of my car. We rode toward Hollywood Boulevard. He spread himself like a flying angel on the cycle, with his feet up on the back mudguard, his arms outstretched. With that reckless maneuver, he sped off with a roar."

Jimmy never lived to read his reviews.

***

Doran later said that about a week after the film was wrapped, she heard someone calling up to her bedroom window at three o'clock one morning: "Mom! Mom!"

She looked down to see that her porch light was dimly illuminating Jimmy standing in her front yard.

"It's your son, Jimmy!" he called up to her after she raised the window.

"He was drunk," she said. She let him in and poured some black coffee into him "as he spoke of his fears and talked about his dreadful loneliness."

***

The last time Steffi Sidney saw Jimmy was when he came into the Villa Capri, right before his death.

Frank Sinatra had thrown a party there. A few months before, he had mocked Jimmy, but now he'd apparently accepted him as a member of the Hollywood elite. Jimmy staggered in, obviously drunk.

He stopped first at the table of his friend, Sammy Davis, Jr., before heading to the men's toilet, trailing behind Sinatra.

When he emerged, his fly was open. "You could see his dick, as he wore no underwear," Davis said. "He complained to me: 'I stood at the urinal beside Sinatra. And now I'm jealous. His dick is bigger than mine.'"

"Then he made his way over to Sidney's table and put his arm around her. His hair had been shaved back from his forehead so he'd resemble a more accurate rendition of the aged character he'd portray at the end of *Giant*."

"You know, Steff," he said. "We've never had our picture taken together. Let's go for it." He summoned the on-site photographer, who snapped several pictures of them, shooting Jimmy, for the most part, from the waist up.

He placed one arm around her, holding a cigarette in one hand, and rubbing his belly with the other.

[The ironies associated with that photo was that eight-by-ten glossies of Jimmy with Steffi arrived at her house on the morning of September 30, 1955. Jimmy would be dead in the afternoon of that same day.]

This photo of **James Dean** with **Steffi Sidney**, an actress, was the last picture ever snapped of him. It was at a party given by Frank Sinatra at the Villa Capri.

A copy of it arrived on her doorstep on September 30, 1955 as a news bulletin came over TV that Dean had died in a car crash.

***

It was on that September 30, 1955, in New York that Natalie Wood was dining with Sal Mineo, Nick Adams, and Dick Davalos, who had portrayed Jimmy's tormented older brother in *East of Eden*. All of them talked about Jimmy, and how he flirted so dangerously with death. To a person, they agreed that he would probably die one day in a car crash.

Before the end of their dinner, news reached them that Jimmy had died in a car crash on a lonely road in California on his way to Salinas.

***

Rebel Without a Cause was released on October 3, 1955. Jimmy had died just a few days before. For the most part, Jimmy's performance elicited rave reviews.

Author Lawrence Frascella wrote: "Ray and Company offers up a romantic, charismatic, sexually charged archetype—a heroic ideal of what being a teenager might mean in *Rebel Without a Cause*. The film took teenagers as seriously as they took themselves."

Writing for *Esquire*, Joy Williamson said: "*Rebel*'s appeal is obvious. We were watching the intense, doomed performance of a dead youth, a myth, the myth of those who would wish to see themselves dead without dying. Dean was dead, pre-dead, dead upon our discovery of him. His vivid presence projected a fathomless absence. It was thrilling."

Film historian Jeanine Basinger wrote: "*Rebel* hits home because the teens in it understood their situation at a level the adults could not even imagine. The film is true emotionally, setting up the world of teenagers as a separate universe. It treated their pain seriously, respecting it, instead of turning it into the subject of a cute little comedy about growing up."

Arthur Knight in *Saturday Review* said: "The late James Dean reveals completely the talent seen in his *East of Eden* performance. Gone are the Brando mannerisms, gone the obvious Kazan touch. He stands as a remarkable talent, and he was cut down, it would seem, by the very passions he exposed so tellingly in this strange and forceful picture."

William K. Zinsser, in *The New York Herald Tribune*, said: "The movie is written and acted so ineptly, directed so sluggishly, that all names but one will be omitted. The exception is James Dean, the gifted young actor. His rare talent and appealing personality shine through, even in this turgid melodrama."

Wanda Hale, of the *New York Daily News*, interpreted the picture like this: "As an honest, purposeful drama of juvenile hardness and violence, it doesn't measure up. Nonetheless, Dean gives a fine, sensitive performance of the unhappy teenager, tormented by the knowledge of his emotional instability."

Variety asserted, "As a farewell performance, James Dean leaves behind, with this film, genuine artistic regret, for here was a talent which might have touched the heights."

Milton Schulman, in London's *Sunday Express*, wrote: "Again, one is impressed by the effects of powerful emotions so harnessed and controlled that if it were not carefully rationed, it would explode."

Bosley Crowther, in *The New York Times*, delivered his usual attack on Jimmy's performances, leveling the familiar charge that he imitated Marlon Brando in his characterization of Jim Stark. "This imitation grows monotonous at some point," he lamented.

Alan Brien, in London's *Evening Standard*, wrote, "James Dean, alas, is dead. But his ghost on the screen in what was only his second film will remain among the immortals of cinema."

Dilys Powell, in London's *Sunday Times*, claimed, "There has been no player of his or any other generation to rival James Dean's interpretation of the desperation of youth."

The novelist, William Faulkner, weighed in, too: "*Rebel Without a Cause* will remain a masterpiece, because it is the only American cinema's Greek tragedy."

***

When the Academy Awards announced its Oscar nominations, it came as a surprise that Mineo was nominated as Best Supporting Actor and Natalie was nominated as Best Supporting Actress. Both of them lost to Jack Lemmon in *Mister Rogers* and to Jo Van Fleet in *East of Eden*.

Jimmy was not nominated, presumably because he'd already been nominated for *East of Eden*.

Elvis Presley was fascinated with James Dean and would endlessly watch *Rebel Without a Cause*. So when he got to Hollywood, he sought out and befriended Nick Adams, who had been Jimmy's friend.

After only a few weeks, Nick became best friend to Elvis, launching a troubled relationship that witnesses claimed turned sexual. Nick himself loudly proclaimed that he'd had affairs both with Jimmy and later with Elvis.

Their bromance began when Elvis accepted an offer to be Nick's "date" for a preview of *The Last Wagon* (1956).

Nick was known as a "star-fucker." His closest friends said he'd go to bed with any star – male or female – who might advance his career. Rock Hudson. Director John Ford. Natalie Wood. James Dean. Elvis Presley. It didn't matter to Nick as long as the fuckee was a star or even better, a director.

In the words of Albert Goldman, Nick was "forever selling himself: a property which, to hear him tell it, was nothing less than sensational—'the greatest little actor to hit this town in years.' In fact, he had very little going for him in terms of looks or talent or professional experience. He was just another poor kid from the sticks who had grown up dreaming of the silver screen."

The handsome, blonde-haired actor became the fourth member of the doomed young crew of *Rebel Without a Cause* who would die young and violently.

In death, he joined the actual stars: James Dean (died September 30, 1955), Sal Mineo (February 12, 1976), and Natalie Wood (November 29, 1981).

James Dean's Effect on Elvis Presley

Elvis Presley was fascinated with James Dean and would endlessly watch *Rebel Without a Cause.* So when he got to Hollywood, he sought out and befriended Nick Adams, who had been Jimmy's friend.

After only a few weeks, Nick became best friend to Elvis, launching a troubled relationship that witnesses claimed turned sexual. Nick himself loudly proclaimed that he'd had affairs both with Jimmy and later with Elvis.

Their bromance began when Elvis accepted an offer to be Nick's "date" for a preview of the film *The Last Wagon* (1956).

Nick was known as a "star-fucker." His closest friends said he'd go to bed with any star – male or female – who might advance his career. Rock Hudson. Director John Ford. Natalie Wood. James Dean. Elvis Presley. It didn't matter to Nick as long as the fuckee was a star or even better, a director.

Born on July 10, 1931, in the gritty coal-mining town of Nanticoke, Pennsylvania, actor Nick (whose name at the time of his birth was Nicholas Aloysius Adamshock) was the son of Ukrainian immigrants.

A close bond between Elvis and Nick Adams was established on the first night they met. Nick told Natalie Wood, "Elvis is going to replace Jimmy in my life."

Right from the beginning, Nick offered his services to Elvis: Friendship, a guide to "Inside Hollywood," a bosom companion, a homosexual lover. "Whatever it is you want, I've got it ... and plenty of it," Nick told Elvis. "If you want to meet movie stars, I know them. Want to fuck Natalie Wood? I can set it up." And so he did.

When Elvis arrived in Hollywood in 1956 to make *Love Me Tender*, the mega-star fell in love with his co-star, Debra Paget. She gave him his blue suede shoes and told him to keep on walking.

Elvis asked Nick to show him Hollywood, and Nick readily agreed. When Elvis and Nick met, "the chemistry exploded" between them and an instant friendship developed.

Within a week, as Nick later told another lover, Sal Mineo, Nick and Elvis were sleeping together. Elvis preferred oral sex and mutual masturbation. Penetration, apparently, was never an option between them.

In those days Elvis could drive his white Cadillac all over Los Angeles with Nick beside him. There was never any fear of molestation from fans. Fan magazines of that era were quick to pick up on this new friendship. However, they misinterpreted its real purpose and accused Nick of riding on Elvis' coattails to promote his own career. (Previously, the same accusations had been leveled about Nick when he developed his friendship with Jimmy.)

Nick took Elvis to the same places he'd frequented with Jimmy, including the old Villa Capri when it was on McCadden Place. They were seen dining frequently at Googie's Restaurant on Sunset Boulevard. Elvis wanted to know what foods Jimmy had liked, and he asked for the same dishes.

When Elvis had to return to Graceland, he left Nick an airplane ticket. To avoid suspicion, Nick flew to Tennessee two days later, telling friends that he was going to New York to seek work on the stage.

Sometimes at Graceland, Elvis would have a lover's quarrel with Nick, and Nick would be forced to sleep in a room with Vester Presley, Elvis's uncle.

A tabloid ran a story that Nick and Elvis shared the same bed at Graceland. When that news broke, Elvis—ever sensitive to charges of homosexuality—ordered that a cot be brought into his bedroom. He told friends that Nick slept on the cot and not in the same bed with him, which—according to the hired help—was not true. A maid later told the press that the covers on that cot were never turned down the mornings after Nick slept over with Elvis.

Late at night, Elvis and Nick would be seen together on the streets of Memphis, riding their twin Harley Davidson motorcycles.

Elvis's girlfriend, June Juanico, claimed that when she dated Elvis all he ever did was talk about Nick Adams.

To legitimatize their relationship, Elvis hired Nick to accompany him on cross-country tours. Nick came out first to warm up the audience by doing his

By the time **Elvis Presley** (right) got to Hollywood, James Dean was dead. Elvis had wanted to bond with Jimmy and become his most intimate friend. He even wanted to play him on the screen.

In lieu of Jimmy, Elvis "settled" for **Nick Adams** (left), based on the assumption that Nick—for a while, at least—had been Jimmy's best friend.

In the photo above, Adams and Presley pose as judo antagonists against the backdrop of an American Airlines logo after disembarking from a flight together at the Memphis Airport in 1956.

impressions of the famous actors he'd learned to mimic as a kid, notably Cagney and Bogart. Elvis warned Nick not to allow them to get trapped alone together by a photographer. Elvis always insisted that he be photographed with some pretty young girl in the picture, most often a fan. On several occasions that pretty little girl was Natalie herself.

In the hotel suites they co-inhabited during their tours, Elvis also insisted that Nick walk around in a pair of tight-fitting white jockey shorts, arranged so that his pubic hairs would peep out. He confessed to Nick that this was his ultimate turn-on.

"Elvis was into oral sex and enjoyed getting a blow-job more than intercourse," Dennis Miller, a former friend and companion, confirmed. Nick later claimed that while Elvis was watching a sci-fi flick, *Queen of Outer Space* [a campy 1958 bomb co-starring Zsa Zsa Gabor] he was "getting head" from Nick.

Nick later revealed some of Elvis's sexual secrets, claiming that the star was uncircumcised. Nick went on to assert that Elvis had told him that during sexual intercourse with a woman, or even masturbating, his tight foreskin would often tear, causing him to bleed.

Elvis constantly bragged to Nick about his conquests with women. But he claimed that he could not have sex with a woman who had borne a child. "Fucking a woman who's given birth is like plowing your dick into a tub of fat," Elvis said. "She's too loose to provide any enjoyment for a man."

In the months following Jimmy's death, Nick learned that Robert Altman was going to film *The James Dean Story*. Elvis was excited and intrigued, eventually lobbying to portray his hero on film. "This would be my greatest achievement," Elvis told Nick.

Elvis was bitterly disappointed when he learned that Altman had decided to configure the film as a documentary with still photographs, film clips, and narration by everyone from Natalie Wood to Clark Gable (of all people).

Nonetheless, Elvis persisted, insisting that he wanted to be the narrator, for which he agreed to appear free. Altman wanted Marlon Brando for the job, but he turned down the job, which eventually went to Martin Gabel instead. [*The most sardonic moment in the documentary, released in 1957, occurred when the filmmakers inserted a commercial of Jimmy, with Gig Young, wherein he urged viewers to drive safely. As a promotional device, Warner Brothers hired Nick to travel to Marion, Indiana (James Dean's birthplace) for the premier of the Altman film. On site, Nick visited Jimmy's aunt and uncle, Marcus and Ortense Winslow.*]

***

At Graceland, Elvis became obsessed that "I look like a faggot on film." Night after night he sat with Nick watching his own movies. He asked Nick to warn him if he were "making any limp-wrist moves like one of those god-damn effeminate swishes." To his male friends, Elvis, in spite of his own nocturnal adventures, often attacked "swishes" or "faggots," never wanting to be identified with them in any way.

When Nick pointed out some scenes where Elvis raised his wrist limply, Elvis would go into a rage and denounce Nick. At one time Elvis got so angry that he ordered Nick from Graceland and tore up his return ticket home. But the next day he forgave his friend and welcomed him back.

Elvis's manager, Colonel Tom Parker, handled the Elvis/Nick affair calmly. "At least he's not impregnating another gal and leaving me to abort another brat."

Col. Parker appreciated Nick's support of Elvis after the death of his mother, Gladys Presley, on August 14, 1958. "Nicky Admas [sic] came out to be with Elvis last Week wich [sic] was so very kind of him to be there with his friend."

During his period of mourning, Elvis locked himself in his darkened bedroom with Nick for three days and nights, refusing to eat or to see anyone.

Years after Jimmy's death, **Nick Adams** was still a working actor in Hollywood. He's depicted above as one of at least a half-dozen other actors in this poster for *Hell is for Heroes* (1962).

Natalie Wood was just a teenager when she took up with **Elvis Presley** for a brief fling. He was so enamored with her that he flew her to Graceland and introduced her to his family and friends.

She found his love-making "boring" and hurriedly flew back to Los Angeles to pursue love affairs with Robert Wagner and Warren Beatty.

News about the co-dependent and unhealthy emotional and sexual links between **Nick Adams** and **Elvis** have been widely bruited within other books. Here's just one of them.

The notorious **Col. Tom Parker** was the greedy business manager of Elvis Presley, taking fifty percent of all his earnings—and anything else he could get away with.

The Murky, Suspicious, & Unexplained Death of Sex Kitten/Screen Goddess
NATALIE WOOD

Death in a Dinghy   WHO DID IT?

Editor's Note: Immediately following the mysterious death of Natalie Wood, reporter Darwin Porter went to Catalina Island, where he remained for ten days, filing the investigative report that follows.

Natalie Wood
When she was a child, a fortune-teller told her that she'd die by drowning. Ever since, she'd been terrified of "dark water."

News of the still-unexplained drowning of Natalie Wood at the age of 43 off Catalina Island made headlines around the world on November 29, 1981. Her body was pulled from a choppy sea about 30 miles off the southern coast of California and one mile south of the Wagners' 55-foot cabin cruiser, *Splendour*. She became the third star of *Rebel Without a Cause* to die violently, in the wake of, first, the fatal car crash of James Dean in 1955 and the murder of Sal Mineo in 1976.

Her death remains one of Hollywood's darkest mysteries. Not since Marilyn Monroe's death by suicide or murder (take your choice) had Hollywood speculated so wildly about the passing of a movie star. Public interest in Natalie's death was understandable. Many of her fans had grown up with her. After all, she'd made 25 films before she turned 18, including the wildly successful *Miracle on 34th Street* in 1947. Mostly she's remembered for the films she made in the 1960s, the decade of her greatest success at the box office where she reigned as America's second most favorite sexy superstar, bowing only to the champ herself, Elizabeth Taylor. Dubbed "Hollywood's Princess," Natalie had earned three Oscar nominations and had immortalized herself in such films as *West Side Story* in 1961 and *Gypsy* in 1962.

By drowning, Natalie was fulfilling the long-ago prophecy of a Russian gypsy who warned her to "beware of dark water" and death by drowning. Over the years, Natalie had become so frightened of water that she even feared having her hair washed because her head would be submerged.

Much of her fame, and many of the fans who adored her, derived from **Natalie Wood's** performance as a tragic "modern-day Juliet" in the 1961 film adaptation of *West Side Story* by Leonard Bernstein and Jerome Robbins.

in the poster above, Natalie and **Richard Beymer** demonstrate, on a fire escape, the kind of passionate but doomed young love that some critics defined as Shakespearean.

Her drowning followed a jealous, drunken row with her husband, Robert Wagner, feuding with her over her excessive attention to her on-board guest, Christopher Walken, who was co-starring with her in the sci-fi flick *Brainstorm*, a film nearly completed before her death.

Some of the cast of *Brainstorm* had reported that Natalie had "fallen big" for her co-star, the son of a baker and a former teenage lion-tamer. She said that she "loved his different-colored eyes"—one was blue, the other hazel.

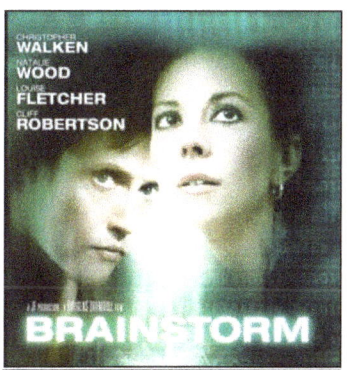

Although **Natalie Wood** found **Christopher Walken** (her co-star in *Brainstorm*; 1983) charming and fascinating, not all critics agreed with her.

Stephen Lemons found that Walken's eyes "looked part cadaver, part Muppet. Those glassy, bulging eyes look like they might entice sex from a bobcat. No one plays the kook, the psycho, the fallen angel, the deadly crime lord, the blood thirsty ghoul better than Walken."

On the set and in her dressing room, they'd talked for hours about acting. He encouraged her return to the stage after *Brainstorm* in which she was going to star in *Anastasia*, the story of the tragic Romanov duchess. Natalie herself was of Russian descent and was eager to play the part. She expressed a dream to friends, "Chris and I might become the Alfred Lunt and Lynn Fontanne of the 90s."

Privately Natalie confessed that she'd been mesmerized by Walken after he played the psychotic Vietnam veteran in *The Deer Hunter*, for which he won the 1978 Best Supporting Oscar. Once she met him, Natalie told him that "no one, but no one, can play the malevolent WASP like you."

Five years her junior, he gave her a renewed feeling for life, awakening a renaissance in her. She'd been putting on weight and had fired a stylist who suggested that she might be getting "a bit too matronly" for the camera. Walken had rekindled a rebellious streak in her and had relit her artistic spirit. She'd already told friends that Wagner was drinking far too much and "becoming even more boring than usual."

Even the second time around, Natalie and her R.J. hardly had a dream marriage. There were rumors of a near fatal suicide attempt, infidelity, a dependence on pills, and the anxiety that every middle-aged actress faces in a search for decent film roles. She was so desperate near the end of her life that she told her sister, Lana, "You know what I want? I want yesterday. Bring back 1960."

Natalie throughout her life, even while married, was promiscuous. As a teenager, friends called her "boy crazy," or perhaps man crazy would be more apt. When she was 15, Frank Sinatra, a ripe 38, had seduced her. On a few occasions, she'd have three heavy dates within a period of 24 hours. "There is nothing wrong with having James Dean in the afternoon, Nick Adams as an after-dinner treat, and Nicky Hilton for midnight champagne." Hilton, of course, was the first husband of Elizabeth Taylor.

Her lovers had ranged from James Dean to Elvis Presley to Warren Beatty. Yet she was not a *femme fatale*. Steve McQueen said. "I never saw what was so great about Natalie. She was short and lousy in bed." Natalie herself could be equally candid about her bedfellows. "Elvis can sing but he can't do much else."

With Walken aboard, Wagner and Natalie set off for Catalina on their ill-fated Thanksgiving sail during a break in the shooting of *Brainstorm*. Natalie may have been deliberately flirting with Walken to make her husband jealous. She was, in fact, furious at him for all the attention he was paying to his *Hart to Hart* co-star Stefanie Powers, following another not sufficiently explained death of her lover, William Holden, only two weeks before.

Wagner had been playing Power's super-rich, private-eye partner, Jonathan Hart, in the crime drama for TV, *Hart to Hart* (1979-1984). His friendship with Powers had actually begun in the late 1950s when the actress was in her teens. "We've coped with the highs," Power reportedly said, "and God knows RJ and I have been through the lows together."

Fans knew little about the marital discord within the Wagner family. "They had to live out the dream the world had imagined for them whether or not it went sour," said Lana Wood, Natalie's sister. Natalie had married Wagner in 1957 but had divorced him in 1962. After a brief second marriage to Richard Gregson, the British producer, she'd remarried Wagner in 1972.

After others turned down the invitation, only four people were on board at the debut of the ill-fated crossing to Catalina—Natalie, of course, plus Wagner, Walken, and the New Jersey captain, Dennis Davern, who would later give conflicting stories of what really happened that weekend. Both Walken and Wagner were less than candid following Natalie's death and have mostly remained silent about what really happened aboard the *Splendour*. Most of the participants were so tanked up that their memories, at best, would be unreliable.

The departure just before noon on the Friday after Thanksgiving met cold, gray November skies. Natalie had always liked the island, having honeymooned there with her heartthrob, Wagner, in 1958.

The *Splendour* anchored at Avalon where Wagner, Walken, and Natalie went ashore for a booze-filled afternoon at a Mexican restaurant and later at a waterfront bar, El Galleon.

At one point they went shopping, Wagner buying his wife a one-karat diamond necklace. Halfway through the jaunt, she disappeared, ostensibly to go to the women's room. She was gone for about thirty minutes, later explaining that she had a mild case of Montezuma's revenge.

The reason for her disappearance, if her friend Roddy McDowall was to be believed, was that Natalie had spotted her off-the-record lover (name unknown) who, to her surprise and dismay, had followed her to Catalina for a showdown, since she was trying to drop him now that her outside romantic interest had shifted to Walken.

McDowall had by chance run into Natalie with her handsome young heartthrob

Christopher Walken...
What did he know?

The Splendour
One dark and stormy night, Natalie fled from it in a dinghy. She never returned.

Gossips had surmised that Natalie was "psychotically jealous" of **Robert Wagner's** vibes (and TV success) with **Stephanie Powers.**

They're seen above on the cover of *TV Guide* for their co-starring roles in the mystery and crime series, *Hart to Hart* (1979-1984)

only weeks before in Los Angeles. To Rock Hudson, writer Tommy Tompson, and others in the gay Hollywood grapevine, he'd described the stranger as a "combination of Troy Donahue and Tab Hunter as they looked in the 50s." Natalie did not bother to introduce her lover to her long-time friend and hurried on her way. Later, she called McDowall and told him that, "I'm just having a little fling—nothing serious. As we both know, R.J. has his flings. Why not *moi*?"

A waitress at Catalina's El Galleon bar where Walken, Wagner, and Natalie had downed margaritas, said that Natalie had returned unexpectedly with a young, blonde-haired man. They'd taken a seat at a concealed table where they had an animated conversation that looked like it was going to break into a violent argument, although they kept their voices down. Even so, a waiter saw Natalie kissing the young man on the lips before she hurried away to rejoin Walken and Wagner.

That night, Natalie had dinner aboard the *Splendour with* her husband and Davern. Walken, feeling seasick, had retreated to his cabin. Davern recalled that Natalie argued with Wagner about whether to move the *Splendour* to more tranquil waters to avoid the rough waves washing in.

Natalie demanded that Davern take her ashore. She'd decided to spend the night in a hotel, the Pavilion Lodge, where she rented rooms 126 and 219. She asked the captain to sleep with her in 126 because "I'm afraid." Acting as Natalie's bodyguard, he fell into a drunken sleep on the floor beside the star's bed. At some point Natalie must have slipped out of the room, because a maid later told some of the staff at the hotel that she'd seen her coming out of room 219 around four o'clock that morning. About five minutes later a young man left the same room. The maid had watched the comings and goings from room 219 through a partially opened broom closet door. When the maid came into room 219 later in the day, she found that the bed had been disturbed. And during her cleaning of the accommodation, she found a semen-filled condom discarded on the floor of the bathroom.

The *Splendour's* captain, **Dennis Davern**, who would later give conflicting stories about what really happened that weekend.

Upon Natalie's return to the *Splendour* the next morning, she tried to wake up Walken, urging him to return with her to the mainland. He refused. Later that morning, she abandoned her plans to go back to Los Angeles and seemed in better spirits as she cooked *huevos rancheros* for Wagner and Walken, "the two men in my life."

Walken was informed that the *Splendour* was being moved over to the Isthmus at Two Harbours on the remote side of the island where the waters were calmer. As the men slept, Davern went for a short ride in the dinghy. It was later speculated that he was delivering a note from Natalie to the young man on shore about their plans to move the craft, but Davern has never confirmed that this was the case.

Buffetted by gusting winds and choppy seas, the *Splendour* moored at Two Harbours with about 55 other pleasure craft. As Wagner slept, Walken and Natalie went ashore, leaving him a note. At a bar/restaurant, Doug's Harbor Reef, Walken and Natalie were seen flirting with each other by Don Whiting, the manager. "It was obvious to all of us that they were in love," he said. Whiting is now dead and, of course, can't be questioned more extensively.

On board the *Splendour*, Wagner woke up and found the note. In a jealous rage, he went ashore to find the pair. As the winds gusted even stronger outside the bar, Wagner joined his wife and Walken. Natalie reportedly continued her "outrageous flirting" with Walken. Whiting, a homosexual, later claimed that Wagner, "perhaps to get even with Natalie began flirting with Walken himself, even more outrageously than Natalie had done, making me wonder if those bisexual rumors about him were true. Those rumors go back to the 50s when he was promoted by the king of the casting couch, Henry Willson, who did a lot for Rock Hudson's career."

Whiting said that he was under the impression that Wagner, Natalie, and Walken "were gearing up for a three-way later that night." At the time of their dinner reservations when he ushered them to table at seven o'clock, he claimed that all three of them were drunk.

The drunken dinner lasted for three hours. At one point Natalie excused herself and was later seen in the women's toilet befriending a young girl and telling her how she missed her own children. It was around this time that Natalie left the restaurant and walked down by the shore.

Whiting, who lived on a boat, had to retrieve something. On his way to the boat, he saw Natalie in what appeared to be a confrontation with a young man. He watched the pair from a concealed position. The young man seemed to win the argument, forcing her to disappear with him. Whiting got the impression he was demanding money from her, "but he also seemed to be trying to force her into sex with him at the same time. I wanted to stick around but my presence was due in the restaurant. I noticed that Natalie came back about thirty minutes later. Her hair was in slight disarray, but I don't think Walken and Wagner even seemed to take notice that she'd been gone for a long time."

Walken, Walker, and Natalie closed down the bar at around 10 o'clock and headed back to the *Splendour*. On board, and on deck, Walken and Wagner got into a violent and jealous argument over Natalie. Although allegedly the two actors did not attack each other, Wagner in his fury broke a wine bottle. Natalie ran below to her cabin, and Walken disappeared into his room slightly later.

Here the story gets murky. Apparently, Wagner went below to search for his wife to make up, but he found her missing. He then began a search of the boat, finding that the only dinghy, *Valiant*, was also missing. It seems improbable that he or the captain would not have seen Natalie when she came back on deck and lowered the dinghy into the water. Wagner must have known that there was nothing open at that time on shore, as the only restaurant and bar had closed. Yet he later claimed that Natalie may have lowered herself into the dinghy in the dark, turbulent waters to go ashore for a drink.

Roddy McDowall
A chance encounter

Natalie was discovered missing around 10:30pm. But it was not until 1:30am that Wagner radioed for help. Why he waited so long may never be known.

It was "exactly at 11:05pm" that a woman's scream for help was heard aboard a cruiser called the *Capricorn*, which was moored about eighty feet from the *Splendour*. On board were Marilyn Wayne, a commodities broker, her eight-year-old son, Anthony, and her boyfriend, John Payne (not the actor, of course). All three later claimed that they had heard an unknown woman screaming, "Help me! Please help me! I'm drowning!"

All three passengers aboard the *Capricorn* reported that she kept screaming that she was drowning. The trio also reported that they heard either one or two men calling to the woman that they were jumping in to help her. Could those voices have been that of Wagner and Davern? The press would speculate about that for months.

Wayne later claimed that the screams for help were coming from the direction of the *Splendour*. Wayne was discouraged against going into the water herself. There were fears that the drowning victim would clutch her and pull her to her death, and since the waters were cold there was also the fear of hypothermia.

Payne called the harbormaster at Two Harbors but there was no answer. The woman kept screaming for help although her calls grew weaker. Payne turned on the light topping their mast and scanned the area. But the crew aboard the *Capricorn* spotted no one.

In desperation Wayne called the harbor patrol at Avalon on the other side of the island. The harbormaster there promised to send a search helicopter. As time went by and no copter appeared, Wayne placed yet another call to Avalon. Again, there was no answer. Right before 11:30pm, Wayne, her boyfriend, and her son heard no more screams.

The *Capricorn*'s crew concluded that someone aboard the *Splendour* had rescued the drowning woman. In testimony the next day, Wagner, Walken, and Davern claimed that they had heard no screams that night. Then who was the man—or men—promising to come to the aid of the drowning Natalie? It was not until the following morning when listening to a radio broadcast that Payne, Wayne, and her son heard that it had been Natalie Wood, the famous movie star, screaming for help in the middle of the night.

Although Roddy McDowall apparently never went to the police, he later told friends, including Tommy Thompson, that he felt the young man, whom he called Natalie's "stalker/lover," had gone to Catalina for a final showdown. He wanted to prolong the sexual liaison he'd formed with her, but, if not, he wanted a pay-off.

McDowall speculated that the young man was threatening to take a small boat over to the *Splendour* for a confrontation with Wagner if Natalie did not come through for him. "I'm sure the kid would have taken $25,000 in hush money," McDowall said. "Natalie did not have that much, of course, aboard the *Splendour* but she could probably have raised a thousand in cash to hold the kid off until she got back to the mainland. Perhaps she promised him she'd find some cash aboard the Splendour, and slip off the boat later that night and deliver it to him."

McDowall, victim of several blackmail attempts during his life, owing to his homosexuality, had been threatened by boyfriends in his time. McDowall also speculated that Natalie's stalker had heard rumors that her husband was a bisexual. "Perhaps he was pressuring Natalie to arrange a three way," McDowall said. "I know R.J. He would never have gone for that."

When he learned that Natalie's body was clad in garments that included a nightgown, McDowall provided what he thought might have been a likely reason: "If Wagner caught her on deck, she could always claim that the dinghy was banging against the *Splendour* and keeping her awake. She could say that she had risen from bed to adjust it. That would explain the nightgown. He would never suspect that she was going to shore in an outfit that included a down-filled jacket, a flannel nightgown, woolen stockings, and no panties."

Aboard his houseboat, Whiting had overheard Wagner's drunken radio call for help to the Harbor Patrol at 10:30pm, 35 minutes before the *Capricorn* crew heard a woman screaming. Knowing the patrol office was closed for the night, Whiting intercepted the call and spoke to Wagner.

Once Whiting determined that Natalie was missing, he agreed to search for her in his own boat. Wagner did not want to call the Coast Guard, fearing "unwanted publicity," a strange reaction from a husband who knew his wife was missing in a dark sea.

In his frantic search onshore for Natalie, Whiting was joined by both Paul Wintler, a maintenance man, and by Wagner himself. Amazingly, all three men seemed to think they might find Natalie on land. Wagner returned empty-handed to the *Splendour* at 2:30am.

It should have been apparent, even to drunken men, that Natalie had been lost at sea. Still Wagner did not want to call Baywatch or the Coast Guard. Whiting and Wintler, however, woke up Doug Oudin, the harbormaster at Two Harbors. Setting out in his own craft, Oudin went aboard the *Splendour* to confront Davern and Wagner, both of whom were still drinking. The men told Oudin that Natalie was attired in her nightgown when she left the cruiser.

How could they have known what she was wearing if they hadn't seen her leave? That comment would later cause much speculation in the tabloids. Rumors spread that Wagner and Natalie had fought on deck and that she'd accidentally fallen aboard. According to that tall tale, he'd been too drunk to rescue her.

Speculation was getting out of hand. A London reporter, Peter Rydin, suggested in an article in *The Globe* that Natalie might have been "murdered" by Walken, with the blessing of Jill St. John, whom Wagner later married. Of course, there was no hard evidence for any of these wild claims, but the public devoured these theories, believing what readers wanted to believe.

If Natalie had indeed fallen overboard in the wake of violence on the deck, that would have accounted for the bruises on her body which were documented during an autopsy.

For an actress who had relentlessly courted the press throughout the course of her long career, the tabloid treatments of her death were loaded with ironies.

Even as dire as the outlook appeared, Wagner demanded that Oudin not call the Coast Guard. Oudin left the *Splendour around* 2:45am, continuing the search for Natalie with some local boatmen. He abandoned the hunt within an hour and put through a radio call to the Coast Guard himself. He did not mention Natalie by name, knowing that if someone were listening in, the person might notify the Associated Press, which would immediately send a bulletin around the world and might possibly make headlines in afternoon editions in Europe or in late editions along the East Coast.

The Coast Guard learned at 3:30am that a woman aboard the *Splendour* had been missing since around 10:45pm in shark-infested waters. It was not until 5:16am that Baywatch was notified. As dawn was coming up at 6am, a truly professional search for Natalie at long last had begun. Helicopters with search lights, Harbor Patrol vessels, and Baywatch boats were scanning the coastline in the vicinity of Isthmus Cove.

Trapped in kelp, the empty *Valiant* was discovered at Blue Cavern Point around 5:30am by Whiting himself. Its key was in neutral. The body of Natalie was found at 7:45am, floating face down in the ocean. She was wearing a flannel nightgown and a red eiderdown jacket that, when waterlogged, weighed forty pounds. The "coroner to the stars," Dr. Thomas Noguchi, later speculated that this heavy jacket might have led to her death. Had she removed it, she might have been able to climb back into the floating dinghy and safety.

Scratch marks were found on the side of the dinghy, indicating that in her desperation she'd tried to climb aboard but the jacket weighed her down. Her blood contained .14 percent of alcohol and that might have prevented her from thinking clearly. If she were more in control, she might have slipped off the jacket or else swam only a few feet back to the safety of the yacht. In a tantalizing and still-unexplained statement, Dr. Noguchi concluded that, "I don't believe drunkenness caused her to fall into the water."

The announcement of her death launched a media-feeding frenzy. There was almost unprecedented speculation, as various candidates were suggested by Natalie's fans as the possible murderer. At the head of the list of suspects was Robert Wagner himself. Fans also accused Walken of murdering Natalie. And in some of the most outlandish charges imaginable, Stefanie Powers was suggested as the murderer, her motive being that she'd killed her lover, William Holden, and replaced him with Wagner, whose job it now was to do Natalie in. That scenario evoked Hitchcock's *Strangers on a Train* (1951), starring two bisexual actors, Farley Granger and Robert Walker.

Fans around the world mourned Natalie's death and wanted answers as to how or why she'd died. So-called "official" announcements raised far more questions than they answered. It didn't help that all parties intimately connected with Natalie's death contradicted themselves over the years.

Even as honorary pallbearers such as Frank Sinatra, Fred Astaire, Rock Hudson, Gregory Peck, and Sir Laurence Olivier were attending Natalie's funeral, listening to the strains of a balalaika (in honor of her Russian background), speculation around the world remained rampant.

In spite of all Dr. Noguchi's official reports, he himself admitted that "scandalous stories and weird sexual allegations were spreading like brushfire."

A popular speculation was that Natalie had gone to bed but had awakened later to discover Walken and Wagner making love to each other. In jealousy and frustration, she'd fled the boat, so the story goes. However, Dr. Noguchi himself suggested that Walken and Wagner were far too intoxicated that night to have had sex with each other.

Right after the drowning was reported, there was immediate suspicion that Natalie was the one having an affair.

Dr. Noguchi in his findings postulated that it "could not be ruled out" that Natalie was attempting a clandestine affair on the night of her death.

Although there was an attempt to suppress this evidence, the autopsy found traces of semen in Natalie's genital area. Allegedly, the semen did not match that of Walken, Wagner, or Devern. How Noguchi determined this is not known, as the three men aboard were not asked to provide samples. One report suggested that the coroner, through a court order, obtained medical records of the possible suspects.

If the semen found on her body was not that of her husband, Walken, or the captain, then the conclusion was that it had come from this mysterious lover who had shown up on Catalina. During her disappearances from the table with Walken and Wagner, had Natalie engaged in quickie sex with the handsome heartthrob? The restaurant manager, Whiting, suspected that she had.

The swabs taken from Natalie's genital area were later "lost" before an attempt could be made to determine who might have had sex with her shortly before her death.

The case of the mysterious semen was never sufficiently resolved, and too many questions left unanswered.

On December 11, the Sheriff's Department told the press that the "case of the accidental drowning of Natalie Wood" was officially closed. The case might be officially closed, but it was hardly closed unofficially. Lurid speculation about what happened that night remains today.

Noguchi, in discussing the role of a medical examiner, talked of the "Five W's." What was the cause of death? Where did it happen? When did it happen? Why did it happen? The last W, of course, is Who—the person responsible."

That final W may never be answered unless there is a death-bed confession from some party.

Frank Salerno of the Sheriff's Department claimed, "We may never figure out exactly what happened."

Long after Natalie gave her life to the sea, Wagner expressed his grief. "When Natalie died, I was embittered. I still get angry about it and I wonder why it had to happen. I have all those feelings of grief and anger that people who've lost someone they love always have. I had lived a charmed life, and then I lost a beautiful woman I loved with all my heart."

As for Walken, he said, "At its best, life is completely unpredictable." So is death.

One journalist wrote that "the death of Natalie Wood was about as accidental as the shooting of John F. Kennedy in Dallas."

"Every death is a homicide until proven otherwise," Dr. Noguchi said.

In the case of Natalie Wood, her death was never proven otherwise.

Years After Natalie's Mysterious Death,
DENNIS DAVERN
Captain of the *Splendour*, Speaks

In 2009, the captain of The Splendour, Dennis Davern, with his friend Marti Rulli, published a controversial book, *Goodbye Natalie, Goodbye Splendour*. Originally a native of New Jersey, and an enlisted member of the U.S. Navy until 1971, Davern became the California-based captain of *The Splendour*, piloting Natalie Wood and Robert Wagner across the waters of the Pacific. He was in command of the boat the night Natalie died.

Referring to Natalie's death, he said: *"It's the kind of story that never goes away. A year or two can pass, then—BOOM!—there she is, walking down the dock, smiling at you when you're ready to fall asleep, and you know you just have to do this for her."*

The book's jacket asserts that "the police investigation was insufficient, that the parties involved received special treatment because of their celebrity status, and that a grave injustice occurred when Natalie Wood's death was brushed under the rug as an accident." It raises additional speculation about the night Natalie died, revives the rumors of the past, and reinforces the suspicions associated with her drowning. Presented as a "confessional," it articulates a damning indictment of Wagner, albeit in a format that would fall short of definitively convincing a jury.

In his book, Davern charges:

My first reaction was that Wagner had everything to do with Natalie's death, and it is my belief to this day that Natalie is a victim of her husband. I saw too much that

As we move deeper into the 21st Century, it appears that the exact truth about the mysterious drowning of **Natalie Wood** will never be known, unless **Robert Wagner** makes a death bed revelation about what really happened. That is, if he knows exactly what happened.

When **Christopher Walken** was interviewed by *Playboy*, he dodged an important question by responding with: "If there had been anything wrong, certainly the police would have looked into it."

night to ever believe it was an accident. I witnessed R.J.'s drunkenness. I witnessed R.J.'s anger and outburst. I heard the stateroom fight and saw that it carried over onto the back deck. I know that Wagner was with Natalie when she left the boat. Wagner knows how and exactly why she left the boat.

Yet despite the book's length (335 pages), there is no smoking gun delivering definitive proof of anything. Yet some of its readers, on the other hand, thought that the book carried an argument that was strong enough to justify a reopening of the investigation into Natalie's death.

The book is filled with shaky innuendo. For example, it attaches unmerited importance to the fact that immediately after Natalie drowned, a TV episode of *Hart to Hart* was based on a (fictitious) murder victim who, coincidentally, drowned. No final "payoff" in terms of definitive answers ever emerges from a reading of the book.

Many of Natalie's fans, including Peter Winkler of North Hollywood, greeted the book with skepticism. "Suspicion that Robert Wagner threw his wife overboard or intended to murder her is ridiculous. He notified the harbor patrol in enough time to find his wife alive, when she could have conceivably accused her husband of attempted murder."

Winkler's assessment is not true. As mentioned previously, Natalie was discovered missing at around 10:30pm, but it wasn't until three hours later that Wagner called for help.

Surely, after the passage of three hours, no one expected to find Natalie alive. She would either have drowned or succumbed to hypothermia.

Another reader who identified herself only as "Jeanne," summed up the case logically. "We are supposed to believe that Walken slept through both the loud music and the loud violent fight between R.J. and Natalie. [I'm] not buying that one. If Davern saw/heard the violent fight, why did he not come to Natalie's defense? He could have gotten Walken to help. In another biography, Davern stated that he saw/heard Natalie in the water, crying out for help. Now he says he never saw her in the water. I think everyone involved is still lying. The very sad truth is that there were three men on the boat and not one of them did anything to save Natalie."

Many readers felt that lurid speculation about Wagner's possible involvement in Natalie's death is not fair either to him or to his children. Jason Crawford posted a statement on Amazon.com, saying that he hopes there will be "no more books about the death of Natalie Wood until one of the three men aboard the yacht that night is ready to tell the truth—and all of it."

In the wake of new revelations, Natalie's sister, Lana Wood, has asked the Los Angeles coroner to re-open the case of her sister's drowning.

Lana told CNN that she believed an animated argument between her sister and Wagner on the yacht's rear deck occurred right before Natalie's drowning. Dennis Davern also claims that Natalie's death was a direct result of the fight with her husband.

"My sister was not a swimmer," Lana claimed. "She did not know how to swim. She would never go to another boat or to shore dressed in a nightgown and socks."

In their respective accounts of the drowning, Davern and Wagner gave two very different accounts in their memoirs. But regardless of which account is accurate, the title of the Davern/Rulli book (*Goodbye Natalie, Goodbye Splendour*) evokes its sadness.

In our view, the death of Natalie Wood will forever remain a mystery, evoking the shadowy demise of another screen goddess, Marilyn Monroe, and the legends her passing evoked as well.

One of her most famous roles was that of a stripper-in-training under the tutelage of her tarantula mother, as portrayed by Rosalind Russell in *Gypsy* (1962). Reviewed by some as "a musical case history of nice girls who strip," it retained (amazingly) a PG audience rating suitable for families. In her role as a young Gypsy Rose Lee onstage, **Natalie Wood,** many said, was "a natural. show-biz pro"

RIP Natalie Wood
1938-1981

ROCK HUDSON: EROTIC FIRE

A Truck Driver and Master Seducer
Invades Hollywood to Become a
PHALLIC SYMBOL and OBJECT OF LUST
To Love-Starved Teenage Girls and Gay Men

The Influencers He Beds Include Elizabeth Taylor, Liberace,
Errol Flynn, Tyrone Power, Joan Crawford, James Dean,
& Marilyn Monroe

Impossibly handsome, charming and cool, he was America's favorite phallic symbol. Here's **Rock Hudson** as he appeared in 1953.

"The boulder he was named for must have been a big one."
—**Mamie Van Doren**

"What a waste of a face on a queer. You know what I could have done with that face?"
—**John Wayne**

"Just because it wiggles, you don't have to fuck it."
—Advice from Rock's best friend, **Mark Miller**

Henry Willson first met Roy Fitzgerald in 1947. After a tour of duty in the U.S. Navy, working as a mechanic, he decided to try his luck in Hollywood. The 21-year-old got a job driving a truck and delivering frozen peas and carrots to various outlets.

"Nothing major ever happened to me until I walked into the office of Henry Willson," he recalled. Our meeting was followed by a long weekend at his home. He promised that he'd make me a star. The following week, he told me that my new name would be Rock Hudson."

Not only did Willson do that, but he provided Rock with a new wardrobe, fitting the jockey shorts on him personally. He took him to the dentist and paid for fixing his crooked teeth. He also taught him to stop saying, "He don't."

In addition to all that, he paid for acting and vocal training, providing that Rock would "put out every day or night, sometimes both love in the afternoon followed by commando sex in bed that night."

Rock, as his conquests were discovering, was a "top."

Henry would not always make the best decisions for Rock. For example, he rejected any involvement for his client as *Ben-Hur*, the role going to Charlton Heston, which brought him the 1959 Best Actor Oscar.

As was inevitable, Rock eventually fired Willson as his agent. On their last phone call, when learning of his dismissal, Willson told him, "The next time I meet up with you, I'm going to be carrying a bottle of flesh-eating acid which I'll toss in your face. After I do that, you can revive the Frankenstein franchise."

***

Rock was already a star when Darwin met him at a party at Willson's residence in the early 1960s. "He was friendly, outgoing, and loved gossiping about what was really going on in the movie colony. What I learned—or at least sensed—was that he did not want to talk about his own private life."

Although Darwin got no personal revelations from him, he learned what he wanted to know from former lovers, acquaintances, enemies, and fellow actors who had plenty to reveal about the superstar.

It wasn't until 2017 that Darwin, with me, his co-author, Danforth Prince, assembled Hudson's epic saga into a 668-page book published by Blood Moon Productions. Its title was ***Rock Hudson: Erotic Fire.***

After its publication, *Erotic Fire* received massive coverage in the press, both in America (especially in New York and California) and in the U.K.

The most intriguing review was written by Paul Bellini:

Here's How One of the Writers at Canada's Most Popular Comedy Series reviewed Blood Moon's biography of Rock Hudson

Paul Bellini (born September 1959) is a Canadian comedy writer and television actor best known for his work on the comedy series **The Kids in the Hall** and **This Hour Has 22 Minutes**. According to author Raymond Helkio, "Paul Bellini has created his own underground following of intellectuals, groupies, misfits and actors to rival even Ingmar Bergman."

Bellini's on-screen presence in **The Kids in the Hall** began when CBC Television suggested that the troupe conduct a sweepstakes as a promotion for the show's fanbase. Rejecting such conventional ideas as a cash prize, his colleagues decided that the "prize" would be Paul Bellini in a towel. Thus the "Touch Paul Bellini" contest was born, wherein the winner was granted the chance to gently poke the betoweled Bellini with a stick

During these and other appearances on the show, Bellini would wander into a sketch wearing nothing but a towel and never speaking, thus himself becoming an absurd character in the show.

Bellini was later a columnist for **fab**, a gay magazine in Toronto. In 2012 he self-published *The Fab Columns*, a compilation of his writing for the magazine. He also appeared in nonsexual roles as "Paul" on the defunct website **his-firsthugecock.com** at least 15 times, sometimes as a priest or minister and performed at *Awkward*, a storytelling event about embarrassing experiences at **Buddies in Bad Times**, a leading destination for "artistically rigorous" alternative theater. Around the same time, he was also a radio host on **Toronto's CIRR-FM**.

Here's what Paul Bellini wrote about Porter and Prince's biography of Rock Hudson:

"Rock Hudson was the ultimate movie star—gorgeous, manly, sufficiently talented, charming, and hung. The whole world loved him. What they didn't know at the time was that Rock Hudson was gay. And not just any kind of gay, but a real slut who had sex almost daily and racked up numbers in the thousands. Studio head Ed Muhl once said, 'Rock saw sexual intercourse as little more than a handshake.' **Rock Hudson Erotic Fire** *is juicy beyond words."*

***

Usually, the Table of Contents of a book is either vaguely boring or boringly vague.

BUT! What we crafted for *Erotic Fire*, however, is worth replicating. We posted it here as an ulta-condensed overview of Rock Hudson's spectacular rise, fall, and decline:

HERE'S THE "TELL-ALL" TABLE OF CONTENTS WE CRAFTED FOR
ROCK HUDSON, EROTIC FIRE

Chapter One
A Depression Era Kid, Roy Fitzgerald Grows Up in Illinois. He joins the U.S. Navy, sails to the Pacific, falls in love, and fights during World War II. On leave from the Navy, he fathers a son in Illinois.

Chapter Two
A Truck Driver and Navy Veteran Emerges as the Future Movie Star, Rock Hudson. The young stud lies on the casting couch of the notorious starmaker, Henry Willson. Rock seduces his first movie stars: Joan Crawford and Rory Calhoun.

Chapter Three
Rock Joins Willson's Stable of Studs and manages to seduce Judy Garland. Rock & Vera-Ellen shock Hollywood at a Photographer's Ball, appearing in gold paint as Mr. and Mrs. Oscar. A nude Rock is a sensation at the star-studded Finlandia Baths.

Chapter Four
Hungry Starlet Marilyn Monroe Sways her Shapely Hips into Rock's Life. Nancy Reagan merely flirts, but matinée idols Errol Flynn and Tyrone Power seduce Rock. He lands a role in a James Stewart Western and becomes a co-star with the Queen of Technicolor, Yvonne de Carlo.

Chapter Five
Rock and Guy Madison Introduce Beefcake to Tinseltown. Rock & Liberace become "The Odd Couple." He "boxes" Iron Man Jeff Chandler on and off the screen. He has a reunion in Hollywood with his Navy flight instructor and sex partner, Robert Taylor.

Chapter Six
Rock Becomes the Baron of Beefcake and a Dashing Leading Man—Raw Meat for She-Wolves. An encounter with James Dean. He's "too fast" on the draw for Mamie Van Doren. He "drops trou" at Universal for both the studio chief and his director.

Chapter Seven
Box Office Dynamite, Rock Joins the Hollywood Pantheon. Fans Morph Him Into a "Magnificent Obsession," Phallic Symbol, & Lust Object. Stardom at last as Rock emotes with Jane Wyman. Ronald Reagan's ex falls for him big time. The emerging Rock beds everyone from Steve Cochran to Anita Ekberg.

Chapter Eight
Rock Enjoys the Trappings and Dangers of Movie Stardom. Orgies with Tyrone Power, a love affair with "My Italian Stallion," & a sexual tryst with Lana Turner. To conceal his private life, Rock pursues Henry Willson's lesbian secretary.

Chapter Nine
Celebrities Flock to Rock—Elizabeth Taylor, Monty Clift, Truman Capote, and Garbo. No longer enjoying the "favors" of his wife, Michael Wilding "worships" Rock, who turns to Tony Perkins.

Chapter Ten
GIANT: In His Oscar Nod, Rock Heats Up the Screen in Hollywood's Ultimate Ode to Texas. He seduces his co-stars Elizabeth Taylor & James Dean. He beats out Hollywood's fading matinée idols for the role of Bick Benedict. Sal Mineo becomes a footnote, and so does the aptly named Rod Taylor.

Chapter Eleven
Rock Launches a Seven-Year Reign as King of Hollywood. He's celebrated as the world's most desirable male. He enters a tumultuous marriage to his gay agent's lesbian secretary. He rescues Monty Clift from the jaws of death and puts on a show for Marlon Brando by the pool.

Chapter Twelve
When his Marriage Crashes, He Flies to Italy to Star as a Hemingway Hero. Love scenes with Jennifer Jones by day and with his "Roman Romeo" at night. He travels to Kenya to battle the Mau Mau before winging back to Hollywood and a gangster's blackmail.

Chapter Thirteen
PILLOW TALK with America's *La-Di-Da* Happy-Go-Lucky Virgin Who Really Wasn't. Rock's secrets are threatened as his lesbian wife heads for the divorce court. Ricky Nelson gets ready for "A Teenager's Romance," hoping Rock will be his "Be-Bop Baby." Mae West & Rock bring down the house on Oscar night.

Chapter Fourteen
Rock Fires Henry Willson and Proposes Marriage to Marilyn Maxwell. More Doris Day! *Lover Come Back!* In Monaco in her Royal Chambers, Rock plays Prince Charming to Grace Kelly. Rock faces *The Last Sunset* with Kirk Douglas and *Come September* with Gina Lollobrigida. *Man's Favorite Sport* isn't what you think it is.

Chapter Fifteen
Rock Bids *Adieu* to Universal and Meets a Handsome Stockbroker Who Becomes "The Love of My Life." Making screen love to Claudia Cardinale & Leslie Caron. More Doris! More Gina! Tired of romantic comedies, he films *Blindfold* and *Seconds*, disappointing thrillers which threaten his reign as Box Office Champion. He and George Peppard find solace together.

Chapter Sixteen
Rock Feuds with Mary Poppins (*Darling Lili*), then Hosts the Last Great Hollywood Party. A handsome gas jockey/college student meets "The Man of My Dreams," & moves into The Castle. J.Edgar Hoover orders F.B.I. agents to investigate Rock's sex life. Julie Andrews and Blake Edwards tangle with Rock on set of *Darling Lili*.

Chapter Seventeen
In Paris, Rock Seduces the Former Queen of Iran as Rumors Fly in Hollywood that He's Marrying Jim Nabors. Rod McKuen's scheme to turn Rock into a "rock star" ends in disaster. Roger Vadim casts him as a sex-obsessed serial killer in *Pretty Maids All in a Row*.

Chapter Eighteen
How Television (the Little Black Box) Rescued Rock's Career, Introduced him to Millions of New Fans, and Made Him Rich. His new lover, Tom Clark, rules The Castle. *McMillan and Wife* is a hit among TV viewers as Rock as a police commissioner solves murder after murder. Rock faces a *Showdown* with Dean Martin.

Chapter Nineteen
A Middle-Aged Rock at Fifty looks for Love in all the Wrong Places. On screen, he creates a test-tube woman and seduces her off-screen. He spends cozy nights with HRH, Princess Margaret Rose and with her counterpart in Monaco, Grace Kelly. Elizabeth Taylor & Rock reunite on the screen.

Chapter Twenty
Rock Endures Quintuple Bypass Heart Surgery & Bravely Confronts the Last Sunset of a Fabled Career. Doctors deliver a death sentence: "You have AIDS, and there's no cure." At the White House, Nancy Reagan spots a red sore on his neck.

Chapter Twenty-One
Rock's AIDS Shocks the World. Widely Broadcast, the Syndrome and its Stigma Destroys His Carefully Cultivated Image. Last-minute treatments in Paris fail. He suffers a slow, agonizing death. Friends flock to his bedside.

Rock Hudson on the plains of West Texas in *Giant*

As the 20th Century reached its midpoint, there was no leading man as popular as Rock Hudson in both comedy and drama. For seven consecutive years (1957-1964), he was one of the Top Ten Stars of the year.

He repeatedly beat out all "the bubblegum boys," such as blonde Tab Hunter or blonder Troy Donahue, at the box office, not just in the United States, but around the world.

For raw masculinity, he was a walking mass of testosterone. He fitted into that leading man category previously occupied by Clark Gable, Burt Lancaster, and Robert Mitchum. Women by the millions wanted him, and men wanted to be like him. Other men just wanted him.

Just released from the Navy, the muscled, 6'4" hunk, then known as Roy Fitzgerald, arrived in Hollywood with a clear understanding of what he wanted: "I don't want to be an actor…I want to be a movie star! And I don't give a damn how many casting couches I have to lie on!"

To that end, between gigs as a truck driver, he donned very tight, faded jeans and seductively stationed himself near the entrances to Warners and Universal. Eventually, he was "discovered."

Almost from the moment he set foot in Tinseltown, young Rock set off an "erotic fire" that blazed all the way to the Hollywood Hills. He was given such appellations as "Hollywood's Sexiest Man" and "The Reincarnation of Apollo." Columnist James Bacon said, "If Hollywood ever makes a film called Adonis, it should star Rock Hudson."

Always after the new boy in town, Joan Crawford was the first diva to lure him into her boudoir, later pronouncing him "a cross between Gary Cooper and Robert Taylor." Others followed, including a drunken Judy Garland and a very young Marilyn Monroe. His affair with Elizabeth Taylor, his co-star in *Giant* (1956), developed into a life-long friendship.

Rock Hudson with the former Mrs. Ronald Reagan (aka **Jane Wyman**) in *Magnificent Obsession* (1954)

Also during the production of *Giant*, his affair with James Dean turned sour.

While making two soap opera dramas with Rock, Jane Wyman, the ex-Mrs. Ronald Reagan, wanted to marry Rock. Among his (arguably) most bizarre seductions were Tallulah Bankhead and Liberace.

Matinee idols of yesteryear also wanted him—Tyrone Power, Errol Flynn, Robert Taylor, Jeff Chandler, Tony Curtis. Rock also seduced many of the emerging young stars of the 1950s: Marlon Brando, Monty Clift, Jeffrey Hunter, Troy Donahue, Steve McQueen, and Tony Perkins.

Early in his career, he was assigned roles in a string of B-pictures, playing handsome Apaches, easy-on-the-eyes sea captains, and "Ordinary Joes" whose charm moviegoers remembered way beyond the limited scale of his roles. Meanwhile, power players in Hollywood clamored for him up close and personal, too.

Stardom finally arrived based on a performance opposite Jane Wyman in that tear-jerking melodrama, *Magnificent Obsession* (1954).

Three eventful years later, his status as one of the most popular (and most consistently profitable) actors in Hollywood was reinforced, based on his co-starring performance opposite Doris Day in the spectacularly successful *Pillow Talk* (1959). Together, as a captivating duo, they went on to appear together in other "artfully campy" battles of the sexes.

Compiled as a memorial for the 30th anniversary of his death, *Rock Hudson Erotic Fire* is based on dozens of face-to-face interviews with Rock Hudson's friends, co-conspirators, and enemies. Researched over a period of a half century, it reveals the secretive actor's complete, never-before-told story within a context of scandal-soaked and historic ironies, many of which have never been fully explored—until now.

Although maligned by the media because of the stigmas associated with his AIDS-related death, Rock showed inner courage and manly grace as he lay dying. "This is my shining hour," he told his closest friends, as the media rushed to "Out" him as a "celebrity bisexual" who'd been stricken by the then-stigmatizing scourge. His death on October 2, 1985 at the age of 59 made headlines in America and Europe.

Today, beloved by hordes of cultish fans and film buffs around the world, Rock Hudson is the often misunderstood (until now) Golden Icon of a glamourous bygone era.

TONY RANDALL
Life in the Closet Isn't Funny

Secretly Gay Offscreen and Secretly Gay Onscreen, Too

"That Jack Parr was right. On nationwide TV he said 'What's ruining television are those big productions—the fairies who come in and sing with the big balloons. It's the fairies who are going to ruin television.' I myself always felt there are too many pansies on TV. Let's face it. The gay boys—I call them camera-swishes—are dictating what you see on TV. It's appalling. TV is going to pervert America's teenage boys to their perverse world. It's odd when you turn on the TV and don't see a limp wrist."
—**Tony Randall**

"The limpest wrist on television belongs to Tony himself. If they were the same size, he and J. Edgar Hoover could exchange gowns."
—**Rock Hudson**

A talented specialist in light comedy, the late Tony Randall was born on February 26, 1920, in Tulsa, Oklahoma, the same state from which emerged the homophobic orange juice queen, Anita Bryant.

He became a brilliant character actor, usually playing an articulate, obsessive, and well-meaning schlub. Postmortem (he died in 2004), he's best remembered for his interpretation of fuss-budget Felix Unger in *The Odd Couple*, the TV serialization (1970-1975) adaptation of Neil Simon's play.

His greatest screen success came in 1959, when he played Doris Day's "unsuitable suitor" in that smash hit *Pillow Talk*. As seen today by more sophisticated audiences, Randall appears to be more interested in Rock Hudson, the film's co-star, than in the bouncy, chirpy, strong-willed blonde, as played by Doris.

Indeed, he was. Hudson told his buddy George Nader and others that "Tony came on to me real strong. I think he fell in love with me one day when I was dressed in a bathing suit. The elastic of the athletic supporter inside the suit was loose. One of my balls fell out. Tony was entranced. Knowing how much he wanted it, I let him give me a blow-job. In fact, he gave me quite a few."

Hudson also revealed that Randall told him that he'd had an active gay past, particularly in the 40s and early 50s. He also said that "like Marilyn Monroe and her calendar shot, I've posed nude. But I never showed it erect. Only tasteful nudes. You know, the Greek ideal. Classical."

Universal was so delighted with the Day-Hudson-Randall *ménage à trois* that they re-teamed them in *Lover Come Back* (1961) and again in *Send Me No Flowers* (1964). That meant a lot more blow-jobs for Hudson.

In 1981-83, Randall did another series for TV called *Love, Sidney*. It was spun off from a telefilm in which his character is clearly gay. But TV suits "cleaned it up" for its weekly projection into America's households.

One TV critic claimed that Randall always played it gay, most definitely as Felix Unger in *The Odd Couple*. "If Felix isn't a gay man, I don't know who is. Those prissy characters he played were a 1950s and 60s version of Edward Everett Horton or

It seems that everyone **Tony Randall** (photo above) worked with, from blonde bombshells Jayne Mansfield to Marilyn Monroe, from Jack Klugman to Rock Hudson, knew that Randall was gay. But in spite of his closeted private life, he could never admit that he was a homosexual.

Nonetheless, when he appeared in the situation comedy, *Mr. Peepers*, he had an affair with its star, Wally Cox. Cox took time out from servicing Marlon Brando to devote some time to Randall.

Cox was a foot fetishist. Years later, Randall confided to Hudson, "During the time I knew Wally, I had the cleanest feet in town – no toe jam when you're in bed with Wally."

Merv Griffin (of all people) also seduced Tony when they made the campy *Hello Down There* (1969), but it was a one-night stand. The two entertainers decided it was "better to remain sisters than lovers."

To celebrate the life and legend of Lucille Lortel in 1976 as the Queen of Off Broadway, she hired director/producer Gil Hodges. Darwin was named assistant producer.

"Right from the beginning, Tony was a disaster to work with," Darwin claimed. "He tossed out the script and ad-libbed."

His opening remarks were, "We're here to celebrate the life and legacy of Lucille Lortel...She never offered ME a job!"

Franklin Pangborn, most definitely Clifton Webb. In fact, Randall was following in Webb's footsteps. Webb lusted after that beautiful Robert Wagner, and Randall went for that handsome hunk with the super-sized dick, Rock Hudson."

Perhaps as a means of concealing his own homosexuality, Randall gave a number of interviews on the subject of homosexuals, many of them decidedly homophobic. One such interview, bizarrely entitled "Evening Out the Odd Couple," was delivered to journalist David Johnson, who printed it in the September 1972 issue of *After Dark*.

In the article, Randall described the time when he took a group of friends to what he described as "an all-male house in Los Angeles."

> RANDALL: *"Oh, that was really bad, really bad. Just terrible. Just disgusting. But also not good. Oh, guys sucking each other's cocks. There's nothing to watch in that. It confirms something I've always suspected about homosexuality—they don't like it. These guys never got aroused. Whereas in today's modern straight porn, these kids really go at it. Yeah. Oh, it's awful to see great big guys . . . definitely not my bag. There's no such thing as homosexuality—it's just something invented by a bunch of fags."*

At this point in the interview, Randall broke into hysterical laughter, as if at his own wit. *"I believe that!"*

In the same interview, Randall went on to claim that he had been bitterly attacked by homosexuals for an interview he gave in *Opera News*, which had expressed "my attitude toward faggotry." In the article, he complained about "hordes" of homosexuals who went to the opera to "scream and squeal and support broken-down sopranos. They're a self-appointed claque. This is absolutely true. Same guys that follow Bette Davis movies and all that."

When Rock Hudson was shown a copy of this rambling and disjointed interview, he remarked, "Tony is a very funny man, but this is about the most ridiculous piece of shit I've ever read. Homosexuals don't like getting it on? Tell that to millions of gay men around the world. I no longer think Tony is smart. From that throat does not emerge the wisdom of the ages. But he certainly opened up that throat to me. I'd rank him as one of the best cocksuckers of all time, even better than Liberace—and that's a high compliment indeed."

Rock went on to say, "Tony once told me that he was caught sucking off a teenage boy in a New York T-room—that's a toilet—but the cop let him off because he thought Tony 'was a riot' in *Pillow Talk*."

Two views of **Tony Randall:** *Upper photo:* with **Rock Hudson** in ***Pillow Talk*** (1959)**;** and *(lower photo)* with **Jack Klugman** in ***The Odd Couple*** (1970-1975)

Was Tony Randall All That Funny?

Here is what Tony Randall considered his all-time favorite joke.

Q: How do you wash a genital?
A: The same way you wash a Jew.

GAY EXTORTION
How Rock Hudson Coped with Blackmail
From the Unscrupulous Lesbian He Married

GETTING A PIECE OF THE ROCK: How Hudson Was Pushed Off the Casting Couch & Into a Lavender Marriage

James Frey's so-called memoir, *A Million Little Pieces*, about drug addiction and alcoholism, became a national scandal and bestseller in spite of its infamy. Oprah Winfrey first promoted the book to millions of her fans, then turned on Frey, exposing him on TV as a fraud and a liar.

But fake memoirs are old hat to insider Hollywood. Bennett Cerf, publisher at Random House, once told Marlene Dietrich that in her memoirs she must have confused her own infamous life with the saintly days of Mother Teresa. Joan Crawford privately admitted that her self-serving 1962 *Portrait of Joan* "was only fodder for fans."

The world took little note in 2006 of the death of another fake memoirist, Phyllis Gates, who died of cancer at the age of 80 in Marina del Rey. On November 9, 1955, this beautiful "farm girl from Minnesota" married Rock Hudson, who at the time was the most popular movie star in the world. In 1985, he died of AIDS at the age of 59. Two years later, Gates wrote *My Husband, Rock Hudson*, portraying herself as an innocent victim who didn't know her husband was gay at the time of their marriage.

Ironically, in ways that were even more shocking than the AIDS-related death of Hudson himself, the innocent-faced Gates was a blackmailer and an extortionist, the memoir a lie. Her boss was Henry Willson, a notorious homosexual agent who ruled the male flesh market of 1950s Hollywood. Almost single-handedly, he created "Rock Hudson" (actually Roy Fitzgerald) as well as Guy Madison, Rory Calhoun, Tab Hunter, and various other goodlooking heart-throb male stars. Willson paid Gates $50,000 of Hudson's money to enter into this sham of a marriage before scandal-mongering *Confidential* magazine exposed the handsome macho star as a homosexual.

Before working as a secretary for Willson, Gates was known in lesbian circles of the 1950s. She'd been the "girl toy" of the cross-dressing heiress, Joe Carstairs, whose grandfather had left her mega-millions in petroleum dollars he'd amassed alongside John D. Rockefeller.

After her divorce from Hudson in 1958, Gates became infuriated at the meager terms she'd agreed to, and eventually demanded more money—millions, in fact. She threatened to blackmail her former mate, demanding 75 percent of his future earnings. She warned him that "25 percent of something is better than nothing." She could have destroyed Hudson's burgeoning career.

Willson to the rescue. He presented Hudson's lawyers with a five-inch file on the nefarious blackmailing schemes Gates had attempted with some of her more famous lesbian friends, an activity that brought her to the attention of the FBI. "It was a Mexican standoff," one of Hudson's lawyers once told reporter Darwin Porter. "She had us, and we had her." Gates called off her blackmail threats, returning to a quiet life with her lesbian girlfriends—she referred to them as "my sewing circle."

As many a Hollywood star painfully knows, not all blackmailers look like a white-suited Sidney Greenstreet in an old Bogie film. Some of them, as in the case of Phyllis Gates, looked like she could have reigned as queen of a 1950s senior prom.

"A marriage made in hell." That's what **Rock Hudson** told George Nader on the second day of his so-called "honeymoon," following his arranged marriage to **Phyllis Gates** on November 9, 1955.

The problems began with the wedding dress—while Rock insisted on "cocoa brown," Phyllis demanded white. Rock won out.

To dispel stories tht Rock was a homosexual, Henry Willson, the mega-agent with whom the hunk was sleeping, forced him into this disastrous "shotgun wedding."

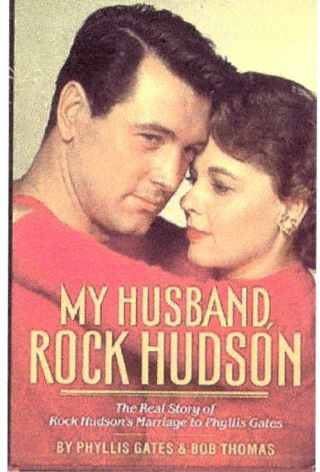

"There is nothing true in this book," said friends of Rock's former wife, **Phyllis Gates.** An interior decorator and secretary to Rock's agent, Henry Willson, she pretended to be shocked to find out that Rock was gay, when in fact she knew that and more all along.

Exposed intimately to his secret, she eventually used it to blackmail him. Incidentally, in addition to being a gold-digger and a hypocrite, she was also a lesbian.

 #1  #2  #3  #4

In the 1950s fan magazines such as *Screen,* with **Ava Gardner** and **Rock** on the cover *(see above)*, were getting suspicious and asking, "Why Rock Hudson hasn't married."

Of course, these articles were just for a gullible public; most screen writers knew that "The Rock" was gay. He gave out fake quotes, "If I think of Lana Turner, I can't go to sleep."

WAS THERE LIFE FOR HIS EX-WIFE AFTER ROCK?

For **Phyllis Gates** (*photos #1 and #2 with* **Rock** *"at home"*), there certainly was, in her case in the form of **Marion (Joe) Carstairs** (*photo #3 above, from the 1920s, and photo #4 above from the 1960s*), the ultra-eccentric Texas-born heiress who inherited part of the Standard Oil fortune.

Butch and brilliant, she ruled with a bemused but iron grip over her own private Bahamian island, Whale Cay, which she had converted from a wilderness into a flourishing, mostly self-reliant private fiefdom. Years after Marlene Dietrich had terminated an emotional involvement with her—it was noted by biographers as one of the most flamboyant lesbian affairs in the history of same-sex love—Joe invited Phyllis into her life as a companion and "kept woman," a relationship that endured for years.

More macho than most sailors, Carstairs documented scores of affairs with other women, including Dolly Wilde —the niece of Oscar—and a string of actresses, among them Tallulah Bankhead. "I was never a little girl," Carstairs declared. "I came out of the womb queer."

But despite Phyllis' prom queen good looks, Carstairs' true love, or at least obsession, was "**Lord Tod Wadley**," a 12" tall doll that's visible, despite the 40-year span in the chronology, in each of the photos below. At the time of her death at the age of 93, she was virtually never seen without it, having attached very personal fetishistic powers to it. As a friend observed, "Wadley was her religion."

"I was never entirely honest to anyone," Carstairs confessed later in her life, "except to Wadley."

According to Kate Summerscale, Carstairs' biographer, when Wallis Warfield Simpson, the Duchess of Windsor first saw Wadley, she asked "Who is that?". Carstairs introduced her: "That's my boy, that's Wadley."

"My God!" said the Duchess, for whom her husband had abandoned the British throne: "He's just like my husband."

Two cute guys, **Rock Hudson** (*above*) and **Ronald Reagan** (*right*) try to give cancer to the American public. A very macho-looking Rock, smoking a Camel, had been drinking heavily and lost his six-pack abs.

Reagan eventually gave up smoking and Hollywood altogether, and went on, with his actress wife, Nancy Davis, to preside over the Free World.

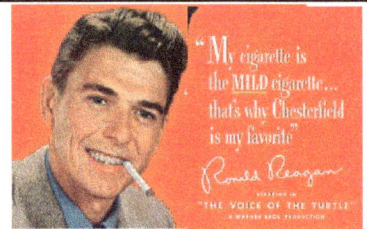

In a scene from *Pillow Talk* (1959), **Doris Day** and **Rock Hudson** played footsies with each other in their respective bathtubs, separated from one another with either a wall or with a split screen, depending on how you interpreted screen technologies at the time.

That was reel life. In real life, between marriages, Doris pursued other men. One of them was a failing young actor, Ronald Reagan, who—until another of his dates (Nancy) told him she was pregnant—considered marrying her. Romantic gossip at the time linked Doris to black men.

At least part of their success as politicians involved the Reagan's deep familiarity with show-biz and the press and PR that made it work. Here, photographed at the White House in May of 1984 are **Rock Hudson**, the former B-list starlet **Nancy Davis Reagan**, and "the Great Communictor" himself, the 40th President of the United States

In 1971, the **Prudential Insurance Company** inaugurated an ad campaign promoting itself as being as solid as "**The Rock**" of Gibraltar. Many Hudson fans credited its success, in part, to the widespread fame and desirability of Rock Hudson

In Sickness and in Health: Two views of the celebrity who "jet propelled, on steroids" the public's awareness of the ravages of AIDS.

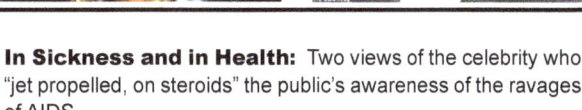

At a reception at the White House, it was **First Lady Nancy Reagan** who first spotted an open sore on **Rock Hudson's** neck. He dismissed it as a minor infection. But it wasn't. In time, the world would learn that the big, strapping, sexy hunk of male flesh known as Rock Hudson, a former sailor and truck driver, had AIDS.

He was the first major celebrity known to have come down with the disease, which was thought at the time to attack "only limp-wristed fairies, junkies, and Haitians." The public was much more naïve in the 1980s. Many did not realize that macho he-men could also be gay.

Hudson was the first personal friend of the Reagans to contract the disease, and as such, it made the President painfully aware that it could strike anywhere. Up until then, in the words of Brigadier General John Hutton, the White House physician, Reagan believed that AIDS "was like measles and would go away." In an ill-conceived move, Hudson agreed to join his longtime friend, Doris Day, for the launch of her cable show, *Doris Day's Best Friends*. Because of her invitation, the world saw a shockingly diminished version of the Rock Hudson they thought they knew. No longer the macho beauty they knew from *Pillow Talk*, his image was broadcast virtually everywhere. It was *Variety* that first broke the news that Rock Hudson had Kaposi's sarcoma. Doris, regretting the invitation she'd extended, but with compassion and grief, said, "Rock shouldn't have come."

Flown to Paris for experimental treatment at the American Hospital there, Hudson finally issued a formal statement admitting that he was not only gay, but that he had full-blown AIDS. At the time, he hadn't yet informed his lover, Marc Christian. When authorities realized he didn't have long to live, Hudson was flown back to Los Angeles on a private chartered jet, where he died on October 2, 1985. One of his last public statements was, "I can at least know that my own misfortune has had a positive worth." Perhaps he meant that his association with the disease would give AIDS a face. However, it took two additional years before President Reagan would even acknowledge the existence of AIDS, much less provide funding for research. By then, AIDS was claiming the lives of both men and women, gay and straight, and children as well. In time, millions would die, and in some parts of the world, continue to do so.

After Hudson's death, since he had continued to have unprotected sex with his lover for a year after he knew he had contracted AIDS, Marc Christian sued his estate for $5 million. The jury awarded Christian $14.5 million—almost three times more than he had asked for. Soon thereafter, the Prudential Life Insurance company abandoned forever its long-standing (but by now, inappropriate) advertising slogan, *Get a Piece of The Rock*.

In Memory of a Great American Movie Star
Rock Hudson
Rest in Peace

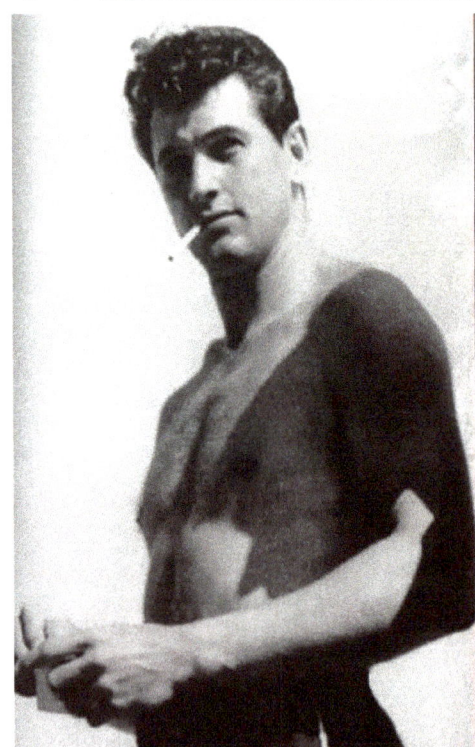

Rock Hudson Erotic Fire

Darwin Porter & Danforth Prince
Another Outrageous Title in Blood Moon's Babylon Series

PART THREE

Blood Moon Productions Proudly Presents

ANITA FINLEY

The Guiding Light Behind
Boomer Times & Senior Life Magazine

A Tribute from Danforth Prince

Anita Finley, founder and publisher of Senior Life & Boomer Times with her friend, **Jack**, in 2024.

Anita Finley, "The Voice of South Florida," met author Darwin Porter, the world's leading travel guide writer, at the right time: The 21st Century was still in diapers. Together, they evolved into a team whose columns and broadcasts evoked the journalistic styles of Barbara Walters and Walter Winchell.

During the course of their 22-year collaboration, on the air and in print, they revealed a LOT of media secrets. Some of them were picked up by other media outlets that included both the *New York Daily News* and London's *Daily Mail*.

That was a trend that developed gradually over the course of many of Blood Moon's book releases. After previews in *Boomer Times*, Darwin's overviews of Humphrey Bogart, Katharine Hepburn, and Marlon Brando later generated "Second Coming" headlines in bigger, more widely distributed publications. *Example?* The *Daily Mail* devoted three full pages (none of them interrupted with ads) to Darwin's *Brando Unzipped*. Ditto, in different variations, for Darwin's literary treatments of Bogart and Hepburn.

Before she met Darwin, Anita had established 1) a popular monthly magazine for senior citizens in South Florida, and 2) a distribution deal for it with *The Miami Herald*. Of headlined interest were overviews of current trends in books and entertainment. *[Those, of course, are subjects on which Darwin speaks and writes about (some say, "obsesses about") frequently.]*

But with the exception of Darwin's humor, glitter, and flash, *Boomer Times* usually focused its coverage on practical subjects of everyday merit, enriched with advice from experts.

As examples of her editorial focus, 'lo those many years, here are some sample headlines that appeared during the creative evolution of her monthly magazine:

"You are the salt of the earth. You have borne the pain and joy of motherhood and have earned every beautiful wrinkle and laugh line...so keep smiling and make time for your children and other children. Everyone needs a mother, but especially a grandmother. If you have reached that glorious age, don't regret it...salivate it."

—**Anita Finley,**
addressing mothers everywhere

HOW TO RESOLVE MARRIAGE CONFLICTS CAUSED BY RETIREMENT
TERM Vs. PERMANENT LIFE INSURANCE
THE PROMISE OF MEDICAL BREAKTHROUGH IS NOW!
HOW TO REVERSE BRAIN AGING
NEW BEGINNINGS FOR YOUR FINANCIAL WELL-BEING
DO YOU BANK ON SOCIAL SECURITY FOR YOUR RETIREMENT INCOME?

***

When Anita's magazine "diversified" its content to include gossipy commentaries from Darwin, he was (oddly enough) the most widely read author of travel guides in the world. Beginning in 1960, he'd written dozens upon dozens of Frommer guides *[hotel recommendations, restaurants, shopping, nightlife, museums and attractions]* to cities, regions, and countries of Europe, the Caribbean, and to

Baby Boomers are defined as any child born between 1946 and 1964. After World War II, they morphed into the most poowerful consumer group in human history.

Anita Finley usually aimed her editorial and marketing focus at them directly

states or regions of the U.S.

Remarkably, during their early months laboring together as a team, it was immediately obvious that his skills were more varied than those of a "run of the mill" travel and leisure advisor. His God-given calling (and talent) involved the composition of non-conformist overviews of the entertainment industry

"Anita, you know," Darwin said to me often, *"helped me blossom as a commentarian, a public speaker, and an 'on the air' critic."*

***

In reference to her inbred sense of optimism, Anita says, "I am very encouraged about life, even with some tragedies, but when one looks up at the sky in the morning, with the billowing clouds, shades of blue, the landscape becomes a painting. Many early mornings, when I was at the radio station prepping for our Saturday morning shows, the view of the sunrise was magical. The hues of reds turning into other subtle colors were breathtaking. Nature, in all its fantasy, can start your day with joy and appreciation. Whenever your night has been dark, open your blinds and look outside, up, down, and all around you—and wish yourself a bright future."

Who is Anita Finley? In my view, she's a modern-day Amazon, a Renaissance woman capable of thriving wherever she happens to land. A woman of influence, she spreads tolerance and love and, very importantly, has kept abreast of (and alert to the implications of) changing times.

Under her administration, *Boomer Times* always focused on ways that Baby Boomers could enrich and extend their lives. In her words, "It's never too late to learn something new," was one of her most oft-expressed monikers.

Her optimism was expressed, in one of her columns, like this:

"April has finally come with beautiful weather, showers for the flowers, lovers strolling arm in arm, restaurants serving delicious Epicurean delights, dogs walking their owners, boaters beating the waves, bikers and walkers getting their exercise. It's almost Easter or Passover—and time to celebrate with family and friends."

"Calling all mothers, grandmothers, and great-grandmothers: May is your month to sing, stomp, and scream about how great it is to be a mom and more! It offers you a lot of privileges and joyful moments."

She greeted June that year with a song from the 1956 movie musical (and before that, the 1945 stage play) **Carousel**: *"June is Bustin' Out All Over."* In her words, *"With the advent of an oncoming summer, it's time for renewal. Life-sustaining energy is flowing."*

In 2023, **Anita** made marital news after a fast-paced late-in-life romance (and sudden marriage) to one of the most eligible bachelors in South Florida.

He's former Naval Commander **John Patrick Derr.** After his retirement from active duty in 1977, he worked for ten years as the Emergency Management Director of Charlotte County, Florida.

He's pictured in the lower photo in 2024 *(post nuptial)* with Anita on the driveway of their home in Port Charlotte, FL.

In the wake of their wedding , dozens of Anita's fans screamed BRAVISSIMA! and sent heartfelt congratulations.

HOW TO BECOME A MEDIA-SAVVY GERONTOLOGIST
by Anita Finley

From age 18 until 30, I modeled on Miami Beach and participated in fashion shows throughout South Beach. Once, I was a guest on *The Tonight Show* with Steve Allen when he broadcast it from the Sea Isle Hotel.

At age 37, with 50 credits from the University of Miami, majoring in literature, I attended Sam Houston State University in Texas. Enrolled in its Radio, TV, and Film program, I interviewed retired professors for college radio shows, and co-founded a Senior Center. For a period of four years, I wrote a weekly column for a local newspaper. It featured elders in the community.

I moved to Boca Raton, Florida, in 1981, and became a real estate broker. On the side, I interviewed elders in Delray Beach as a weekly radio talk show host.

After that, I wrote a senior-specific newspaper column I developed for the *Palm Beach Post*. I promoted it as *"**STARS: Seniors Taking Active Roles in Society**."* A different "Star" was featured every week. In tandem with my work as a realtor, I morphed into a featured speaker in condos and senior communities throughout South Florida making speeches, usually twice a week.

Fascinated as I've always been by the aging process, I enrolled in the Master's program for Gerontology at the college of Boca Raton (now called Lynn University), graduating with a Master's Degree in 1990.

In 1992, I started a magazine dedicated to the growing population of seniors flooding into South Florida. One of the names it bore until its final incarnation as Boomer Times & Senior Life Magazine was *Senior Power News*.

For three hours every week, I collaborated with WSBR/WWNN, a radio station broadcasting my shows (*STARS,* as noted above) throughout South Florida. Every week, in-depth, 30-minute interviews with six informed guests were featured back-to-back. Voices from informed locals were broadcast along with visiting celebrities, personalities such as Jane Fonda and Engelbert Humperdinck along with nationally recognized authors such as Darwin Porter. It also starred a roster of pros whose expertise (medical, legal, or whatever) was specifically aimed at seniors. One of my 'regulars' (we survived as radio colleagues for seven highly visible years) was a British-Canadian doctor whose conversations focused on breakthroughs in male geriatric sexuality and erectile dysfunction.

Press and PR highlights became more frequent after the publication, in 1992, of my book, *Live to 100 Plus*. Producers from all three of that era's networks (ABC, NBC, and CBS) invited me to New York for promotions. Other guests I met in green rooms included George Plimpton and Eartha Kitt.

As a spinoff of that year's Christmas-season buzz, a PR agency arranged a "ten-day, ten city" nationwide tour, with appearances on early morning talk shows (ABC, CBC, and NBC). Its theme involved my spin on what their viewers could buy their elders for the holidays.

Eventually, my radio-based venues morphed into video. For a period of six intense months, my show was broadcast every week throughout South Florida, with ad revenue coming in as part of the setup. Weight watchers was one of my sponsors.

SUNRISE, SUNSET, WHERE HAVE ALL THE YEARS GONE?
By Anita Finley

Where do I begin?
Senior Life, our magazine's original name, was an early idea that turned into a living accumulation of messages, formulas, interviews, and new information and tactics that were put into print, packaged as a newspaper and delivered to a small group of seniors living in South Florida.

It was 1990, and seniors were about to explode across the U.S. South Florida was a destination for many of these retirees. They were smart, upbeat, active and rarin' to go, wanting to know all about what was in store for them as they were aging. It was a powerful opportunity for entrepreneurs to offer senior services and products.

Growing up in Miami Beach, I found myself curious and infatuated by the elder population living on South Beach, in small hotels on the beach, in tiny apartments sprinkled throughout the city and enjoying the beautiful weather and safe, carefree living. In fact, my grandmother lived in one of the first senior retirement hotels on Washington Avenue, the heart of what became known as "a ghetto of elders." She lived there until she died at 95. That left quite an impression on my psyche.

In 1992, I co-authored a book with my late husband Bill Finley, *Live To Be 100 Plus*, made hundreds of speeches throughout South Florida, and appeared on national TV and radio explaining how denser concentrations of elders was the future of our society.

Looking back, it was destined that, in tandem with my husband Bill, I'd start a newspaper aimed specifically at seniors, many of them baby boomers.

Senior Life morphed into *Senior Life & Boomer Times*. Suddenly, we were a full-fledged lifestyle and wellness magazine with monthly deadlines, smart and talented writers and health professionals, and advertisers competing for the attention of seniors and baby boomers in South Florida. Lightning struck when *The Miami Herald* 'discovered' us and asked us to include *Boomer Times* as a monthly supplement of their newspaper.

My business acumen flew into high gear. I organized seminars, symposiums, and EXPOS and hired a talented, dedicated staff. Each of them became "enrolled" in my mission of assisting seniors. In retrospect, applause for my production team is heartfelt. Also, I must applaud our fantastic writers, some of them famous in their own right.

Co-authored with her previous husband, **Live to be 100 Plus**, has proven, again and again, Anita's competence as a gerontologist.

Still Waters Run Deep

Anita, contemplating the ironies of creativity, passion, and age.

In 1998, our hard work and creative ideas brought us an exciting opportunity to expand our multi-media company. dedicated to all the seniors and beamers in the U.S. We were on the verge of being inserted in all the major newspapers, with methodologies similar to our insertion success in *The Miami Herald*. We were about to receive $18 million to insert our magazine in styles equivalent to what's happening with *Parade* and *USA Today* magazines. Everything looked like we'd scored big but unfortunately, the 9/11 tragedy occurred and our investors bailed out! Those three years of planning caught us and we went backwards! What a great disappointment!

In business and in life, change is inevitable. After my multi-talented husband passed in 2017, it was more difficult to operate *Boomer Times* (its shortened name). His death led to inevitable changes in sales and our organizational structure. Ironically, despite our hard work and good intentions, it was COVID that ultimately led to their nose dive.

Commander John Derr taking care of active naval duties in the 1960s.

***

The sun always comes out after a storm and GOOD NEWS! I was introduced, through the Internet, to a 93-year-old smart, kind and youthful man who has changed my life for many reasons. We dated for one year and fell in love. We got married on November 21, 2022.

The next change involved combining our homes (one on the West Coast of Florida, another on the East Coast of the same state) into a single, smoothly functioning unit.

His name was (and is) **John P. Derr**, a retired Naval commander based in Port Charlotte, Florida. He was (and is) a prize. You can Google him and see how this Annapolis graduate, originally from Idaho, has an incredible spirit and the body of a 75-year-old. His one condition for our marriage was that I retire with him and not continue *Boomer Times*. During this, our retirement, we read, play racquetball, visit museums and the gym, travel, and tend to the "growing pains" of our devoted families.

As matriarchs wiser than I have said, "Man proposes, but God disposes," and I am grateful for the wrinkles and laugh lines my joys and sorrows have etched.

So, as a farewell to our advertisers and devoted readers, listeners, and EXPO attendees and exhibitors: You are special and have been a superb group! Go with God, and may he or she bless all of you. **X from Anita.**

The Flames of September vs. The Embers of December
by Danforth Prince

The columns from Anita Finley's *Boomer Times* that we included within our 2024 showpiece, *Hollywood Remembered*, reflect **the American obsession with fame**. Many of them focused on scandals aggressively suppressed during Hollywood's Golden Age.

Darwin composed most of *Hollywood Remembered* when the "Flames of September" burned gently within his heart. Now, he's "Deep in December," awake, alert, and spectacularly productive. And we're in a radically different era.

So—because it seems crucially important at this late stage in our lives—let's take a journey back to yesterday.

When Darwin composed the first of his inaugural bios (subjects included Humphrey Bogart, Katharine Hepburn, and Marlon Brando), Anita was the first newsperson to discover his *oeuvre*.

At the time, her magazine, *Boomer Times* was distributed within both Broward and Palm Beach Counties by *The Miami Herald* and other major outlets in South Florida.

To their delight, many of the "breaking news" revelations he included within Anita's *Boomer Times* were picked up, re-configured, and re-distributed by major-league media which included *The New York Post* and the *Daily Mail*.

Thanks in part to that publicity, Darwin's fans, over the years, have been saturated with insider-ish data about the private lives of, among others, Marilyn Monroe, Michael Jackson, Rock Hudson, James Dean, Tennessee Williams, Zsa Zsa Gabor, Frank Sinatra, Lana Turner, Marlon Brando, Howard Hughes, Merv Griffin, and more recently, Debbie Reynolds, Carrie Fisher, Playboy's Hugh Hefner, Kirk Douglas, Judy Garland, Desi Arnaz, Lucille Ball, and both Henry and Jane Fonda.

Five of Darwin's biographies focus on U.S. Presidents: John F. Kennedy, Bill and Hillary Clinton, Donald Trump, and Ronald Reagan and his two wives, Jane Wyman and Nancy Davis. Yet another is an overview of a Presidential wife and mega-celebrity: *Jacqueline Kennedy Onassis, Her Tumultuous Life & Her Love Affairs*.

Insights and revelations that appeared within many of them, have, over the years, been published within

 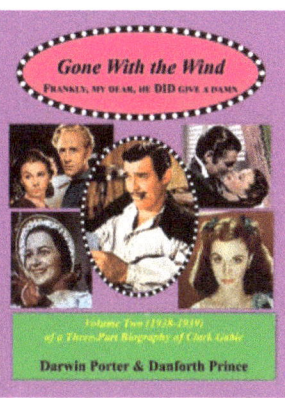 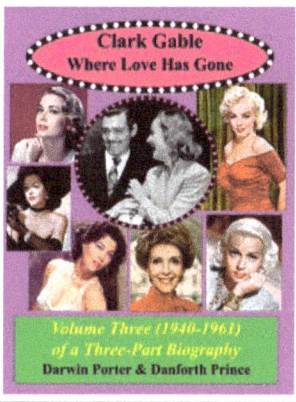 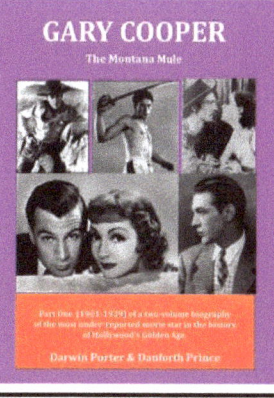 

IS IT TRUE? That **Darwin Porter, Danforth Prince,** and to some degree **Anita Finley** are obsessed with books that reflect **"The Way We Were?"**

YES!, as noted in titles *(see above)* scheduled for release at six-month intervals beginning in 2026. Four of them are already written, and await editorial processing. All of them are described in greater detail in the final pates of this catalogue.

various editions of *Boomer Times*

WHY DO WE CONTINUE TO WRITE AND PRODUCE BOOKS ABOUT "THE WAY WE WERE?"

We do it "before memory fades" as a celebration of the Darwin/Anita collaboration, as a formal statement of our production history, and as an "autobiography" of Blood Moon Productions.

Listed below are examples from *Hollywood Remembered* that Darwin, through Anita, premiered to the world at large, over the course of many years, through *Boomer Times*. Many of them appear in this book in formats which we've amplified from their original presentations.

Burt Reynolds: How a Nude Centerfold Seduced Hollywood
Steve McQueen & Paul Newman Were Lovers
Liz Taylor: Her Teenage Dalliance with Ronald Reagan
The XXX-Rated Life of Peter O'Toole
Kirk Douglas: A Century of Sexual Conquests
Linda Lovelace Deep-Throated Frank Sinatra
Elvis Presley Got Down and Dirty with Marilyn Monroe
Michael Jackson became infatuated with a young (very young) Prince William
June Allyson Slept with Two (Future) U.S. Presidents
Marlon Brando, the Master; James Dean, the Slave Boy
Rock Hudson on the Casting Couch
Judy Garland's Gay Husbands
Movie Stars Reveal "Their First Time"
Vivien Leigh Bedded Guys—and Girls
Katharine Hepburn & Spencer Tracy: Platonic Lovers in Public, LGBTQ "Buddies" in Private
Future First Lady Nancy Davis wanted Clark Gable, but Settled for Reagan
Merv Griffin Seduces Tarzan
Revenge Porn
Bogie May Have Slept with 1,000 Women

One of Darwin's most ironic revelations, as printed within the pages of *Boomer Times,* was the "outing" of President **Abraham Lincoln** as a homosexual. A Daguerreotype replica of his most committed lover, Joshua Fry Speed, was also published.

Lincoln's "lavender" side has now been exposed to millions of Americans through books and television documentaries. A recent example is *Lover of Men: The Untold History of Abraham Lincoln* (2024).

More recent political dramas were also presented within the pages of Anita's *Boomer Times,* notably that involving **Marilyn Monroe**'s murky involvements with **John F. Kennedy**. When his brother, **Robert F. Kennedy**, was "enrolled" to inform her that the President was breaking it off from her, she began an affair with the then Attorney General, too.

After the assassination of JFK, **RFK** launched an affair with the widowed **Jacqueline**. The late **Ethel Kennedy** surely found out about it.

Another revelation that appeared within *Boomer Times* involved JFK's curious co-dependencies with his best friend, **Lem Billings**, a homosexual. Lem's enchantment with young Jack began in prep school (in 1933) and lasted until the end of the President's life in Dallas. Lem had his own room within the White House, and enjoyed, publicly, the title of "best friend."

Because of his injured spine, and often in agonizing pain, JFK engaged Lem as something of a personal aide, advisor, information gatherer, problem-solver, and valet. Lem helped him get dressed most mornings, tending to personal duties, making arrangements, and helping him into his shoes.

Others of Darwin's columns, as they appeared in *Boomer Times*, derived from the distant past, as in how the world's most famous painting **Leonardo Da Vinci's** *Mona Lisa*, was stolen from the Louvre on August 21, 1911. It was eventually "re-discovered" and returned. The thief turned out to be the glazier who had made the painting's protective glass case.

Darwin's columns, as they appeared within *Boomer Times*, had many surprises, including what happened when **Nikita Khruschev** visited Hollywood in September of 1959. When it was announced, as a press & PR triumph—that he'd be hosted by 20th Century Fox, he made a special request to have a private (very private) rendezvous with **Marilyn Monroe**.

Either as a broadcast or as a column, one never knew what Anita and Darwin would feature. Their topics and themes included "The Sexiest Man in the World."

One of their columns featured **Hedy Lamarr**, marketed by her movie studio as "The Most Beautiful Girl in the World." A lot of fans assumed that anyone who looked that good was probably stupid, but something she invented during World War II catalyzed the invention of the cellphone.

Sometimes a column would "time travel backwards" to reveal latter-day surprises. **Sir Isaac Newton** (1643-1727), one of the most influential scientists of all time, predicted that the end of the world would occur in 2060.

The way things are going today, perhaps he was right.

One column within *Boomer Times* led readers on a tour of medical oddities from years passed. Two or three centuries ago, "a cure for anything" involved blowing pipefuls of tobacco into a patient's bowels through a tube inserted in the anus.

Baby Boomers [*i.e., anyone who entered the world between 1946 and 1964, therefore a significant percentage of the world's population*] became the chief consumers of the Anita/Darwin columns and broadcasts.

One item noted that Baby Boomers have already catalyzed a "Silver Tsumani," *i.e.,* a fast-emerging and powerful force in American politics and disposable income. Alarming for its medical complications, the number of people aged 85 and older is projected to more than double from its 6.5 million population of today to 14.4 million in 2040.

The last of the Baby Boomers are expected to say *"Sayonara"* in 2083. That means that some of them will have reached the age of 119. "Impossible!" you say. Actually, Susan Kraus, born in 1880 during the presidency of Rutherford B. Hayes, lived to see the presidency of Bill Clinton.

What's Next from the Legacy of Boomer Times?

It's Blood Moon's **MEDIA BUZZ**, a name coined by Darwin as the theme of many of the columns he submitted to Anita for publication in *Boomer Times*. **Its components are gonna vaguely resemble what we did with Blood Moon's BABYLON series.**

WHAT IS MEDIA BUZZ?

News is that it's an all-new, upcoming series from Blood Moon Productions. Whereas its tone evokes the trio already within our Babylon series, its scope won't be limited to just the naughty indiscretions of Hollywood. It will also lampoon politics, the art world, religion, foreign leaders, and foreign celebrities.

MEDIA BUZZ: Coming Soon From Blood Moon Productions.

PART FOUR

Who Is?

Danforth Prince

*Behind the Scenes of a
Celebrity Exposé Publisher*

Danforth as a young Turk

For years, Danforth Prince was one of the "Young Turks" of the post-millennium publishing industry. He's president and founder of Blood Moon Productions, a firm devoted to researching, salvaging, compiling, and marketing the oral histories of America's entertainment industry.

One of Prince's famous predecessors, the late Lyle Stuart, founder of Barricade Press, was self-described as "the last publisher in America with guts." Stuart once defined Prince as "one of his natural successors." In 1956, that then-novice maverick launched himself with $8,000 he'd won in a libel ludgment against gossip columnist Walter Winchell. It was Stuart who published Linda Lovelace's two memoirs—*Ordeal* and *Out of Bondage*.

"I like to see someone following in my footsteps in the 21st Century," Stuart told Prince. "You publish scandalous biographies. I did, too. My books on J. Edgar Hoover, Jacqueline Kennedy Onassis, and Barbara Hutton stirred up beehives. You do, too."

Prince launched his career in journalism in the 1970s at the Paris Bureau of *The New York Times*. In the early '80s, he resigned to join Darwin Porter in the research, development, and publishing of various titles (including *Frommer's France* and *Frommer's Paris*) within *The Frommer Guides*. As a collaborative team, they reviewed the travel scenes of more than 50 nations for Simon & Schuster. Authoritative and comprehensive, the guides they spearheaded were perceived as indispensable "travel bibles" for millions of readers with recommendations (hotels, restaurants, shopping, nightlife, and "what to see and do" for the nations of Western Europe, the Caribbean, Bermuda, New England, The Bahamas, Georgia, the Carolinas, and California.

Danforth's role model, avant-garde publishing iconoclast and "shock jock," **Lyle Stuart,** publisher of Linda Lovelace's double-barreled memoirs and founder of Barricade Press.

Prince, with Porter, is also the co-author of many celebrity biographies, each configured as a title within Blood Moon's Babylon series. These have included *Hollywood Babylon—It's Back; Hollywood Babylon Strikes Again; The Kennedys: All the Gossip Unfit to Print; Frank Sinatra, the Boudoir Singer*, and *Elizabeth Taylor, There is Nothing Like a Dame*.

Prince, in tandem with Porter, has also co-authored four books on film criticism, along with provocative "postmodern" biographies of, among many others, Lana Turner and Peter O'Toole. With Porter, he also co-authored *Pink Triangle: The Feuds and Private Lives of Tennessee Williams, Gore Vidal, Truman Capote, and Famous Members of their Entourages.*

Prince, a graduate of Hamilton College and a native of Easton and Bethlehem, Pennsylvania, is the president and founder (in 1996) of the Georgia Literary Association, and of the Porter and Prince Corporation. Founded in 1983, the Porter and Prince Corp. produced dozens of travel titles for both Prentice Hall and John Wiley & Sons. In 2011, he was named "Publisher of the Year" by a consortium of literary critics and marketers spearheaded by the J.M. Northern Media Group.

According to Prince, "Blood Moon provides the luxurious illusion that a reader is a perpetual guest at some gossipy dinner party populated with brilliant but occasionally self-delusional figures from bygone eras of the American Experience. Our success at salvaging, documenting, and articulating the (till now) orally transmitted histories of the Entertainment Industry—in ways that have never been seen before—is one of the most distinctive aspects of our backlist."

During the years he published in collaboration with the National Book Network, he electronically documented some of the controversies associated with his stewardship of Blood Moon. From that collaboration emerged more than fifty videotaped documentaries, book trailers, public speeches, and TV or radio interviews. Any of these can be watched, without charge, by performing a search for Đanforth Prince" on YouTube.com; checking him out on Facebook [either "Danforth Prince" or "Blood Moon Productions], on Twitter (now X) (#BloodyandLunar); or by clicking on BloodMoonProductions.com.

During the rare moments when he isn't writing, editing neurosing about, or promoting Blood Moon, he works out at a New York City gym, rescues stray animals, talks to strangers, and maintains the physical plant and gardens of his historic home on Staten Island.

Awards & Honors

Since 2004, under Danforth's stewardship, Blood Moon titles have been awarded dozens of nationally recognized literary prizes. They've included both silver and bronze medals from the IPPY (Independent Publishers Assn.) Awards, four nominations and two Honorable Mentions for BOOK OF THE YEAR from Forward Reviews; nominations from the Ben Franklin Awards; and Awards and Honorable Mentions from the New England, the Los Angeles, the Paris, the New York, the San Francisco, and the Hollywood Book Festivals. Two of its titles have been Grand Prize Winners for Best Summer Reading, as defined by the Beach Book Awards.

Anatomy of an Exposé
The Donald, as Never Seen Before

The Donald, vengeful subject of a bio originally conceived by Danforth Prince

In 2016, Donald Trump was running for President for the first time. The dumpster fires of that election prompted Blood Moon's production and publication of one of the boldest political commentaries of that election cycle, *Donald Trump: The Man Who Would Be King.*

This was the first major book to explore the origins of the Trump Dynasty and its links to The Donald's grandfather and his ventures into Alaska during its Gold Rush. The Trump family's "seed money" was founded on the sale of mining supplies; meat salvaged from dead pack animals which were worked to death hauling supplies over high-altitude passes; and the "rental" of over-the-hill prostitutes to horny (and half-frozen) new arrivals from "Back East."

The book went on to relay the cringeworthy moments and media gaffes of Donald Trump in the years prior and during his 2016 campaign.

It won top prizes ("BIOGRAPHIES OF THE YEAR") from the Hollywood Book Festival, the New York Book Festival, and the Florida Book Festival.

Years later, in 2024, Blood Moon's then-latest memoir, *Hollywood Remembered* (a book aimed at Media Studies) won the Best Biography of the Year Award from the Hollywood Book Festival, and Best Anthology of the Year from the New York Book Festival.

Puritanical America the Way It Used to Be
(*i.e.*, the Genealogical Origins of a Publishing Maverick)

Whereas everyone's family has a past full of interesting and exciting stories, the Prince family of Flatbush in Brooklyn was unusual because their New World saga began early in the history of the United States.

It started in the then-Dutch stronghold of Brooklyn 1657 and continued to unfold there—at least until the family migrated to the then-booming industrial stronghold of Cleveland—through three-and-a-half centuries of unimaginable upheaval and change.

Many of Danforth's early male ("America-born") ancestors "took to the sea," becoming skilled sailors in the Anglo-Dutch tradition. One of them, Christopher Prince, having

Miniature portrait, on ivory, in a gold frame, of the 18th century sea captain **Christopher Prince**, father-in law of (*right photo*) **Gertrude Helen Martense Prince** (1818-1894). She married the sea captain's son 1835, around the time this portrait of her was painted. .

attained the rank of captain sailing routes between New York, Capetown, and Marseilles, saw action against the British during the War of 1812.

The uncrowned "Queen of Flatbush" was Gertrude Martense Prince. It was said that every summer, her farm provided vegetables for half of the residents of Flatbush. She was only 16 when she married John Duffield Prince (son of the above-mentioned Christopher Prince) in 1835. Together, in 1837, they erected (at the corner of what's now Fulton and Clarkson Streets in present-day Brooklyn), an elegant private home with Ionic columns and space for entertaining. Flowering magnolia trees graced its front yard. It became the center of some of the most elegant celebrations in Flatbush, with the gowned Gertrude presiding as one of her era's reigning hostesses.

Another distinguished ancestor of Danforth was the philosopher/theologian, **Jonathan Edwards** (1703-1758), a leading figure in the "American Enlightenment" and one of its most widely respected orators. His literary output included "Sinners in the Hands of an Angry God," viewed today as a (subliminally terrifying) classic of early American literature. Another of his works was *The End for Which God Created the World,* an evangelistic tract that motivated thousands of missionaries in the decades that followed his death.

He was the maternal grandfather of **Aaron Burr,** the third U.S. Vice President and the murderer of Alexander Hamilton.

Another distinguished ancestor was **Harriet Beecher Stowe** (1811-1896), the American author and abolitionist who immortalized herself as the author of *Uncle Tom's Cabin* (1852). One of the most incendiary books ever written, it depicted the harsh conditions experienced by enslaved African Americans. Reaching an audience of millions it was "required reading" in North American schools for at least a century. It's still considered a book that essentially altered the course of the American Experience.

On November 25, 1862, at the approximate midpoint of "The War of Northern Aggression," as some called it, Stowe was received at the White House by then-President **Abraham Lincoln**. In front of everyone within earshot, he delivered a line that went "zing" to the collective consciousness of many of her descendants: "So you're the little woman who wrote the book that started this great war."

The scariest theologian in the American Colonies, father of "The American Enlightenment;" author of "Sinners in the Hands of an Angry God;" and grandfather of Aaron Burr.

Jonathan Edwards (1703-1758)

Would he have approved of Danforth's backlist?

ALL IN THE FAMILY

The abolitionist activist blamed for starting America's Civil War, the author of *Uncle Tom's Cabin*

Harriet Beecher Stowe (1811-1896)

The Complicated Celluloid Saga of *BUTTERFLIES IN HEAT*

During his tenure at *The New York Times* in Paris, *[then located on the rue Scribe, Paris 9e, near the Paris Opera]* Danforth was awarded a two-week vacation. As a change of scenery, he flew to Rome and Naples.

He had rented accommodations near the Via Veneto. One sultry night in Rome, he strolled along the fabled (and then, very theatrical) pavements recently "experienced" by Elizabeth Taylor and Richard Burton.

At a newsstand, he was surprised to see a rack devoted to paperback copies of an English-language novel, *Butterflies in Heat*. Selling for the equivalent of $1.95 in U.S. currency, it had been written by Darwin Porter. Although they hadn't met, it was a name already familiar to Danforth, since he had "experienced" Morocco using that author's travel guide.

That night, he read *Butterflies in Heat*, surprised at how memorable its characters were. They included a blonde (male) hustler (Numie Chase); an American version of Coco Chanel (Leonora de la Mer) living in imperial and autocratic retirement in Key West.

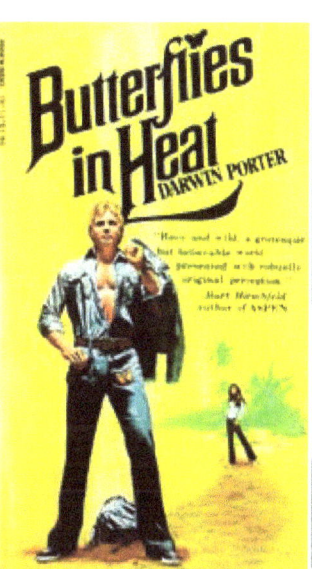

MARKETING VARIATIONS OF A CULT CLASSIC

As the boundaries of censorship grew more lenient, the front cover of one of publisher Danforth's "staples" became more permissive. Years after its inaugural publication in 1976, Darwin Porter's evocative novel is still selling.

Other characters he remembered, long before he ever actually met Darwin, included Lola La Mour, an outrageously campy African American trans-sexual who was shacked up with The Commodore, her perverse lover. Also memorable was Tangerine: 300 pounds of compassionate Southern womanhood. Even Key West itself emerged as a character within *Butterflies in Heat,* configured as it was into "The Last Resort," a seedy end-of-the-line favored as a refuge for the mending of broken hearts.

Chasing Butterflies
(Celebrity Endorsements)

Butterflies in Heat had already been publicly endorsed by a number of then-famous authors, notably Tennessee Williams and James Kirkwood, who would later win a Pulitzer Prize for his hit Broadway musical, *A Chorus Line* (1975, with a film adaptation a decade later).

In Key West, Tennessee was both sullen and intoxicated when he delivered his endorsement for *Butterflies:* "I'd walk the waterfront for Numie any night of the week."

As part of yet another recommendation of *Butterflies in Heat,* the novelist, James Leo Herlihy, asked, "How does Darwin Porter's garden grow? Only in moonlight, and only at midnight, when man-eating vegetation in any color but green bursts forth into full bloom to devour the latest offerings."

In 1969, Danforth had seen *Midnight Cowboy* written by Herlihy and starring Dustin Hoffman and Jon Voight. *[Each of them was nominated for a Best Actor Oscar, losing to John Wayne for* True Grit. Midnight Cowboy *also won an Oscar for Best Picture of the Year, the first and only X-rated film to do so.]*

 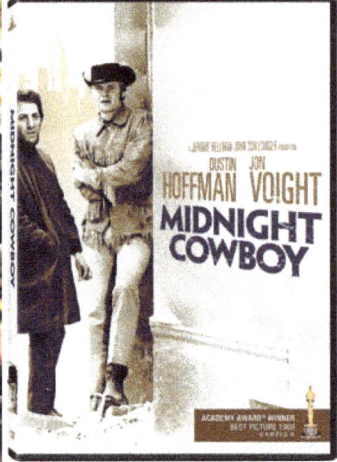

Many critics wrote that *Butterflies in Heat* was the "logical continuation" of *Midnight Cowboy,* and that it revealed what happened to the hustler (Joe Buck) after he reached Florida and both the end of his dream and the end of that movie.

For years, Herlihy, was one of Darwin's best friends, a mentor to whom Darwin had showed his first novel (*an early version of* Butterflies in Heat) which he'd written when he was a prodigy of 17. He had never, to that point, submitted it to either a literary agent or a publisher.

[In other words, years before Herlihy's crafting of "sex for sale" Joe Buck, Darwin had conceived of Numie Chase, his blonde hustler and the motivating force within Butterflies in Heat.*]*

Darwin's composition of **Butterflies in Heat** and its theme of desperate hustlers at the end of the line coincided with the spectacular success of equivalently earthy projects that had attained unimaginable success after their adapation into films

Two of them were **James Kirkwood's** musical (later a movie), *A Chorus Line*, and **James Leo Herlihy**'s novel, *Midnight Cowboy*.

Midnight Cowboy's adaptation into a film about (guess what?) sex for sale from streetwalking hotties later made millions and won some Oscars—the first X-rated movie to ever be so acknowledged.

Both **Kirkwood** (*photo top left*) and **Herlihy** (*photo top right*), each a frenemy of Darwin from "the hood" in Key West, endorsed **Butterflies in Heat**.

Literary License
The Sordid Story of Jay Garon

In the 1970s, Darwin was introduced to Jay Garon, a "notoriously iconoclastic" (and sometimes larcenous) literary agent who would later "discover" (and hugely profit from) the best-selling novelist, John Grisham.

Garon began to shop *Butterflies in Heat* to publishing venues, receiving nothing in return but rejections.

Although even conservative editors agreed with one of Kirkwood's endorsements, ("Hot enough to singe the wings off any butterfly") they were afraid of its unconventional characters (Hustlers! Trans-sexuals!), context (*burnt-out love for sale at the end of the line!*), and theme (*beauty, pain, and postmodern pop searches for redemption*).

After many tries, Manor Books bought reprint rights to the novel, and ultimately, its president was glad that he did. It went on and on for years, eventually selling one million copies throughout North America and Europe.

Manor Books widely advertised it, taking out a two-page color ad in *Publisher's Weekly*, a promotion they duplicated in other publications. During the summer of 1976, an airplane was hired to fly over the resorts of Fire Island, trailed by a banner that advertised BUTTERFLIES IN HEAT in huge red capital letters. *Butterflies* became THE summer read for Fire Islanders that summer. Permissive cocktail hours resounded with premises about what really made Numie hot.

Based on this avalanche of publicity, a young film producer, Jerry Wheeler, rushed to acquire the novel's screen rights.

Provocatively, he even went so far as to announce that the film would star Warren Beatty and Lauren Bacall as the male and female leads. But whereas Bacall's agent loudly asserted that her role as "the American version of Coco Chanel" would suit her style and mannerisms. Beatty's agent did not respond.

Readers submitted suggestions and recommendations of replacements for Beatty: perhaps Perry King or Jan-Michael Vincent.

Left photo: **Lauren Bacall**, older but still seductive, glamourous, and demanding. Darwin thought she'd be perfect as Leonora de la Mer; and (*right photo*) **Warren Beatty,** one of the most promiscuous actors in Hollywood, seen here with **Faye Dunaway** in *Bonnie and Clyde* (1967).

Some of his abandoned *inamorata* thought he'd be perfect as the washed-up hustler, Numie Chase. Jerry Wheeler, the film version's producer, even announced to the press that they'd been awarded the parts.

Perry King

Jerry Wheeler had seen King's performance in his film debut (*Slaughterhouse 5; 1972*), and he thought he might make a good Numie. But his agent never responded. Wheeler told Darwin that he didn't know whether King had even been shown the script or not.

Jan-Michael Vincent

As for Jan-Michael Vincent, when he was asked to play Numie, he responded, "Why in the hell not?"

Wheeler had been impressed with Vincent's performance opposite such stars as John Wayne, Rock Hudson, Robert Mitchum, and Charles Bronson. Alas, Wheeler was slow in getting him a contract, and during the delay, Vincent signed to make *Shadow of the Hawk* (1976) opposite Marilyn Bassett.

Interestingly, in offers that Darwin interpreted as having enormous artistic and commercial merit, two major-league porn stars (each an X-rated "King" during the late 70s) eagerly solicited the role of Numie. They included Jack Wrangler and Cal Culver (aka Casey Donovan). Wheeler (rather squeamishly, everyone thought) rejected both of them. "We're not making that kind of picture."

Perry King (left) and **Jan-Michael Vincent.** Potential dreamboats for those who could pay the price.

Christopher Jones

Darwin's choice for who would play Numie was actor Christopher Jones. They had met in 1961 when Jones had a minor role on Broadway in Tennessee Williams' *The Night of the Iguana* opposite Shelley Winters. From 1965 to 1968, he'd been married to actress Susan Strasberg.

Born in Tennessee, Jones had become known for his performances in such films as *Wild in the Streets* (1968) and *Ryan's Daughter* (1970). *The New York Times* suggested that he had the star power and talent of the late James Dean.

Darwin visited Jones when he occupied a cottage behind 10050 Cielo Drive in Los Angeles. He had been having an affair with Sharon Tate, who lived in that property's "big house," [*i.e., the main residence associated with the "rental" cottage in back.*]

She'd soon make headlines, worldwide, when she was "butchered" by psychotic members of the Charles Manson gang, who killed her other guests, too.

"Based on Sharon's murder in 1969, poor Chris seemed to be coming unglued," Darwin said. "Before the afternoon ended, he claimed he never wanted to act in a film ever again, even though offers were coming in."

Darwin "vibed" with the affable and charismatic **Christopher Jones** better than any other candidate for the role of Numie.

Here, he appears with **Pia Degermark** in *The Looking Glass War* (1970).

Matt Collins

Wheeler's final choice for the character of Numie was Matt Collins, America's top male model of the 1970s. Lean, chiseled, and blond, his million-dollar portfolio seemed to be aimed at ads for cigarettes, beer, and suits. At the time, Collins was receiving 30,000 fan letters a month from ardent fans. He'd also been voted the most handsome man in the world, with Catherine Deneuve polling as the world's most beautiful female.

Collins was graceful and sinewy, with sandy hair, dark eyes, strong cheekbones, and a sullen demeanor. His casting as Numie landed him on the front cover of *After Dark,* an arts & entertainment revue aimed at GLBTQ audiences.

Left photo: Here's **Matt Collins,** the highest-paid male model of the 1970s, on the cover of Charles Hix's Guide for Men, *Looking Good.*

It was Matt who was eventually persuaded to play Numie, a self-absorbed "gay for pay' hustler in Key West (i.e., the end of the line) in the film adaptation of Darwin Porter's *Butterflies in Heat.*

Right photo: NUMIE (aka Matt) IN LOVE after his character was "safely heterosexualized" in a (failed) attempt to render the film adaption more commercially acceptable to the general public.

A flock of extraordinary women engulf **Numie Chase (Matt Collins)** in a whirl of sexual escapades. Roxanne Gregory is the conquest.

Gloria Swanson
Egomaniacal, Temperamental, and Very Very Grand

Nearly everyone agreed that the role of Leonora de la Mer would be ideal for Gloria Swanson, since it evoked comparisons of her as Norma Desmond in *Sunset Blvd.* (1950). In *Butterflies,* however, instead of a faded vamp of the silent screen, she'd be a once-fabled fashion designer whose *avant-garde* couture was, by now, outdated.

Darwin personally delivered the filmscript of the newly in vogue *Butterflies in Heat* to Swanson in Manhattan. After reading it, she said, "I've been looking for, but not finding, a role like this. However, I must insist that your producer, Mr. Wheeler, greatly enlarge my part. My fans will want to see more of me…not this male model."

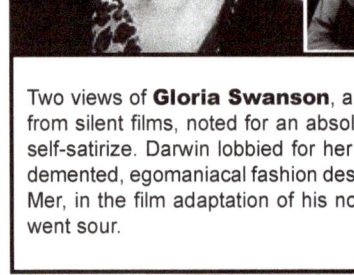

Two views of **Gloria Swanson**, an "over the hill diva" from silent films, noted for an absolute lack of ability to self-satirize. Darwin lobbied for her involvement as the demented, egomaniacal fashion designer, Leonora de la Mer, in the film adaptation of his novel. Things quickly went sour.

Then, another ego-driven disaster struck: A misinformed reporter for New York's *Daily News* broke the fake news that Swanson "Will return to the screen in the porno version of *Sunset Blvd."*

Swanson's involvement with the substance and dialogue of the screenplay had nothing to do with porn, but the damage was done. She was inundated with protests, enough so that she felt compelled to buy a full page (and much gossiped-about) announcement in *Variety.* In it, she loudly insisted that "I will not be playing Leonora de la Mer in the upcoming film rendition of *Butterflies in Heat."*

Rita Hayworth
The Decline and Fall of the Love Goddess

Now dealing with a full-blown production crisis, Wheeler, accompanied by Darwin, paid a call on Rita Hayworth, presenting her with an opportunity to turn to the screen as the upcoming film's female lynchpin, Leonora de la Mer.

[*Hayworth, rivaled only by Betty Grable, had been the top pin-up girl for G.I.s during World War II. Eventually, she*

Rita (The Love Goddess) **Hayworth:** Although negotiations were polite, age had taken its toll

morphed into one of the greatest stars of the 1940s. Hailed as that decade's "love goddess," she's remembered as the enigmatic—and unforgettable—lynchpin of the 1946 film noir, Gilda.]

As a film production team, Wheeler, with Darwin and the film offer, were at first received gracefully, and they elaborated at length about their vision both for the film and for Hayworth's involvement. They even digressed into speculation about which designer might handle her wardrobe, since she'd be playing a character inspired by Coco Chanel.

"But after an hour of gracious chatter," Darwin recalled, "Miss Hayworth seemed to come unglued. She rose unsteadily to her feet and rudely ordered us out of her home. Frankly, her sudden emotional shift (was it a mood swing?) shocked us. Was it something one of us had said?"

In 1980, some light was shed on the aborted deal. She had been diagnosed, as revealed in the press, with an early onset of Alzheimer's disease. It contributed to her death in 1987 at the age of 68.

And the role of the grandest dragon in couture went to:

Left photo: **Barbara Baxley**, as she appeared in a 1955 stage production of *Bus Stop*, a role that Marilyn Monroe later made famous, and

Right photo: The cover of the first edition of *Period of Adjustment*, by Tennessee Williams. Her interpretation of its female lead won her a Tony Award in 1961.

Barbara Baxley

For the role of Leonora, several other fading stars were suggested, but Wheeler settled for Barbara Baxley. She was a very talented actress and had been nominated for a Tony for her performance on Broadway in Tennessee Williams' dark comedy, *Period of Adjustment* in 1961. [*Tennessee himself admitted that the play's very existence had derived from "a rush of activity partly induced by drugs."*]

"She might have evoked a great Leonora," Darwin said, "but her role as a seething and ruthless egomaniac was cut down and ended up as bland and rather harmless. Baxley—and what could have been a fabulously viperish performance—deserved better."

Joan Blondell vs. Pat Carroll

For the role of Tangerine, Darwin suggested that his long-standing friend, Joan Blondell, would be ideal. He visited her with a proposal and spent a "working afternoon" going over it with her. When he finished, she said, "Sign me up! I can play that role. I might even get a Best Supporting Actress Oscar for it."

Alas, before filming began, she developed health issues and had to bow out. She died on Christmas Day of 1979 of leukemia.

The role of Tangerine went to Pat Carroll, a talented actress and a much-awarded one, winning an Emmy, a Drama Desk Award, a Grammy, and a nomination for a Tony Award.

Two views of **Joan Blondell**

Folksy and relentlessly cheerful **Pat Carroll**

"She was lovable as Tangerine," Darwin said. "Perhaps a bit too lovable. My version of Tangerine had a much darker side and wasn't quite as jolly as Carroll made her in the film adaptation."

Gay? Gay-for-Pay?

As sales for the original (book) version of *Butterflies in Heat* soared, members of the press began referring to it as "the gay versions of both *Sunset Blvd.* and *All About Eve.*"

Actually, as Darwin himself frequently said, "It wasn't a gay novel, as such, since most of its lead characters were straight. Even Numie, a 'gay for pay' hustler, ends up falling for a woman."

As dictated by the novel, the movie was set in Key West. Regrettably, during pre-production, Wheeler—as he later admitted—got "cold feet," fearing that the script and the subject matter were too controversial.

According to Darwin, "Thus, in decisions he made that I'll forever regret, he devised what I call 'a vanilla downplay' of what had been a shocking and avant-garde breath of fresh air with blockbusting potential. Wheeler eventually succeeded at watering my novel into a rather conventional (and boring) heterosexual love story. We argued about it at the time, with me telling him, 'If you want a love story, revive Ryan O'Neal with Ali MacGraw.'"

Years before his death in 1990, Wheeler phoned Darwin, telling him that he'd made a huge mistake in not sticking to his novel's original vision. By then, of course, it was too late. Wheeler compounded his bad judgment by opting to change even the film's title from *Butterflies in Heat* to the more flaccid *The Last Resort*. Compounding matters, when it was released on CD, its name was changed again to the even more flaccid *Tropic of Desire*.

The Commodore

During their pursuit of the perfect cast, Wheeler, with Darwin, also visited Orson Welles, hoping to lure him into an onscreen involvement as the perverse Commodore. He received them politely and (correctly) evaluated the role as intriguing.

"It's something new and different for me," he said, "especially if you go through with your casting of Eartha Kitt as 'my little hottie.'"

Ironically, Welles confessed that he'd had, years before, an affair with her.

As negotiations continued, to his frustration and regret, Wheeler learned that because of his obesity and fast-declining health, Welles (and any film project in which he'd be featured) could not be insured.

[*Welles, during inaugural discussions, at least, was fully supportive of the context of his character as part of a ménage à trois with Numie and Lola. Regrettably, in the final, watered-down version of the script, his role was rendered less controversial and he became little more than an eccentric, self-indulgent, egomaniacal drunk without the ménage à trois. Ditto for Lola La Mour. In the final cut, the role went to Don Porter, best known for his TV portrayals of Peter Sands, the boss of Ann Sothern's character in* Private Secretary, *a 1950s sitcom.*]

Darwin conceived of **The Commodore** as a malevalent, alcohol-soused, overweight, and over-the-hill letch. **Orson Welles** (upper photo) would have been perfect. In his place, because he was "uninsurable" the producers cast the affable and handsome staple from the golden age of TV, **Don Porter** (lower photo).

Eartha Kitt as a Black Trans-sexual

During pre-production, Wheeler spent lots of effort figuring out how to cast the trans-sexual, Lola La Mour, fretting that the character—as portrayed by Darwin in his novel—would lead to the commercial ostracization of any film adaptation. During conversations with Eartha Kitt, she accepted the role, and a contract was drawn up. Orson Welles had already referred to her as "the most exciting woman in the world."

Thus Eartha Kitt flew to Key West and into Darwin's life. Her part included a provocative (some censors called it "sexually suggestive") bar routine in which she begins a cadenced seduction of "the new man in town"…in this case, Numie (aka Matt Collins).

[*Eartha was well-known at the time, in part because of her casting, a decade before, as Catwoman in the 1966-1968 TV series* Batman, *the one that featured Adam West.*]

The original screenplay for *Butterflies in Heat*, like the novel on which it was based, spun around strong, powerful interactions between vivid characters involved in tangled sexual trysts. To everyone's disadvantage, before filming began, Wheeler ordered a "more vanilla" rewrite that would be less controversial and less raw.

As Darwin later described it, "The filmmakers loved everything iconoclastic and unconventional about my original version of *Butterflies in Heat*. Later, much to the detriment of its commercial appeal, they became deathly afraid, paralyzed, even, by its unconventionality. Ultimately, they watered down and rendered 'harmless' everything they'd originally interpreted as compelling. Ultimately, the film adaptation morphed into a

Campy enough to play a drag queen: **Eartha Kitt** as Catwoman in *Batman* (1966-68)

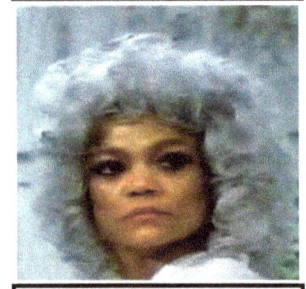

Eartha as an "implied transsexual," **Lola La Mour** in the film adaptation of *Butterflies in Heat*.

somewhat conventional love story between two emotionally damaged heterosexuals."

Fudkicker Malloy, an internet critic, wrote: "Darwin Porter's *Butterflies in Heat* was a defining piece of gay literature and a bestseller, receiving praise from the likes of Tennessee Williams, James Kirkwood, and James Leo Herlihy. The story centered on a hustler, Numie Chase, and his diverse clientele: A black drag queen, an aging, domineering fashion designer, an alienated gay man, and a run-of-the-mill nice girl in search of love. Each of them is vying for a piece of Numie, who is in search of himself. Its film adaptation starred the top male model of the decade."

Released in 1979 and retitled *Tropic of Desire*, the film was highly enjoyable and campy, with touches of borderline soft-core pornography. It didn't fare too well with critics, but fans embraced it. Since its release, *Tropic of Desire* has become something of a cult classic.

Little did Danforth know that the night he bought that $1.95 paperback, *Butterflies in Heat*, from a newsstand on the Via Veneto, that it would change his life.

The Georgia Literary Association

In 1997, he'd purchased the historic former home of Robert Toombs, famous for previously serving as Secretary of State to the Confederate States of America. It stood in the town of Washington, Georgia, the site of Jefferson Davis' signing of the papers that dissolved the Confederate States of America. He then fled, disguised in drag and deeply humiliated. Somehow, he was nonetheless arrested (and briefly imprisoned) by the Yankee "invaders."

It was during his sojourn in Washington, Georgia, that Danforth established the Georgia Literary Association. As one of its first releases (and in collaboration with the Florida Literary Association), he factored and released a new edition of the notoriously best-selling *Butterflies in Heat*, replete with a "somewhat provocative" front cover. (see illustration…)

[*Buying a historic home in the Deep Dark South seemed like a good idea at the time. Porter and Prince had opted to station themselves there, far from the editorial pressure cookers of Manhattan, during their research and composition of the well-reviewed* Frommer's Guide to Georgia and the Carolinas, *a title they developed, nurtured, and sustained though each of its five editions.*]

Once again, *Butterflies in Heat* became a counterculture bestseller, especially in New York, L.A., San Francisco, and this time, thanks to some local press and PR, "the fleshpots of Atlanta."

As stated by Prince, "The re-release of *Butterflies in Heat*, in collaboration with Darwin (who still held the copyright) catalyzed a change in my career goals forever. I became a publisher—and a controversial one at that. First came the novels, then the movie bios, then political tomes devoted to scandal-soaked iconoclasts like JFK and later, Donald J. Trump. Ironically, it would be our bio of Jacqueline Kennedy that outsold those of any of the male politicians we crafted."

The Georgia Literary Association was established in the late 1990s in Wilkes County, Georgia. Following its initial success, it was relocated to New York City.

Its literary output focused on controversial novels by Darwin Porter, Danforth's co-author. Darwin's novels were crafted, in part, as a diversification from too weighty a dependence on the crafting and research of many dozens of Frommer travel guides.

One reviewer maintained that "Darwin Porter's literary niche is set midway between one-handed eroticism and the literary canons of D.H. Lawrence and E.M. Forster. He specializes in artfully brutal sagas, often with overtones of psychosis, sexual obsession, money, power, personal transformation, religion, and love."

Entrepreneurial Danforth & The Georgia Literary Assn.

It grew out of Porter and Prince's on-site research for *Frommer's Guide to Georgia & The Carolinas.* Setting it up seemed to justify the release of a new breed of entertainment aimed at the counter-culture South.

The upper photo shows the company logo, and the *lower photo* shows the outfit's headquarters within Danforth's historic home in **Washington, Georgia**. It's address? **408 South Alexander Avenue**.

It was built after the Civil War by Robert Toombs, the "Unrepentant Confederate" who served as Secretary of State to the Confederacy, According to rumor, it was funded with gold looted from the Confederate Treasury as wagons hauled it to (supposed) safety, near Washington, during its flight from Richmond.

Danforth radically enlarged and renovated it during his occupancy.

Razzle Dazzle
A Libertine Romp as a Sequel to *Butterflies in Heat*

On the heels of *Butterflies in Heat*, Danforth published *Razzle-Dazzle*, also authored by Darwin. Configured as a sequel to *Butterflies*, it was marketed with taglines that included: *"Super-rich Sherry and her boys set out on a gay romp to film Butterflies in Heat in Key West. But an ill wind was blowing north from the Caribbean."*

It was also bolstered with review quotes (in this case, from *Time Out* in London): *"Darwin Porter makes Truman Capote look like a Disney-boycotting redneck at a Southern Baptist Convention."*

Razzle-Dazzle rose to No. 2 on counter-culture polls in New York and San Francisco and reinforced with praise from reviewers in underground Atlanta and Savannah, it almost topped the continuing sale of *Butterflies*. It also developed an international gay following, especially in Toronto, Berlin, Munich, Helsinki, Copenhagen, Zurich, London, Paris, and Edinburgh.

The German periodical *Siegessaule* wrote: "There's something for everyone in *Razzle-Dazzle*: Sadists, size queens, romance readers, thrill seekers, gossip mongers, defenders of the *paparazzi*, and bedmates of Cuban men."

Fan mail arrived, some suggesting that a film adaptation might star both Elizabeth Taylor (as a grand diva and matriarch) and Madonna as her competitive, rebellious, and immoral daughter.

A script for it was devised and "shopped." Agents of Taylor expressed interest, in part because their client would portray a woman more alluring than her daughter. Agents for Madonna, however, requested such an outrageous price that any collaboration became impossible.

For Danforth, it marked the beginning of what thousands before him had experienced: Hollywood is, indeed, the Boulevard of Broken Dreams."

[Fortunately, for him, the dreams that were shattered were not the only ones being crafted, as he was having one success after another in publishing. The shattered dreams had, for the most part, been nurtured by Carolina and Georgia-based filmmakers who had labored over scripts and production issues for a dream that never came true. "If all the failed scripts were stacked up, they'd be a mountain high!" Danforth told a reporter. "No matter how good the script, everything depends on money, money, money. That's the game in Hollywood. Whereas great scripts lie on shelves, gathering dust, some really trite and tacky ones get filmed. Everyone is aiming for the jackpot but a few are the lucky ones who see their dreams come true."

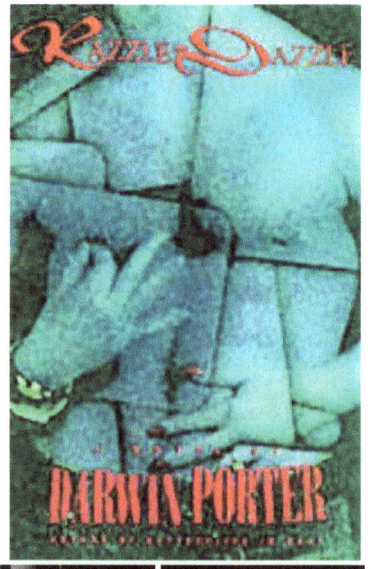

Then Came a Razzling, Dazzling Casting Dilemma

In the film adaptation instigated by investors in Nashville, everyone wanted to know who would play super-rich Sherry, the novel's Tarantula Mother, and who would play her rebellious, nymphomaniacal daughter?

Outreach was inaugurated to **Elizabeth Taylor,** the megastar who brilliantly portrayed a harridan in ***Who's Afraid of Virginia Woolf***, and **Madonna,** who wanted WAY too much money.

SILENT DEBAUCHERY
Soundless Films "on the Down Low"

Darwin's epic novel, **Hollywood's Silent Closet**, published in 2001 by the Georgia Literary Association, was a lusty saga of the Roaring Twenties, an incredible era when movie stars morphed into legendary figures around the world. In what was going on behind the scenes, it spares no one, especially Rudolph Valentino and Charlie Chaplin.

Time Out for Books proclaimed, "There has never been a juicy read like this one on Hollywood in the flapper era of the 1920s."

Fab magazine claimed, "Darwin Porter does everything but stick our fingers in a light socket to give us a sexual buzz."

G-Scene found *Hollywood's Silent Closet* "Unbuttoning or unzipping the flies of men and reaching inside to sample the goodies of every actor from Valentino to Clark Gable."

Rudolph Valentino with **Vilma Banky** in *The Son of the Sheik* (1926). In audiences across America, women swooned as they imagined Valentino's luscious lips meeting theirs.

Homosexuals with Southern Twangs
Rhinestone Country
A Novel about Closeted Lives South of the Mason-Dixon Line

As the third novel in its published repertoire, The Georgia Literary Association released *Rhinestone Country*, one of the most controversial books ever published about the music industry in Nashville. It centered on country singer Pete Riddle, a closeted bisexual making it massive in the country-music industry. Many readers saw shades of a young Elvis Presley.

Outrage called it "The most provocative, hard-hitting novel ever written about country-western stars who scaled the mountain, then crashed to the bottom."

Tyrone Maxwell described it as, "a sexual kick in the groin." *Inferno* defined Pete Riddle as "the most fuckable man on earth.:" Mississippi Pearl wrote, *"Rhinestone Country* reads like a scalding gulp of rotgut whiskey on a snowy night in a bow-jacks honky-tonk."

RHINESTONE COUNTRY
A publicity poster aimed at the then-flourishing market for GLBTQ print and celluloid entertainment

BLOOD MOON
A Novel about What Happens When the Moon Turns to Blood

Blood Moon (the novel after which Blood Moon Productions was eventually named) was released in 1999, just as the 20th Century came to an end. An epic with 800-plus pages, it became a best-seller, even in Germany. A few years after its release, Danforth re-named the Georgia Literary Association in its honor. That original, "region-specific" entity, after that, was "re-baptized" as Blood Moon Productions, Ltd.

Between the Covers defined it like this: "This is pure novelistic Viagra, an American interpretation of Arthur Schnitzler's erotic masterpiece, *La Ronde*. Never have I read of such interlocked lovers pursuing sex, money, and power. Take a hostage for ransom, or let your father have his way with you—just raise the $14.95 to purchase this dazzling, seductive novel."

It elicited a lot of buzz among Hollywood producers, and film scripts were written with hopes that it would be adapted into celluloid. Regrettably, it was never produced.

The novel was so successful that Danforth made a decision. Since it was no longer headquartered in Georgia, the Georgia Literary Assn was, by now, an out-of-date moniker. With that it mind, its name was changed, in honor of its most recently released novel, to Blood Moon Productions, Ltd. The new entity would move in powerful new directions that eventually generated "Second Coming" headlines.

What's New in Fiction defined **Blood Moon** as "A stylish thriller expertly written and gripping. The corruption of the Far Right, religion, obsession, and the siren song of the flesh—it's hot, hot, and hotter."

Blood Moon "Discovers" the Fine Art of Biography with
A Double Dose of Humphrey Bogart

For decades, Darwin had been gathering boxes of data about the stars of Golden Age Hollywood, with the intention of switching from novels to biographies. "After reviewing the staggering numbers of records he'd maintained, I signaled to him to go ahead, a move that would vastly affect my future as his publisher."

"Our first biography became one of the company's most successful. Published in 2003, it was entitled *The Secret Life of Humphrey Bogart: The Early Years (1899-1933)*. It was hailed as a "myth-shattering bio that gives a controversial closeup of a young, hot, and humpy Bogart—that is, pre-*Casablanca*, pre-Bacall, pre-*African Queen*. It reveals for the first time what lay under the trench coat of history's most famous movie star."

It created a sensation, making headlines in various publications. Lauren Bacall told a writer at *Vogue* that she didn't like it. Perhaps she learned more about her hus-

Double-Whammied Bogie

Hot, Horny, Pissed-Off, and Footloose

band than she wanted to know.

In 2010, in the aftermath of letters from fans who wanted to read a continuation of Bogie's life, Blood Moon issued *Humphrey Bogart: The Making of a Legend*. A kicker headline read: BOGIE'S DEAD, BUT HE WON'T LIE DOWN."

It was so successful that there have been several attempts to turn it into a film. Pressure remained rather persistent to make a film version until as late as 2025.

KATHARINE THE GREAT
The Secret Life of Katharine Hepburn

The Bogie bio was followed by a probe into the heretofore unknown private life of Katharine Hepburn. It was *Katharine the Great…A Lifetime of Secrets Revealed*.

Its first edition was released in February of 2004. It, too, generated much controversy and many headlines, since it exposed Hepburn's true identity as a lesbian and re-defined her association with the bisexual actor, Spencer Tracy, as mostly platonic.

Today, all these secrets about Hepburn and Tracy are frequently bruited about on YouTube.

In the opening pages of *Katharine the Great*, Danforth formally defined the "mission statement" of Blood Moon Productions:

> *Blood Moon Productions, Ltd. is administered and staffed by writers who were formerly associated with The New York Times, United Press International, and The Miami Herald, and who are presently involved with the production of editorial copy for many of The Frommer Guides.*
>
> *It was established as a "type S Corporation" in 2003 as a spinoff of another publishing venture, The Georgia Literary Association (The GLA). The GLA was conceived in 1997 in the rural hamlet of Washington, Georgia, quickly evolving into a small but commercially viable publishing enterprise that eventually moved to New York City, a more appropriate venue.*
>
> *Blood Moon Productions is devoted to mainstream literary treatments of hard-core revelations about the history of Hollywood, always with an abiding respect for the creative talent that fueled Hollywood's Golden Age.*
>
> *Its name derives from the title of one of the Georgia Literary Association's most successful novels, Blood Moon, by Darwin Porter, an artfully brutal thriller packed with cinematic images. It's about love, psychosis, a deviant evangelist, sexual obsession, money, power, pornography, and evangelical Christianity in America today. It contains, in the words of one critic, "erotica that's akin to Anaïs Nin on Viagra with a bump of meth."*

"When I originally negotiated with Darwin Porter for the distribution rights to *Katharine the Great*," Danforth said, "I was keenly aware of the reams of sometimes trivial material that had been previously published about Katharine Hepburn. Frankly, if I hadn't had access to so much incendiary, never-before-published material about her, I would never have attempted to re-define such a shopworn subject."

"But now that the child (i.e., this book) has been birthed, I freely admit that we nearly drowned in the deep and murky lake associated with the life and psyche of Katharine Hepburn. EVERYONE who ever met her seemed to have a strong, and sometimes violent, opinion or anecdote about her. So, in synch with our role as social historians, we're honored to have been the first to publish the revelations contained within this book."

Katharine Hepburn as Eleanor of Aquitaine (1124-1204), Duchess of Aquitaine, Queen of France, Queen of England, and heiress to the House of Poitiers, as she appeared in *The Lion in Winter* (1968) with **Peter O'Toole**

Bad Boy, Megastar, Sexual Outlaw

UNZIPPING MARLON BRANDO

Blood Moon's third bio, *Brando Unzipped,* published in 2005, became one of the all-time best sellers about the actor who was considered the greatest in the history of Hollywood.

It generated massive publicity and still sells well today, as each new generation discovers Brando. *The New York Daily News* defined it as "The definitive gossip guide to the late, great actor's life."

As the 21st Century moved on, Danforth Prince, as publisher of Blood Moon, became more secure in his decision to focus on biographies of rich, famous, and notorious celebrities. Others quickly followed, each expressing long-suppressed facts.

Marlon Brando with **Vivien Leigh** in Tennessee Williams' *A Streetcar Named Desire.* He conquered with his penis.

They were met with both rave applause and attacks. Some readers wanted to cling to frothy perceptions of long ago, when studio press agents created false bios of its stars, especially if they'd had a notorious past, like Joan Crawford, who launched her movie career in porn.

For growing numbers of fans, Blood Moon could not release its products fast enough. Danforth was bombarded with requests for tell-all books about some of the leading stars in the galaxy. The most requested were Clark Gable, Gary Cooper, Errol Flynn, Tom Cruise, Brad Pitt, Johnny Depp, Clint Eastwood, Jack Nicholson, William Holden, Sean Connery, Fred Astaire, and especially, Elvis Presley.

As a surprise choice, many readers wanted to read a full bio of Lex Barker, the former husband of Lana Turner, and a former star in a series of Tarzan movies. During that period of his career, he showed off his sculpted body in loincloths. A poll in a gay magazine voted him "the sexiest man in America."

As for actresses, the most desired subjects included Greta Garbo, Marlene Dietrich, Grace Kelly, Lauren Bacall, Barbara Stanwyck, Audrey Hepburn, Hedy Lamarr, and even Madonna. Many requests came in for a double bio of the doomed lovers, Robert Wagner and Natalie Wood.

HOWARD HUGHES
Is What Happens When a Demented Billionaire Pulls Strings in Hollywood

Encouraged by the success of Blood Moon's earlier bios, Danforth published, in 2005, with reprints about a year later, *Howard Hughes: Hells's Angel* and subtitled: *America's Notorious Bisexual Billionaire: The Secret Life of the U.S. Emperor.*

It took Darwin many years of tough research to write this epic 814-page book. It revealed the Aviator's megalomania, as well as bartered sexual trysts with Gary Cooper, Bette Davis, Marlene Dietrich, Robert Taylor, Errol Flynn, Jean Harlow, Katharine Hepburn, Rita Hayworth, Carole Lombard, Randolph Scott, Cary Grant, and Marilyn Monroe.

Joan Crawford expressed her opinion, too: "Howard Hughes would fuck a tree."

Billionaire aviator and movie-making mogul **Howard Hughes** with the then-hottest female star in Hollywood, **Jean Harlow.**

Producer Roger Corman was a trailblazer in the world of independent cinema. Hailed as the King of Pop Cinema, he assigned a pithy (and accurate) title to his memoir: *How I Made a Hundred Movies in Hollywood and Never Lost a Dime.*

In 2004, Corman had seen the widely touted film, *The Aviator,* starring Leonardo DiCaprio. He was very disappointed at how it failed to reveal most of the pithy intrigue of Hughes' private life and sexuality. In his opinion, the filmmakers had concentrated more on his experiments in aviation than with his love life.

Corman wanted to film a script—one that incorporated the information and points of view of Blood Moon Productions and that focused on Hughes trysts with, among others, Jean Harlow and Errol Flynn.

The press hinted previews about Blood Moon's involvement in "a follow-up to Scorsese's *Aviator.*" But like so many other film projects, its production collapsed, and the idea was relegated to one of the potholes pitting the surface of the Boulevard of Broken Dreams.

Jacko

In 2007, while Michael Jackson was still alive and thriving, Blood Moon published a pioneering bio entitled *Jacko: The Social and Sexual History of Michael Jackson*. After his death, a member of his household staff told the press that a copy of it was on his nightstand.

It was highly praised, especially in the U.K., but also subjected to harsh attacks from the singer's devoted fans in L.A., many of whom didn't want the memory of their idol sullied.

Critics found it unexpectedly fascinating: In reference to *Jacko*, Blood Moon's biography, Virginia Haynes Montgomery, a writer and PR pro, said, "I think the story of Michael Jackson reflects our times perfectly and will be something historians in future centuries (provided there's still a planet) will explore. He has been destroyed by success. I worked on the fashion promotion of the movie *The Wiz* in the 1970s and Michael was the Scarecrow. Met him at the studio and found him to be normal, quiet, and very sweet. Not a prima donna at all. But this was before the first nose job and the skin-bleaching."

Richard LaBonté at *Books to Watch Out For* reviewed it like this: "I'd have thought that there wasn't one single gossipy rock yet to be overturned in the microscopically scrutinized life of Michael Jackson. But Darwin Porter's exhaustive (but always zippy) hybrid of celebrity bio and solid reporting proves me quite wrong. It's all here: The abuse Jackson suffered as a boy from the fists of his father; rough early years on the "chitlin' circuit;" his rocky relationship with Diana Ross and his quirky relationship with Liz Taylor; his sham marriages and his oddly conceived three children; unflagging rumors of his homosexuality; and his scandalous affection for generations of adolescent boys. Definitely a page-turner. But don't turn the pages too quickly: Almost every one holds a fascinating revelation."

NEVERLAND

Here's **Michael Jackson,** a photo associated with the 2014 release of *Xscape*, a medley of remixed and "contemporized" songs originally written and recorded by him between 1983 and 1999. Even now, more than a decade later, his memory burns bright.

Paul Newman

Paul Newman, The Man Behind the Baby Blues, His Secret Life Exposed created a sensation when it was published in 2009. Focusing on his tempestuous rise from obscurity, it defined him from the perspective of "an impossibly good-looking young actor, climbing the lavender ladder and on the make on Broadway and in Hollywood."

In reference to Newman, and not without touches of envy, Marlon Brando said, "Paul Newman had just as many on-location affairs as the rest of us, and he was just as bisexual as I was."

Everything about Newman was abundantly revealed, with sources that derived from a gaggle of lovers, friends, frenemies, and admirers.

Blue-Eyed and Enigmatic:
Paul Newman

Steve McQueen

Newman was followed by the life story of an even more controversial actor, *Steve McQueen, King of Cool, Tales of a Lurid Life* (2000). His tumultuous personal history was far more controversial than that of Newman.

America's most scandalous star made rebellion hip. As McQueen proclaimed, "I live for myself. I answer to nobody."

His sexual conquests and style became legendary. Early in his career, he sampled all the girls from a whorehouse in the Dominican Republic where he was employed as a "laundry assistant." In Hollywood, he was famously married to Ali MacGraw, but sampled the charms of Barbra Streisand, Ann-Margret, Lee Remick, the doomed Sharon Tate, Tuesday Weld, Mamie Van Doren, and—among many others—Natalie Wood.

King of Cool
Steve McQueen

Heeeere's Merv!

Merv Griffin, A Life in the Closet, was also published by Blood Moon in 2009. Shortly after the Griffin estate learned of its upcoming publication, it threatened a lawsuit. Of course, as attorneys, they knew full well that dead people can't be libeled.

Ignoring their threats, Danforth continued his publishing venues, and Darwin continued his pioneering research. He had first met Merv when he hired him as the "entertainment" for one of the proms at the University of Miami. *[Darwin, in case you didn't know, was head of the student body at the time, and the job naturally fell to him.]* On and off, girded with that early memory of him, Darwin spent years researching his (closeted but very gay) life and his gift for "The Midas Touch."

Publication of that bio catalyzed a banner headline in *The New York Daily News*. Sales soared. Richard LaBonte in *Book Marks* asserted that "Darwin Porter tears the door off Merv Griffin's closet with gusto in this sizzling, massively researched bio."

Merv Griffin, once the most popular talk show host in the world, interviewing **Eva Gabor**, on his weekday talk show, watched by millions, every day

Heathcliff & Scarlett (aka Larry and Viv)

Damn You, Scarlett O'Hara—The Private Lives of Vivien Leigh and Laurence Olivier, published in 2011, set off a firestorm in both the U.S. and in England. One of its marketing slogans was *"Heathcliff and Scarlett O'Hara, In Love and Together on the Road to Hell."*

It was advertised as "the saga of the most romantic couple in England, the darlings of the gods."

As Britain desperately held against the Nazi's "Invasion of the Huns," during World War II (and during the war's aftermath) they were hailed by the English as the Romeo and Juliet of their era, the doomed Lord Nelson and Lady Hamilton, the tragic Hamlet and Ophelia.

The Book Editor of *The Washington Times* wrote: "*Damn You, Scarlett O'Hara* is a dazzling read, the prose unmannered and instantly digestible. The author's ability to pin scandal upon scandal after seduction can be impossible to resist."

Fire Over England (1937)

Before there was Heathcliff (hero of *Wuthering Heights (1939)*, and before there was Scarlett O'Hara (lynchpin of *Gone With the Wind* (also 1939), there were **Vivien Leigh** and **Laurence Olivier,** thrilling English-speaking audiences worldwide with their talent, passion, and beauty.

Blood Moon published a well-reviewed overview of their tormented lives in 2011.

THE KENNEDYS
The Gift that Keeps on Giving, with All The Gossip Unfit to Print

In 2011, Darwin and Danforth co-authored one of their most highly publicized books, *The Kennedys: All the Gossip Unfit to Print*.

Of course, its focus was for the most part aimed at the principal actors ("Jack and Jackie") in that family's drama, but other members of the clan also come into (cringeworthy) focus. Its texts were riddled with quotes, sometimes from members of their own brood:

THE KENNEDYS
Left to right, **Jack, Bobby,** and **Teddy**
No woman was off-limits to them.

"Joe Kennedy is the height of vulgarity. He's horny all the time." **(Columnist Doris Lilly)**
"I'm afraid my son is going to grow up to be a fruit," **(Jacqueline Kennedy)**
"Lem Billings, my brother's closest friend, should be called the second Mrs. John F. Kennedy," **(Robert F. Kennedy)**
"Everybody talks about Marilyn Monroe being seduced by my two brothers, Jack and Bobby. They never gossip about Marilyn and me. She told me that I was better in bed than either of them." **(Teddy Kennedy)**
"A vulgar slut. A publicity seeker. An egomaniac. A self-promoter. A vicious bitch. An unbalanced drug addict. An alcoholic whore. A dime-a-dance floozie." **(Jacqueline Kennedy, referencing Marilyn Monroe)**

Fabulous Frank
(SINATRA)

Darwin and Danforth combined their research and writing talents to create the 2011 bio, *Frank Sinatra, The Boudoir Singer*. It was advertised and promoted, accurately, as a "hot, unauthorized, and unapologetic *exposé* of Ol' Blue Eyes."

In Toronto, Paul Bellini of *Fab* magazine wrote: "I'd like to think that if Sinatra were still alive, he'd be taking a swing at Darwin and Danforth for spilling so many of his juicy secrets."

David Hartnell, an entertainment columnist in New Zealand, wrote: "Every page turn of this book is brimming with shocking situations and scandalous stories. It's like a pressure cooker that just blew its lid."

Seemingly everyone who came into contact with Sinatra had an opinion about him. He was one of the great seducers of Hollywood. Just to cite a few: Marilyn Monroe, Jacqueline Kennedy, her sister, Lee Radziwill, Natalie Wood, Lana Turner, Elizabeth Taylor, Zsa Zsa Gabor, Judy Garland, Grace Kelly, Shirley MacLaine, Nancy Davis Reagan, Gloria Vanderbilt, Kim Novak, and numerous prostitutes. Seemingly, EVERYBODY had something to say about him:

Frank Sinatra with **Ava Gardner**
Who didn't they seduce?

I was not impressed with the creeps and Mafia types he kept around him," **(Prince Charles II of England)**
"When Sinatra dies, they're giving his zipper to the Smithsonian." **(Dean Martin)**
"Mais oui! The Mercedes Benz of Men!" **(Marlene Dietrich)**
"A complete shit!" **(Lauren Bacall)**
"There's only ten pounds of Frank, but there's 110 pounds of cock." **(Ava Gardner)**

J. EDGAR HOOVER & CLYDE TOLSON
High Jinx and Gay Trysts at the FBI

In 2011, Blood Moon published one of its most controversial books, *J. Edgar Hoover & Clyde Tolson*. It described how the FBI director spent most of his career voyeuristically investigating the sexual secrets of the idols then dominating America's culture and *zeitgeist*: Marilyn Monroe, Elvis Presley, Eleanor Roosevelt, Robert F. Kennedy, Errol Flynn, and Martin Luther King, Jr., among countless others. It also revealed the dynamics of his life as a closeted homosexual, and his enduring affair with the lover he elevated to the highest ranks of the FBI: Clyde Tolson, "The Gary Cooper of the FBI."

Bed Buddies & Comrades-in-Arms

Clyde Tolson with **J. Edgar Hoover**

Here's what a trio of former presidents had to say about him:

"Hoover rules as head of the American Gestapo." **(Harry S Truman)**
"He's got us by the cojones, and he'll never let go." **(Lyndon B. Johnson)**
"Jesus Christ! That old cocksucker?" **(Richard Nixon)**

A truth that had only been whispered about by his closest associates—until Porter and Prince blasted it across the media landscapes of a world that remembered him with bitterness— was that Hoover was a (frequent) cross-dresser. His close friend, the loudmouthed Broadway star Ethel Merman, supplied him with gowns, hosiery, makeup, and shoes that actually fit him.

"LA LIZ," SUPERDIVA
Elizabeth Taylor, There Is Nothing Like a Dame

Many books have been written about Elizabeth Taylor, but none quite like the revelatory, best-selling *Elizabeth Taylor: There is Nothing Like a Dame,* published in 2012 by Blood Moon.

It probes into her private life as no bio had before. She admitted on a televised talk show that she'd never write her real bio "because too many people would sue me."

She was Hollywood's most mercurial actress, the central figure in a whirlpool of world-class scandals. She confessed, "I'm called a scarlet woman. That's wrong. I'm positively purple. My biographers have revealed only half of my story."

That certainly changed with the publication of *There Is Nothing Like a Dame.*

Richard Burton, who married her twice, claimed, "Her best-known asset is her breasts." He called them "apocalyptic. They will topple empires before they wither."

Howard Hughes proclaimed that "every man should have the privilege of sleeping with Elizabeth Taylor. At the rate she's going, every man will."

Taylor confessed, "I often fucked actors who liked to fuck each other—Peter Lawford, Monty Clift (at least I tried), Rock Hudson, James Dean, Paul Newman."

"My wife had the face of an angel and the morals of a truck driver," claimed Eddie Fisher.

"I know I'm vulgar," she said. "But would you have me any other way?"

"Elizabeth was a faithful wife—at least for the first week." So said rival Lana Turner.

Elizabeth Taylor as Cleopatra (1963)

"I demanded that my co-star, Richard Burton, rape me every night."

PORNOGRAPHIC AMERICA
Inside Linda Lovelace's Deep Throat

A historic overview of the "apocalyptic" rise of pornography arrived in 2013 with the release of *Inside Linda Lovelace's Deep Throat: Degradation, Porno Chic, and the Rise of Feminism.*

It answered two questions: Was the fellatio specialist a sex-crazed nymphomaniac? Or a tragic victim of sexual abuse?

Deep Throat (the film in which Linda Lovelace starred) became the most popular and most-watched porn film in history. As a by-product, it transformed Lovelace into one of the most famous (and personally sought-after) actresses of her era.

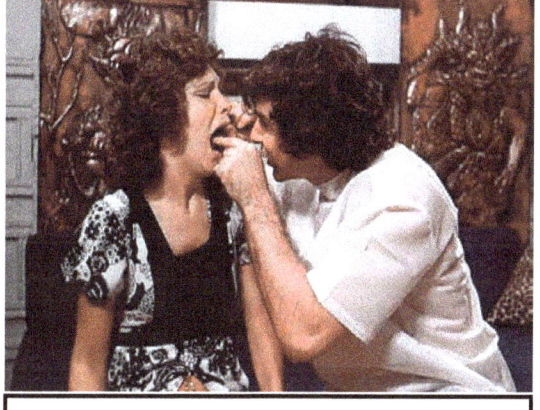

Porn star **Harry Reems** (as her doctor) examines **Linda Lovelace's Deep Throat**

"It changed America's attitudes about sex more profoundly than anything since the first Kinsey Report in 1948," wrote journalist Bob Briggs. "And it altered the lives of everyone associated with it. It supercharged the feminist movement. It also gave the Mafia its most lucrative product since Prohibition, and it changed America's views on obscenity forever."

"After the release of *Deep Throat,* Linda Lovelace became the reigning Queen of Porn," columnist James Bacon said privately. *[He knew much more about her private life than he could print in his column.]* "She became the party favor of movie stars, sports figures, one U.S. senator, and one vice president of the United States. She performed fellatio on such stars as Sammy Davis, Jr., baseball's Joe DiMaggio, Frank Sinatra, Elvis Presley, Marlon Brando, and Johnny Carson, among others."

According to Danforth, "Our tell-all about Linda Lovelace was delayed for years because of threatened lawsuits. Darwin had researched and written it years before we felt it was safe to publish. Finally, since the rage associated with her evolution had, by then, subsided a bit, we timed its release to coincide with the debut of the 2013 film (*Lovelace*) that starred Amanda Seyfried."

As the Lovelace saga unfolded in the early 70s, Darwin had been horrified when the government threatened Harry Reems, the co-star of *Deep Throat,* with a jail term. Reems was the only actor ever prosecuted on a charge of obscenity based on a performance as an actor in a film.

Darwin spearheaded a fundraiser at Backstage, a restaurant in the theater district of Manhattan. Its clientele was stylish and show-bizzy, and many contributed to the payment of Reems' daunting legal fees.

Deep Throat and its implications has never died. It's still for sale or rent in at least 170 countries around the world.

As part of its marketing, Danforth issued the following statement about Linda Lovelace:

"A Bronx-born brunette, the notorious Linda Lovelace was the starry-eyed Catholic daughter in the 1950s of a local cop who called her Miss Holy Holy. Twenty years later, she became the most notorious actress of the 20th Century.

She'd fallen in love with a tough ex-Marine, Chuck Traynor, and eventually married him, only to learn that she had become his meal ticket. He forced her at gunpoint into a role as a player within hardcore porn, including a 1971 bestiality film entitled Dogarama.

Her next film, shot for $20,000, was released in 1972 as Deep Throat, *It became the largest-grossing XXX-rated movie of all time, earning an estimated $750 million and still being screened all over the world. The fee she was paid was $1,200, which her husband confiscated. The 'Sexy 70s' went wild for the film. Porno chic was born, with Linda as its centerpiece.*

Traynor, a sadist, pimped his wife to celebrities, charging them $2,000 per session. It became a status symbol to commission an individualized film clip of Linda performing her oral specialty. Clients included Elvis Presley, Frank Sinatra, Milton Berle, Desi Arnaz, Marlon Brando, William Holden, Peter Lawford, and Burt Lancaster. The Mafia had found its most lucrative business—pornography—since Prohibition.

After a decade of being assaulted, beaten, and humiliated, Linda, in 1980, underwent a Born Again transformation. She launched her own feminist anti-pornography movement, attracting such activists as Gloria Steinem and scores of other sex industry professionals who refuted their earlier careers."

"THIS BOOK IS A WINNER!"

The Beach Book Festival Grand Prize Winner. "Best Summer Reading of 2013"
Runner-Up to "Best Biography of 2013, The Los Angeles Book Festival
Winner of a Sybarite Award from Lola Bastinado and her crew from HedoOnline.com
"This book drew me in...How could it not?" Coco Papy, Bookslut.

Eva, Magda, and Zsa Zsa
THE GABORS, BOMBSHELLS FROM BUDAPEST
Great Courtesans of the 20th Century

WOMEN WE LOVE
Eva, Magda, and **Zsa Zsa Gabor**

During their on-site research for *Frommer's Austria & Hungary*, Darwin and Danforth met many people who knew the Gabors: Jolie, their matriarch, and her vivacious, much-married daughters, Magda, Zsa Zsa, and Eva. LOTS of socially connected matrons in Budapest and Vienna had a LOT to say about their early years, before they fled from the Old World to America.

In the United States, their research into the private lives of these fabled sisters culminated in the production of an epic triumph of fact checking and storytelling: *Those Glamorous Gabors, Bombshells from Budapest.* It was published in 2013.

"For this major bio, we came up with lurid inside information—lots of it—about those man-eating Magyars, those endearing Hungarian Hussies from Hell," Danforth said.

"Zsa Zsa's list of lovers beat out her sisters' by a country mile," claimed James Bacon.

In addition to her eight husbands, Zsa Zsa seduced—to name only a few—Sean Connery, Porfirio Rubirosa, Frank Sinatra, her stepson, Nicky Hilton, William Paley (head of CBS), John F. Kennedy, Mario Lanza, and Prince Aly Khan.

Her two most famous husbands were hotel mogul Conrad Hilton and actor George Sanders. After he divorced her, Sanders later married Zsa Zsa's older sister, Magda.

Quick-witted Zsa Zsa was always adored by the press because of her gift for memorable lines:

"I don't mind sleeping with him, dahlink, but I don't want to be seen with him. Imagine! He's only a headwaiter."
"I'm often asked how many husbands I've had. I answer: 'Do you mean my own or those of other women?'"

Danforth signed an option with a film producer to bring their saga to the screen. During the negotiations, he speculated about which actresses might play the lead roles. Eventually financing proved too much of a problem, and the film was never made. But, as Darwin later said in speeches about them at Cinema Paradiso, a film society in Fort Lauderdale, "Even though the film adaptation I strived for never happened, I'll always have Zsa Zsa."

UNHOLY TRIO: PINK TRIANGLE
The Feuds and Private Lives of Tennessee Williams, Gore Vidal, & Truman Capote.

Darwin's friendship with Tennessee Williams dated back to the day he was named as Bureau Chief of *The Miami Herald* in Key West. The celebrated playwright turned out to be his neighbor. Thus began the young reporter's introduction to the world of Southern Gothic drama *à la* Tennessee.

Knowing him well, as Darwin did, it was inevitable that he would come into contact with (and collect stories about) two other famous authors of that day, Gore Vidal and Truman Capote.

It was Danforth's idea that Blood Moon pursue, in 2014, the compilation of a triple bio entitled *Pink Triangle, the Feuds and Private Lives of Tennessee Williams, Gore Vidal, Truman Capote and Famous Members of Their Entourages*...i.e. Jacqueline Kennedy, Elizabeth Taylor, Marlon Brando, Bette Davis, Marilyn Monroe, Katharine Hepburn, and others.

In Danforth's words, "The *enfants terribles* of America in the mid-20th Century challenged the sexual censors of the day while elevating 'bitchfests for love and glory' into something approaching an art form."

Many scholars agree that **Gore Vidal** *(left)*, **Truman Capote** *(center)* and **Tennessee Williliams** *(right)* were among the greatest writers of the 20th Century.

This photo, snapped in the months immediately following World War II, belies their ferocious competition for better reviews, better sales, better invitations, and better boyfriends.

Blood Moon's PINK TRIANGLE, built on information gleaned through years of contact with virtually everyone who knew them, is a rich banquet of literary feuds, egomaniacal vanities and the kinds of gossip that shook both Broadway and Hollywood.

Blood Moon's Presidents Club
(This Time, It's THE REAGANS)

Blood Moon followed *Pink Triangle* with another triangle *exposé*. This one, published in 2014, focused on the early lives of Ronald Reagan and the double-whammied actresses he married, Jane Wyman and Nancy Davis. It was entitled *Love Triangle*. It was riddled with provocative quotes, including a thinly veiled, artfully phrased confession from the "horndog," Ronald Reagan, when he first arrived in Hollywood in the late 1930s. "During every picture I made, I developed *Leading-Lady-itis*."

Ronald Reagan, a former Hollywood actor, was the first divorced person to ever attain the rank of U.S. President. *LOVE TRIANGLE* is about what he and his wives did in Hollywood BEFORE they began rehearsing for his role as leader of the Free World

Left photo: Wife #1, megastar **Jane Wyman,** as she appeared during the early years of her gig as a dynastic matriarch on *Falcon Crest*. *Right photo,* **President Ronald Reagan** with wife #2, Hollywood starlet **Nancy Davis**.

"He's about as good in bed as he was on the screen,"
—Reagan's first wife, movie star Jane Wyman
"Clark Gable turned Nancy down, so she had to settle for Ronald Reagan."
—Adolphe Menjou
"As a starlet at MGM, Nancy Davis became known as 'the fellatio queen of Hollywood,'"
—George Cukor
"Nancy was one of those girls whose phone number was passed around a lot."
—Biographer Anne Edwards
"He would never have become president if Hollywood had given him better parts."
—Lauren Bacall

"From politics to betrayal to romance, infidelity, and sordid affairs, Love Triangle *is a steamy, eye-opening story that blows the lid off of the Reagan illusion to raise eyebrows on both sides of the big screen."*
—Diane Donovan, Senior editor, *The Midwest Book Review* and *California Bookwatch*

MORE from Blood Moon's "Presidents Club"
THE CLINTONS (*So This Is That Thing Called Love*)
Get a Celebrity Exposé of Their Own

"Bill Clinton is a…Baby Boomer from Hell"
—George H.W. Bush

Blood Moon ventured once again into the political arena when, in 2015, it published *Bill & Hillary: So This is That Thing Called Love.*

Midway through the book's production, Hillary made a surprise visit to Staten Island. Darwin lined up to greet her and confessed that he was writing a book about her. She shook his hand, smiled, and asked, "Please be kind."

Danforth, its co-author, marketed it, in part, with provocative titles for each of the chapter headings: "Caligula of the Ozarks," "Hillary Defines Herself as Neither a Lesbian nor a Sandra Dee Slut." "Bill Compares Hillbilly Peckers to Elvis." "Skirt-Chasing Bill Confesses to Hundreds of Girls." "Horniest of Horndogs Becomes Governor of Arkansas." "Bill Contemplates Divorce." "Lounge Singer Gennifer Flowers Tells All—and Then Some." "Paula Jones as the Dogpatch Madonna." "Monica Lewinsky Should Have Had that Blue Dress Dry-Cleaned."

The book was filled with comments from people who either admired or hated the Clintons. George H.W. Bush delivered an idiosyncratic private opinion: "Bill Clinton is a womanizing, Elvis-loving, non-inhaling, truth-shading, war-protesting, draft-dodging, abortion protecting, gay-promoting, draft-dodging, gun-hating Baby Boomer from Hell."

Larry Klayman wrote: "It became well-known during the Clinton years that while the President was a certified sleazeball, the most evil partner of this Bonnie and Clyde duo was Hillary. She is the *consigliere* of the couple, the one who executes their dastardly plans and deeds."

Gail Sheehy weighed in, too: "The story of the Clinton Presidency has always been the story of a marriage. Their relationship is both supportive and destructive. Hillary is addicted to Bill, and he desperately depends on her to bring him back again from the political dead."

PETER O'TOOLE
Hellraiser, Sexual Outlaw, Irish Rebel

Peter O'Toole

"There is nothing on earth as good as a man and a woman."

Peter O'Toole: Hellraiser, Sexual Outlaw, Irish Rebel was published by Blood Moon in 2015. It received wide attention in the press after news of its arrival first broke in New York's *Daily News.* It was billed as "an unprecedented new look at the 20th Century's most talented (and most outrageous) actor."

As O'Toole himself confessed, "If there's a dame on the set I can't screw, my name's not Peter O'Toole…God put me on this earth to raise hell. And I did!"

The book was filled with provocative (and sometimes very personal) comments, either from O'Toole or from those who encountered him.

"If Peter had been any prettier, he'd have been billed as Florence of Arabia," said Noël Coward, who developed a crush on him.

"Princess Margaret was insatiable," O'Toole claimed. "Calling every day. Couldn't get enough of me."

"My greatest sexual thrill was going to bed with Peter and some girl at the same time," said Richard Burton.

"Peter was the only man I preferred in bed to Richard Burton," claimed Elizabeth Taylor

"Katharine Hepburn called me a pig and a drunk. She even bashed my head a few times with an empty liquor bottle. But I adored her. I told her that one night with me would cure her of her lesbianism." —Peter O'Toole

In reference to it, *Celebrity Dish* weighed in with: "This is the grittiest, most unvarnished, and most comprehensive biography of the dashing, charismatic, movie star *roué* ever written."

Fab magazine gave this provocative assessment: "Insouciant, offensive, brilliant, promiscuous, and brash, Peter O'Toole was said to have matched Don Juan's legendary total of 1,033 seductions. It's all here in this latest blockbuster biography from those blokes at Blood Moon, no doubt hellraisers themselves when it comes to stirring up scandal."

Jimmy, Lad, We Hardly Knew 'Ye
The Public vs. The Private James Dean

According to Danforth, "One of my proudest achievements was publishing and co-authoring the most complete life of the iconic James Dean ever published."

It was released in 2016 on the 60th anniversary of Dean's violent and early death. Its title was *James Dean, Tomorrow Never Comes*. It took until the 21st Century until the last major players in Dean's life revealed their secrets about the charismatic actor.

James Dean
"A young man must be courageous in the bedroom. Life's too short to worry about what's perverted."

In many instances, Dean kept silent about his sexuality, but he did utter a few comments: "You know, I've had my cock sucked by some of the biggest names in Hollywood. I'm certainly not going to go through life with one hand tied behind my back."

Rodgers Brackett, a friend of Darwin's, was a TV producer who discovered Dean in a parking lot in Hollywood, fell in love with him, and brought him to New York. Brackett virtually launched his career, which began in television. At the time, most of Dean's seductions were rigorously concealed from the general public.

His most famous conquests included Elizabeth Taylor, Sal Mineo, Rock Hudson, Woolworth heiress Barbara Hutton, director Nicholas Ray, Susan Strasberg, the prissy actor Clifton Webb, composer Alec Wilder, Natalie Wood, Eartha Kitt, Nick Adams, Ursula Andress, Tallulah Bankhead, Betsy Palmer, plus an African-American man he fellated in front of thirty other guests at a Hollywood party.

Opinions about him were varied, most of them unfavorable: "I don't mean to speak ill of the dead, but Dean was a prick," said Rock Hudson, his co-star in *Giant* (1956).

Nicholas Ray said, "He was intensely determined not to be loved or to love."

"The little son of a bitch was one of the most unspeakably detestable fellows I ever knew in my life," claimed producer Ruth Goetz.

"I once told a reporter that Jimmy and I never became lovers," said Sal Mineo, his co-star in *Rebel Without a Cause* (1955). "Forgive me. I lied. He was the love of my life."

Even Marlene Dietrich had an opinion about Dean: "He was a small, ugly, hunchback with a potbelly and bow-legged. If he'd have lived, he'd have a larger potbelly, wear a wig, and have died of AIDS."

"He was a walking streak of sex and had seduced half the male and female population of Hollywood…even yours truly," claimed Elizabeth Taylor.

President's Club Bad Boy
THE DONALD
The Man Who Would Be King

Months before he was elected President of the United States in 2016, Blood Moon published *Donald Trump: The Man Who Would Be King*. Intensely controversial, it remains noteworthy, even today, as the most thorough overview of the origins of the Trump dynasty ever published. Called both "America's Savior" and "The Anti-Christ," The Donald is presented in all his glory (or vainglory): Boardroom swashbuckler, 21st Century Midas, master wheeler-dealer, cult TV celebrity, Gilded Age mojo, guru for wannabe millionaires, master of *schmaltz*, global real estate magnate, the wizard of hype, a smoke-and-mirror casino operator, and a model-seducing "Don Juan of the boudoir."

Trump in 2013
"A dictator from Day One."

Opinions about The Donald are eclectic. Televangelist Jerry Falwell Jr. claimed "Donald Trump embodies the best qualities of Jesus Christ and Martin Luther King, Jr."

Bloomberg Politics wrote, "Donald Trump is a disgusting jerk, a comedian character assassin, and a solipsistic blatherer."

[In 2023, based partly on growing interest in Europe about how "Only in America" Trump wangled his way to the presidency, Blood Moon released an abbreviated edition entitled The Donald: How Did It Happen? The Gathering Storm.*]*

One critic cited the book as "A Trumpocalypse—How a loud-mouthed, pussy-grabbing TV star, failed casino kingpin, and real estate mogul climbed out of frequent bankruptcy to lose a popular vote to Hillary Clinton and emerge as President of the United States in 2016."

Blood Moon cites it as a research source for Media Studies, a road map for scholars trying to understand him as a Media Guru; a blow-by-blow of cringe; and an orchestrator of the most psychotic presidential candidacy in American history.

LUSCIOUS LANA
Hearts and Diamonds Take All

Lana Turner
The Ultimate Movie Star

In 2017, Blood Moon turned its focus on the production of a tell-all book about one of the 20th Century's most extravagant movie stars, *Lana Turner: Hearts & Diamonds Take All*. Here at last was the first complete overview of the actress once defined as "The World's Most Desirable Woman."

Luscious Lana, the Celluloid Venus, was *The Bad and the Beautiful,* the last great Love Goddess of the Silver Screen. Her life was a kaleidoscopic tale of passion and scandal that included murder. She inhabited a real-life soap opera laced with romance, betrayals, *paparazzi,* and high drama.

Her motto? "So many men, so little time."

In addition to seven husbands, Lana seduced some of the most famous men in America: Desi Arnaz, Richard Burton, Sean Connery, Kirk Douglas, Clark Gable, John Garfield, John Huston, Howard Hughes, John F. Kennedy, Robert Taylor, Frank Sinatra, Victor Mature, Dean Martin, Mickey Rooney, and Tyrone Power.

Opinions about her were varied: "She was not an actress, only a trollop," or so claimed Gloria Swanson.

Robert Taylor said, "She was the type of woman *[for whom]* a guy would risk five years in jail for rape."

"She was amoral," asserted MGM executive Benny Thau. "If she saw a stagehand in tight pants with a muscular build, she'd invite him to her dressing room."

Getting a Piece of the Rock
EROTIC FIRE

Rock Hudson
Only Mickey Rooney turned him down.

Based on a foundation of decades of research by Darwin, Danforth joined him to co-author the most explosive book ever written on the box office megastar, *Rock Hudson*. Subtitled *Erotic Fire*, it was published in 2017. In part because of its tagline ("*In the dying days of Hollywood's Golden Age emerged "The Rock," a former truck driver who became the reigning phallic symbol of America. This book describes his rise, fall, and the Entertainment Industry that created him.*" It immediately created a sensation and hailed as Best Biography of the Year at both the Northern and Southern California Book Festivals.

Rock seduced everyone from Joan Crawford to Liberace. "For Rock," according to his best friend, actor George Nader, "sex was just as casual as a handshake." Throw in Vera-Ellen, Errol Flynn, Marilyn Maxwell, Sal Mineo, Jim Nabors, talent agent Henry Willson, Tyrone Power, and Elizabeth Taylor, and you have quite a stewpot from the 50s— especially when you include dozens of other men and women not associated with the film industry.

Playboy's HUGH HEFNER
Empire of Skin

Hugh Hefner: "My biggest regret? That I never fucked Marilyn Monroe, but I'll be buried next to her."

In a departure fron his usual subjects, Danforth moved ahead to work with his co-author, Darwin, to create the most explosive book ever written about *Playboy's Hugh Hefner: Empire of Skin.*

Hefner, the Playboy of the Western World, was a visionary publisher, an empire builder, an avatar of pleasure, and a pajama-clad pipe smoker "with a pre-coital grin."

This groundbreaking bio was the first published since Hefner's death at the age of 91 in 2017. As publisher of *Playboy* magazine, Hef studded it with nudes and centerfolds, starting out with a naked Marilyn Monroe as part of its first edition. At its zenith, *Playboy* reached eight million readers. Hef became a cultural warrior, his battle against censorship even reaching the U.S. Supreme Court.

Lauded by millions of readers, he was also denounced as "the father of sex addiction," "a huckster," "a lecherous low-brow feeder of our vices," and, near the end of his life, "a symbol of priapic senility." It traces the evolution of how America interpreted its centerfolds: What began as an act of clandestine shame (for the models, we mean) evolved into a major status symbol as celebrities like a late-in-life Joan Collins ferociously lobbied for the gig. Like Hefner himself, *Empire of Skin* is rich, provocative, historic, and tantalizing.

Princess Leia and Unsinkable Tammy in Hell

In 2018, Blood Moon invaded the private lives of movie star and casino magnate Debbie Reynolds and her daughter, Carrie Fisher. The bio was subtitled *Princess Leia and Unsinkable Tammy in Hell.* A hit with fans of that mother-daughter team, it won "Best Biography of the Year" at the New York Book Festival.

It probed into the inner life of Debbie, whom some detractors have called "Tough as Nails with more balls than five guys." It also featured Carrie, one of the smartest, hippest chicks in Hollywood.

Debbie Reynolds with **Carrie Fisher**

Here's the "*boop-boop-a-doop* girl" linking up with her intergalactic daughter.

Loaded with never-before-published revelations about who was doing what to whom during the final gasps of Golden Age Hollywood, the bio was one-of-a-kind, an All-American saga about the price of glamour, career-related pain, family anguish, romantic betrayal, lingering guilt, and the volcanic shifts that affected a scrappy, wryly funny mother-daughter team—and everyone else who ever loved the movies.

Death of a Hollywood Horndog

It was said that the last book an aging Kirk Douglas ever read was Blood Moon's bio of his own life. It was published in 2019: *Kirk Douglas, More is Never Enough.* At his death, many newspapers headlined his passing as HOLLYWOOD HORNDOG DIES.

Kirk Douglas
"An erection is a mysterious thing."

He not only made some of the most memorable films in Hollywood history, but he seduced some of its biggest stars: Pier Angeli, Lauren Bacall, Joan Crawford, Linda Darnell, Marlene Dietrich, Rita Hayworth, Evelyn Keyes, Ann Sothern, Patricia Neal, Gene Tierney, and Lana Turner.

Issur Danielovitch (Douglas' birth name) was the son of an illiterate Russian "ragman." He survived poverty and anti-semitism to pursue the American dream—and achieved it beyond all expectations. Over the course of many decades, he immortalized himself in film after film, with one memorable performance after another.

En route to his status as a legend, he was beaten to a bloody pulp in *Champion* (1949). As a sleazy, heartless reporter in *Ace in the Hole* (1951), he was stabbed with a knife in the gut. As Vincent Van Gogh in *Lust for Life* (1956), he sliced his ear off with a razor. He lost an eye in *The Vikings* (1958). In *Spartacus* (1960), as a Thracian slave leading a rebellion against Roman legions, he was crucified. This book, as many reviewers concluded, tells it all.

The Highest-Grossing MegaStar of the 1980s
BURT REYNOLDS

Burt Reynolds
"Let's face it: I'm God's gift to females."

As the second decade of the 21st Century came to an end—that is, in 2019—Blood Moon published *Burt Reynolds, Put the Pedal to the Metal: How a Nude Centerfold Sex Symbol Seduced Hollywood.*

Burt sometimes left the disquieting impression that he had lost control of the direction of his life and career. As he, himself confessed, "I became a redneck icon but really wanted to be the next Cary Grant."

He seduced some of the most famous women on the planet, notably Marilyn Monroe and Elizabeth Taylor. An older woman, singer Dinah Shore, became his longtime companion. For five years, he was the number one box office star in the world.

The nude centerfold and heartthrob to millions graced screens with his foot on the gas. In his own words, "I was a hellraiser hotter than a firecracker."

He became tabloid fodder to his generation, garnering "Second Coming" headlines. And he pursued, frantically, the American Dream—at least until it became a nightmare.

GOING GLOBAL
(*Selling Celebrity to the Chinese*)

Printed in English, Blood Moon biographies attracted readers around the globe, especially Canada, the U.K., Australia, and New Zealand. Books sold well in Germany and France, too.

Occasionally, a publisher—say, in the Netherlands—would translate and publish a Blood Moon title in Dutch as was the case with *Brando Unzipped.*

Some bios we published were almost as popular in the U.K. as they were in America. Such was the case of *Damn You, Scarlett O'Hara,* which focused on the tumultuous lives of the British icons, Laurence Olivier and Vivien Leigh.

"Then a surprise market opened for us in China," Danforth said. "The three of our books whose Chinese editions we know about (and were paid for) focused on JFK, Marilyn Monroe, and Elizabeth Taylor. JFK has always fascinated the Chinese, much more than less flashy presidents like Jimmy Carter, Gerald Ford, or George H.W. Bush."

"As for Taylor and Monroe, they're the biggest (Hollywood) stars in the Chinese constellation. All of their films have been popular in China for decades, and as icons, all of them have been scrutinized by millions of Chinese, perhaps as part of an effort to understand the sometimes bizarre assumptions and values of The American Experience. As such, we've entered a collaboration with a publisher based in Chengdu, Southern China, for translations into Chinese of some of them: Notably, our bios of Marilyn, the Kennedys, and 'La Liz.'"

GLOBE TROTTERS

For years, during the heyday of the world as a "relatively unproblematic" touristic playground, Darwin Porter and Danforth Prince were the most widely read travel journalists in the world. Here's the territory they covered:

Long ago and far away two reporters working for *The Miami Herald* and *The New York Times,* respectively, decided to quit their jobs at those papers and switch to the research and crafting of travel guides. During their deep immersion in that field, the world's geography opened to tourism. Suddenly, every nation on earth began more or less frantically marketing the charm and allure of their respective tourist scenes.

As a collaborative team providing travel overviews from publishing venues that included Simon & Schuster, they "discovered" venues stretching from Greenland to Patagonia. They sailed the China Seas and "invaded" every country within what used to be the Soviet Union. Most of their attention was devoted to the staples of Europe, which they covered, in depth and through dozens of annual or bi-annual Frommer editions, from Iceland to Romania. Nor did they overlook Africa, traveling within, and writing about that continent's northern tier, from Morocco to Egypt.

Here, below, is a list of the countries and regions whose travel scenes they wrote about, in nuts-and-bolts detail:

Many Editions and Many Variations of *The Frommer Guides, The American Express Guides, and/or TWA Guides, et alia* to:

Andalusia, Andorra, Anguilla, Aruba, Atlanta, Austria, the Azores, The Bahamas, Barbados, the Bavarian Alps, Berlin, Bermuda, Bonaire and Curaçao, Boston, the British Virgin Islands, Budapest; Bulgaria, California, the Canary Islands, the Caribbean and its "Ports of Call," the Cayman Islands, Ceuta, the Channel Islands (UK), Charleston (SC), Corsica, Costa del Sol (Spain), Denmark, Dominica, the Dominican Republic, Edinburgh, England, Estonia, Europe, "Europe by Rail," the Faroe Islands, Finland, Florence, France, Frankfurt, the French Riviera, Geneva, Georgia (USA), Germany, Gibraltar, Glasgow, Granada (Spain), Great Britain, Greenland, Grenada (West Indies), Haiti, Hungary, Iceland, Ireland, Isle of Man, Italy, Jamaica, Key West & the Florida Keys, Las Vegas, Liechtenstein, Lisbon, London, Los Angeles, Madrid, Maine, Malta, Martinique & Guadeloupe, Massachusetts, Melilla, Morocco, Munich, New England, New Orleans, North Carolina, Norway, Paris, Poland, Portugal, Provence, Puerto Rico, Romania, Rome, Salzburg, San Diego, San Francisco, San Marino, Sardinia, Savannah, Scandinavia, Scotland, Seville, the Shetland Islands, Sicily; St. Martin & Sint Maarten, St. Vincent & the Grenadines, South Carolina, Spain, St. Kitts & Nevis, Sweden, Switzerland, Turks & Caicos, the U.S.A., the U.S. Virgin Islands, Venice, Vienna and the Danube, Wales, and Zürich

Their advice? Travel widely and read.

Why? Because travel and reading are the best antidotes ever invented for the avoidance of complacency and stupidity.

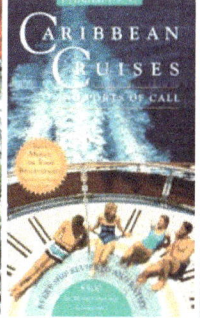

TIRED of HORROR STORIES ABOUT DONALD TRUMP?
Cheer Up, because here's
BOOK AGENDA NEWS about Blood Moon Productions'
NEWEST BOOK RELEASES--Biographies to Die For!!!
CELLULOID NOSTALGIA, HOLLYWOOD GLAMOR, & SEX
THEY'RE BACK!!!

Blood Moon proudly announces the release of radical new biographies of two of the sexiest stars of Hollywood's Dream Machine:

LANA TURNER & ROCK HUDSON

Drawing on firsthand interviews and on information never before published, each is the most complete, comprehensive, and unvarnished portrait of these great American movie stars ever published.

LANA TURNER: Everything that no one ever told you about The Sweater Girl, Hollywood's OTHER most famous blonde, LANA TURNER, Hearts & Diamonds Take All. Available everywhere now. Softcover, 6" x 9"; .622 pages with hundreds of photos and dozens of unvarnished insights into LUSCIOUS LANA. ISBN 978-1-936003-53-2, and

ROCK HUDSON: A former naval ensign & truck driver, Roy Fitzgerald charmed every casting director in Hollywood (and movie-goers throughout America) as the mega-star we most wanted to share PILLOW TALK with. ROCK HUDSON EROTIC FIRE--a biography loaded with never-before published information about America's Sexiest and Most Secretive All-American Heartthrob, delectably available for consumption by enquiring minds on 32nd anniversary of his death in November of 2017. Softcover, 6" x 9", 650 pages with hundreds of photos. ISBN 978-1-936003-55-6.

Award-winning Entertainment about how America Interprets Its Celebrities

For more information, click on
BloodMoonProductions.com

or contact
DanforthPrince@
gmail.com

Blood Moon's Invasion of Babylon and its Detour to Gomorrah

An Overview of Exhibitionism, Sexuality, and Sin as Filtered through 85 Years of Hollywood Scandal

Kenneth Anger (1927-2023) was an experimental and underground filmmaker and author of two scandalous editions of books named *Hollywood Babylon.* The first was banned shortly after its publication in 1965. A decade passed before it went into general distribution. *The Daily Beast* called it "essentially a work of fiction." He later came out with a second edition.

In 2006, Darwin Porter and Danforth Prince published a better-researched and more thorough treatment of "Babylon." Reportedly, Anger was so enraged by the competition that news of his placing a curse on them was widely bruited around both the publishing world and the Satanic cells of California. *[In case you didn't known, Anger was a self-proclaimed Satanist and a magician of a devilish sect self-identified as "the Thelema."]*

Blood Moon, in time, amplified its release of Babylon titles to three. Each became a best seller and, for the most part, garnered good (*i.e., spectacular*) reviews.

"Anger always promised a third edition, but perhaps clouds got in his way," Danforth said. "I guess I pre-empted him with the three Hollywood Babylon titles issued by Blood Moon. It seemed like a very natural thing to do at the time. My co-author, Darwin Porter, knew more about Hollywood scandals than anybody I'd ever met. He was the obvious choice to outdo anything Anger ever fumed and fought over. In fairness, his Babylons were written in a wildly different (and tamer) era. Today, many of the so-called 'scandals' he trumpeted look harmless—something you could probably safely read to a kindergarten. Standards of journalism—and censorship—had radically changed by the time we entered the clash. I mean, even the formerly staid *New York Times* made news in the aftermath of publishing the penis size of actor Hugh Grant!"

"Volume One of our Babylon trio (Blood Moon's *Hollywood Babylon—It's Back*) was released in 2008 and imediately caused a sensation. Our stuff *[which, of course, doesn't reflect an iota of Satanism]* was a LOT more radical in the subjects they covered than Anger's. We not only arrived, with klieg lights, after dark in Babylon, but accessorized the texts with what we call 'side tours' to Sodom and Gomorrah."

Kenneth Anger (born **Kenneth Wilbur Anglemyer;** 1927-2023) was an American actor, writer, and experimental filmmaker who produced almost 40 ultra-*avant-garde* short films, some of which (bizzarely) illustrated homosexuality tinged with sadomasochism and the occult.

As he aged, he became fascinated (some said "obsessed") by the Satanic writings of the English occultist **Aleister Crowley** and **Thelema**, the demonic Satan-based religion that Crowley promoted and publicized.

Despite the fact that Anger's writings occupied much less of his time than his filmmaking, his two editions of *Hollywood Babylon*, published in France, were banned in the U.S., despite the fact that the information they contained was relatively tame—some said "non-committal and lackluster." Nonethelss, they became part of the postwar American *Zeitgeist.*.

When Anger heard about Porter and Prince's release of Blood Moon's more amusing, more informative, and less dark *Hollywood Babylons*, news broke in the underground press that he'd placed a Satanic curse on the authors. Many surmised at the time that it was nothing more than a saber-rattling publicity ploy,.

When asked for a response to his condemnation to emotional agony and a brutal early death, **Danforth Prince**—in an interview with a journalist pursuing the issue at a Libarrian's convention in Pasadena.—responded "*Pooey and Phooey*—Anger is a vicious and jealous out-of-touch queen and his curse is gonna boomerang and hit him back, HARD."

Anger died shortly afterward, bitter and broke, still muttering imprecations to anyone who would listen.

Blood Moon's "matched pair" of Babylon books, and the spectacular praise they elicited from the literary press—absolutely enraged Kenneth Anger.

What were the reviews that particularly enraged **"that old Satanist sod," Kenneth Anger**? According to the sales staff at a leather/fetish store in West Hollywood, it was from Barry Lowe (SX News Australia) who called it "one hell of a gossip bible."

"We didn't just write about penis sizes," Danforth continued. "We ran pictures of them. One was of Victor Mature's during his service in the Coast Guard. He's lying in bed reading, with his most prized asset dangling over the edge of the cot. *Oooh-la-la!* as the French might have said at the time."

Candidly shocking stories were unearthed and published:

James Dean had been a child molester. Bette Davis was an off-screen murderess. Errol Flynn committed incest with his son. Marilyn Monroe had a few "tosspot" sexual trysts with Elvis Presley.

Rock Hudson expressed things beautifully: "In Hollywood, you can keep a mistress or a boyfriend. Maybe both. You can be gay, bi-, or pansexual. Just don't tell anybody and don't get caught. What do you expect after you bring the most beautiful men and women together to work in the same industry?"

According to Danforth, "Frankly, I was amazed at how whole-heartedly the foreign and domestic media embraced and endorsed our spin on sex and scandal in Hollywood. Perhaps everyone had become both bored and numb by Anger's repeated associations with Satanism. But the reviews these books generated were joyfully irreverent, fulsome, and loud. For example, In reference to Blood Moon's Babylon, *The London Daily Express* claimed, 'Many of the most outrageous secrets in Hollywood have remained hidden. UNTIL NOW. This book will set the graves in Hollywood cemeteries spinning.'"

Volume One (2008) morphed into such a success that two years later, Blood Moon came out with Volume Two: *Hollywood Babylon Strikes Again.*

Its opening chaper presents an overview of Hollywood whorehouses of yesterday and some of their clients. (They included both Clark Gable and Errol Flynn.) Some of them were defiantly omnisexual, catering to a wide spectrum of gender preferences.

Golden Age secrets? Van Johnson and June Allyson were widely publicized as "America's Sweethearts"—an aggressive concealment of the fact that he was gay and she was a nymphomaniac.

Light is shed on Walt Disney's being a homosexual; starlet Liz Renay defiantly promoting herself as "a girl who—after sleeping with 200 actors—had 'evaluated' how each of them had performed in bed."

Other issues were raised, too: Audrey Hepburn and Capucine (an actress and model for *haute couture*) had an affair. *Ma Kettle* (Marjorie Main) was a dyke. And in addition to discussing Hollywood's biggest endowments, the Babylon books added a section on "shortcomings." Poor John Wayne.

Eventually, the "Babylon of Babylon" books was issued by Blood Moon in 2022. It was entitled *Hollywood Babylon, with Detours to Gomorrah.*

Critic David Hartnell said, "This is the best classic scandal book on Hollywood ever published. And believe me, I've read hundreds."

Blood Moon's Jockstrap awards were given to winners of the Battle of the Bulge. Readers also got a detailed rundown on Lucille Ball's gig, during her early days at RKO, as a hooker.

Perhaps most shocking of all were revelations about what happened to Judy Garland's corpse as a plaything for necrophiles. Self-acknowledged vampires will find it fascinating.

Rudolf Nureyev appears frontally nude, showing off what those ballet tights concealed. At last, we learn what Harry Potter (Daniel Radcliffe) was hiding in his undies.

We read about Marilyn Monroe's sexual trysts with Elvis Presley. What about horndog Ronald Reagan's seductions of ALL those actresses during his early days in Hollywood? And did you know that his First Lady, starlet Nancy Davis, was known as "The Queen of Fellatio."

Clark Gable commanded attention wherever he went. Here's how he looked during his filming of *White Sister* in 1933.

Hollywood's illusion of heterosexual passion: **June Allyson** with **Van Johnson** in the provocatively (some said "obscenely') titled *The Bride Goes Wild* (1948)

Daniel Radcliffe as *Harry Potter*

Walt Disney

Audrey Hepburn

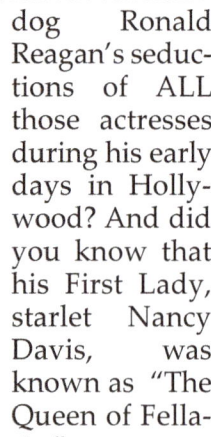

"The Most Beautiful Woman in Europe," **Capucine**

> THIS YEAR AT THANKSGIVING, BLOOD MOON PRODUCTIONS WILL PROUDLY
> RELEASE A NEW AND EXPANDED EDITION
> of the SCANDALOUS ANTHOLOGY THAT MADE IT FAMOUS WHEN
> ITS PREDECESSOR FIRST APPEARED IN 2008. THIS TIME, WE'RE CALLING IT:
>
> # *HOLLYWOOD BABYLON*
> # *WITH DETOURS TO GOMORRAH*

Making America Great Again: For Immediate Release, from Blood Moon Productions

In the tradition of GREAT AMERICAN GOSSIP that's about to explode this Thanksgiving amid the turkeys and cranberry sauce, Blood Moon offers this COMPELLING ANTHOLOGY OF GOSSIP to anyone who ever had any nagging questions about Show-biz indiscretion, mendacity, and excess.

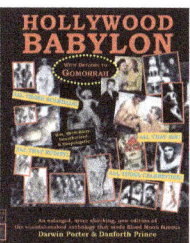

WHAT IS IT?   According to Blood Moon's President, Danforth Prince, "It's the best feature-length compendium of Hollywood gossip ever compiled, lavishly illustrated, and loaded with examples of the PR hurricanes generated by the false gods of fame, physical beauty, lust, greed, narcissism, and exhibitionism. This book might not be everybody's fantasy about what they really wanna crawl into bed with, but as a publishing phenomenon, it's the very best of its genre."

HOW HAS IT BEEN REVIEWED SINCE ITS FIRST EDITION?
ANSWER: With spectacular praise and enthusiasm from publications that include the NY DAILY NEWS, London's EXPRESS, a passel of entertainment-industry publications "Down Under," and show-biz blogsites around the world.

HOW BIG IS IT AND HOW MUCH DOES IT COST?
ANSWER: This anthology was conceived and designed as a softcover **COLLECTOR'S ITEM** for placement on COFFEE TABLES in living rooms that need a little nudge. It has a BIG footprint—something akin to an 8 1/2 x 11" news magazine—and the central image of its front cover is Fritz Lang's 1920s 'perhaps demented' image of THE WHORE OF BABYLON. Debauched and persuasive, she hovers over a passel of spectacularly famous, partially undressed celebrities culled from a century of show-biz mania. In this case, you can acquire her "favors" for $60.

Danforth Prince continued: "We're marketing this as the most lewdly sophisticated 'coffee table book' of the holiday season. It's a one-of-a-kind 'conversation stopper' or (depending on your point of view) 'conversation starter.' This is a 'hipster to hipster' gift you'd give to an embittered survivor who's already deeply familiar with the casting couch.   It's the best accumulation of tabloid trauma ever published....a drunken sorority party's first prize; a 'I'm ready for another martini' cocktail *klatsch's* most embarassing panty raid."

"We've doubled its content from its previous edition," Prince continued, "by adding the 'concentrated cream' from rip-snorting OTHER biographies within Blood Moon's (very extensive) backlist. This anthology is what happens when Classic Hollywood gets down and low with the literary *avant-garde* of the Fabulous 50s, the Free Love Sixties; the Sexy Seventies, and the big-haired teledrama-driven Eighties."

"WHO'S NEW? There's More about Ronald Reagan and "fellatio Nancy" than you might wanna know, and a cross-section of ONCE AGAIN IN THE NEWS stars you might, if not for this book, have forgotten."

IT'S BACK.! IT'S BABYLON! And it's available after Thanksgiving through **Amazon.com, Barnes & Noble.com** and other online booksellers worldwide.

HOLLYWOOD BABYLON with DETOURS TO GOMORRAH
By Darwin Porter and Danforth Prince   www.BloodMoonProductions.com
488 pages, 8 1/2" x 11" softcover. ISBN 978-1-936003-88-4
A ONE-OF-A-KIND COLLECTOR'S ITEM AND COFFEE TABLE SHOWPIECE. MSRP $60.

Blood Moon's Magnolia House Series

Volume One—Celebrity and the Ironies of Fame
&
Volume Two—Glamour, Glitz, and Gossip at Historic Magnolia House

Magnolia House. Its name was assigned after the Civil War by its builders as a reminder of their native Virginia

In 2018, as part of complicated marketing maneuver, Danforth created yet another publishing spin-off, "The Magnolia House Series." The inspiration for its name derived from Blood Moon's corporate headquartrers within a historic building known for more than a century as Magnolia House.

Built in stages between 1830 and 1870, it's a historic landmark on Staten Island, the least-visited Outer Borough of New York City.

Set within a 10-minute walk from the (free) Staten Island ferry that accesses Manhattan at intervals of every thirty minutes or less, it's the headquarters of the widely distributed independent press, BLOOD MOON PRODUCTIONS, a feisty wordsmith noted for celebrity biographies that have been reviewed in THE DAILY MAIL, the New York DAILY NEWS, show-biz news reports, and literary journals across the country.

Some visitors liken Magnolia House to a *grande dame* with a centuries-old knack for nourishing high-functioning eccentrics. Many of them have lived or been entertained here since New York's State Senator Howard Bayne, a transplanted Southerner, moved in with his wife, the daughter of the Surgeon General of the Confederate States of America, in the aftermath of that bloodiest of wars on North American soil, the War Between the American States.

Since then, many dozens of celebrities—some of them notorious—have whispered their secrets and rehearsed their ambitions within its walls. They've included movie vamps from the silent screen, *MIDNIGHT COWBOYS*, dancers from the dance, *BUTTERFLIES IN HEAT*, a heavyweight boxing champ, writers from every hue, faded film goddesses, playwrights who crafted blockbusters for both Marilyn *(Monroe)* and Elizabeth *(Taylor)*, ultra-avant-garde diarists *(including Anaïs Nin)*, every

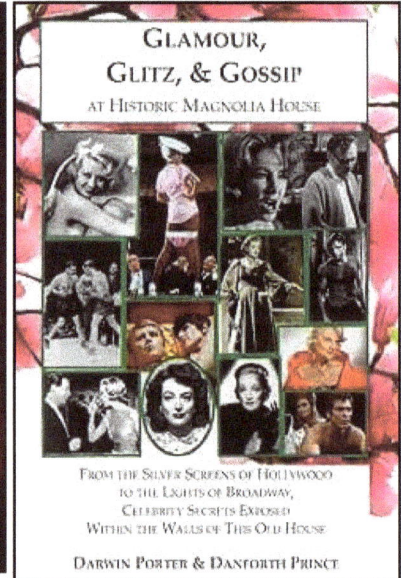

Documenting the show-biz scandals associated with a landmark which by anyone's standards is a a *grande dame*: These were the first two volumes within **Blood Moon's Magnolia House Series**. Is Magnolia House still occupied by the spirits and memories from "other voices" and "other rooms?" **Yes.**

Early celebrities associated with Magnolia House: *Left photo*: **The Vanderbilts.** Here's a view of their mausoleum on Staten Island. Modeled after a Romanesque church in Arles, France, it was a testimonial to their influence over the development and residents of Saint George, Staten Island, during their 19th-century heyday.

Center photo: **Staten Island, circa 1888,** Children, perhaps from affluent families of Saint George, being exposed to the social graces. Photo by Alice Austen.

Right photo: **Julia Gardiner Tyler** before her marriage to U.S. President, John Tyler. A short-term resident of Magnolia House, she was a controversial celebrity hated for her ostentation, her sense of privilege, her support of slavery, her lavish spending, her *coquetteries*, and for what her contemporaries defined as "sexually equivalent to the loosest morals of the Napoleonic courts of Europe."

known variety of prima donna and diva, including some from the world of opera; and a world-class Olympic athlete.

They've also included Darwin Porter and Danforth Prince, who spent decades here renovating it and producing a stream of FROMMER TRAVEL GUIDES and award-winning celebrity biographies.

The first volume within the Magnolia House series, published in 2018, was *Celebrity and the Ironies of Fame.* It revealed intriguing stories that were uncovered as Darwin and Danforth traveled the world researching the Frommer guides.

For example, in Sweden, the director of that country's tourism department arranged for Darwin to visit Ingrid Bergman at her summer home on an island off the coast of Stockholm. She revealed to him what had really happened during the filming of *Casablanca* (1942) in which she co-starred with Humphrey Bogart.

Ingrid Bergman, as she appeared in *Notorious* (1946).

The writers also stayed at the Villa Taylor in Marrakech (Morocco). It's the Moorish/Art Deco villa where Sir Winston Churchill and Franklin D. Roosevelt met, in secret and with intense security, during the darkest days of World War II.

Ripped directly from Darwin's diaries were details of his encounters with Eleanor Roosevelt during his gig as a reporter for *The Miami Herald.* He also writes of his morning walks with ex-President Harry S Truman during his final visit to Key West.

It also includes a report of how Darwin worked for the campaign of Florida's Senator George Smathers. Known to women throughout Washington as "Gorgeous George," he drove Darwin to Palm Beach to meet a young senator from Massachusetts, John F. Kennedy, and his wife, Jacqueline. On the day of their meeting, both of them were attired in (then terribly fashionable) pink pants. *En route* back to Miami, Smathers revealed that JFK was going to run for President of the United States.

Another chapter reveals what happened when Darwin and Tennessee Williams drove together to Mexico where his play, *The Night of the Iguana,* was being adapted into a movie with Ava Gardner and Richard Burton. Elizabeth Taylor was in (intensely competitive) residence there, too, and she made it a point to entertain the playwright and Darwin.

Magnolia House developed an inferiority complex after its emissaries, Darwin Porter and Danforth Prince, spent a week at the very posh and historically spectacular **Villa Taylor** in **Marrakech, Morocco.**

Name any newsworthy celebrity from Europe's *haute monde* in the 70s who wasn't aware of what was happening in Marrakech? Check out what happened when Magnolia House got magical with Madame la Comtesse Boul de Breteuil at the most secretive hotel in Africa.

The beat goes on and on: One tantalizing encounter after another.

A second volume, *Glamour, Glitz, and Gossip at Historic Magnolia House* was published in 2019. Inserted below is a brief preview of what it contained:

Glamour, Glitz, & Gossip at Historic Magnolia House

CONTENTS

PROLOGUE
LITERARY OUTLAWS OF THE POSTWAR AMERICAN CENTURY   PAGE 1
    Tennessee Williams, Gore Vidal, and Truman Capote ("The Pink Triangle') were *Enfants Terribles* from the Golden Age of American Literature. Their biographer and archivist, Darwin Porter, describes their thwarted ambitions and ferocious infighting.

CHAPTER ONE   PAGE 5
    Portrait of the Artist (Tennessee Williams) as a young man. His feuds with the Über-divas of Hollywood: Tallulah Bankhead, Joan Crawford, and Miriam Hopkins.

CHAPTER TWO   PAGE 33
    Broadway Remembers Audrey Wood, the most Influential literary and show biz agent in the history of the American Theater. How Darwin hosted a black tie mega-party in her honor at Magnolia House.

CHAPTER THREE   PAGE 63
    Joan Blondell: Portrait of a movie star and a Magnolia House "regular." How she seduced Errol Flynn and Clark Gable, transitioned from Pre-Code Hollywood to TV sitcoms, and how she married "double trouble' Dick Powell and Mike Todd.

CHAPTER FOUR   PAGE 95

MURDER AHOY with Bette Davis: Did she kill her second husband?

CHAPTER FIVE   PAGE **101**
When prostitutes were named after flowers: How Truman Capote's avantgarde, all-black cast danced the Mambo all the way to Broadway.

CHAPTER SIX   PAGE **115**
Myra Breckinridge: Gender-fluid, pink, and crafted by Gore Vidal, he/she became America's foremost literary transsexual.

CHAPTER SEVEN   PAGE **129**
Crazy October: Tricking, treating, arguing, and on the road with Tallulah Bankhead, Joan Blondell, & Estelle Winwood.

CHAPTER EIGHT   PAGE **135**
Midnight Cowboy: The first X-rated movie to win an Oscar, and its link, through its author, to Magnolia House.

CHAPTER NINE   PAGE **151**
When Divas Clash: The real-life fight for Robert Taylor, starring Tamara Geva (the ex-wife of George Balanchine) and how she was assaulted, backstage, by Barbara Stanwyck. PLUS the tormented sexual intervention of the billionaire film producer, Howard Hughes.

CHAPTER TEN   PAGE **175**
Rudolf Nureyev: from Russia with Love (*Tales of Tatar Tail*). His links to Gore Vidal & America's literary *avant-garde*.

CHAPTER ELEVEN   PAGE **181**
More about Rudolf Nureyev: Seducing his way through the Kennedy clan.

CHAPTER TWELVE   PAGE **191**
Nureyev's homage to Rudolph Valentino. How an insanely popular icon from the 1970s reinterpreted the doomed life of a legend from the 1920s.

CHAPTER THIRTEEN   PAGE **203**
How the Opera Diva, Eleanor Steber generated headlines at a "black tie, black towel gala" at a gay bathhouse in Manhattan, and how she dished the music world's juiciest dirt, including how Adolf Hitler molested boys in Bayreuth.

CHAPTER FOURTEEN   PAGE **217**
Greta Keller: Hitler's favorite cabaret singer (Europe's "other" Lili Marleen), and her long-term residency at Magnolia House.

CHAPTER FIFTEEN   PAGE **233**
Edward Albee at Magnolia House: *Who's Afraid of Virginia Wolff?*.

CHAPTER SIXTEEN   PAGE **239**
Grace Kelly: Beauty, good manners, lucky breaks, & the triumph of myth over reality.

CHAPTER SEVENTEEN   PAGE **267**
Hedy Lamarr: The bizarre story of the political loyalties and censorship problems whirling around the most beautiful woman in the world.

CHAPTER EIGHTEEN   PAGE **279**
Jack Dempsey: The world's heavyweight boxing champ, his widely publicized romp with Mae West, and his links to Magnolia House.

CHAPTER NINETEEN   PAGE **289**
Bombshells from Budapest: The Gabors, their formidable mother, Jolie, and her links to Magnolia House

POSTSCRIPT FROM THE EDGE: BOOMER TIMES & MEDIA BUZZ   PAGE **299**

SCRIBES & MESSENGERS (AUTHORS' BIOS)   PAGE **321**

WHO MURDERED SHOW BIZ'S MOST FAMOUS BLONDE?

Marilyn Monroe as a floozie with marriage on her mind in *Bus Stop*

As his publisher, Danforth had frequently pressured Darwin to write a biography of Marilyn Monroe. Darwin had been present on the set of *The Misfits* (1961), invited there by his mentor, Stanley Mills Haggart, a longtime friend of its author, Arthur Miller.

Darwin's first revelations appeared in *Marilyn at Rainbow's End*, published in 2012 by Danforth's Blood Moon Productions.

Before writing it, Darwin had spent time with master detective Milo A. Speriglio, who spent twenty years investigating Marilyn's mysterious death. It's estimated that he handled more that 35,000 cases over the course of his career—more than all those television sleuths combined.

Over the years, Darwin, too, interviewed numerous people, even those only remotely connected to Marilyn's death.

As a component within the then recently launched Magnolia House series, Danforth reissued (in 2020) a revised version of Darwin's original (2012) Marilyn biography, entitling it *Marilyn: Don't Even Dream About Tomorrow*. He subtitled it *Sex, Lies, Her Murder, and the Great Cover-Up*.

We've incorporated some of its revealations into the pages that immediately follow. It's a meticulously researched, intricately detailed account of what happened that long ago night in August of 1962, headlines for which were blasted across the front pages of newspaper around the world. It encapsulates our version of who murdered Marilyn Monroe. You decide. **Rest in Peace, Norma Jeane. Rest in Peace, Marilyn.**

***

In Chicago, Sam Giancana had assigned the "contract" to murder Marilyn to Felix Alderisio, whose nickname was "Milwaukee Phil." Within the Chicago outfit, he was the underboss to Sam Giancana, whom he called "Momo" or "Mooney."

Alderisio's career as a criminal had been launched during Prohibition. His first minor arrest had been for vagrancy, since he was seen every day waiting outside Al Capone's headquarters at Chicago's Lexington Hotel, hoping to get a job as a messenger. Eventually, he broke into the mob, who employed him as a "bagman," bringing cash payoffs to Chicago judges and police officers.

By the 1950s, he'd risen to the position of "the enforcer," working with his partner, Charles ("Chuckie") Nicoletti, who would also be hired to kill Marilyn.

As enforcers, the two men made gangland hits on merchants and others who did not pay the Mafia insurance money. They became known for their own version of a "Batmobile," except that in their case, their black vehicle was a "hit mobile," with special switches that controlled taillights and headlights as a means of obscuring the car's license plate and helping avoid police detection. In a concealed compartment within the vehicle, they carried pistols, shotguns, rifles, and plenty of ammunition.

Two editions of Darwin Porter's overview of the conspiracies associated with **the murder of Marilyn Monroe**. In the pages that immediately follow, we replicate the text of what really happened on the violent and tragic night of August 4, 1962 in Brentwood.

Alderisio and Nicoletti also directed a gang of "cat burglars" who broke into homes in Chicago's upscale Gold Coast district, looting jewelry for the most part, and whatever cash was on hand. Alderisio and "Chuckie" eventually expanded their operations to Milwaukee, where they ran bordellos, striptease joints, nightclubs on Rush Street, and three small hotels.

From their collection of payments from various restaurants and nightclubs on the North side of Chicago, Alderisio and Nicoletti handed over millions to the Mafia after their cut was taken out.

As one of Giancana's top aides, Alderisio was probed by the Permanent Subcommittee on Investigations of the U.S. Senate looking into organized crime. Alderisio developed a personal hatred for Attorney General Bobby Kennedy, who had him hauled before the committee, where he refused to testify, pleading the Fifth Amendment twenty-three times.

Sometimes, Alderisio and Nicoletti arranged for the smuggling of heroin into the United States, traveling, at Alderisio's insistence, to Italy, Turkey, and Greece as a means of expressing his passion for classical ruins. While Alderisio wandered among the ruins of yesterday, Nicoletti preferred to stay in his hotel room "fucking the local broads and giving them a treat," as he immodestly put it.

Alderisio was also involved in the CIA-Mafia link to the failed Bay of Pigs covert operation in Cuba aimed at toppling Fidel Castro.

During May of 1962, weeks before being hired to murder Marilyn, Alderisio directed an infamous mob torture incident. Billy McCarthy and Jimmy Miraglia had ambushed and shot two Mafiosi. Alderisio and Nicoletti captured McCarthy and tortured him until he revealed Miraglia's name. Alderisio and his henchmen extracted information from McCarthy by placing his head in a vise, slowly tightening it until one of his eyes popped out of its socket. After McCarthy revealed Miraglia's name, Alderisio slit his throat. Nicoletti then trailed Miraglia, eventually catching up with him and cutting his throat too.

Felix Alderisio
("Milwaukee Phil")

Over a period of several decades, Alderisio was arrested three dozen times for bombing, racketeering, gambling, hijacking, counterfeiting, bootlegging, extortion, bribery, and murder for hire. By the late 1960s, years after his assault on Marilyn, he was convicted and sent to prison, where he died of a heart attack on September 25, 1971.

When not involved with Alderisio, Nicoletti often worked with Francis Schweihs ("Frank the German"). Giancana also selected Schweihs as a hit man to murder Marilyn.

Tom Knight, Assistant U.S. Attorney, would later refer to Schweihs as "one of the most violent people ever to stand before a judge."

As another of his cohorts, Frank Cullotta, would later testify, Schweihs wanted to rape and torture Marilyn before her execution, but Giancana demanded, under threat of death, that her killing be relatively painless.

When not murdering people, Schweihs sold "insurance" for the Mafia in Chicago, and was considered the best salesman among Giancana's henchmen.

Charles (Chuckie)
Nicoletti

Schweihs, or so it is believed by law enforcement officials, would later be the hitman who killed Nicoletti, with whom he had joined forces during the night of Marilyn's murder. Giancana had by this time turned against Nicoletti, accusing him of skimming money from the Mafia, and ordered Schweihs to murder him.

Long after Marilyn's murder, Schweihs was convicted of extortion in 1989 and sentenced to a thirteen-year term in prison. Schweihs, along with his partner, Angelo J. LaPietra, nicknamed "The Hook," were caught skimming millions from Las Vegas casinos in the 1980s.

After prison, Schweihs was known to have lived for a while in Dania Beach, Florida.

Sought on a charge of murder in April of 2005, he became a fugitive, but was eventually caught in Berea, Kentucky, just before Christmas of that same year. In prison, he was diagnosed with cancer, and moved to a federal medical center at Rochester, Minnesota, where he seemed to recover, at least slightly, after a series of operations. He was set to go to trial on October in 2008, but died that summer on July 23.

Francis Schweihs
"Frank the German"

When questioned by the police about the death of Marilyn and its link to Sam Giancana, he said, "Marilyn Monroe? Never heard of her. I always jerked off to the pictures of Jayne Mansfield with her tits hanging out. As for Giancana, someone once pointed him out to me in a restaurant."

Schweihs has the dubious distinction of being the longest surviving member of the gang who killed Marilyn, most of whom ended up murdered themselves. Giancana himself was murdered in 1975, assassinated in his Chicago kitchen, his brains splattered over the tile floor. Later that year, Roselli ended up in a barrel dumped into a Florida bay.

Anthony ("The Ant") Spilotro was the fourth mobster assigned to the Marilyn hit. The Chicago-born hood was only twenty-four years old when he joined in Marilyn's murder.

FBI agent William F. Roemer, Jr. called him "that little pissant," but the media didn't want to use the word "piss" so they shortened his nickname to "Ant."

Spilotro met Giancana because of his frequent meals at Patsy's Restaurant in Chicago, which was run by his parents, Pasquale and Antoinette Spilotro. In fact, Giancana often held mob meetings in the parking lot of Patsy's.

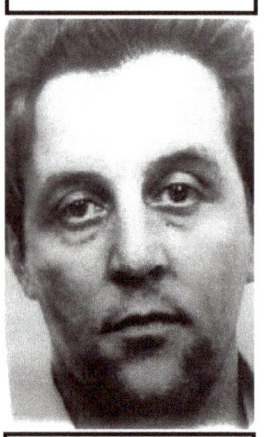

Anthony ("the Ant")
Spilotro

After Marilyn's death, Spilotro's mob career took off, and by 1971, he was the Chicago mob's link to its operations in Las Vegas.

Spilotro embezzled ("skimmed") profits from the casinos and sent the money back to the Mafia in Chicago. Ten years after Marilyn's murder, Spilotro orchestrated one of the most vicious murders in America's mob history. He killed Leo Foreman, a real estate agent and loan shark by repeatedly stabbing him with an ice pick, cutting out chunks of his flesh. Before that, as an act of psychotic sadism, he castrated Foreman, removing one of his testicles and chomping down on it with his teeth, as Foreman, screaming, looked on as blood dribbled from the corners of Spilotro's mouth.

In spite of overwhelming evidence, Spilotro was later acquitted of Foreman's vicious murder.

Frank Cullotta

"The Ant" often worked with his brother, Michael Spilotro. Together, they established "The Gold Rush, Ltd." a Las Vegas operation for the fencing (distribution and sale) of some of the most valuable stolen goods in the country.

In 1979, Nevada's Senator Harry Reid, Majority Leader of the U.S. Senate beginning in 2007, got Spilotro blacklisted from all Nevada casinos.

The Spilotro brothers, in yet another venue linked to "The Gold Rush," eventually spearheaded a burglary ring known as "The Hole in the Wall Gang," because of their penchant for drilling through the exterior walls and ceilings of buildings they burglarized.

Frank Sinatra knew the Spilotro brothers and actually suggested that some of their criminal antics be used as plot devices in *Ocean's 11*, a movie released in 1960 that featured some of his fellow Rat Packers.

Eventually, Spilotro was indicted for his role in at least twenty-two murders, including that of Bill McCarthy.

In Martin Scorsese's 1995 film, *Casino*, McCarthy's murder was depicted, albeit in a less gruesome way, through the murder of an onscreen character named "Tony Dogs."

Spilotro's murder of San Diego real estate heiress Tamara Rand was another event depicted in *Casino*. Rumors on the street also implicated Spilotro, along with Johnny Roselli, in the murder of Giancana.

In 1986, both of the Spilotro brothers were killed in the basement of an abandoned hunting lodge in DuPage County, Illinois. They were beaten and strangled to death before being buried in a cornfield beside Highway 41 in northwestern Indiana. Their former comrade, Frank Schweihs ("Frank the German"), was arrested in 2005 and charged with their murders.

The fifth and most unlikely member of Marilyn's murder squad was Frank Cullotta (sometimes spelled "Culotta"), a former Las Vegas detective who "switched sides." He had been a childhood friend, growing up in Chicago, of the Spilotro brothers.

Cullotta was arrested in July of 1981 during a botched robbery and was tried and convicted. In prison, he learned that Spilotro, "The Ant," had ordered his execution.

"The Ant" had once trusted Cullotta to handle Mafia money, but he learned that Cullotta had been "skimming" the illegal profits before turning them over to the Mob. Cullotta was stashing a lot of the money in his own offshore bank accounts.

In nearly all cases when the Mafia discovered that one of their members was doing that, a death sentence was issued.

"The Ant" chose Lawrence Neumann, nicknamed "Crazy Larry," to execute Cullotta. Neumann and Cullotta had been comrades-in-arms when they worked together murdering and robbing for the Hole in the Wall Gang.

Unaware that Cullotta had been tipped off that he was going to be murdered, Neumann believed that his Mafia comrade still trusted him. He arranged to pay Cullotta's bail and to have him released into his custody. But Cullotta wasn't having any of that, fearing that if he accepted a release into Neumann's custody, that he'd be murdered that very night.

As his only chance for survival, Cullotta approached the warden and volunteered to become a state witness against his former comrades, who included both "Crazy Larry" and "The Ant." When "The Ant" learned of this, he renamed Cullotta "The Canary."

Interviewed by state law enforcement officers, Cullotta revealed "The Ant's role in the brutal murders of both Miraglia and McCarthy, and he also testified that "The Ant" had engaged in a number of other notorious murders, including the 1979 slaying of Las Vegas mob member Sherwin ("Jerry") Lisner.

Johnny Roselli

Based on Cullotta's charges, Spilotro was indicted (but not convicted) on murder and racketeering charges. Criminal Court Judge Thomas J. Maloney ruled that the case could not be proven beyond a reasonable doubt. However, the judge himself, in 1992, was convicted for accepting bribes.

Cullotta was rumored to have been the only mobster to testify about the men who murdered Marilyn Monroe on the night of August 4, 1962.

His testimony was sealed and delivered to the Department of Justice in Washington. His revelations were never released, and his confidential report has never been made public under the Freedom of Information Act. It remains sealed to this day or else was destroyed by some official in government, perhaps a Kennedy loyalist, although that is pure speculation.

After his release from prison, Cullotta was assigned to the witness protection program and relocated somewhere in Heartland America with a new identity. He was never heard from since then, and presumably died years ago.

These were the mobsters that Giancana sent to kill Marilyn, turning the matter over to Roselli to choreograph.

Sam Giancana

***

On the evening of August 4, 1962, the arrival of Johnny Roselli on Marilyn's doorstep was not an immediate cause for alarm. He was known to have visited her on several previous occasions, even when she lived in apartments. He often bragged to his henchmen, "I've got to pop in at Marilyn's to pop her one."

Alone in the house except for her poodle, Maf, Marilyn answered the door. Perhaps eager to learn about what important message he had for her, she invited him into her living room for a glass of champagne.

When he came in, he must have flicked open the lock on her front door, as later, there would be no sign of forced entry.

It can be assumed that no threatening dialogue occurred between them because Roselli already knew that anything he said to her would be recorded. What survived on the Bernard Spindel tapes has long ago been destroyed…perhaps. The only record we have of this is Spindel and Otash's memory of the recording, as relayed to witnesses and interviewers after the event.

Marilyn's psychiatrist, **Dr. Ralph Greenson**

Maf began to bark, and Roselli got up and took the dog and removed him to another room, perhaps asking her permission to do so because the poodle seemed highly agitated. An hour or so later, the barking dog would be released from his captivity in the telephone room by Norman Jeffries, who'd been hired as a handyman.

Roselli and Marilyn idly chatted for no more than five minutes before two of the hit men, perhaps "The Ant" (Spilotro) and Schweihs ("the German"), came into the room.

Slipping behind Marilyn, one of these men removed a chloroform-soaked washcloth from his bag. Perhaps at this point, alerted by the smell, she quickly turned around, but it was too late. The cloth was forced over her nose and mouth. Her struggle was useless. Giancana had issued orders that her body was not to be bruised.

Knowing that the living room was bugged, Roselli ordered the other hit men, who by now had entered the living room, to remove her body to the guest cottage at the far end of the compound. Apparently, no one had ever bugged the cottage.

Before invading her home, Giancana's henchmen had prepared a solution of liquid Nembutal, chloral hydrate, and water.

Marilyn's mendacious housekeeper **Eunice Murray**

She changed her story many times in the years that followed.

All struggle gone from her, Marilyn was stripped, and her nude body was placed on the bed. A bath towel was put under her buttocks. The solution had been transported in a Thermos bottle.

A bulb syringe was filled from the contents of the Thermos bottle, and the tip of the syringe coated with petroleum jelly for easy insertion into her rectum.

The poisonous concoction was then released into her colon. She was then given a second dose of the deadly solution.

Another hit man had gone into her bedroom and emptied the contents of her medicine bottles into his bag and had left the empty bottles. Apparently, the mob wanted it to appear that she'd swallowed all the capsules.

The entire assault had taken less than thirty minutes, or so it seemed. Perhaps hearing a noise, the men rushed out so fast they even left the door to the guest cottage ajar and a lamp turned on.

At approximately 10:15pm, Eunice Murray and Norman Jeffries returned from dinner. Marilyn had insisted that they call first before returning to the house, but when they tried, they had found both lines busy.

Getting out of the car, Jeffries was the first to notice that a light was on in the cottage and its door was ajar. Had Marilyn put an overnight guest in there?

The mother-in-law and the son-in-law went to investigate. As Murray opened the door, she shrieked in horror to find a nude Marilyn on the bed, lying in her own waste.

As a trained nurse, she immediately checked Marilyn's pulse. She was still alive. "Call an ambulance," she yelled at Jeffries.

"She rushed to the other phone and placed an emergency call to Dr. Greenson. "Marilyn's dying. Come at once. Get Engleberg." She slammed down the phone and rushed to attend to Marilyn. She didn't know whether the ambulance or Greenson would arrive there first.

At this point, the scenario becomes the subject of debate. Murray obviously realized that Marilyn's death would become an international headline, and she didn't want to be left alone with Jeffries to manage the press, the photographers, and the police.

It was at this point that it is believed that she called Pat Newcomb in spite of her hostility to her. Someone trained in public relations had to manage the crisis. Murray didn't want to be in the spotlight.

Pat Newcomb

The sound of an arriving vehicle could be heard. Murray pulled back the curtains of the guest cottage and looked out at the street. It was an ambulance. Two men were getting out and rushing toward the house with a stretcher.

She stood outside the cottage signaling the young men to come toward her and not to go in through the front door of the main house, which was being held open by Jeffries.

James Hall, the ambulance driver, later gave much disputed testimony, although any statement from anybody—all parties, in fact—is much disputed.

Some biographers have placed Bobby Kennedy at the murder scene, but this claim later seemed outrageous to Hall, who was actually there.

Hall claimed that his fellow ambulance driver was Murray Liebowitz, who later denied that he was Hall's partner, and denied, for a while, that he'd even been at the scene. "We were returning from a run to UCLA Hospital, when we received a call to rush to 12305 Fifth Helena," Hall said. "We were told it was an emergency. We were real close, practically around the corner. We were at the house within two minutes."

Marilyn
gloriously alive

"I'm her housekeeper," the unknown woman told Hall. "Come in here."

"It was the single most memorable moment of my life, a vision that would be with me forever, when I came into that cottage on that hot August night back in 1962," Hall recalled years later. "I looked down at the body on the bed."

"My God!" he said. "This woman is a dead ringer for Marilyn Monroe."

He remembered the hostility reflected on Murray's face. "It is Marilyn Monroe, you idiot. Save her!"

"Marilyn Monroe?" he asked. "You gotta be kidding me!"

"Save her life, you goddamned fool!" she shouted at him.

Hall was nervous and inexperienced, and he was only twenty-two years old and new to the job. He felt Marilyn's pulse and determined that it was "very weak, very rapid, her respiration almost nonexistent. A classic symptom of overdose. In Los Angeles, I'd already seen a lot of that."

Hall and his partner decided to apply CPR. "The bed is too soft. We've got to put her on her back, a hard surface," Hall told his assistant.

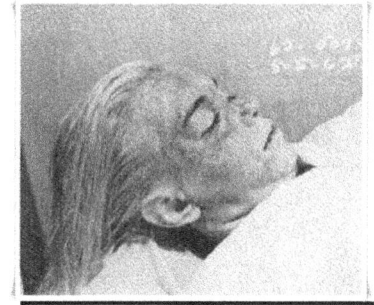

Marilyn
as photographed in the morgue by an unauthorized paparazzi

The floor in the guest cottage was too cramped, so both men picked up her body to move her to the foyer. "Unfortunately, I dropped her on her fanny. It was my fault. Later, I heard that the coroner found two unexplained bruises on her body. The one on her upper arm was probably caused by my fingertips. I'd gripped her really hard. The other bruise, I'm sure, definitely came from dropping her. All the time, my partner had held onto her feet. We then picked her up again and moved her into the foyer. She was still breathing, but I thought [she was] going fast."

The fact that she bruised showed that she was still alive," he said. "I'd recently learned that dead bodies don't bruise."

While Leibowitz went back to the ambulance for a resuscitator, Hall inserted an airway into her throat to aid her intake of oxygen. The housekeeper helped hook up the resuscitator.

"I felt the CPR was starting to work," Hall said. "We were getting a good exchange of air from her body. Some of the color was coming back to her face. When I first saw her, she looked like she was still wearing that graveyard white makeup she wore in *Bus Stop*. I thought it was safe now to move her. I called out 'get the gurney.'"

It was then that a hysterical woman in raincoat and pajamas ran down the hallway, screaming 'SHE'S DEAD, SHE'S DEAD!'"

"She came and butted in," Hall said, "hovering over the body. I wanted to knock the crazy bitch on her ass because I feared she'd fuck everything up."

"Who in the hell are you?" Hall asked.

"I'm her publicist," the woman shouted at him.

He later said, "At that time of my life, I didn't even know what a publicist was."

"We're not ready for you yet," he told the woman. "She's not dead. You can publicize it if she's dead. But we're going to save her."

As Hall and his partner were getting ready to remove Marilyn, a man appeared in the hallway, carrying a black leather bag. "I'm her doctor," he shouted at me. "Give her positive pressure."

"Turkey, what in the fuck do you think we're doing?" an angry Hall said. He was tired of all this interference. "She's breathing, thanks to me."

"When I took the job, I had been instructed to follow doctor's orders at the scene of any emergency—or else get fired," Hall said. "I took the resuscitator off, put an extension on the airway, pinched her nose, and then started to give her mouth to mouth. You can't get any god damn more positive than that."

"At that time, this doctor guy began to give her CPR," Hall said. "I thought he should apply it to her chest. Instead, the fucker was applying it to her lower abdomen."

"Look, doctor, you blow and I'll push," Hall suggested. "He didn't pay me any attention. He opened his bag and pulled out this hypodermic syringe with a heart needle attached."

Hall claimed he heard the doctor say, almost to himself, "I have to make a show of this."

Then, according to Hall, the doctor removed a pharmaceutical bottle from his bag and then inserted the needle into the bottle, filling the syringe. "I'm sure it was Adrenalin."

"He told me he had to inject her between the sixth and seventh ribs. He counted down her rib cage, pushed a breast to the side, and stuck the needle into her chest. He sure got it wrong. He entered at a bad angle, and the needle hit something, no doubt her rib. Instead of taking the needle out, he pressed down hard, and I heard this 'snap.' The fucking needle probably had broken a rib. He shoved the needle right into her heart. I knew at this point that it was curtains for Marilyn."

"The doctor stood up and confronted me," Hall said. "He looked like I had killed Marilyn. 'She's dead,' he told me. 'You guys can leave now.'"

"As we were heading out, he came up to me, standing very close like he was trying to intimidate me. "Whatever you do, don't report one word of what happened here tonight. Don't call the newspapers. We've got it handled. If you don't follow my instructions, things will go very, very bad for you.' He gave me the creeps."

As Hall was gathering his paraphernalia, to the sounds of that publicist screaming hysterically in the hallway, two men appeared on the scene.

"One was a police officer, and the other guy was dressed in a suit," Hall recalled. "The guy in the suit looked familiar, but like he was coming off a forty-day drunk. I thought he might have been a detective summoned from some bar.

"Later, when I saw his picture in the paper, I recognized Peter Lawford," Hall said. "He was no damn detective. I'd heard he was a movie star, but I'd never seen one of his films. The papers said he was married to one of President Kennedy's sisters."

Twenty years from the night of Marilyn's murder, Hall said, "I firmly believe that Dr. Ralph Greenson—by then I knew his name—murdered Marilyn Monroe, who was already at death's door. But he finished her off. Had he not shown up, and with me in charge, we might have gotten her to the hospital."

"All that shit that appeared in all those books about her being rushed to the hospital is just so much bull," he said. "We never put her in that ambulance. It never happened."

Hall would be the only person at the scene of the crime who volunteered to take a Polygraph test. All the other people on the scene never even had to testify under oath, and most of them denied even being at the scene shortly before dawn that Sunday.

[In 1982, Hall was flown to Florida, where he was introduced to John Harrison, the co-inventor of the Polygraph (a device popularly referred to as a lie detector). "I administered six tests on Hall," Harrison claimed. "I asked him, 'On the evening of August 4, 1962, did you attempt to administer life-saving techniques to Marilyn Monroe?' He was not lying. He passed each of the tests I gave him with flying colors. It seemed that everybody, even those remotely connected to Monroe, lied, told some more lies, and even changed their stories. I'd love to have given some of them my Polygraph test, especially Eunice Murray, Bobby Kennedy, Johnny Roselli, Peter Lawford, and Dr. Greenson...and that would be just for starters. My money's on Hall."]

The Seductive Sapphic Exploits of

MERCEDES DE ACOSTA
Hollywood's Greatest Lover

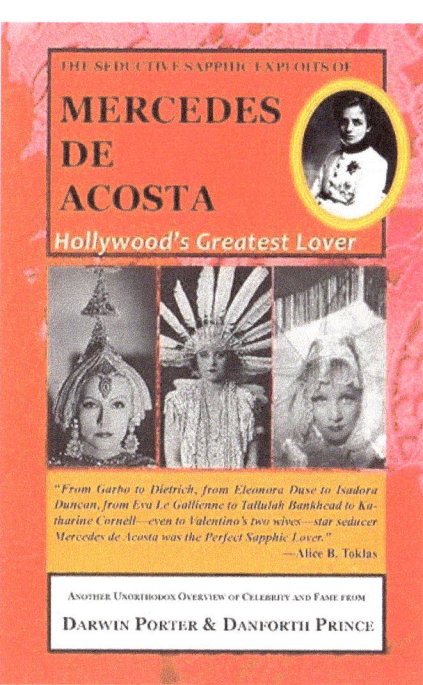

Men are not alone when it comes to seductions of the fabled actresses of the 20th Century. In Blood Moon's biography of **Mercedes de Acosta**, published in 2020, we meet the legendary socialite of the first half of the 20th Century. Configured as a biography, it focuses on the libertine sense of *avant-garde* that permeated the arts of the early 20th century.

"From Garbo to Dietrich, from Eleanora Duse to Isadora Duncan, from Eva Le Gallienne to Tallulah Bankhead to Katharine Cornell, even to Valentino's two lesbian wives—star seducer Mercedes de Acosta was the perfect Sapphic Lover." Or so said Alice B. Toklas, the longtime lover of Gertrude Stein.

During the final years of her life, Mercedes was a frequent visitor at Magnolia House. To Darwin, she confessed tantalizing tales of her fabled sexual exploits in New York, London, Paris, and Hollywood.

"Our book is the biggest name-dropping bio we've ever published," Danforth claimed. "Mercedes did not only seduce these famous women, but she moved in a circle that included some of the most famous artists and celebrities of the early to mid-20th Century. Along the way, readers are introduced to Ethel Barrymore, Nazimova, Beatrice Lillie, John Barrymore, Rita Lydig, Sergei Diaghilev, Vaslaw Nijinski, Jean Cocteau, Igor Stravinsky, Aldous Huxley, and countless others, the cream of the *literati* and *avant-garde* in a world now gone forever."

**NEWS: BLOOD MOON'S CONTRIBUTION TO LESBIAN STUDIES
WILL BE RELEASED IN TIME FOR HALLOWEEN**

THE SEDUCTIVE SAPPHIC EXPLOITS OF MERCEDES DE ACOSTA
HOLLYWOOD'S GREATEST LOVER

IF YOU ASSUMED THAT THE GREATEST LOVERS ARE MEN,
some of the most famous "cult goddesses" of the early- and mid-20th-Century might emphatically disagree.

At Magnolia House, in the final years of her life, the celebrated, notorious, and once-fabled Spanish beauty, **MERCEDES DE ACOSTA** (1892-1968) was a frequent visitor. To Darwin Porter, she confessed and recited fabulously indiscreet stories about her romantic same-sex exploits among the theatrical and cinematic elite of New York, London, Paris, and Hollywood.

It reveals "Sapphic Standards" from the heyday of Silent Film and the early Talkies that no other book—even her own (Here Lies the Heart, published in 1960)—ever dared to make public.

| Rita de Acosta Lydig | Katharine Cornell | Isadora Duncan | Nijinsky *(right)* with Tamara Karsavina, dancers with the *Ballets Russes* | Jean Cocteau | Nazimova |

TOO MANY DAMN RAINBOWS

Judy Garland and her daughter, Liza Minnelli, live again within the torrid pages of *Too Many Damn Rainbows*, Blood Moon's 2020 exploration of their private lives. The dynamic duo survived to love and laugh again in the tear-soaked pages that were their lives.

Liza said about Judy: "She was the world's greatest entertainer and lived eighty lives during the short time she was with us."

In reference to herself, Liza said, "I'm not just Judy Garland's daughter: I'm me. I've made it on my own."

"This mother and daughter act—the greatest in show biz—lived a live of triumph and tragedy," claimed Mickey Rooney. "I screwed Judy when she was just a kid and would have married her had not that sultry tarheel, Ava Gardner, walked into my life."

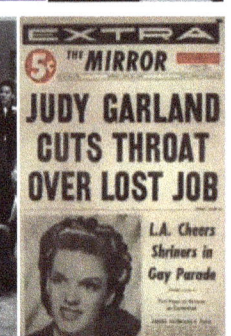

Both mother and daughter lived scandalous lives. Judy lost her virginity as a teenager to the much older actor, Spencer Tracy. "All my life, I've done everything to excess," Judy said. "In some way, Liza at night was even more outrageous than 'dear 'ol Ma.'"

Like her mother, Liza had a penchant for marrying gay husbands. Her affairs ranged from Peter Sellers to Desi Arnaz Jr. Once, in Manhattan, at Studio 54, she was caught in the basement fellating the ballet superstar Mikhail Baryshnikov.

Judy had far more big-name affairs that her daughter—in Judy's case, with celebrities who included Eddie Fisher, Tyrone Power, Ethel Merman, and Prince Aly Khan. She had a philosophy of life that she wanted to convey to her daughter: "You've got only one life to live, so make it a hell of a ride!"

Liza had her own suggestion for living: "What good is sitting alone in your room?"

"I've never seen a show-biz life that was studded with as many ironies as **Judy Garland**'s," Danforth Prince said. "The same entertainer who could hold both cast members and audiences enthralled for hours could also morph into an anguished wreck pleading for understanding, compassion, and approval."

"Our double biography of this mother-daughter team examines, more than any of the others we've crafted, the fine line between artistic genius and psychosis— all of this from a writing team that absolutely, positively adored Judy Garland."

JACKIE-O!

One of the best-selling of the many books Blood Moon published first emerged as *Jacqueline Kennedy Onassis, A Life Beyond Her Wildest Dreams."* It was such a success that Danforth re-published it in 2021 with a new title: *Jacqueline Kennedy Onassis: Her Tumultuous Life and Her Love Affairs.*

It created something of a sensation, as it contained revelations about her private life heretofore never published, everything played out against a backdrop of America's unofficial Queen.

Many of her love affairs had been relatively unheralded. Did you know that she had affairs with three famous actors? (*Hint: Marlon Brando, Paul Newman, and Warren Beatty.*)

Author John P. Marquand, Jr. took her virginity. When he was finished, she asked him, "Is that all there is?"

After an affair with Frank Sinatra, she told her sister, Lee Radziwill, "I much prefer William Holden."

JFK's closest friend, George Smathers, said, "Don't feel sorry for Jackie because she's married to Roto-Rooter. Jack may be a *wham, bam, thank you, ma'am* type of husband, but she, too, had outside resources."

She ignored a note she got from Marilyn Monroe: "Jack is going to marry me and make me First Lady after the divorce."

When Jackie married Aristotle Onassis, she got a note from Gloria Swanson. "I had Ari first, dearie."

At one point, Onassis tricked her and paid a photographer to snap (without her knowledge) photos of her, nude, on his private Greek island. For more than a year, it outsold Marilyn Monroe's nude calendar.

Jackie's stepdaughter, Christina Onassis, said, "What amazes me is that she survives while everyone around her drops. She's dangerous. She's deadly."

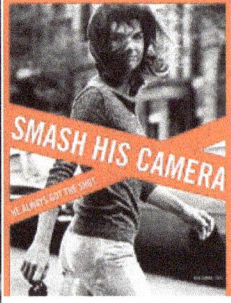

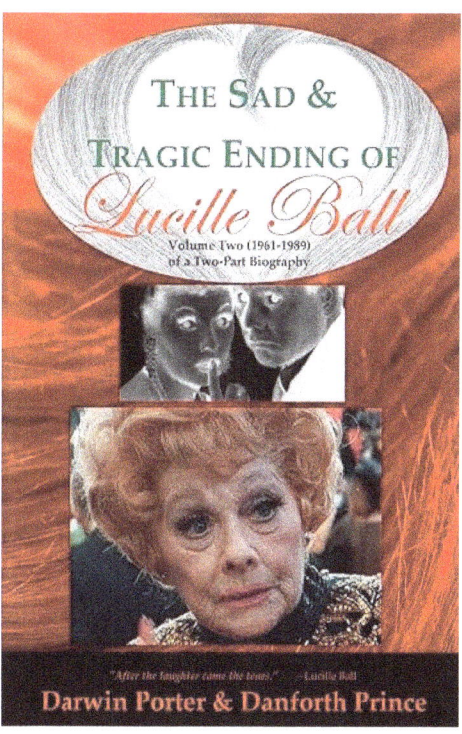

Porter and Prince's biography of Lucille Ball and Desi Arnaz wouldn't fit into just one bio. "It took two volumes," said Danforth. "The dividing point was their divorce, after which both of them admitted that they'd never be the same again. Their covers are inserted above. For a change of pace, It seemed easiest to let others (including Lucy and Desi themselves) weigh in with their opinions of this fabled pair. "

Everyone Had Something to Say About Lucille Ball & and Desi Arnaz

Here's How They Were "Reviewed" by Some of their Contemporaries, and How They Viewed Themselves.

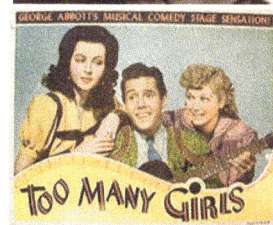

"Lucille Ball and Desi Arnaz were known around the world as Lucy and Ricky Ricardo. The public confused these two television characters as a real-life couple. I had a fling with Lucille myself in the late 1930s, and I think she wanted to marry me. I knew Arnaz very well, too. Let me tell you, those two had a tempestuous marriage from Day One. Lucille accused Desi of cheating, but she did, too, although she denied everything. During the eight-year run of I Love Lucy, it was hell. Often, they were not speaking to each other except on camera."
—Milton Berle

"Lucille Ball looked like a two-dollar whore who had been badly beaten up by her pimp. She had a black eye, her hair was hanging down in her face, and her skin-tight dress was coming apart at the seams."

—Desi Arnaz, remembering his first glimpse of Lucille. At the time, she was dressed for her role in *Dance, Girl, Dance*

"Lucille wasn't the kind of girl you could take home to meet mother."

—Monroe Greenthal, publicist

"When Lucille broke off our engagement, I tried to get my diamond ring back. She refused to give it to me. I gave her a black eye."

—Broderick Crawford

"Love! I was always falling in love."

—Lucille Ball

"Desi Arnaz was a lech! Anything female from thirteen to thirty, he'd go after."

—Actor Roger C. Carmel

"Desi didn't know the difference between sex and love. To put it bluntly, love was a good fuck. Desi could get that anywhere—and did."

—Fred Ball

"The world was my oyster. What I wanted, I had only to ask for it."

—Desi Arnaz

"I don't take out other broads. I take out hookers."

—Desi Arnaz

"Your wife is your wife. Your fooling around can in no way affect your love for her. Your marriage is sacred, and a few peccadilloes mean nothing."

—Desi Arnaz

"I brought laughter to millions. But privately, I cried a lot."

—Lucille Ball

"Desi once told me that he would always love Lucy—but Lucille Ball was another thing."

—William Frawley

"Lucille was not the type of gal to throw herself at a man. But if a guy put the make on her, and he was good-looking enough, chances are he had a damn good chance of getting somewhere."

—Kay Vaughn, a friend

"I hate failure and that divorce from Desi Arnaz was the number one failure in my life. My

divorce from him was the worst period of my life. Desi or I have never been the same since, mentally or physically."

—Lucille Ball

"My mother and father had one of those historical marriages, like Napoléon and Josephine, Richard Burton and Elizabeth Taylor—destined to be trouble but destined for them to never find anyone as passionate or fabulous."

—Lucie Arnaz

"We had our daughter, our son, and two people could not have been in love or happier than we were. Then the shit hit the fan."

—Desi Arnaz

"In addition to Desi Arnaz, I got to suck off some of the most beautiful men of my era—Tyrone Power, John Payne, George Montgomery, Scott Brady, and Gary Cooper. Do I have regrets? I sure do. I didn't get to make it with Lex Barker, Johnny Weissmuller, Sterling Hayden, Steve Cochran, John Derek, Errol Flynn, and Robert Taylor."

—Cesar Romero

"I guess I'll have to learn to love the bitch."

—Vivian Vance on Lucille Ball

"Desi was like Dr. Jekyll and Mr. Hyde. He drank and gambled, and he went out with other women….and in a few cases men as well in his early days trying to break into show biz. It was always the same—booze, broads, and Cesar Romero. Desi's nature is destructive. When he builds something, the bigger he builds it, the more he wants to tear it down. That's the scenario of his life."

—Lucille Ball

"George Sanders is a polished seducer. Desi has more passion, but George has more boudoir flair. He knows how to flatter a woman and make her feel she is the Czarina of Russia. Too bad he's married to that ghastly Hungarian bombshell, Zsa Zsa Gabor."

—Lucille Ball

"I spent hot nights evoking Old Havana with the uncut salami of Desi Arnaz. He told me that since he had a redhead at home, he preferred well-stacked blondes when he committed adultery. The first time he took me out on a date at the racetrack at Del Mar, he told me he had something in common with a race horse. Even a blonde bimbo could figure that one out."

—Liz Renay, Hollywood's leading "Star Fucker"

"When I appeared on her Lucy show, I came to loathe Ball. Tonight, as I write this, I merely pity her. After that episode I did with her, I made a vow never to see her again. She can thank her lucky stars that I wasn't drinking back then. I might have killed her."

—Richard Burton

"I loathed William Frawley, and the feeling was mutual. Whenever I received a new script, I raced through it, praying that there wouldn't be a scene where we had to be in bed together."

—Vivian Vance

"Vivian Vance is one of the finest gals to come out of Kansas. But I often wish she'd go back there."

—William Frawley

"After appearing on that stupid Lucy show, I decided that Ball is a bigger bitch than me."

—Joan Crawford

"The secret of staying young is to live honestly, eat slowly, and lie about your age."

—Lucille Ball

"Desi was a boozer, a philanderer, and a gambler who lost most of his millions. Technically, their marriage lasted two decades. Maybe five years of that were spent away from each other. I thought he was a dirty little Spic, not worthy of my daughter. She should have married William Holden."

—DeDe Ball

"I am a real ham. I love an audience. I work better with an audience. I am dead, in fact, without one."

—Lucille Ball

"How *I Love Lucy* was born: We decided that instead of divorce lawyers profiting from our mistakes, we'd profit from them."

—Lucille Ball

"I'm sometimes scared of everything that has happened to us. We didn't think that Desilu Productions would grow so big. We merely wanted to be together and have two children."

—Lucille Ball

"I will never do another TV series. I couldn't top *I Love Lucy*, and I'd be foolish to try. In this business, you have to know when to get off."

—Lucille Ball

"Women's Lib? Oh I'm afraid it doesn't interest me one bit. I've been so liberated it hurts."

—Lucille Ball

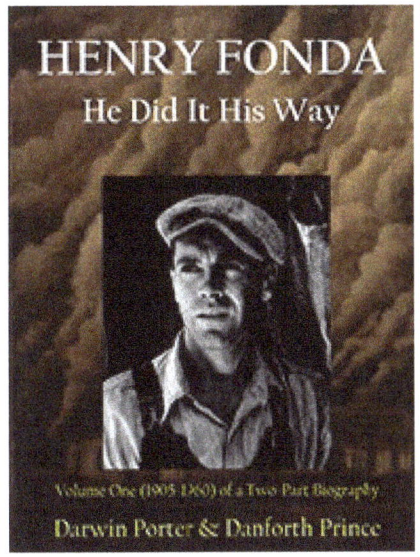  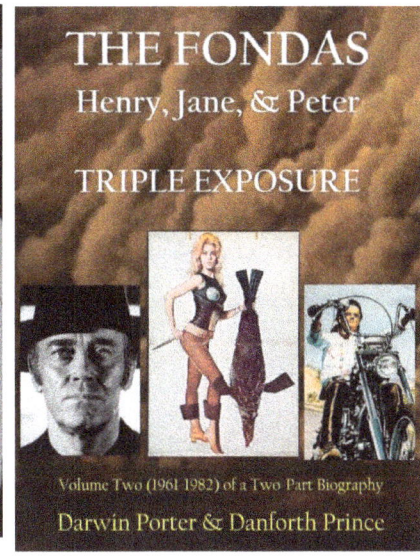

In 2022 and 2023, the Magnolia House series released a two-part bio of **the "Fabulous Fondas"—Henry, his daughter Jane, and his son, Peter.** Theirs was a saga of triumph, family discord, and tragedy. The covers, with their respective **Tables of Contents**, appear here and on the pages that follow:

THE FONDAS
Volume One (1905-1960)

Chapter One
　　FOUNDATIONS OF THE FONDAS
　　Henry, a Son of Nebraska, Embarks on a Brutalizing Road to Stardom; Brouhahas with the Bourgeoisie; Summer Stock with the Sea Monsters of Cape Cod

Chapter Two
　　SURVIVING MARGARET SULLAVAN & THE GREAT DEPRESSION
　　Henry Gets Dramatic, Onstage and off, sometimes with players who became independently famous in their own right. The Twentieth Century Roars

Chapter Three
　　YOUNG HENRY FACES THE PERILS AND DEBAUCHERIES OF THE GREAT WHITE WAY and THE PEOPLE WHO LABOR WITHIN

Chapter Four
　　REACTING TO HOLLYWOOD—Henry becomes a working movie star in *The Farmer Takes a Wife, Way Down East, I Dream Too Much,* and *Trail of the Lonesome Pine*. Roommates Henry and James Stewart meet and seduce Greta Garbo. Henry's on-screen romances or off-screen trysts star Marlene Dietrich, Jeanette MacDonald, Lily Pons, and Sylvia Sidney.

Chapter Five
　　LOVE, POLITICS, & SHOW BIZ
　　Between "Play Dates" with the Natives of La-La Land, Henry Meets, Seduces, and Marries FRANCES BROKAW SEYMOUR, and celebrates more or less "parallel career success" with JAMES STEWART

Chapter Six
　　HOW, ONCE UPON A TIME IN HOLLYWOOD, HENRY FONDA DID IT HIS WAY WITH: Frances Seymour Brokaw, Bette Davis, Margaret Sullavan, Joan Bennett, and

at least a dozen other pre-eminent "Supernovas and Starlettes" of the late 1930s and early 40s.

Chapter Seven
STARTING A DYSFUNCTIONAL FAMILY; BECOMING A MOVIE STAR; and Coping with Bette Davis (*Jezebel!*), Loretta Young, Dorothy Lamour, "Bloody Babs" Stanwyck, half-truths about Abraham Lincoln, and a film with Dolores Del Rio about a haunted refugee priest.

Chapter Eight
WAR IN EUROPE, THE GRAPES OF WRATH, a competitive "Bromance" with James Stewart, a Flirtation with David Selznick about a possible role in Gone With the Wind, and Henry's escape from a "Slave Contract" with "Fuck-it-All" (Henry's words) Darryl Zanuck.

Chapter Nine
MORE ABOUT ZANUCK, LILLIAN ("The Queen of Broadway') RUSSELL, LOVING LUCY ("Lucille Ball was the love of my father's life," said his daughter Jane), TALES OF MANHATTAN, and that grim but memorable classic, THE OX-BOW INCIDENT

Chapter Ten
A MATURE & DOMESTICATED FATHER OF THREE JOINS THE NAVY
How Henry Fonda, a low-ranking "Quartermaster, Third Grade" got drenched in the blood baths of the South Pacific, and the obstacles he faced, after the war, back in Hollywood.

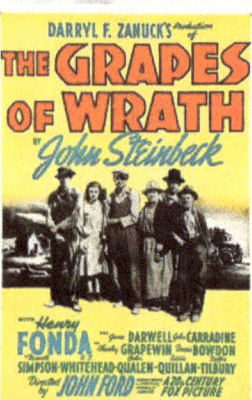

Chapter Eleven
ONSTAGE WITH MR. ROBERTS, BATTLING COCHISE & THE INDIANS WITH JOHN FORD, and the stupid, pointless suicide of Frances Seymour Fonda. *Daisy Kenyon* with volatile Joan Crawford. Introducing Susan Blanchard, "Almost Losing" Peter Fonda after a prep school gunshot accident, and stage and film offers that didn't always work.

Chapter Twelve
HENRY RETURNS TO BROADWAY. More about Joan Crawford, Rita Hayworth, John Wayne, Gary Cooper, Dick Powell, June Allyson, and a sometimes unsavoury Charles Laughton, "Tedium at Sea" (a Cinematic adaptation of *Mr. Roberts*), and Dino De Laurentiis' big-budget blockbuster rendering of Leo Tolstoy's WAR AND PEACE

Chapter Thirteen
HOLLYWOOD ON THE TIBER: THE FONDAS INVADE ROME Henry's Divorce from Susan Blanchard and his marriage to the "socially voracious vampire," Afdera Franchetti, and How Things Went with Anthony ("Psycho") Perkins when father Henry and daughter Jane each co-starred with him in separate movies.

Chapter Fourteen
PLAYTIME ON THE FRENCH RIVIERA, and MORE ABOUT AFDERA FRANCHETTI. Susan Strasberg, gilded, well-connected *wünderkind* of Method acting, appears with Henry in *Stage Struck*. Henry's co-starring gig with Anne Bancroft on Broadway launches her as a superstar. Henry picks some bad scripts as Afdera is suspected of "inaugural intimacies" with JFK.

Chapter Fifteen
JANE: Sleeping around Paris with the New Wave, Warren Beatty, and Anthony Perkins. Arguments with Shelley Winters and Andreas Voutsinas, and what happened when she inherited a chunk of her late mother's estate.

Chapter Sixteen
HENRY DIVORCES HIS BARONESS and marries the woman of his dreams, then

228

forcefully portrays Olivia de Havilland's cancer-ridden husband, onstage. WHO's AFRAID OF VIRGINIA WOOLF? rocks movie audiences nationwide, and Jane's bordello flick, WALK ON THE WILD SIDE, raises paternal (and censorship) concerns.

THE FONDAS
Volume Two

HENRY

Prologue
An Abbreviated Rundown of Henry Fonda's Life

Chapter One
As one of the few surviving superstars of Pre-War Classic Hollywood, Henry Works. *The Longest Day, The Best Man, Fail Safe, Sex and the Single Girl, In Harm's Way, The Rounders, Battle of the Bulge, Welcome to Hard Times.*

Chapter Two
Horrified by newfangled social trends, Henry Fonda changes with changing times: *Firecreek; Yours, Mine, & Ours; Madigan; The Boston Strangler; Once Upon a Time in the West; Our Town*

Chapter Three
The Movies Change—and to some degree, so does Henry:
The Cheyenne Social Club; Too Late the Hero; There Was a Crooked Man; Sometimes a Great Notion; The Smith Family; Night Flight from Moscow; Ash Wednesday; My Name is Nobody; Clarence Darrow.

Chapter Four
Ignoring health concerns, Henry works until he can't.
The Decline and Collapse of Henry Fonda.Midway, Tentacles, The Great Smokey Roadblock; Killer Bees: The Swarm; Fedora, Roots, The Next Generation; Meteor; City on Fire; The Oldest Living Graduate; Gideon's Trumpet; Summer Solstice.

JANE

Chapter Five
Lady of Contradictions, Mistress of the Unexpected
The Chapman Report; Period of Adjustment; Marilyn Monroe; In the Cool of the Day; Sunday in New York; Cat Ballou.

Chapter Six
Jane and her French Invasion
America's Answer to Brigitte Bardot moves to France and inaugurates an affair with the French actor voted, prior to their meeting, as "The Handsomest Man in the World." (Alain Delon). Roger Vadim, the avant-garde director, enters Jane's life. BARDOT (Vadim, not God, created her.) DENEUVE ("the most beautiful woman in the world.") How the producers of La Ronde display an effigy of Jane, nude, above Times Square. Back in California, The Chase teams Jane with Marlon Brando and Robert Redford.

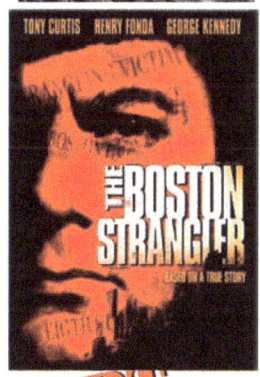

Chapter Seven
Jane Gets Morphed into the Sex Kitten of the 22nd Century
Barbarella. Jane and Roger Vadim host the "celebrity shindig of the year" at Malibu. Any Wednesday. Jane gets married! *The Game Is Over; Hurry Sundown; Barefoot in the Park, Myra Breckinridge.*

Chapter Eight
The Enchanted Couple and the Vagaries of Vadim.
Jane meets the cream of *avant garde* Europe: Jean Marais; Jean-Paul Belmondo; Louis Jourdan; Luchino Visconti; Gunter Sachs, Marcello Mastroianni, Jean-Louis Trintignant, and Roman Polanski.

Chapter Nine
Jane becomes the preferred actress of both the commercial and avant-garde film industries: Existential anguish during the Great Depression (*They Shoot Horses, Don't They?*). Rock Hudson: Vadim directs him in an celebration of nymphet allure, *Pretty Maids All in a Row*; *Klute* (Jane plays a whore); *Steelyard Blues* (Jane plays another whore); the most respected director in France (Jean-Luc Godard) directs Jane in a socialist comedy, *Tout Va Bien*; Jane does Ibsen in *A Doll House*; Even Jane can't rescue the USSR's sloppy, confusing remake of *The Blue Bird. Fun with Dick and Jan.* Jane teams with Vanessa Redgrave in Lillian Hellman's fantasy version of an anti-Nazi activist in *Julia*.

Chapter Ten
Jane Gets Aggressive: ***Barbarella*** **Morphs into Hanoi Jane**; Her marriage to Tom Hayden. Henry Fonda (*père*) is not amused—neither is the American public.

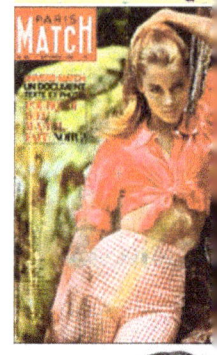

Chapter Eleven
Jane Ages Gracefully: *Coming Home; Comes a Horseman; California Suite; The China Syndrome; The Electric Horseman; 9 to 5.*

PETER

Chapter Twelve
An entitled child of Hollywood, Peter is "resentfully royal" from birth.
Tammy and the Doctor. (WHAT? Peter Fonda in a Tammy rip-off?), *PT 109* (Peter doesn't get to play JFK); *The Victors* (Before the final reel, Peter doesn't become one of them); his scandals with the draft board; Peter's rival (Warren Beatty) dates Peter's ex-stepmother, Afdera Franchetti; Peter hangs out with (and gets high with) the deeply depressed sons of other famous movie stars; Peter gets batty with Adam West (aka TV's campy *Batman*); Peter's competitive maneuverings with Tom Jones, George Hamilton, and *the Rifleman*, Chuck Connors.

Chapter Thirteen
Sex and Drugs and Rock and Roll: Peter vs. Hollywood's Other "Heartthrobs of the Moment," Nick Adams, Tommy Kirk, Brandon deWilde; and Michael Pollard. Then-daring feature films about teenaged pregnancies (*The Young Lovers*); Peter's cultivation of the King of B-List Filmmaking, Roger Corman; Motorcycle Mania and *The Wild Angels*; Romantic Dramas, played out publicly, with Nancy Sinatra. Peter drops Acid, publicly and Willfully, in *The Trip*.

Chapter Fourteen
Peter Bites Hard (and Swallows) the Commercial Potential of the Counter-Culture. Certain *Honorable Men*; Anachronistic Sex with Celebrities from the Past (Billy the Kid! Jean Harlow!) in a stage play, *The Beard* (Peter doesn't get the movie role); a politically provocative film (*The Queen*) that Peter covets the lead for never gets made; The Quirks and Private Anguish of Dennis Hopper (*Easy Rider* makes Peter rich): Marital abandonment and reconciliation in *The Hired Hand*; Peter embarasses himself in *The Last Movie*, reviewed by some as "the worst movie ever made."

Chapter Fifteen
Winding Down ("the Slow Goodbye) with Peter Fonda. The embarrassing but inevitable collapse of his screen career, his separation and divorce from Susan Brewer, and *Idaho Transfer; Two People; Dirty Mary, Crazy Larry; Open Season; Race with the Devil*, and *92 in the Shade*. How he emoted with Andy Warhol's self-enchanted porn star, Sylvia Miles, in Key West; and his love affair and marriage with Portia Rebecca Crockett.

Chapter Sixteen
Peter Tunes Out, Drops Out, and Fades Away. *Killer Force*; Navigating his way, aboard his private yacht, through the South Pacific, Portia Crockett, *Fighting* (Ho-Hum) *Mad; Future World; Outlaw Blues;* and *Wanda Nevada*.

Epilogue
Twilight Time on Golden Pond. Henry Fonda, *père*, Joins his daughter, Jane, in a *tour de force* of acting talent, and manage to salvage meaning from their dysfunctional, highly contentious personal pasts. Katharine Hepburn stands by as their Prickly On-Screen Matriarch.

HOLLYWOOD REMEMBERED
Glamour, Glitz, Triumph, & Tragedy

Early in 2025, when this catalogue was released, the final volume in Blood Moon's Magnolia House series was *Hollywood Remembered, Glamour, Glitz, Triumph, and Tragedy.* Reasons for its publication are defined on the press release that appears on the page that immediately follows. In 2024, (the year of its release) it won **First Prize for Biography** at the highly competitive **Hollywood Book Festival** and **Best Anthology of the Year** from the **New York Book Festival.**

Some of the material it contains originally appeared, in truncated formats, within Anita Finley's *Boomer Times.*

Burt Reynolds: How a Nude Centerfold Seduced Hollywood
Steve McQueen & Paul Newman Were Lovers
Liz Taylor: Her Teenage Dalliance with Ronald Reagan
The XXX-Rated Life of Peter O'Toole
Kirk Douglas: A Century of Sexual Conquests
Linda Lovelace Deep-Throated Frank Sinatra
Elvis Presley Got Down and Dirty with Marilyn Monroe
Michael Jackson became infatuated with a young (very young) Prince William
June Allyson Slept with Two (Future) U.S. Presidents
Marlon Brando, the Master; James Dean, the Slave Boy
Rock Hudson on the Casting Couch
Judy Garland's Gay Husbands
Movie Stars Reveal "Their First Time"
Vivien Leigh Bedded Guys—and Girls
Katharine Hepburn & Spencer Tracy: Platonic Lovers in Public, LGBTQ "Buddies" in Private
Future First Lady Nancy Davis wanted Clark Gable, but Settled for Reagan
Merv Griffin Seduces Tarzan
Revenge Porn
Bogie May Have Slept with 1,000 Women

During the 21st Century, Darwin Porter and his co-author, Danforth Prince *(photo, right)* have written and published more biographies than any other American. As of this writing, they're also in pre-production on ten additional books. Awaiting final edits and formatting, each of them has already been written.

FOR MORE ABOUT THEM, PLEASE REFER TO THIS VOLUME'S NEXT (AND FINAL) CHAPTER, **COMING ATTRACTIONS**

> Here's how we defined our motivation for writing
> *Hollywood Remembered.*

BOOK RELEASE NEWS

Blood Moon's
Hollywood Remembered
Glitz, Glamour, Triumph, & Tragedy

How Blood Moon Productions captured the attention of The American Tabloids during the decline of The Entertainment Industry's Golden Age

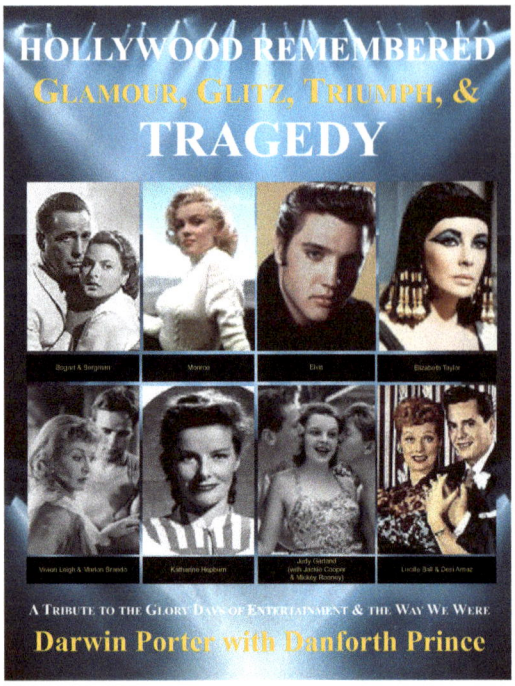

Blood Moon Productions (www.BloodMoonProductions.com) proudly announces the release of *Hollywood Remembered*, a 500-page compendium of "short stories" inspired by **Darwin Porter's** long exposure to the backlot intrigues of the entertainment industry's "Hollywood Heyday."

It's envisioned as an oversized coffee table book of enduring interest to anyone who ever loved classic films and the scandalous intrigues associated with its players. It's not for the timid. Pages are splashed with incisive commentary and photographs of a fabulous era swept away by changing times.

Its inspiration derived from twenty years of Darwin Porter's monthly contributions to *Boomer Times*, a glossy magazine and "Sunday supplement" of *The Miami Herald's* subscribers in Dade and Broward Counties, Florida. It was spearheaded by **Anita Finley**, a South Florida gerontologist who doubled as a spokesperson for her state's "politically connected' population of Baby Boomers.

According to Blood Moon's president, Danforth Prince, "The core values of **Anita Finley** and **Darwin Porter**—who define Baby Boomers as "Old-Time Hollywood's Greatest Fans"—always dovetailed neatly. This book is envisioned as a joint celebration of the staggering literary output of both *Boomer Times* and **Blood Moon Productions**. As such, we've dedicated it to **Ms. Finley**. The *Grande Dame* of Florida's Boomers.

"We also envision this as an **autobiography of Blood Moon Productions** and an end-of-life tribute to its creative director, **Darwin Porter**. If not for his archival skills, many once-underground truths about The American Century would have died with their last first-hand witnesses. But thanks in part to Porter's staggering descriptive output, thousands of once-repressed facts have been recorded and digitalized for future historians and fans. In fact, for the Library Trades, we've categorized this one-of-a-kind new book as a resource for MEDIA STUDIES.

"With a release expected on that Greatest of American Holidays, The 4th of July, Blood Moon's HOLLYWOOD REMEMBERED will challenge traditional beliefs about celebrities and the sociologies that nurtured them. "

With a special tribute to the celebrities whose luminous images still enthrall us on movie screens today, thanks for taking a look at this portrait of the ferociously unfettered "indie" that briefly reigned as a magnet for tabloid publicists, and as one of the hottest independent publishing ventures in the world.

Blood Moon's HOLLYWOOD REMEMBERED:
Glitz, Glamour, Triumph, & Tragedy

By Darwin Porter with Danforth Prince
ISBN 978-1-936003-92-1

PART FIVE: COMING ATTRACTIONS		

It's 2025. Time is Fleeting and Short.

What's New and What's Next from
Blood Moon Productions?

ANSWER:
HISTORY'S MOST CANDID AND COMPREHENSIVE BIOGRAPHY OF

Clark Gable, in Three Volumes

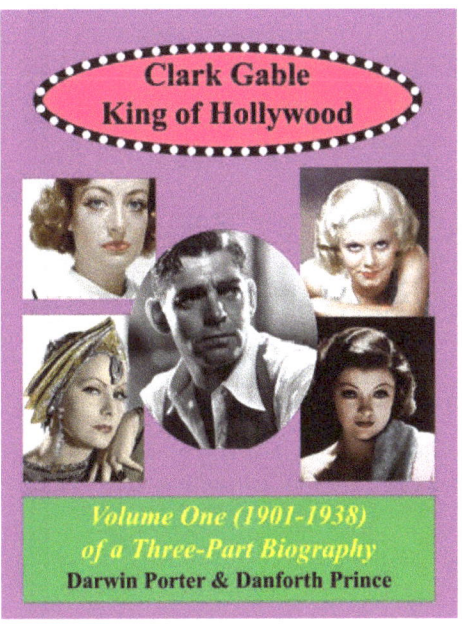
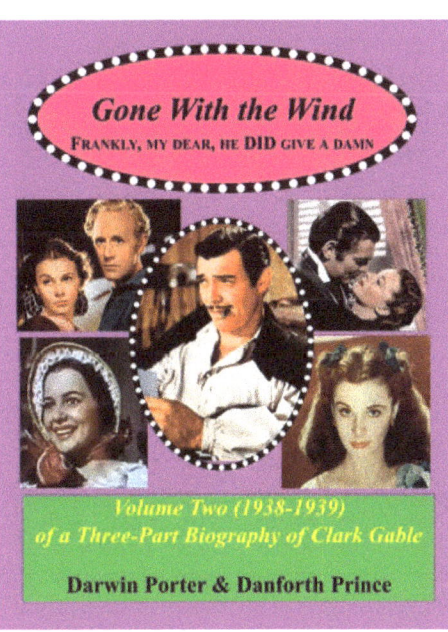
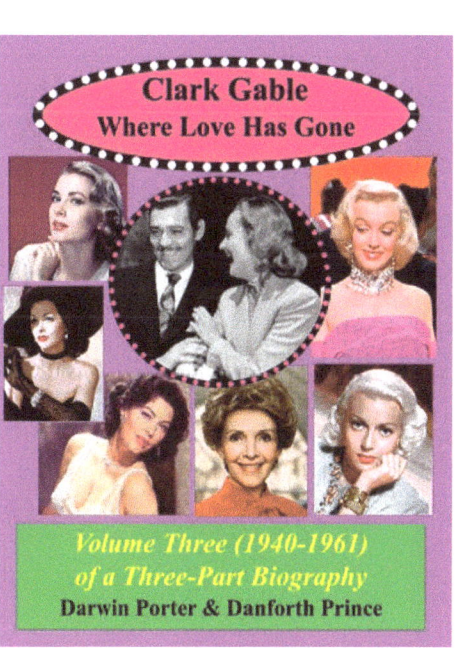

No one in Publishing Has Ever Tried this Before,

but it's NEXT on Blood Moon's Agenda

He Was the King of Hollywood. He's Clark Gable.

Although Clark Gable was probably the most-watched, and most-emulated actor of Golden Age Hollywood, no one has ever really explored his meteoric but opportunistic rise to fortune and unparalled fame. Beginning in 2025, the authors at Blood Moon Productions will change all that, thanks to the release of a three-volume trilogy exposing THE KING OF HOLLYWOOD, uncut, unclothed, stripped of his camouflage, and exposed.

More than any other actor of his era, he influenced America's definition of Manhood; he became a Mega-Celebrity before they invented the word; and despite intense rivalry with lesser actors, his career survived (and thrived) throughout vastly different eras of America's film-industry priorities and values.

He led a mind-bending life which Blood Moon will configure into THREE SPECTACULAR VOLUMES, each choreographed in ways never achieved, despite multiple hackneyed attempts from other publishing venues. He was THE KING, and despite many shocking revelations about the eras in which he thrived, we treat him like one.

Gable, In Three Volumes, Like He's Never Been Seen Before

At the peak of his career, flush with the success of his starring performance in history's most poignant film about the end of the Old South (*Gone With the Wind*), **Clark Gable** had become a symbol of American pride and power itself. His role as an icon was so pronounced that Adolph Hilter placed a bounty on his head and stated his intention of capturing him alive and dragging him, caged and in chains, as a trophy through the streets of Nazi Berlin.

GABLE! He's here, alive and thriving, the beneficiary of years of research from the creative team at Blood Moon. So complicated is his story that no single tome can contain all that's needed to say in this ULTIMATE OVERVIEW of CLARK, GLORIOUSLY GABLED, the focal point of a major trilogy spearheaded by film historian **Darwin Porter**.

Volume One (1901-1938): Clark Gable, King of Hollywood, Available in the summer of 2025

Volume Two (1938-1939): Gone With the Wind, Frankly My Dear, He DID Give a Damn

Volume Three (1940-1961): Clark Gable, Where Love Has Gone

WHAT'S COMING AFTER GABLE?

ANSWER: A Double-Barreled Overview of the Sexiest, most Fantasy-Adaptable actor in Golden Age Hollywood

GARY COOPER

In two unforgettable, sometimes shocking volumes

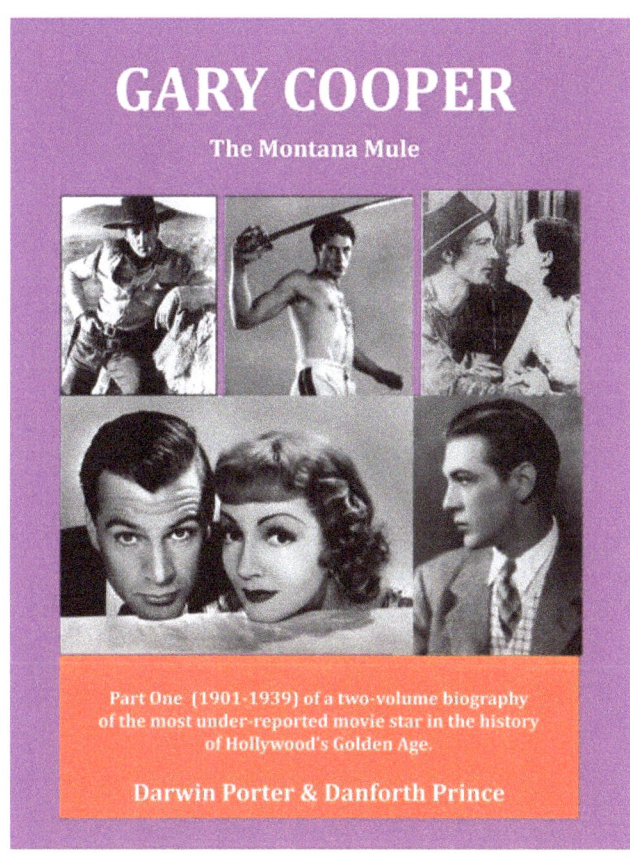

Gary Cooper symbolized the American hero—a national icon of self-reliant integrity. Yet in private, he was tempestuous, passionate, a raging bull traveling a path of seductions of some of the most famous leading ladies in Hollywood—and some male stars, too.

For him, day or night, it was always "High Noon" in the bedroom.

As his director, Stuart Heisler proclaimed, "Coop was probably the greatest cocksman who ever lived."

What Will We Be Plotting After That?

Media

Buzz

We're Gonna Call it

MEDIA BUZZ

and it's gonna vaguely resemble what we did with Blood Moon's BABYLON series

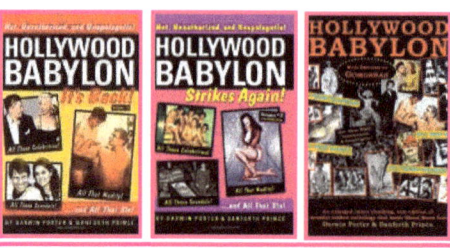

**MEDIA IS BUZZING
FOR WHAT'S NEXT AT BLOOD MOON**

This all-new multi-volume series looks a bit like the illustrations above,
Its scope, however, won't be limited to just the naughty indiscretions of
Hollywood. It will also lampoon politics, the art world, religion, and foreign events.

Titillating chapters (just a few examples) within the first of this new series will include:

- Sir Isaac Newton's Predictions about the End of the World (Hint: It's scheduled for 2060)
- Marilyn and Nikita Khruschev at 20th Century Fox: The Odd Couple
- The Saga of the Gay Computer Genius who Shortened World War II by Two Years and Saved 14 Million Lives. After the war, English Police chemically castrated him.
- From the Slammer to the Glamour: The Sexiest Man Alive
- The Return of the Woolly Mammoth: DNA can't do everything, but it can do a LOT
- Young Men Who Marry Older Women
- Lady Liberty is No Lady
- America's Much-Married Bluebeard
- JFK's best gay friend: Lem Billings
- Franklin & Eleanor: Omnisexual Adultery in the White House
- Genocide & Racial Substitution: Einstein's Clearly Articulated Fear That the Chinese Will Demographically Supplant Other Races
- How Lady Jeanne Campbell, a forcefully well-funded newspaper columnist, Seduced JFK, Nikita Khruschev, and Fidel Castro
- A Horrifying Tour of Yesteryear's Medical Oddities
- Hedy Lamarr: Her (self-repudiated) marital links to an Austrian Nazi; Her triumph as a Pro-American sex symbol; and her unprofitable links to the invention of the cellphone.
- How and Why "The Broadway Belter" (Ethel Merman) Assisted and Encouraged the FBI Director, J. Edgar Hoover, as a cross-dressing female impersonator.

Announcing Blood Moon's "STARDUST" Series
A Startling Overview of Why NYC was, During its Theatrical Renaissance of the 60s, and 70s, Truly Great
"Only in New York, Kids, Only in New York."

Quirky, informative, and meticulously researched, each of the two books envisioned for this series has already been conceptualized, plotted., and written. They're at the point in their development where they're merely awaiting editorial processing.

Blood Moon's Stardust Series
Volume One of Two

Stardust, From Off-Off Broadway to Hollywood:
Lucille Lortel, Joseph Papp, and the Explosive Birth of the Modern Theatre

Danforth Prince

Darwin's mentor, **Lucille Lortel** during her heyday as a B actress in Hollywood's early Talkies.

Stardust is about the arbitrary, ego-driven disasters (and occasional triumphs) of the American Theater, as transcribed by the "Ultimate Insider," Darwin Porter as relayed to his partner and publisher, Danforth Prince. They derive from Porter's role as a friend, companion and advisor to two of the moguls who redefined the term "Off-Broadway" during the peak years of New York City's dominance of the American *zeitgeist*.

They included **Lucille Lortel**, the imperial, flamboyantly eccentric and very rich Queen of Off-Broadway, and **Joseph Papp**, the most controversial and widely acclaimed theatrical visionary in the history of the mid-20th Century.

It captures the Renaissance of the American theater that arose outside of NYC's traditional *(i.e., West Side, Midtown)* Theater District during the mid-20th Century. The movement witnessed the birth of future movie stars, great playwrights, and brilliant directors.

LUCILLE LORTEL
SOCIALITE, OFF-BROADWAY PRODUCER
& ARTS PHILANTHROPIST

Theatrical producer and philanthropist **Lucille Lortel** (*inset photo*), against a backdrop of the theater she bought, and from which emanated a string of *avant-garde* classics

LUCILLE LORTEL provided a showcase for the emerging talent that flooded through New York in the 60s, and 70s. As a young man fresh out of the university, Darwin and Lortel struck up a friendship from the first night they met, morphing into something akin to a mother and son, waching the same plays and meeting (and interviewing) the same emerging new talent. Lortel introduced Darwin to Richard Burton, Helen Hayes, Lillian Gish and Lotte Lenya, the star of her long-running (and fabled) *Threepenny Opera,* and dozens of other "heroically" pertinent players.

In this "transmission" of Darwin's memoirs, and aimed at devotees of the American theater, Prince recaptures, through Darwin's eyes and ears, many dozens of Off-Off Broadway maneuvers, love couplings, feuds, triumphs, and tragedies. With Lortel, Darwin shared front-row seats to productions that either crashed and burned or headed on to glory. All of them, accessorized with additional commentary that Prince gleaned during his 40+ year partnership with Porter, are included within the pages of this book.

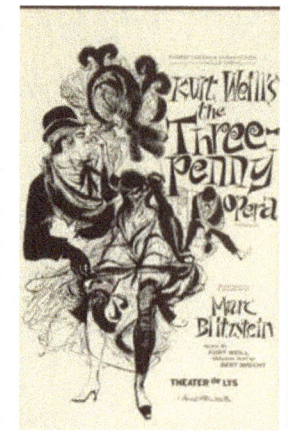 

WHO WAS LUCILLE LORTEL? A forceful Hollywood *ingénue* during filmdom's tricky transitions from Silents to Talkies, she married well—some say brilliantly—to the mogul who invented the modern cigarette. Yearning to keep her creative juices alive (and by then, supremely well-funded), she bought the "way Off-Broadway" **Theatre de Lys**, on Christopher Street in Greenwich Village, and through it, successfully morphed herself into one of NYC's most visible theatrical producers. Eventually, she became a target (and according to some, a victim) for the artistic yearnings and ambitions of virtually EVERYONE with a Broadway dream.

One of the first plays Lortel produced in her theater was the long-running hit, *The Three-Penny Opera*, by Kurt Weill. As she confessed to Darwin, "It was an immediate but unexpected hit, which was wonderful except for limiting the creative scope of my theatre for the next nine years. I couldn't book anything else."

A *grande dame* with a disposable fortune and an artistic temperament, she knew EVERYONE (stars, has-beens, and wannabees). AND EVERYONE (slavishly and obsequiously or not) KNEW HER, vying for invitations to her celebrated parties within her permanent residence within Manhattan's Sherry-Netherland Hotel. Darwin, in the seventies, became her escort, her "walker," her adviser, her scribe, her collaborator, her friend…and ultimately—in the form of this new title from Blood Moon—her biographer.

Lortel was a magnet for faded *grandes dames* of the stage and screen, introducing many of them to Darwin. Two of them included **Helen Hayes** (left) and **Lillian Gish** (right).

JOSEPH PAPP
KING OF OFF-BROADWAY

JOSEPH PAPP, of course, was the founder of **The New York Shakespeare Festival (***aka* **Shakespeare in the Park)**; founder of the Public Theater in what had been the Astor Library in Lower Manhattan; and producer of the Pulitzer Prizewinning musical, *A Chorus Line.* Conceived by Michael Bennett, its plot centered on 17 Broadway dancers auditioning and hoping to get cast. Papp borrowed $1.6 million to produce it within the Public Theater. In July of 1975, it moved to Broadway, where it ran for 6,137 performances, the longest-running Broadway production in history until *Cats* in 1997, surpassed it.

As a young man recently relocated to New York, Darwin Porter occupied the top floor and terrace of the landmark John J. Astor home, part of the historic Astor Colonnade, an interconnected crescent of Greek Revival Buildings. His apartment overlooked the former Astor Library, which was set to be demolished. It was rescued by Brooklyn-born Joseph Papp (1921-1991), the son of Jewish immigrants. From the City, he rented it for $1 a year and adapted it into the Public Theater. In the months and years that followed, it attracted "culture vultures" from across America.

Papp also launched the **New York Shakespeare Festival** (aka **Shakespeare in the Park)**, offering free performances with such stars as Meryl Streep and George C. Scott. Papp believed that theater should be for everyone, not just the rich. Soon, Papp became the unofficial "King of Off-Broadway."

Papp at the Public. Latter-day reviewers credit him as one of the most forcefully effective theatrical producers and promoters in the history of the American theater. Darwin knew him well.

During the period when Darwin knew him best, Papp produced the notoriously provocative musical, *Hair*, a celebration of nudity and free love that sent uptown theatrical traditionalists into apoplectic frenzies. *[It eventually moved to Broadway, where it ran for 1,750 performances.]* Around this time, Darwin, his neighbor, emerged as his friend, advisor, collaborator, quasi-publicist, and co-host—within his apartment in penthouse of the Astor Colonnade—of many of his cocktail parties and fundraisers.

Joe Papp was viewed as the greatest theatrical impresario since Florenz Ziegfeld. Displayed above are posters for plays and/or theatrical events he organized. Each was mind-bogglingly successful.

Darwin's friendship with Papp began on their first meeting. "He enriched my life, not only as a beloved friend, but as a cultural icon who introduced me to actors, playwrights, aspirant directors, an emerging troupe which collectively sparked a theatrical Renaissance far from the lights of Broadway.

"Joe felt that emerging playwrights should be given as much attention as The Bard himself." Darwin said. "You never knew knew what he was going to stage next. He was a devotee of multiculturalism. I had a front row seat to *For Colored Girls Who Have Considered Suicide When the Rainbow Is Enuf.*"

"Joe introduced me to theater unlike any I'd seen before," Darwin said. "He was a cultural icon deserving of his unofficial crown as King. More important than that, he taught me what friendship really was. You stand by your friend through both tragedy and triumph. Both Joe and I witnessed plenty of both."

Darwin Porter (never one to miss an arts industry *brouhaha* when he saw one) was privy to the insider maneuverings of both Lortel and Papp, their couplings, their insecurities, their feuds, their ambitions, and their plots—the kind that kept Off-Broadway's footlights and klieg lights blazing

In this upcoming "biography" of Off- and Off-Off Broadway , Darwin's voice is present and in some cases, loud. Texts are peppered with vignettes of faded Broadway and Hollywood stars from yesteryear, back when people went to parties, wore furs and jewelry, and competed ferociously for parts, stage roles, and acclaim. This book, which we envision as a resource for Theater Studies, will be loaded with the kinds of insider "Off Broadway to Hollywood" gossip that has never been committed to print before.

The core texts of this book have already written. All that remains is some editorial processing. It represents a unique overview of value systems and ways of life that will never return.

Public Works, an ongoing arts project of Joe Papp's Public Theater, continues its outreach to the citizens of NYC and the USA.

Blood Moon's Stardust Series
Volume Two of Two

Sex and Drugs: X-Rated Manhattan in the Jaded 1970s
Sybaritic Denizens of the Night Thrive in an Emporium of Exotica & Erotica

Danforth Prince

Darwin Porter's best friend, James Leo Herlihy, wrote a novel, *Midnight Cowboy, about the travails of a male hustler.* It was adapted into a motion picture in 1969 with stars who included Jon Voight and Dustin Hoffman, with Sylvia Miles in a supporting role as a Times Square prostitute. To the surprise of many in the film colony, *Midnight Cowboy* was voted the Best Picture of the Year, the only X-rated film ever to take home an Oscar.

Both of its male stars, Voight and Hoffman, competed for the Best Actor Oscar, losing to John Wayne for *True Grit.* Miles was nominated for the Best Supporting Actress Oscar, losing to Goldie Hawn for *Cactus Flower.*

Darwin and Herlihy, by invitation, attended the set where directoer John Schlesinger ordered Voight and Miles to strip naked for a sex scene. It was rumored that Voight developed an erection as he lay on top of her. The segment that ensued was very explicit and the director kept the camera rolling. Of course, much of the scene was XXX rated and ended up on the cutting room floor or, more likely, in the director's private files.

In the movie's final cut, after her (implied) sex with Voight, Miles is seen applying lipstick as she faces a mirror. She seems oblivious to the greenhorn hustler who is awkward about getting paid for his sexual services.

With indignation, Miles croaks, "You're gonna ask *me* for money? Who in hell do you think you're dealing with? Some slut from 42nd Street? I'm one hell of a gorgeous chick!"

Herlihy had met Miles two years before, and she invited him, with Darwin, into her dressing room as she changed. Herlihy had to depart early for a date, and Darwin remained behind. When she was fully dressed, Miles turned to him and asked, "Where are you taking me to dinner? I'm starved!"

Thus began a decades-long relationship that launched them into the 1970s in Manhattan, a city widely known as "**Gomorrah on the Hudson**." Many couples could be seen having sex in doorways before rushing off to work in an office.

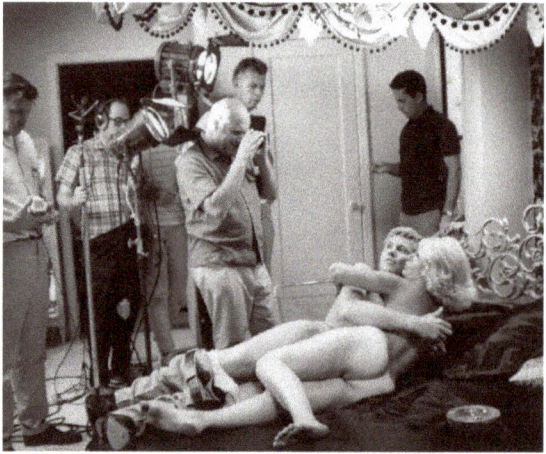

Jon Voight, playing a prostitute, embraces **Sylvia Miles**, also playhing a prostitute, under the glare of cameras, kleig lights, and the judgmental gaze of an armada of technicians—including director **John Schlesinger**—on the set of *Midnight Cowboy* (1969), the first X-rated movie to ever win an Oscar.

After hookers f*** other hookers, there's that embarrassing detail about who gets paid: **Jon Voight's** post-coital fleecing by **Sylvia Miles** in *Midnight Cowboy.*

Sylvia and Darwin set out to live every X-rated minute of that turbulent decade. " It was in New York where anything goes (and did). For pervasive decadence, historians cite Paris as a trendsetter in the 1920s, Berlin in the early 1930s, Rome in the 1950s, London in the 1960s. But for sheer sexual depravity and exhibitionistic frenzy, it was New York in the 1970s. As one writer phrased it, "Manhattan became the pace-setting world captial of the sybaritic taste-makers of the time, dominated by Andy Warhol at his 'Factory.' Manhattan was the Cheshire cat grinning through the Apocalypse."

Promiscuous sex—usually without gender preference—spread even beyond the exclusive domain of jaded hedonists.

Sylvia Miles got invited everywhere, and she most often showed up with Darwin on her arm. They wandered through all the parties, the galas, that celebrated "The New Gomorrah." Much time was spent at Warhol's Factory, where they met one celebrity after another.

On any given night, you might meet and talk with Mick Jagger, Federico Fellini, Calvin Klein, Mia Farrow *(what was she doing here?)* Mama Cass, Truman Capote, John Lennon, James Baldwin, Madonna, Jack Kerouac, William Burroughs, even a young horndog named Donald Trump, a future TV star. Bob Dylan and Rudolf Nureyev were regulars. The ballet dancer had posed nude for Warhol for his private collection, which also included a frontal nude of Yul Brynner in all his uncut glory. As such, Sylvia and Darwin became closely acquainted with many of Andy Warhol's "superstars," including Ultra Violet, Viva, Edie Sedgwick, Brigid Berlin, and Warhol's "Trio of Transsexuals," Candy Darling, Holly Woodlawn, and Jackie Curtis.

As such, in Danforth's epic, life at Warhol's "Factory" lives again in glittering detail and glittering depravity.

As Warhol predicted, "Everyone, in the future, will be famous for 15 minutes."

Tuned to trends, and never willing to miss out on "megatrends of the minute," Sylvia and Darwin never missed a performance of "The Divine Miss M" (Bette Midler) at the Continental Baths.

With or without Sylvia, Darwin also became something of a regular at Studio 54, where one night, during their explorations of that Club's lower depths, they spotted Liza Minnelli fellating the ballet star, Mikhail Baryshnikov.

Sylvia would once again be nominated for a Best Supporting Actress Oscar for her ten onscreen minutes in Raymond Chandler's *Farewell, My Lovely*. A week after its filming, Darwin arrived at Sylvia's Manhattan apartment, letting himself in with the key she had given him.

As he was making coffee, a nude man suddenly emerged from Miles' bedroom. At first Darwin was startled, although he quickly realized that it was Robert Mitchum as he'd never seen him before. "What's the matter?" Mitchum asked. "Never seen a nude man before? What's for breakfast? I'm one hungry man after that workout last night."

Andy Warhol cast Sylvia alongside Joe Dallesandro in the 1976 film, *Heat*. It was a parody of the 1950 film classic, *Sunset Blvd.* starring Gloria Swanson and William Holden. In *Heat*, Sylvia did her take on the demented silent screen star, Norma Desmond.

Danforth Prince's book about gossip, glitz, and glamour covers the 1970s in Manhattan as no book has done before. It details the decade when a replicated can of Campbell's soup would be hailed as great art.

One magazine compared the era to "Disneyland on an acid trip: The atmosphere Fellini-esque. A time of Narcotic Nirvanas and sweaty bodies, often semi-nude, dancing to throbbing sound systems."

Late night joints featured the kinkiest of kinks, even young men performing sadomasochistic gymnastics on stages, and, in the S&M corners of leather bars, bathtubs into which acolytes could recline for repeated dousings of urine.

The Seventies came to a raw and bitter end. The party ended with the advent of AIDS, a life-changing epidemic that descended onto, and in many ways paralyzed, the raunchiest of the city's nightlife options. But before it fades from memory, though, much of it is recorded within the pages of this book.

Andy Warhol *(left)* with the era's most famous transsexual, "Warhol Superstar" **Candy Darling**

Left: **Bette Midler** in a commemoration of her gigs at the Continental Baths; *right*, **Mikael Baryshnikov** with **Liza Minnelli** onstage.

Announcing Blood Moon's "INSIDE BROADWAY" Trio

Anticipating Publication, in this order, beginning in 2027:

Volume One of Three

Broadway Actors, Directors, & Playwrights:
Who Lit Up the Great White Way

Darwin Porter & Danforth Prince

Volume Two of Three
Broadway Damsels, Dames, & Divas:
They Gave Us So Many Enchanted Evenings

Darwin Porter & Danforth Prince

Volume Three of Three

Babes (Male and Female) on Broadway
Mystique, Ego, Triumph, and Tragedy

Darwin Porter & Danforth Prince

During many of the peak years of the American Theater, **Tennessee Williams** *(a neighbor and close friend of Darwin Porter)* was the virtual King of Broadway. Inserted below are scenes and players from productions of his plays that sparked envy, applause, consternation, and sometimes violence. Insider gossip about many of them are liberally scattered throughout the pages of Blood Moon's upcoming triptych,

INSIDE BROADWAY

Gertrude Lawrence and **Jane Wyman** in the 1950 film adaptation of *The Glass Menagerie.*

Margaret Leighton and **Bette Davis** in the 1961 Broadway version of *Night of the Iguana.*

Maureen Stapleton and **Eli Wallach** in the 1951 Broadway production of *The Rose Tattoo.*

Ben Gazzara and **Barbara Bel Geddes** in the 1951 Broadway version of *The Rose Tattoo*.

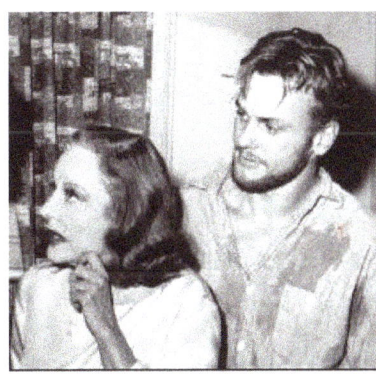

Tallulah Bankhead and **Tab Hunter** "misconnecting" in the 1964 stage version of *The Milk Train Doesn't Stop Here Anymore.*

Marlon Brando abusing **Jessica Tandy** in Broadway's original stage version of *A Streetcar Named Desire.*

BLOOD MOON'S GOMORRAH SERIES
IT'S BACK, AND THERE'S MORE TO COME

You might have heard about Blood Moon's award-winning 2023 spin on America's Gomorrah. Two additional installments are almost ready for their closeup. They include:

Volume Two of Three

Slimelight—Nobody's Perfect
Hidden Tales from Celebrity Boudoirs

Darwin Porter and Danforth Prince

Volume Three of Three

Only Angels Have Wings
More Hidden Tales from Celebrity Boudoirs

Darwin Porter and Danforth Prince

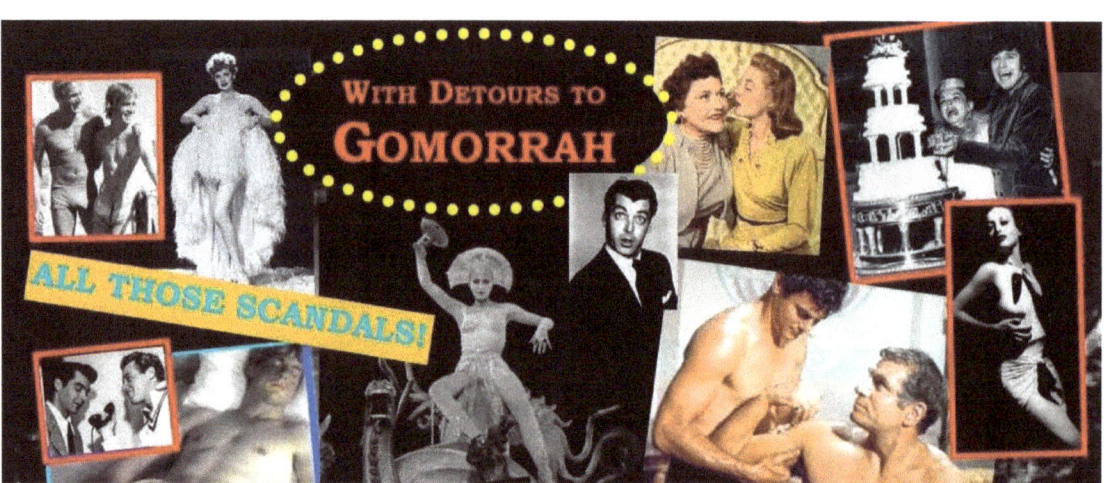

WHO'S IN THE HOPPER, WAITING FOR HIS CLOSEUP?

His biography is presently being developed at Blood Moon Productions.
He's the swashbuckling, wildly promiscuous Golden Age studmuffin of legend and notoriety.

He's

ERROL FLYNN, THE TASMANIAN DEVIL
Golden Age Hollywood's Phallic Symbol

Darwin Porter with Danforth Prince

Seductively gifted and notoriously promiscuous, Errol Flynn was the sex-obsessed arbiter of WHO got invited to the best orgies during the final years of Hollywood's Golden Age. His complete story has never been told…Until Now. Tinseltown's most flamboyant (and most substance-abusive) sailor found—according to his own estimate—14,000 ready, willing, and able "ports of call" until the ravages of time took their inevitable toll.

Celebrity chronicler Darwin Porter spent years researching and elucidating "in like Flynn's" adventures—both in and out of Hollywood. We define it as provocative "background reading" for classic movie fans with enquiring minds—especially the ones who refuse to be easily shocked.

Errol Flynn, The Tasmanian Devil
Golden Age Hollywood's Phallic Symbol

Darwin Porter with Danforth Prince

**All this and more from
Blood Moon Production's
almost inexhaustible list of upcoming titles**

HERE'S A REMINDER ABOUT THE ORIGIN OF OUR NAME

Do You Remember the Erotic Thriller we Published in our Early Days, way back in 1999?
It involved mysterious Events that happen whenever a Blood Moon is sighted.

Inserted below, as photographed by Russell Maynard, is the image we used during promotions
for that Underground, "artfully brutal" novel.
Set in Miami, it was about psychosis, sexual obsession, money, power, religion, and love.

The name we assigned to that book was catchy and easy to remember... so we kept it.

BLOOD MOON

BLOOD MOON PRODUCTIONS

is a Prolific Independent Publishing Venture with a Knack for Challenging the Status Quo's Beliefs about Celebrity and the Ironies of Fame.

It's a tough job, but somebody's got to do it.

Thanks for your interest, and x from
www.BloodMoonProductions.com

www.ingramcontent.com/pod-product-compliance
Lightning Source LLC
Chambersburg PA
CBHW042359070526
44586CB00027B/2820